The Star Creek Papers

The Star

HORACE MANN BOND

& JULIA W. BOND

Creek Papers

EDITED BY ADAM FAIRCLOUGH

FOREWORD BY JULIAN BOND

The University of Georgia Press

Athens & London

© 1997 by the University of Georgia Press
Athens, Georgia   30602
All rights reserved
Designed by Erin Kirk New
Set in 10 on 14 Sabon by G & S Typesetters
Printed and bound by Maple-Vail Book Manufacturing Group
The paper in this book meets the guidelines for
permanence and durability of the Committee on
Production Guidelines for Book Longevity of the
Council on Library Resources.

Printed in the United States of America
01   00   99   98   97   C   5   4   3   2   1

Library of Congress Cataloging in Publication Data

Bond, Horace Mann, 1904–1972.
    The Star Creek papers / Horace Mann Bond and Julia W. Bond ;
edited by Adam Fairclough.
        p.   cm.
    Includes bibliographical references and index.
    ISBN 0-8203-1904-X (alk. paper)
    1. Afro-Americans—Louisiana—Washington Parish—Social life
and customs.   2. Afro-Americans—Louisiana—Washington Parish—
Social conditions.   3. Rural schools—Louisiana—Washington
Parish—History—20th century.   4. Washington Parish (La.)—Race
relations.   5. Wilson family.   6. Afro-American farmers—
Louisiana—Washington Parish—Biography.   7. Lynching—
Louisiana—Washington Parish—History—20th century.   8. Bond,
Horace Mann, 1904–1972—Diaries.   I. Bond, Julia W.   II. Fairclough,
Adam.   III. Title.
    F377.W3B66   1997
    976.3'11—dc21   96-48851

British Library Cataloging in Publication Data available

CONTENTS

FOREWORD

Hanging on a wall of my study are a framed photograph and hand-made certificate, both fifty-five years old. In the picture, three men in academic regalia stand behind two young children; the accompanying fading testimonial, neatly typed, announces to "ALL MEN BY THESE PRESENTS" the consecration of the children to "the high and noble estate of the scholar."

The children are my sister, Jane Marguerite, then three, and myself, aged two. The three men are W. E. B. Du Bois, E. Franklin Frazier, and my father, Horace Mann Bond.

It is arguable whether the long-ago blessing had any real effect on my current status as university professor, or my sister's chosen profession as a lawyer, but the three dedicators represented the pinnacle of scholarship about black Americans then.

Du Bois was the patriarch, in 1942 the dean of black—even white—translators and chroniclers of black struggle against white supremacy. And, as Adam Fairclough notes in his introduction, sociologist Frazier and Horace Mann Bond agreed on much. Frazier's views of the damage slavery did to the black family, now hotly disputed, find support in the *Star Creek Papers*. Like Frazier, for example, Bond contended that black household stability was subverted by white men's easy appropriation of black women, a taboo subject in the 1930s.

The document on my wall, now yellowed with age, serves as testimony to my father's dedication to unfettered and fearless inquiry. "That the estate of the scholar is an ancient and honorable one," he wrote more than half a century ago, "known of olden times, and in each generation, even in the times of distress and human misery and wretchedness, a refuge and a haven for the souls of men."

Horace Mann Bond valued a life of scholarship for his children as much as for himself. He knew, from both his heritage and his examination of history, that the story of black southerners was also the story of southern whites; the relationships, amicable and hostile, between these people was and is the story of the United States.

He wrote in the middle 1930s, and his work was informed by his own life and training as a scholar. Viewed from today's vantage, it may suffer, but the themes from Star Creek resonate today—in calls for land and restitution for the victims of racism past, present, and enduring, concern about and critiques of the stability of the black family, and lynching—by rural Louisiana mobs then and by more respectable rabble today.

The publication now, after more than sixty years, of my parents' manuscripts, written before my sister and I were born, is more than welcome. I am proud that my mother is given due credit for her part in the project. Given her modest nature, what pleases her is that, twenty-five years after his death, this work will confirm her partner's place in the pantheon of intellectuals of the 1930s and 1940s who helped pioneer the modern interpretation of the southern black family after slavery and Reconstruction. For these innovators, families like the Wilsons were resilient, hard working, and ethical. My father and others argued against the racist obfuscation that typified popular and academic descriptions of these people, and he criticized the federal government which had promised to help them out of servitude and peonage.

My father's experiences traveling in the South for the Rosenwald Fund gave him a wealth of dinner-table stories of the people he and my mother had met and the experiences they had shared.

One favorite story placed him in rural Alabama, stuck in a muddy rut on a country road. From nowhere, it seemed, two black men and a mule providentially appeared and pulled his stranded car from the hole they surely had created. They asked how such a well-dressed man driving such a nice car found himself in this forgotten corner. He replied that he worked for the Rosenwald Fund as he nervously waited to see how much his rescue would cost. "You work for Cap'n Julius!" the men exclaimed. There would be no charge for helping someone doing Julius Rosenwald's work.

One of the Wilson kin lived in Atlanta when my father became dean of education at Atlanta University in 1957 and our family moved from Pennsylvania to Georgia. My parents had befriended the family years before my mother discovered the connection; the relationship helped Fairclough trace Wilson survivors now scattered across the country.

Adam Fairclough deserves a huge amount of gratitude, not only from Horace Mann Bond's survivors, but from present-day scholars and other readers who will find in these pages the work of a scholar willing to challenge established wisdom.

Fairclough's previous work on the modern civil rights movement's most prominent leader, *Martin Luther King, Jr.*, and King's organization, *To Redeem the Soul of America: The Southern Christian Leadership Conference and Martin Luther King, Jr.*, and his excellent civil rights history of twentieth century Louisiana, *Race and Democracy: The Civil Rights Struggle in Louisiana, 1915–1972*, demonstrate a commitment to scholarship representative of his modern generation of civil rights historians, who look at the black movement differently than their predecessors, from inside out and bottom up, rather than from top down and outside in. That perspective and his familiarity with and knowledge of the currents of black and white intellectual opinion on race of more than a half-century ago suit his interpretation of Horace Mann Bond's work particularly well. That he is British makes his accomplishments all the more remarkable, or perhaps more understandable. He has both a firm grasp of historical scholarship and an outsider's critical eye and acute ear for nuance that might escape a native.

Just as two rustics rescued my father in Alabama decades ago, Adam Fairclough has revived his long-forgotten examination of a tiny community whose people, through the years, still have large lessons to teach us.

For that deliverance, thankfulness extends beyond Horace Mann Bond's family, to all those interested in America's past, present, and future.

Writing of scholars fifty-five years ago, my father might have been thinking of the work he and my mother did in rural Louisiana, now revived, when he recorded for his children's posterity: "that for the good of humankind such an estate should not be allowed to perish from the earth, but that each generation of Man shall find among their number some who shall cleave to that honorable estate."

Julian Bond

ACKNOWLEDGMENTS

Editing the *Star Creek Papers* has been a fascinating and moving experience. Coming across these long-forgotten manuscripts seemed at first sheer serendipity, but, in retrospect, it was more than pure chance. I had long been interested in the Wilson family of Washington Parish. In 1987, wading through the NAACP's lynching files in connection with my research on Louisiana, I read about the shooting affray on the Wilson farm that took place on July 21, 1934, and the subsequent trial, conviction, appeal, and lynching of Jerome Wilson. I sketched the bare outlines of the story in *Race and Democracy*, but I always wanted to know more about these events. Every lynching was a tragedy, but the fate of the Wilson family seemed especially tragic. John Wilson was a strikingly sympathetic character, and I often wondered what became of him and his family. Were any of his children still alive? Where did they go after Jerome's death? Did any Wilsons still own land and farm in Washington Parish?

In 1994 I was introduced to Julia W. Bond by our mutual friend Connie Curry. Prompted by Julian Bond, who knew that a lynching had occurred in a place called "Star Creek," Louisiana, while his parents had been living there, I asked Mrs. Bond about her recollections of this event. Only then did I learn of the Bonds' personal knowledge of Jerome Wilson's lynching, and of Horace Mann Bond's effort, sixty years earlier, to turn the history of the Wilson family into a book. Mrs. Bond also told me of her friendship with Freddye Henderson of Atlanta, who was a first cousin of Jerome Wilson. When finally I had the opportunity to go through Horace Mann Bond's papers, I read his

Star Creek manuscripts with mounting excitement and enthusiasm. A recent biographer of Bond had, to my amazement, devoted only a page or two to Bond's Star Creek sojourn, and only a couple of paragraphs to the researches and writings that it inspired. I had no doubt in my mind that publication of the Star Creek manuscripts would make an important contribution to both the sociology and history of the American South. Karen Orchard, director of the University of Georgia Press, shared that view and I am grateful for her confidence and support.

In pursuing this project I am indebted to Julian Bond for providing initial encouragement and to Julia Bond for her help and cooperation throughout. In a real sense, Mrs. Bond is the co-author of this book. It is also a pleasure to acknowledge the help of Freddye Henderson, who gave generously of her time and provided invaluable information, based on personal knowledge and memories, about the Wilson and Magee families. Two surviving siblings of Jerome Wilson also helped me to trace the history of the Wilsons since 1935. Felton Wilson of Chicago provided important details of the family, as did Alexzine Wilson Young of Brooklyn. Mrs. Young was particularly obliging, and she freely shared her vivid and painful memories of the events of 1934–35. I am immensely grateful to her.

The task of editing the *Star Creek Papers* was made considerably easier by the fact that I spent 1994–95 at the National Humanities Center in North Carolina. This wonderful institution not only provided that most precious of all commodities, time, but also gave me invaluable secretarial assistance. Two NHC staff members, Karen Carroll and Linda Morgan, contributed many hours of their time to retyping and putting onto disk blurred and dog-eared copies of the original manuscripts. Their cheerful and efficient assistance was a real boon. I also wish to acknowledge the scholarship of E. Russ Williams Jr. of Monroe, Louisiana, whose encyclopaedic *History of Washington Parish* helped me to confirm and amplify important details of people mentioned in Bond's narrative. Finally, my wife, Mary Ellen Curtin, was unstinting in her encouragement and help.

STATE OF LOUISIANA

N

0   10   20   30   40   50
MILES

Oak Grove
Lake Providence
WEST CARROLL
EAST CARROLL
Tallulah
MADISON
TENSAS
St. Joseph
Vidalia

MISSISSIPPI

WEST FELICIANA
St. Francisville
Clinton
Greensburg
WASHINGTON
Franklinton
Bogalusa
EAST FELICIANA
ST. HELENA
Amite
New Roads
EAST BATON ROUGE
Livingston
TANGIPAHOA
PEARL RIVER
W. BATON ROUGE
Port Allen
BATON ROUGE
LIVINGSTON
Covington
ST. TAMMANY
Plaquemine
ASCENSION
Donaldsonville
ST. JOHN THE BAPTIST
Lake Pontchartrain
IBERVILLE
Convent
Napoleonville
ST. JAMES
Edgard
New Orleans
ORLEANS
Chalmette
Franklin
ASSUMPTION
Thibodaux
Hahnville
Gretna
ST. CHARLES
JEFFERSON
ST. BERNARD
ST. MARY
Houma
LAFOURCHE
Pointe a la Hache
PLAQUEMINES
TERREBONNE

RIVER
MISSISSIPPI

INTRODUCTION

In 1934 Horace Mann Bond was in the early years of a distinguished career as a historian, educationist, and university president. Already, at age twenty-nine, a professor at Fisk University with an armful of publications, his expertise as an authority on black education took him to Washington Parish, a corner of southeastern Louisiana bordered by Mississippi on two sides. Under the auspices of the Rosenwald Fund, he and his wife, Julia Washington Bond, lived in a small farming community and studied the operation of the local black schools. Today they would be called "participant-observers"; in 1934 they were dubbed "explorers." This experience, Horace recorded, "proved one of the most valuable of our entire lives." [1]

For three months the Bonds, who had married in 1929 and had no children yet, lived in a wooden cabin in a district known as Star Creek. They rose before dawn to draw water, chop wood, and start a fire. They had no electricity or running water, and cooked in a kitchen where rain entered through a leaky roof. A lime-slaked hole in the ground served as a toilet. Such conditions were no worse than how most blacks—and many whites—still lived in the 1930s. Besides, the Bonds enjoyed the luxury of a secondhand, if rather unreliable, Ford automobile. Julia passed most days in the company of Gabe Magee ("Miss Gabe"), who lived with her husband, Ernest Magee, on the farm where the Bonds' cabin stood. When Horace was not fixing up the cabin and talking with neighbors, he visited nearby farms, made occasional trips to the towns of Franklinton and Bogalusa, and observed the running of the local black schools. As "Portrait of Washington Parish" attests, Washington Parish was not that far from New Orleans in miles but very distant in terms of culture. Bond became fascinated by its peculiarities.[2]

Quickly befriended and accepted, the Bonds became fond of their rustic neighbors. "My wife and I found ourselves liking the people there more than any we had ever known before," wrote Horace. "Honest, self-respecting, [and] hard-working," they were "my idea of what human beings ought to be." He recorded their observations and experiences in a diary. A rich, funny, and evocative description of black life in the rural South, Bond's "Star Creek Diary" is published here for the first time.[3]

"Portrait of Washington Parish" and "Star Creek Diary" are not works of academic scholarship in the vein of such sociological classics of the era as Charles S. Johnson's *Shadow of the Plantation* (1934), John Dollard's *Caste and Class in a Southern Town* (1937), Hortense Powdermaker's *After Freedom* (1940), or Allison Davis's *Deep South* (1941). They are, however, superb social observations written by a black intellectual at the height of his powers. Horace Mann Bond was also a fine writer. "Portrait of Washington Parish" and "Star Creek Diary" have immediacy and literary freshness.[4]

Bond's Star Creek writings reflected his democratic instincts, love of the South, and, above all, deep respect for ordinary black southerners. Bond once explained his admiration for Booker T. Washington by noting Washington's immense popularity among the most illiterate blacks of the Deep South. "These people cannot be fooled, and they know the truth when they hear it—if I had not learned some time ago that instincts were no longer in good form, I should say that they have an instinct for that which is true and genuine." Aided by Julia's observations, Bond captured these qualities in his Star Creek neighbors. Listening to their conversations with a sensitive ear, he faithfully reproduced the rhythms and inflections of their rural dialect. With no hint of condescension, he produced a very human portrait of a rural black community, an account tinged with affection, understanding, and respect.[5]

Bond also illuminated the development of black schools in the 1930s. Indeed, the study of the Rosenwald school and the study of the black community were in large part one and the same. To an extent rarely documented by historians, the "Rosenwald schools" were embedded in the fabric of rural black communities, a fact that their very name—by implying that they were outright gifts of northern white philanthropy—tended to mask. In fact, Rosenwald money furnished only a part—less than a half—of the necessary funding to build Rosenwald schools. The greater portion came from the state government and significant amounts came from blacks themselves.[6]

The contribution made by blacks in the form of money, materials, and labor made these schools more than mere buildings. Drives to build Rosenwald schools, encouraged by state agents employed by the Fund, gave blacks a sense of common purpose and community progress at a time when they were excluded from politics and subjected to gross discrimination in every area of life. Writing of Star Creek, the Bonds reported:

> Immediately after the War, when the price of cotton gave economic security to the community that it has never since enjoyed, the members of the community obtained a Rosenwald grant-in-aid. They then rented a saw mill, bought some timber . . . and cut the trees, sawed the timber, and hauled it to the site of the school where they erected the structure. This community experience is recalled with great pride. . . . They speak of the school as "our school" in a sense that transcends the ordinary use of that term. Teachers have come and gone, but the memory of that united community and of their contribution centers the life of all in the institution.

So important was the school that it, rather than the church, provided the main focus of community activity.[7]

"Star Creek Diary" provides a richly detailed portrait of a way of life that was on the threshold of virtual extinction, although few perceived it at the time. Between 1920 and 1930 the number of black farmers had already declined by 17 percent, the acreage they cultivated by 30 percent. During the next fifteen years New Deal legislation favored large producers at the expense of small farmers, mechanical cotton-pickers dispensed with the need for black labor, and wartime industrial expansion acted as a magnet to rural southerners. As the old cotton economy declined, migration from the countryside to the towns soon reached the proportions of a mass exodus, and it accelerated when peace returned in 1945. By 1960 about half the African American population lived outside the South, and blacks, both North and South, had become an overwhelmingly urban people. "By the 1970s," writes Gilbert C. Fite, "it could be said that blacks had been all but eliminated from farming." [8]

In scattered pockets of the rural South, however, including Washington Parish, black farmers still cling to the soil with stubborn tenacity. "Star Creek Diary" helps us to to understand why.

The third previously unpublished manuscript contained in this volume illustrates both the tenacity of black agriculturalists and the dynamics of migration. "Forty Acres and a Mule" is the history of a family of black farmers that begins in slavery and ends in 1935, spanning three generations of Wilsons and Magees. As a document of social history it is, to my knowledge, one of a kind, for it culminates in a lynching.

Horace Mann Bond had a lifelong interest in black family history, and one question, in particular, always intrigued him: What accounted for the strength, stability, and success of some families? Bond was struck by the fact that so many black farmers in Washington Parish owned their own land, and he wondered why. Searching for the answer in the histories of these families, he gathered information from his neighbors and started constructing detailed genealogies.

Bond focused his research on the family of John Wilson, one of whose sons, Jerome Wilson, languished in Franklinton jail under sentence of death. Jerome's conviction had arisen from a bizarre shooting incident that took place on the Wilson family farm shortly before the Bonds arrived in Star Creek. A seemingly trivial dispute over a mule had led to a fatal exchange of gunfire that left a deputy sheriff dead, one of John Wilson's sons mortally wounded, and another son, Jerome, accused of murder. After a trial of indecent haste, conducted while a lynch-mob bayed for blood outside the court house, a jury of white men convicted Jerome Wilson of murdering deputy sheriff Delos C. Wood. Jerome's brother, Luther, his mother, Tempie, and his uncle, Sammy, were also due to stand trial.[9]

Horace Mann Bond had no intention of involving himself in this affair when he and Julia moved to Washington Parish in October 1934. Quite the contrary: in the tense aftermath of the shooting and trial, he knew that he needed to be prudent. If he showed too keen an interest in the Wilson affair, if he asked too many pointed questions about "race relations," he might easily become an object of suspicion, possibly jeopardizing his own, and his wife's, safety.[10] Still, Bond could hardly avoid hearing about the subject. His neighbor, Gabe Magee, was a cousin of Jerome Wilson. Indeed, it was difficult to find a neighbor who was *not* related by blood or marriage to the Wilson family.

In fact, Bond found the story of the shooting incident and the subsequent trial engrossing. He became fascinated by the history of the Wilsons, by their success in acquiring land, and by the apparently inexplicable shooting affray on the Wilson farm. He discovered that John Wilson belonged to an extended family that consisted of more than a thousand people, most of them farmers, many of them landowners, and most of them direct descendants of a handful of slaves. By the end of 1934 Bond had drawn up a family tree of the Wilsons that started with Jerome Wilson's slave grandparents, Isom Wilson and Mandy Daniels.

The story of the Wilson family took on an unexpected twist, however, when a group of white men dragged Jerome Wilson from his jail cell and killed him. The lynching took place on January 11, 1935, only days after Wilson had been granted a new trial—and the very day the new trial was to open.

This shocking event ended Bond's rural idyll. He and Julia left Washington Parish for the safety of New Orleans. But Bond could forget neither the lynching nor the fate of the Wilson family. John Wilson, a man of bedrock honesty and sturdy independence, now stood to lose everything. His wife suffered a nervous breakdown. Two of his sons were dead and another remained in jail. Bond wanted to help Wilson keep his family together and remain on the land.

In March 1935 John Wilson visited with Bond in New Orleans. "He is an exceptionally intelligent man," wrote Bond, "and talks with great power. If I could only transcribe exactly what he says, it would be a rare piece of literature." The record of their conversations provided Bond with the raw material for a manuscript, which he titled "Forty Acres and a Mule." He planned to write a history of the Wilson family, beginning with their origins in slavery and ending with the lynching of Jerome Wilson. He intended donating the bulk of any royalties to John Wilson. The Wilsons fled Washington Parish, however, most of the family moving to Chicago, and Bond abandoned the project.[11]

Bond's unfinished manuscript has been gathering dust for sixty years. "Forty Acres and a Mule" provides fascinating insights into lynching, race relations, and the history of a black farming community. It also tells us about Horace Mann Bond as a black intellectual and the ideas that influenced him.

Bond disguised his authorial voice in "Forty Acres and a Mule" by creating an omniscient narrator who evoked the vernacular dialect of Washington Parish blacks—in effect, merging his own voice with John Wilson's. However, Bond used the narrative to convey his own ideas and believed he was making an important contribution to the study of the black family. As he jokingly reported to his mentor Robert Park, the well-known University of Chicago sociologist, "I think the individual life histories of each member of these families is enough to make even Frazier turn green with envy."[12]

The reference, of course, was to another of Park's black students, E. Franklin Frazier. On his way to becoming one of the foremost sociologists of his time, Frazier had recently published *The Negro Family in Chicago* and was working on his larger synthesis, *The Negro Family in the United States*. These books remained, for thirty years, the most highly regarded studies of the black family in historical perspective. Their influence was universal. It comes as no surprise, therefore, that Frazier's tragic account of a people whose African culture had been obliterated, and whose family life had been handicapped by slavery, loosened by Emancipation, and disorganized by migration strongly colored "Forty Acres and a Mule." Over thirty years later, Bond remained convinced that Frazier's studies of the black family had "not been surpassed for their penetration and insightful analysis."[13]

Bond's reliance on Frazier, however, poses a crucial problem when it comes to assessing "Forty Acres and a Mule." To state the matter baldly, for the past thirty years scholars have been systematically assaulting Frazier's ideas on the black family. The undermining of Frazier started with the hostile reaction to the Moynihan Report of 1965. It gathered force with the publication of sociological studies of contemporary family structures that stressed community and adaptation rather than pathology and disorganization. Historians, using cliometric techniques, attacked Frazier from another angle, disputing his generalizations about black family life under slavery. The result is a widespread rejection of what is sometimes crudely labelled the "damage" model of the black family. The idea that black family life in the twentieth-century city has been crippled by the legacy of slavery has few advocates. So low has Frazier's reputation sunk that he merits barely a dismissive mention in many studies. For example, Herbert Gutman, in his influential *Black Family in Slavery and Freedom*, flatly stated that Frazier's interpretation of the slave family was wrong on virtually all counts.[14]

This is a remarkable shift in opinion, for to a large extent Frazier had merely systematized beliefs shared by virtually all African Americans at the time. Indeed, the proposition that slavery had cruelly stunted black family life was one of the few things upon which Booker T. Washington and W. E. B. Du Bois agreed.

If Frazier's critics are right, however, Bond would have been following an error-strewn path by following Frazier. Like Frazier, Bond probably overstated the looseness, instability, and matriarchal nature of family life under slavery. And like Frazier, Bond overestimated the extent of family disorganization after Emancipation, and underestimated the number of strong, two-parent families. Rather than constituting a rare example of morality and stability against a background of sexual laxness and disorganization, the Wilsons, if not exactly typical, were a far more common family type than Bond believed.

The supposed disorganizing impact of migration, central to Frazier's sociology, added to Bond's reluctance to see the Wilsons move North. Thus Bond used the history of Jerome Wilson's maternal family, the Magees, as a counterpoint to that of his paternal family, the Wilsons. The story of Tempie's siblings, Bond believed, illustrated the disasters that so often befell black families when uprooted from the land and cast adrift in the city. The Magees had started to migrate North, and they were losing their family cohesion. John's siblings, on the other hand, had enlarged upon the land bequeathed them by their father, remaining intact as a family, their southern roots giving them strength and stability. "I am afraid that if [John Wilson] takes his family to Chicago," Bond wrote, "they will become completely disorganized. His wife's family has moved to Chicago, and they are already completely demoralized there."[15] The realities of migration, however, were much more complex. The Magees who migrated to Chicago, Atlanta, and California surmounted adversity and retained their family identity. Some achieved great success.

Yet "Forty Acres and a Mule" also highlights the continuing vitality of Frazier's ideas. Like Frazier, Bond argued that the privileged access of white men to black women had profoundly influenced and distorted black family life. Arriving in Washington Parish, he had been struck by the fact that the majority of families, both black and white, shared the same surnames. He speculated that kinship ties, not merely sentiment, explained why so many blacks adopted the names of their former masters after Emancipation. He then painstakingly documented, compiling detailed genealogies that stretched back to slavery, how black and white families intertwined.

Bond's description of how blood lines crisscrossed the color line is perhaps the least accessible part of "Forty Acres and a Mule." Today's reader might be confused, puzzled, or even offended by his excessively detailed account of racial intermingling. In the 1930s, however, miscegenation was still a subject of intense fascination for many whites and blacks. White curiosity derived from both the scholarly interest of sociologists and anthropologists, but also from the prurience of a society that regarded interracial sex as exotic and taboo. Indeed, white attitudes to interracial sex embodied many of the feelings of repression and guilt that clouded the murky undertow of racist ideology. The prevention of interracial sex—expressed as a determination to punish and deter black rapists—was the white South's ostensible justification for lynching. Yet the hidden history of miscegenation—usually sexual relationships between white men and black women—was the white South's guilty secret. Miscegenation had also long been a popular theme in fiction, and in the 1930s the "tragic mulatto," although a tired cliché, was still being pressed into service.

For blacks, often themselves the progeny of interracial unions, the mulatto symbolized, in the most acute form, the irrationality and hypocrisy of the white-imposed color line. That line defined as "Negro" a person with *any* traceable black forbears. The mulatto—especially when he or she could "pass" for white—personified the truth that race was an idea defined by white-made law and ideology, not a natural and universal category.[16] The biological imprecision of the South's color line mocked the notion of white racial "purity" and made nonsense of the idea that whites were innately superior to blacks. Bond, in his own writings on the subject, did not spare white hypocrisy. "The dominant group, after destroying the purity of both parent-stocks, blandly hoists the bars against these left-handed children in the sacred name of racial purity."

Bond's own interest in miscegenation also stemmed from a desire to discredit "scientific" racism. In his first published article Bond entered the stormy debate over the IQ tests administered to Army recruits in 1917. Attacking the fallacy of using the test scores to allege black racial inferiority, he pointed out the wide overlap between the scores achieved by individual whites and blacks. Results corresponded to education and environment, not to race. Southern whites, of course, tried to explain away racial overlaps, and to denigrate black achievements, by attributing the undoubted excellence of some blacks to varying degrees of "white blood." But in 1931 Bond studied the IQ scores of mixed-race children in two different mulatto communities near Mobile, Alabama. In the first mulatto group average scores exceeded national norms; in the second, however, average scores fell short of both national norms and the national average for Negro children. Both groups possessed similar racial characteristics, the children ranging in color from brown to white. "Manifestly, the tonic qualities of white blood . . . has no right to be claimed as the basic factor here." [17]

Although interracial unions were rare in the 1930s, Bond shared Frazier's conviction that blood ties to white families helped to explain the pattern of black landownership in the rural South. In slave society white fathers had often favored and sometimes freed their mulatto offspring. Hence mulattoes had formed a high proportion of the antebellum free Negro population, and after Emancipation they tended to achieve a higher economic status than most blacks. The extent to which white fathers helped mulatto children acquire land in the postbellum South is hard to establish. Still, a recent study of Hancock County, Georgia, has asserted that "in the Deep South, where black farmers were systematically impeded in their quest for land, interracial kinship played an important role in opening the first door." [18]

Frazier and Bond both believed that black landholding had promoted family stability. They were correct. Black farmers who owned their land tended to have larger families, and the family heads, invariably fathers, exerted more parental authority by virtue of their ability to employ their children and endow them with land. Indeed, in examining the landowning families of Washington Parish enumerated in the U.S. Census between 1870 and 1920, the similarity between the black families and the white families is remarkable. If the census had not classified people according to race, it would be all but impossible to tell black and white families apart.

Landownership also gave cohesion to black communities. Arthur Raper could have been describing John Wilson when he wrote, in 1936, that "a Negro with land usually considers himself a kind of father to the community. He functions as a mediator between the mass of whites and Negroes. He becomes the spokesman for the local school trustees when they go to the county superintendant for assistance; he intercedes with the court officials for Negro defendants from his community; he explains to the whites any unusual behavior of the local Negroes, and vice versa. . . . [Moreover], the owners are in virtual control of all Negro institutions." Elizabeth Rauh Bethel's 1981 study of a South Carolina black community, which tracked black landowners over a period of one hundred years, came to the same conclusion. Extensive landownership had helped the community to survive boll weevil, crop failures, and declining cotton prices. Moreover, blacks who migrated to the cities tended to remain in touch with their communities of origin if their families continued to own land.[19]

Yet most black families in the postbellum South did *not* become landowners; although common and even predominant in some localities, landownership eluded the great majority. Bond therefore intended "Forty Acres and a Mule" to be much more than a dramatic account of a shootout and a lynching, more even than a treatise on the black family. Developing his own ideas as a historian, Bond turned the tragedy of the Wilson family into a metaphor for the larger historical tragedy of African Americans since slavery.

The title "Forty Acres and a Mule" referred to the aspirations of the emancipated slaves. It also referred to Thomas Dixon's white supremacist novel *The Clansman* (1905). In a chapter titled "Forty Acres and a Mule," Dixon had depicted the freedmen as lazy and gullible, their desire for free land risible. His scornful picture of idle emancipated slaves demanding something for nothing was then immortalized on screen in D. W. Griffith's *Birth of a Nation* (1915).[20] In the 1930s many white historians, echoing Dixon, still treated the freedmen's expectation of free land as a naive and ludicrous delusion.

Bond challenged this view head-on, with Alabama historian Walter L. Fleming as his principal target. The freedmen "knew exactly what they needed," Bond insisted. "They asked for a subsistence farmstead— for forty acres and a mule." It was a reasonable expectation and a realistic goal. Although Bond's assertion went against the grain of the racist-tinged scholarship of the time, it has now become a commonplace among historians of Reconstruction. Indeed, the consensus of modern scholarship is to fault the Republican party for failing to give the freedmen land, not to condemn the freedmen for wanting it. As Bond pointed out more than fifty years ago, Congress's refusal to redistribute land constituted one of the most egregious errors of Reconstruction.[21]

Yet Bond also wanted to document how, even when the federal government turned its back on land redistribution, blacks like Isom and John Wilson had acquired property and become "shifty" (resourceful) farmers. Indeed, by 1910 at least 218,000 blacks—about one black farmer in four—owned land. This was a phenomenal achievement. To Bond, the Wilsons represented all that was admirable among black southerners; they were the acme of self-help in the tradition of Booker T. Washington. "The entire family," wrote Bond, "is a good example of what a Negro owner family can become—unsophisticated, of course, but honest, industrious, ambitious people."[22]

The murder of Jerome Wilson, however, was a frightening reminder that lynching could still wreck even the most virtuous of families. Although the number of lynchings had fallen sharply during the 1920s, in the early 1930s it rose again. The numbers were relatively small, and nowhere near pre–World War I levels. But lynching occurred with sufficient frequency to sustain a climate of fear that touched the lives of all African Americans. Lynching reminded blacks that a judicial system composed of white judges, white prosecutors, and white jurors, and a law enforcement apparatus composed of white policemen, would neither prevent nor punish the "illegal" violence of whites against blacks.

Even as the incidence of lynching declined, moreover, it remained axiomatic that any black person who killed a law enforcement officer would pay with his life, regardless of any extenuating circumstances. "There is an unwritten law in Louisiana," wrote black attorney A. P. Tureaud, "that any man who kills a policeman . . . either goes to the electric chair or the police will kill him." It is unlikely that a second trial for Jerome Wilson would have produced either a different verdict or a different sentence: successful appeals in such cases usually only delayed executions. Nevertheless, the mere possibility that Jerome Wilson might escape with his life was intolerable to nameless whites in Washington Parish.[23]

Bond intended "Forty Acres and a Mule" to make a distinctive contribution to the campaign against lynching. The NAACP, which spearheaded that campaign, did not shrink from describing lynchings in lurid and bloody detail. But its horror stories rarely probed beneath the surface: seeking to maximize the short-term shock effect of lynchings, the NAACP's searchlight briefly illuminated each incident and then moved on to the next. There were scholars who collected statistics on lynching and formulated sociological explanations for the phenomenon. Both the shock approach of the NAACP and the statistical method of the social scientists, however, tended to bury the individual human stories, the one by sensationalizing, the other by generalizing. Even the best recent historical investigations of lynching offer only sketchy portraits of the victims and their communities.[24]

As a contribution to the study of lynching, therefore, "Forty Acres and a Mule" may be unique. Bond placed a single lynching in the context of one black family's history since slavery. He reminds us that behind each life claimed by lynching there was a person, a family, and a community—individual histories that are, in their own way, more informative than statistics, more eloquent than propaganda, and more illuminating than general histories.

Bond also reminds us of a crucial truth that recent studies of lynching—which stress that lynching rates varied from time to time and from place to place—have tended to obscure. The existence of variations *within* the South is less significant than the fact that lynchings occurred *throughout* the South. Washington Parish did not rank high in the county-by-county lynching statistics; it experienced only an "occasional" incident. Lynching did not have to occur with great frequency, however, to remind blacks of their vulnerability. "However considerable the regional variations in mob violence," writes W. Fitzhugh Brundage, "blacks realized that its potential threatened every black in the South."

It is impossible to estimate what proportion of the southern black population personally knew a victim of lynching, but it must have been substantial. In Washington Parish, with its large, complex kinship network of Wilsons, Bickhams, and Magees, Jerome Wilson had hundreds, possibly a thousand, aunts, uncles, cousins, nephews, and nieces. The psychological impact of lynching was profound; the memory lingers.[25]

To Bond, what happened to the Wilsons had no rhyme or reason. Jerome Wilson should never have been lynched because the shooting affray on the Wilson farm should never have happened. The whole train of events seemed senseless, illustrating the sheer contingency of lynching.

Yet Bond perceived a tragic inevitability about the fate that befell the Wilsons. He stopped short of arguing that lynching was a deliberate effort to dispossess black landholders—even though the history of lynching provides numerous examples of blacks being victimized because of their economic success. He did show, however, that lynching could destroy the work of generations in a single day. The lynching of Jerome Wilson shattered the Wilson family, and none of Bond's efforts to put it back together again succeeded. As the story of the Wilson family shows, lynching was a factor of incalculable importance in the northward migration of African Americans.

"Portrait of Washington Parish" incorporates a report written for the Rosenwald Fund and various drafts of Bond's unpublished manuscript, "The First Lynching of 1935." They have been edited to form a coherent whole. "Star Creek Diary" is published here as it was written save for minor editing. "Forty Acres and a Mule" has been edited more substantially, especially in the two middle chapters. The genealogical charts are Bond's own, as amplified and amended by the editor. Horace Mann Bond was responsible for writing the texts in this collection. Julia Bond made a substantial contribution to her husband's research and is hence listed as a co-author of the volume. All endnotes are the editor's.

THE WILSON FAMILY

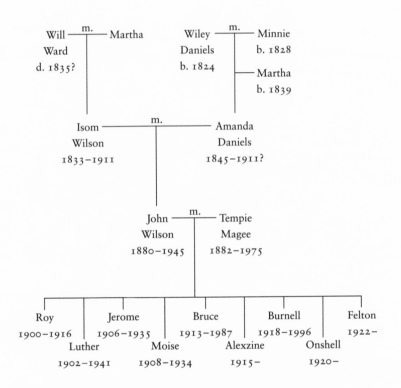

Will ——m.—— Martha   Wiley ——m.—— Minnie
Ward   Daniels   b. 1828
d. 1835?   b. 1824
                              —— Martha
                                 b. 1839

Isom ——————m.—————— Amanda
Wilson   Daniels
1833–1911   1845–1911?

John ——m.—— Tempie
Wilson   Magee
1880–1945   1882–1975

Roy   Jerome   Bruce   Burnell   Felton
1900–1916 1906–1935 1913–1987 1918–1996 1922–
   Luther   Moise   Alexzine   Onshell
  1902–1941 1908–1934   1915–   1920–

THE MAGEE FAMILY

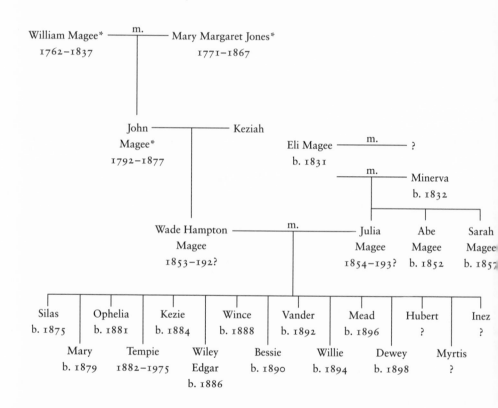

William Magee* —— m. —— Mary Margaret Jones*
1762–1837   1771–1867

John —————— Keziah   Eli Magee —— m. —— ?
Magee*   b. 1831
1792–1877   —— m. —— Minerva
                                                 b. 1832

Wade Hampton —— m. —— Julia   Abe   Sarah
Magee   Magee   Magee   Magee
1853–192?   1854–193? b. 1852   b. 185?

Silas   Ophelia   Kezie   Wince   Vander   Mead   Hubert   Inez
b. 1875   b. 1881   b. 1884   b. 1888   b. 1892   b. 1896   ?   ?

   Mary   Tempie   Wiley   Bessie   Willie   Dewey   Myrtis
   b. 1879   1882–1975   Edgar   b. 1890   b. 1894   b. 1898   ?
                         b. 1886

*White

THE MULATTO CHILDREN

OF JACOB AND FLEET MAGEE

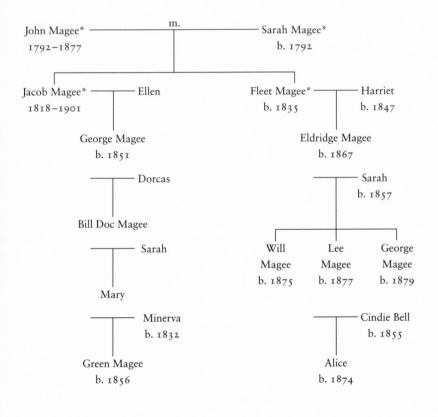

John Magee* —————— m. —————— Sarah Magee*
1792–1877   b. 1792

Jacob Magee* ——┬—— Ellen   Fleet Magee* ——┬—— Harriet
1818–1901   b. 1835   b. 1847

George Magee   Eldridge Magee
b. 1851   b. 1867

————┬—— Dorcas   ————┬—— Sarah
                                                              b. 1857

Bill Doc Magee

————┬—— Sarah   Will   Lee   George
                                      Magee   Magee   Magee
                                      b. 1875   b. 1877   b. 1879
Mary

————┬—— Minerva   ————┬—— Cindie Bell
              b. 1832   b. 1855

Green Magee   Alice
b. 1856   b. 1874

*White

THE CHILDREN OF MINERVA

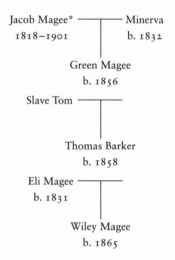

Jacob Magee* ———┬——— Minerva
1818–1901   b. 1832
              │
        Green Magee
          b. 1856
Slave Tom ———┬———
              │
        Thomas Barker
          b. 1858
Eli Magee ———┬———
b. 1831   │
        Wiley Magee
          b. 1865

*White

Portrait of Washington Parish

More than fourteen hundred Negroes have been lynched since 1904, the date of my birth. I remember the month of June, 1913, because of a recurrent nightmare that left me, night after night, screaming with a terrible fear. The nightmare faithfully reproduced, night after night, a cartoon which I had seen in a Negro magazine, *The Crisis*. In the drawing, and in the dream, several Negroes were depicted hanging from a tree, while "Lynch Law," caricatured as a gorilla-like creature with bloody fangs, a rope in one hand and a torch in the other, approached to light a funeral pyre beneath the taut black bodies. The dream had one elaboration of the cartoon: the monster always turned upon me, and I could never move a muscle to escape.

I am willing to leave to the psychiatrists an explanation of the subconscious setting of that nightmare. For me it was the beginning of what may mildly be described as "an interest" in the institution of lynching. That interest has led me to follow closely the immense literature on lynching in newspapers, periodicals, and books; to observe quite carefully the various efforts to enact an anti-lynching bill; and to consider the phenomenon in its relation to the social setting, as well as within the framework of my own emotional reaction to it.

It is difficult not to regard a lynching as an abstraction, a happening that does not really concern you, an incident involving men, both victims and mob members, whom you do not know, will never meet, and who exist apart from your own circle of experience in a little lynching world of their own. Despite my own background, it was so with me; **3** or, at least, it was so until the eleventh day of January, 1935. Early on that Friday morning, in the Washington Parish jail at Franklinton, Louisiana, occurred the death of Jerome Wilson, described by the Coroner's jury as "death at the hands of a person or persons unknown."

The death of Jerome Wilson was the first lynching of 1935. I had not known the victim, but I knew his father and his mother, his brothers, his sisters, his uncles, aunts and cousins. For a brief period I had lived in a cabin three miles away from Jerome Wilson's home. I do not now know who the men were who lynched Jerome Wilson, but I have moved in a community where, doubtless, I have seen one or two of them daily. Under these circumstances it is difficult to maintain either an intellectual or an emotional abstraction toward the incident; it is neither a cold entry in a lynching list, fit for future placement on a graph, nor a cause for a protest parade one thousand miles away.

Jerome Wilson was the son of John Wilson, who married Tempie Magee. His paternal grandfather was one Isom Wilson, who married Mandy Daniels, a mulatto woman, soon after the Civil War. Isom and Mandy had eleven children, ten of whom are living today. First Isom, and then each of his four boys in succession became independent land owners. His seven girls married men who bought or "homesteaded" land in the Northern section of Washington Parish. In the early Summer of 1934 the descendants of Isom and Mandy Wilson included ten living sons and daughters and seventy-seven living grandchildren, forty-three of whom had married and established families of their own.

Isom Wilson's four sons were named Samuel, John, William and Simon. A community of land-owning Wilsons grew up around the Bethel Church, and in 1924 the community had added to it a three-room Rosenwald School built principally by contributions from the Negro farm owners in the neighborhood. During Reconstruction days Isom Wilson was a leader in local Republican politics. The fact that his sons continued his political interest, until the disfranchisement of Negroes by the Louisiana Constitutional Convention of 1898, is remembered by local white persons as the only black mark on the record of the Wilson family. A few Negroes are still registered as Republican voters, although they are not allowed to participate in the Democratic "White" primaries.

The Bethel community is dominated by the Wilson family. There are adjoining Negro communities where Negro owners also predominate, and the second generation of Wilsons is inextricably bound to families similar in origin and circumstances, so that probably one thousand of the five thousand rural Negroes in the Parish belong to one of only three families.[1] Of the living grand-children of Isom and Mandy Wilson, twenty-two lived in the Bethel community, twenty-three in Franklinton, and nine in the Star Creek community. Two lived in the Jemerson Creek community, and one in the Black Jack community. Three lived in the small, nearby Mississippi towns of Picayune, Osyka and Summit. One lived at Kentwood, Louisiana. It is significant of family stability that the industrial city of Bogalusa, which has recruited all of its four thousand Negroes from the surrounding countryside within the last thirty years, failed to attract a single Wilson. On the other hand there are three Wilsons living in Chicago, more than a thousand miles away.

The individual farms are not large, averaging not much more than fifty acres. Isom Wilson homesteaded a "forty" and bought other land. John Wilson added to his small inheritance by homestead and purchase, and in 1934 owned two places totalling almost two hundred acres. On his farm in the Bethel community, on a graveled highway leading from Franklinton to the hamlet of Clifton, he had built in 1926 a new house, the only "painted," "sealed" house owned by Negroes in the community. The land is cut-over timber land, and in this day would be classified as "sub-marginal." On it, however, John Wilson made a good living, what with the aid of a wife celebrated for thrift in the community, and the assistance of a large family of children. Jerome, Luther, and Moise[2] were young men. Felton, twelve, and Bruce, ten, could go to school at Bethel and still find time to help raise a crop. Alexzine, the oldest girl, at sixteen was attending the County Training School at Franklinton as befitted the daughter of a prosperous farmer. The school bus passed the cross-roads just a mile from the Wilson home. Burnell ("Bunch") and Onshell ("Red"), respectively aged thirteen and eleven, were also enrolled in the Bethel Rosenwald school. "Bunch" played on the girls' basketball team.

Washington Parish had in 1934 a stock-dipping ordinance, and the enforcement of this act was always attended by great grumbling by white and black farmers on "Dipping Day."[3] It is no easy matter to interrupt a farming schedule to corral stock before daybreak and drive them several miles to a convenient vat. On July 21, 1934, Range Rider Joe Magee came to John Wilson's home on an inspection tour. A certain mule, he asserted, had not been dipped. The mule had been dipped; and Jerome Wilson, in the absence of his father, became involved in a quarrel with the Range Rider over the mule.

Rebuffed, and angered, Joe Magee went to a white neighbor's house where he telephoned for aid from the Sheriff's office at Franklinton. Chief Deputy Sheriff Delos Wood, Deputy McCauley McCain, and a white citizen named Brad Spears came to support Magee. The Negro family was gathered on the back porch—Samuel Wilson, an uncle, Tempie, the mother, and the young men with their brothers and sisters. According to the testimony offered in the brief trial, Deputy Wood advanced to the porch steps and told the young man Jerome, "Come with me, boy." There are various accounts of what happened thereafter. A dispatch written by a local white reporter for the New Orleans *Times-Picayune*, after the lynching of Jerome Wilson six months later, said that "several of the members of the Wilson family *pounced* upon the deputy sheriff when he attempted to arrest one of their number." (Italics mine)

The trial evidence purported to show that the deputy had drawn his pistol and moved toward Jerome when the latter refused to come with him. Moise, a younger brother, stood in the deputies' path and grabbed for the gun. In the scuffle, the deputy fired two shots into the boy's stomach. The mother, Tempie, tried to shield her son, Jerome. Luther and Jerome were shot. The boy, Felton, was shot in the leg. Jerome is then alleged to have run into the house, and fired through the window at Deputy Wood, killing him instantly.

In the excitement, Luther got away from the scene and hid in the woods. Sisters Alexzine and "Bunch" ran off toward the woods. Commanded by one of the white men to come back, "Bunch" returned. Alexzine jumped over a barbed wire fence, but her naked foot was caught and severely lacerated. She limped across two miles of woods and cotton patches to the home of a white neighbor, who took her in and cared for her wounds, and whose memory is forever blessed in the memories of all of the Negroes in the community for this kindness.

The rest of the Wilsons were lodged in jail. Moise died on the night of the shooting in jail, without medical attention for him or for his wounded brothers. Luther was caught the next morning and the Negro family accused of harboring him was also jailed. An attempt was made to lynch the entire family on the night of the lynching, and the Negroes give the credit for restraining the mob to several white men living near the Bethel community.[4] The confidence of these Negroes in "their own white folks," and their utter conviction that the would-be lynchers were "white folks we don't know" is not without significance.

Nine days after the shooting a special session of court presided over by Judge C. Ellis Ott began the trial of Jerome Wilson for the murder of Deputy Sheriff Delos Wood. Indictments were also drawn against Tempie, the mother, Sammy, an uncle, and Luther, the older brother. Some weeks after Jerome's conviction Tempie and Sammy were released on bond.

The trial opened on the morning of July 30, and the case was in the hands of the jury by the afternoon of the next day. While Jerome Wilson was being carried in a chair from the courtroom to the jail, to await the verdict, a group of men in the courthouse yard attempted to take the prisoner away from the officers. The sheriff relieved tension by an address to the mob in which he asked its members to "give the jury a chance." The jury had its chance; a verdict of "guilty" was returned on the morning of August 1.

The defense filed notice of an appeal, and Wilson was remanded to the Franklinton jail to await the action of the Supreme Court of Louisiana. The Negroes in the community were certain that the appeal would be granted, although they could not understand why the local authorities refused to transfer Jerome to a distant jail for safe-keeping.

I came into the Parish in October of 1934. With my wife I was to live in the Star Creek community, another community of Negro owners some two miles distant from the Bethel community. My business was to be that of community study and school improvement under the auspices of the Julius Rosenwald Fund. The shooting and the trial was scarcely two months old, and our advent was accompanied by easily discernible, and as easily understood, suspicion on the part both of whites and blacks. It was quite generally believed that we were detectives, seeking to uncover some hidden details of the late incident. The Negroes suspected that we might be spies for the white people, and the white people believed that we were sent to investigate the shooting for some organization "from up North" interested in "nigger rights."

It was only by adroit and persistent refusal to meddle with this powder magazine that we were able—or at least, thought we were able—to disarm all of the suspicions of the Negroes, and many of those entertained by the white people. We settled ourselves in a little cabin and proceeded to make ourselves as comfortable as possible. This involved the putting in of screens, a task with which our Negro neighbors cooperated but feebly as they advised us that screens were entirely unnecessary. For the first few nights we could see the stars through our roof; but a few days' work enabled us to "seal" the shingle, weatherboarding walls and ceilings, and at the same time to reach some kind of understanding with our neighbors who dropped in to help and to watch the progress of the work.

When I asked a Louisiana librarian for a history of Washington Parish, he shook his head with scarcely concealed pity for my ignorance. "Nothing has ever happened in Washington Parish. Natchitoches? St. Martinsville? The Teche Country? Opelousas? There's plenty of history I can give you about those places. But *nothing* has ever happened in Washington Parish!" Yet a prominent white man in Washington

Parish told me with awe of the olden times—"They was ignormous things done in them days!"

Both of my informants, it proved, were right. The "Florida Parishes" have no "history" in terms of picturesque records of romantic Spanish Caballeros, or Creole dandies, or the legendary "black Mammy" of the plantation tradition. The isolation of this backwoods area, however, led to deeds whose "ignormity" is sprinkled through the rotting files of newspapers and the yellowed documents of official investigating committees, and in the memories of the old men and women of the Parish. Family feuds were as bloody and persistent as those in any Kentucky mountain county. Bordered both to the North and East by Mississippi, desperadoes from that State found a convenient refuge in the forests of Washington Parish; and black and white lawbreakers within the "Florida Parishes" found it convenient to step across the State line into sanctuary. The Parish bordering on Washington to the West earned the name of "Bloody Tangipahoa."

Washington Parish (county units elsewhere are "parishes" in Louisiana) is, culturally and geographically, an extension of the Coastal Plain that skirts the sea-ward borders of the South from Virginia to Texas. Washington Parish in Louisiana is, in fact, one of the "Florida Parishes" of the State, a part of the old Spanish Province of West Florida. The Spanish colonial influence never reached the "piney woods" of Northwest Florida from the port of Pensacola. The Latin culture of Spanish and French colonials which gives richness to the Louisiana tradition never penetrated the pine forests of the "Florida Parishes," although New Orleans is a scant seventy miles south of Franklinton. While trade and culture followed "The Old Spanish Trail" from East to West, the "piney woods" section was peopled by Scotch-Irish pioneers from the American hinterland. The wealthy slave owners were few in number, and they settled in the fertile river lowlands.

In 1860 Washington Parish numbered in its population only one thousand slaves and two thousand white persons. The slave owners and their slaves formed a "black belt" down the center of the Parish, from North to South, along the lowlands of the Bogue Chitto River. The great mass of the poor white population lived in the piney woods, a sub-region that stretched down from the contiguous uplands of Mississippi. Ten years before the Civil War one hundred and forty-eight white families owned all of the 1,037 Negro slaves. There were two hundred and fifty seven other white families without slaves, and largely without land.

During Reconstruction political riots, assassinations, and "white-capping" were in almost daily vogue. In 1868 Washington Parish reported 646 votes for the Democratic, Seymour presidential ticket, with none for Grant. A Republican Registrar reported that he was shot at three times in Franklinton, and that the Republican vote among whites and blacks was suppressed by open intimidation and frequent murder. A Democratic witness retorted that the Republican had left Franklinton "owing Charley Woods a big bill for Whiskey."

The Balltown riot of 1901 is not celebrated in any history, but it remains in the memory of the old Negroes as a frightful massacre ending with the burial of Negro dead under military guard—"We didn' have nuthin' to bury 'em in; some we wropped in coats, and some we wropped in quilts, and some we jus' had to bury in they clothes." The Balltown riot was an unhappy sequel to Negro participation in politics, and was precipitated by tales told to suspicious whites by a lying Negro. Believing that the Negroes were planning to massacre all of the whites—a belief bedded in the psychoses of ante-bellum slave insurrections—a group of white men surrounded a Negro church and shot down the terrified, unsuspecting worshippers as though they had been squirrels in a cage.[5] The participation of Negroes in politics occasioned bitter and bloody conflicts, but in the end only served to entrench the old families and the old politicians more firmly in control of the Parish. Since the Parish was not an area of large plantations, the minority Negro group occasioned no fundamental disturbance of the economic pattern in their transition to freedom.

There is little obvious structural change in the composition of society in Washington Parish of today as compared to what it was "befo de War." The names of the "prominent white people" of today are the same as those which appear in the random printed accounts of affairs in the Parish in 1865, and in the same relative social strata. The sons of the large slave-owners have become bankers, lawyers, physicians, and store-keepers, in addition to maintaining large land holdings in the rural areas. The "poor whites" of yesterday are the small farmers and tenants of today. The "middle class" of this society has the same relative composition today, the same family membership and the same relationship of retainers to the "upper" class. Its members hold minor political offices, work at skilled trades, and occasionally develop a successful farm.

There were two decisive differences, however, between the status of Negroes in the Parish as compared to other comparable regions in the South. Washington Parish had an abundance of free land, open under the Government to homestead entry; and the emancipated Negroes could achieve the economic emancipation of acquiring "forty acres and a mule" which even so determined a "radical" as Thaddeus Stevens once said to be far more important to the Negro's final freedom than the privilege of voting. Of equal importance was the fact that racial miscegenation was an accepted pattern of life on this raw frontier. No southern community is without instances of open concubinage involving white men and Negro women; and in these instances the relationship has been acknowledged at least tacitly, conferring upon the mulatto sons and daughters such prerogatives as immunity from arrest where a "pure Negro" would be speedily haled before the Courts; and corresponding social and economic favors which gave the mulatto a "marginal status" not only in the minds of white and black, but in his own estimation of his personality and his role in society.

Cheap land and miscegenation in Washington Parish made possible the development of segregated Negro farm-owning communities under the patronage of white relatives, who, in the nature of things, were usually members of the old white families in the community. Mulatto sons were, typically, more restless, and either through temperament or early background unfitted to remain in the rural community. Most of these men are scattered in nearby towns as small tradesmen and teachers. The mulatto daughters were usually married off to progressive black men; and to many of these black tenants their wives brought a dowry of "forty acres," or the patronage of white fathers which aided them in obtaining this escape from tenant life.

The close relations between white and black, which made of concubinage an accepted feature of life in the period following the Civil War, ran through other aspects of life. White owners and Negro tenants worked together in the fields. The children of these parents played together, and, like them, worked together during their early years. Today these children of the post-Reconstruction days are men and women on the verge of old age. They know each other personally, and they have an affection for each other which is difficult to project into an abstracted view of a community in which a lynching can take place. To me it came as a shock to hear a Negro call a white man familiarly by his first name, to observe white families visiting Negro families and "taking coffee" with them, to see a white man sit down to dinner at "hog killing time," while across the table sat a Negro man who was, genuinely, his friend; and who, quite as genuinely, was also eating with no consciousness of the violation of a taboo almost as fundamental as those involved in sex mores.

Franklinton is the seat of government of Washington Parish. Twenty-eight miles to the east is the town of Bogalusa, the capital of an industrial barony that includes most of the "Florida Parishes" and neighboring Mississippi counties to the North and East. The founder of Bogalusa was an Irish lumberman, William Henry Sullivan, who was the agent of "them Goodyear boys from Buffalo," incorporated as the Great Southern Lumber Company. Sullivan died in 1929. He is important to this story because, if he had been living six years later, the first lynching of 1935 would not have occurred, in all probability, within thirty miles of his capital. For Sullivan was an autocrat; ruthless, sometimes whimsical, but always supreme, and lynchings were no part of the program of the process of civilization which he inaugurated in the Parish. Not that he was averse to violence, where the interests of his realm seemed to demand it. He crushed an incipient effort to unionize the Bogalusa mills by playing one race off against the other, and, when that appeared on the verge of failure, by brutal force that left four white union organizers dead on the streets of the town he had made.[6]

Sullivan had no hypocrisies regarding what appeared to him as a necessary control, by his company, over the public officials of the "Florida Parishes." He reminded local rebels that the Great Southern paid sixty-five percent of the taxes in Washington Parish, and suggested to them that there were other attractive places to live if they did not approve of the policies of the Company. These policies were not highly popular among the native citizenry, many of whom were inclined to be ungrateful at the prospect of being civilized. One of the sops thrown to the native Cerberus was to allow the pristine aristocracy of Franklinton to maintain a nominal control over public affairs.

The taxes paid by the company are low enough, in all conscience. They have, nevertheless, brought good schools to a barren wilderness, and, with good roads, truck transportation to carry the poorest children of what was yesterday a wilderness to well built consolidated schools. Even Negro high school children are given free transportation to a central higher school at Franklinton, an expenditure which elsewhere in the South would be regarded as ridiculously wasteful if not dangerously subversive of the public good. Beautiful paved roads stretch through the "Florida Parishes," testifying to the good relations maintained in the past between the dynasty of lumber and the dynasty of the Louisiana Demos. Those roads also symbolize the civilizing process by which the isolation of the backwoods is being destroyed.

Sullivan is dead, the woods are gone for almost a thousand miles around, and the mills at Bogalusa are half emptied by the depression and by labor saving devices. The shrewd Yankees who have succeeded the florid Irishman in the seat of Empire still rule the barony, but they are more interested in cutting operation costs than in the preservation of the aura of autocracy over every aspect of their feudal estate. Washington Parish never had time to become what Sullivan wanted it to be, a completely industrialized, civilized land which would redound to the credit and profit of the Great Southern Lumber Company. The mills, the schools, the roads, the new attitude toward racial conflict that tolerates it only as a device for maintaining industrial peace; these are still new social institutions to the men and women who were born in the time when the "Florida Parishes" were wilderness backwoods.

In our little world of Star Creek, and its adjoining community, Bethel, personal relations between white and black were as varied as between States of the North and the South. I had long appreciated the fact that generalizations about the South could not meet such diverse conditions as are presented by such States as Kentucky and Mississippi; and I recognized, too, the vast separation in culture and the pattern of life between such distinct areas as North Alabama and the Black Belt of the same State. I was not prepared for the realization that gradually dawned upon me; that in our little microcosm there were repeated the differences which set off much larger political units from one another. In our little Negro communities in the Northern edge of the Parish, we were as completely isolated from what in other portions of the same small unit would be the characteristic pattern of "race relations" as though we had lived in the Kentucky mountains and our neighbors, ten miles distant, had lived in Central Alabama.

Our Negro neighbors at Star Creek and at Bethel were admirable persons. They were not the modern proto-types of the Homeric "blameless Ethiopians"—but they were and are responsible, industrious, intelligent and self-respecting men and women. They possessed loyalty and character, humour and a quiet grace in their accustomed behaviour.

The natural leader of the Star Creek community was Old Man Jerry Giles. Hardly literate, Mr. Giles had reared a houseful of children and sent them all out to farm or to work honorably in cities and towns North and South. Just once Mr. Giles told me of his boy who had graduated from Howard University and was working for the Government for $175 a month, when "Tuberculosis got him and he come home to die." It was the crowning sadness of his strong old life, but Mr. Giles did not tell the story for the sake of my sympathy.

It was Mr. Giles who led the drive for the Rosenwald School building, who helped raise a thousand dollars in cash, who rented a saw mill, who directed the men of the community in cutting logs that were finished into lumber for the school at the rented mill. It was Mr. Giles who got the community to set aside every third Saturday to care for the community graveyard, and who thought of ploughing up the whole surface of that weedy spot and sowing it to flowers that made a gorgeous blanket of rich color between the headstones. It was Mr. Giles who organized a Sunday-School in the schoolhouse, to maintain religious interest on every Holy Day of the month in addition to the Fourth Sunday when services were held in the church.

Among our first visitors at Star Creek was a white farmer from close by whose conversation with his Negro acquaintances furnished us with our first shock, as well as our first introduction to the complexities of the situation into which we had fallen. His name, for our purposes here, is Jessie Bent, and when I heard the Negroes calling him "Jessie," and arguing with him on the most intimate terms, I assumed that he was an exceptionally light complexioned mulatto. When I inquired later, however, I found that Jessie Bent was a white man, and the old Negro who told me scoffed at the thought. "Why, me and Jessie was brung up together!" There was in our community another family of Bents—a Negro family; and the two most common family names among our neighbors, the Giles and the Bruces, were parallelled in both races.

Immediately we came to the conclusion that these similarities in family names were the result of the institution of slavery, when the Negroes went by their master's name. It did not take long to find, however, that this conclusion was largely inaccurate. The Negro Bents, and the Giles, and the Bruces, whether white or black, stemmed in most instances from the illegitimate unions of white men with black women in the period after emancipation; and there were still living in the community old patriarchs who directed the destinies of both white and black children and grandchildren whom they had brought into being.[7]

My wife and I found ourselves in a community where gossip was impossible—for us. Let not the unwary join in the general condemnation of Uncle John Bruce, because of his open drunkenness at the community fair. Uncle John turns out to be Jeff Bent's mother's brother—and, while Jeff was loudest in his shocked criticism, everyone took it with a grain of familial salt. And Mr. Fred, who "didn' believe a public man oughta act like that, does you, Perfesser?", would be pained if you agreed with him, for Uncle John is his sister Nellie's cousin. You wonder why Uncle John is not his—Fred's—cousin, and you find that second and third marriages, and even an infrequent "outside" (illegitimate) connection makes all the world akin in Star Creek and Bethel.

The same thing is true where conversation about the white people is concerned. Where there is not actual blood kinship, sometimes openly recognized by the whites, there is likely to be some very personal relationship between white and black that forbids criticism. Mr. Billie is a white country store keeper at a neighboring crossroads, and the temptation to laugh at him with someone else is almost irresistible. But Mr. Billie is credited by the Negroes with having saved the entire Wilson family from being lynched, and they depend upon him for small loans in times of need which he grants without usury.[8] Old Mr. Bent's conduct in having a mulatto mistress fifty years ago may seem scandalous to some, but he was actually Mr. Fred's father-in-law, once helped to get a brother of Fred's out of the penitentiary, and helped the black husband of his mulatto daughter to buy the forty acres upon which the family now lives.

The result was that we kept our mouths shut about everything except the weather. We resolutely refused to be baited into a discussion of white and black. We listened—and we learned.

John Wilson, the farmer and landowner whose life was shattered by the violent deaths of two sons in 1934 and 1935. He provided Horace Mann Bond with much of the material for "Forty Acres and a Mule."

Tempie Magee Wilson, who took her children to Chicago after the lynching of her son Jerome. She never saw her husband, John Wilson, again.

Alexzine, the eldest daughter of John and Tempie Wilson, who fled the family farm after the shootout on July 21, 1934.

Burnell, the Wilsons' middle daughter.

Onshell, the Wilsons' youngest daughter.

Felton, the youngest Wilson son, who was wounded in the shootout of July 21, 1934.

Wade Magee, Tempie Wilson's father. Paterfamilias and Republican politico, Magee was reputedly a son of slaveholder John Magee.

Julia Magee, Wade Magee's wife, the daughter of "old man Eli Magee." Julia Magee ended her days in Chicago.

Ophelia Magee Scarborough, Tempie Wilson's sister, who sheltered the Wilson family in Baton Rouge after they fled Washington Parish.

Rev. A. J. Scarborough, schoolteacher, minister of the Holiness Church, and husband of Ophelia Magee.

Horace Mann Bond while traveling for the Rosenwald Fund.

Horace Mann Bond with his mentor, University of Chicago sociologist Robert Park, and Lewis W. Jones.

Horace Mann Bond as a young man.

Julia W. Bond and Horace Mann
Bond at their wedding party,
October 11, 1930.

Star Creek Diary

October 18, 1934.

Mr. Travis is a white man, a renter who has a farm of sixty acres just beyond Mr. Ernest Magee's place. While we were working on the house today, Mr. Travis showed up with four dogs, two hounds, a bird dog, and a poodle. Mr. Travis has deep set eyes, with an expression almost exactly like the saturnine countenance displayed in the older prints of Andrew Jackson. His hair was thick and brushy, uncut, with a streak or so of grey.

He was talking to Mr. Monroe, whom he called Uncle Monroe,[1] about crops and syrup making. Syrup making is next month. I was not introduced—I never am introduced to white people. Then the conversation veered around to talk of dogs. It seems there are a lot of people who like to poison dogs.

"You know, Uncle Monroe, I don't believe a man oughta keep a mean dog, but I don't believe a feller oughta poison dogs. A man get's a lot of misery keepin' a mean dog. I usedta have a pup that was a bitin' dog—only bitin' dog I ever had. He had scratched up two or three people around the place, and I told 'em all to just pick up a chunk and kill him if he bothered them. None of 'em 'ud do it. I usedta live at a place where my hogs slept right up next to the fence, right in the corner of the yard. Well, somebody chunked three or four biscuits up into the yard, and the next morning three of my hogs were all stretched out, all swelled out. You see, Monroe? That's what a man gets for keepin' a bitin' dog.

19

"Before I moved down here there was a feller who owned some sheep, and he'd go 'round with a bunch of biscuits in his punting pocket and just toss 'em out whenever he passed by a yard. Suppose one of the leetle ones had picked it up and et it? I'm tellin' you, Monroe, he coulda done it—one of these leetle uns coulda picked up one of them biscuits and et it before youda knowed about it.

"Well, me an Bill Smith took our twenty two rifles and we went over where his sheep was pasturin' and then we just sat there and killed sheep til we got tired. We just piled 'em up. We sent word to him who done it, but he never done nothing about it."

(After this tale, which I could not help but shudder at, I believe that Mr. Travis began to put me in my place. He began to use the word "darky" in his conversation, telling about an old darky who used to get drunk with him.)

After he left, Mr. Monroe told me—

"He's a pretty good man, excep' when he's drinkin. He drinks an awful lot. When he's drinkin' with you, he wants you to do anything he wants you to do. But aside from that, he's a purty good man. He'll treat you right."

The next place to Mr. Monroe's twenty acres is owned by a widow woman. Her husband deserted her. "He jus picked up and lef' her. He was sho' doin fine. He had three milk cows, lots of hogs, two fine saddle horses, and they jus lived. But along came this woman and he tuk up with her, and jus left his wife and all his little uns. He's a living down at Bogalusa now, I heerd 'em say. He's gone down to nuthin. He used to make as high as $10 a day. He could do most anything. He could move houses, he could bore wells, he was jus a man who knowed what to do.

"There's another couple used to live in that tin covered house over beyont the school. The woman used to work over on the railroad near Amite. She was doin' well. At last they busted up, and she bought his half the property.

"Then he took up with Boy Bickham's girl, and they been livin' together ever since, ain't been married or nuthin."

October 21, 1934.
Arrived from New Orleans about 2:00. Mr. Monroe and Ernest at home. This is the Third Sunday and we wanted to be back in time for church, the Baptist church. Both barefoot. Taking their rest. When I said I was going to church, both said that it was too late to go to Jerusalem, but that there were services at St. James, the Methodist church. Ernest dressed to go with us. He looked quite debonair in his Sunday clothes, a vest, a green shirt, a blue pair of trousers, well pressed and very clean, and a good hat, with new tan shoes.

On the road to church we passed several groups. Church was over. We passed the preacher's son with two girls, one of whom was a light complexioned girl, the daughter of Luther Graves, whom Ernest said was his first cousin. At the church a few people were still standing around. The preacher was Reverend Downs, a short light complexioned man, probably a mulatto, with grey-blue eyes. I met several deacons—Mr. Manning, a trustee of the school, Mr. Fortinberry, an old man, very old, who, for all his black skin, looked very much like an old Irishman. Fortinberry told me he had been a deacon for forty-six years. I also saw Mis' Lulu, the wife of Mr. Ranse Magee, and Ranse Magee.

On the way back I went to Clifton to get some cigarettes. The filling station and store of Mr. Young was closed. We drove on up to Warnerton. Here Ernest bought a bottle of beer. It is a rural saloon, as Warnerton is just across the line from Mississippi and there were a number of loungers around.

October 22, 1934. Monday.
We went to Bogalusa. On the way I went to see Superintendent Stringfield. "So you're the boy Mr. Lewis[2] sent down here." "Yessir." After a short conversation in which I used my best white folks manners, Mr. Stringfield agreed to help in getting paint for Blackjack and Star Creek. He told me to see Mr. Fletcher Smith, the school board member for my ward.

At Bogalusa we purchased a small wood stove, no. 7, for the house. $10.00 cash. Cash prices are thirty to forty percent lower than time prices. Most of the merchants in Bogalusa are Jews. Our stove was purchased from M. Marx, typically urban. The Jews are the only city people in this country, quite as brisk and as cosmopolitan as they would be in Chicago. Several younger Jews were around, talking about the exploits of "Little Monk" Simons in the Tulane-Georgia game Saturday, in which Simons starred. Probably Simons is a Jew.

The used car in which we went to Bogalusa did very well on the pavement, but coming back on the rough roads the distributor began to miss badly. We just managed to get home.

October 23, 1934. Tuesday.
We gathered up our things and moved up to the house. It took two loads on Mr. Monroe's wagon. Miss Lulu came over and watched vigorously. I put in screens, which are largely ornamental, considering the numerous cracks in the walls, and the open spaces under the eaves.

While we were moving, Miss Lulu told about the news that Mr. Alec Burton died last night. He had been po'ly for some time. Mr. Manning had brought the news around to get some men to help dig the grave. There was mild speculation over the time of the burial. The news was received quite philosophically. "Well, Monroe," said Miss Lula, "he's gone the way all of us have to go!" "Yes," said Mr. Monroe, with great solemnity.

"I guess they'll be buryin' him today" said Mr. Monroe. "Yes," said Miss Lula, squinting at the hot sun. "I'm sure they will."

I went in the old Ford with Ernest to tell some of his cousins to come help with the potato grubbing on Wednesday. The Ford behaved abominably, finally stopping at intervals. Ernest told me on the way of a spot where he had got drunk with a cousin of his off of corn beer, the preparation of which sounds like the formula for what I used to know as "Choc" or "Choctaw Beer" in Oklahoma. It is the vilest drink known to man, actually a simple mash strained, and produces a sick drunk. The cousin on this occasion, after finishing a jug, sat down on a bridge, then crawled into the swamp until he sobered up. There is not much talk of drunkenness, or much evidence of it. The people are too busy to get drunk. Whenever the subject is mentioned, reference is made to Mr. Travis, the white tenant who lives not far off, and whose carouses seem to be classic.

On the way we passed a woman getting peas in the garden. She waved. "That's the woman who likes the beatin's," said Ernest. It appears that this woman claims that she must have her husband beat her once a month, to keep her happy. Whether the people attach more than a casual interest to this phenomenon is unknown to me.

Coming back from Franklinton I picked up a man, a relative of the Mr. Burton who died. The roads were very bumpy, and he sat on the back seat. The bumping made him sick. I stopped to let him heave. He got off two or three miles from home to walk through the swamp. He protested that it was not the bumping, but that he had been dizzy at spells, and was bilious. After he got out, Ernest told me, "I spec' the trouble with him is that he's knocked up his wife again. He's good for that." Although I understood the phrase perfectly, I did not see the question, and asked Ernest what he meant. "I mean, he got his wife in a family way again. You know that gets the men too, like it gets the women."

The bye roads are terrible, but are graveled along wherever a white man lives, even if surrounded with Negroes.

I went to Clifton and Ernest went with me. He advised me to go to Mr. Willie's store, Mr. Willie Bickham. Mr. Bickham is an old country gentleman at whose store I phoned New Orleans from Saturday. His wife was in today. I had on overalls, and it helped me in buying a tub, marked a dollar. She knocked off a dime. Mr. Bickham, Mr. Monroe told me, is a very good white man. He is credited with having helped get the Wilson family off as light as they have, so far, after killing the deputy, and of averting the lynching of the family. Mr. Monroe also told me that whenever he wanted a dollar or two, Mr. Willie would let him have it. Apparently there is a relationship of dependence between these Negro owners and the store keepers much like that dependence between tenants and landlords. Ernest has an account with Mr. Bickham. Most of the Negroes seem to have accounts with one or the other of the store owners in Clifton.

October 24, Wednesday.
Today was devoted to potato picking by the Magees. Several families of their relation helped. They don't seem to have a suitable plow, but borrowed it from a neighbor. (A two horse grubber.)

Thursday, October 25, 1934.
The potato digging, which had been deferred until the last day of the full moon, was not completed Wednesday. Thursday morning a light rain fell beginning at 4 o'clock. Mr. Monroe was greatly disturbed, because to put the potatoes in the potato house while they were wet was an inducement to rotting. Mr. Monroe and Ernest had received cotton tickets, notifying them that they could sell more of their cotton if they got the tickets. I carried them to Franklinton, where they waited in line for the tickets.

At the Ford place, I got my old Ford again. The Negro helper seems to be much more intelligent than any of the white mechanics.

I came back through Black Jack, where I met with the trustees of the school at 2:30 o'clock. The trustees are Mr. Melton Magee, Mr. Nelson, and Mr. Luther Bickham. Mr. Melton Magee takes the lead here as elsewhere.[3] I learned that the people here raised $500 in cash and contributed $600 in labor in building this school. They had raised money at other times to put up additional buildings. The plot is three acres. A demonstration garden is on the lot. There are three buildings—the plot is planted with a hedge around the driveway, there is a canna bed, an excellent pump, and sanitary privies. All are in a state of disrepair.

I was somewhat confused at the fact that evidently I was expected to tell exactly what I was there for. I talked in generalities about my mission, but it was clear that all felt that I had said nothing. It was agreed that we were to go to see Mr. Fletcher Smith, the board member for this district or ward, that afternoon. Mr. Magee, the principal, also a Magee, and myself drove over. The member was not at home. His wife was there. We went to the backdoor. Mrs. Smith was quite polite. We made arrangements to see Mr. Smith the next evening. The Smith home is comfortable, Mrs. Smith plainly dressed. The house has a delco light attachment, is screened, with an artesian well. Most of the white homes in this neighborhood, where of well-off owners, have these conveniences.

I then drove back to Star Creek. My wife told me that a strange man had come in the back yard while I was gone, and had frightened her very much. He was either a white man or a mulatto, but she believed that he might have been a white man, because he didn't talk like a Negro at all. It turned out that this was Mr. Ed Magee, Mr. Monroe Magee's step-son, Ernest's brother, probably a half-brother to Ernest.[4]

As I walked down the hill, I saw Ed in the wagon. He was going to haul potatoes. Evidently he felt a sense of shame at seeing me, a fellow city man (I had on my city clothes), and his first words, although I had never seen him before, were, "They've made a farmer of me already." (Indicating his overalls.) It developed that Ed works in Bogalusa, with a lumber company. Mrs. Gabe says that he is frequently taken for a white man, and it caused a great deal of laughter when it developed that he had thought that my wife was a white woman, and that he too had been frightened or surprised to see a white woman in the place where he expected to see the Magees. Ed seems to be a thoroughly urbanized (small town) individual. His tales of trips to New Orleans and Brookhaven and Mobile quite angered Ernest.

October 26, 1934. Friday.
This morning I got up late, about 8:00. By the time breakfast had been cooked, water drawn, and wood cut, it was about 10. I walked toward the school. On the way I passed by Mr. Monroe's, and found Orsell there.[5] He had come earlier, but they had not seen any fire up at our house (smoke) and so he had just waited. The potatoes were all in the house.

At the schoolhouse Mr. Crane, the vocational teacher, met me effusively.[6] Mr. Crane is a tall, somewhat stout reddish yellow man, of fifty or more. He has only a lower set of false teeth, or perhaps the upper half was just absent when I saw him. The sight of his perfect row of lower teeth against the red gums of his upper jaws reminded me of nothing so much as of carrion against stripped bone. Mr. Crane had met me at Franklinton during the Fair, when I had carried some exhibits for the Star Creek school down there.

He advanced enthusiastically with outstretched hand. "You're Professor Bond, the gentleman working for the Rosenwald Fund, I believe. You know, Barker told me about you. I'm certainly glad to meet you. I was just asking somebody if you were here. I was about to come over to your house. Old Boy Bickham told me, 'Professor, he's a man something like you. Sometime we see him in overalls and sometimes he's dressed up.' "

I answered in between as best I could. I asked him for the estimate on the paint. At Blackjack the young principal, Magee, had prepared an elaborate memorandum figuring out the number of square feet for inside and outside surfaces and the specified number of gallons of paint required. This had come to around 102 gallons, the estimated cost being about $275, a staggering sum in my comprehension, so far as presenting the bill to the School Board for one item for a Negro school.

Mr. Crane seized a piece of scratch paper and on the basis of his memory, figured out 34 gallons. He stated that the school board would give him that. The school board, he said, would give him anything he wanted. They had just given him $100 for three toilets. He scoffed at the Black Jack estimate.

Evidently Mr. Crane, a good white folks nigger, was willing to give the Board an estimate for paint that he knew to be woefully deficient and that would result in inferior results. The young man, Magee, had not yet learned how to do this.

I then asked the other teacher, who was teaching a class in the same room, Mr. W. E. Sibley, to let me see his register. The register was in frightful shape. The roll had not been called for several days. Mr. Sibley comes to school whenever he wants to, apparently, until my arrival, since when he has been more careful. Mr. Sibley told me at once that the register was not quite accurate, as some of the children had been promoted. I then asked him to check the names of those who had been promoted. He took the register and wrote after several names, "po[*sic*]moted."

After copying out some facts from the register, I took my departure. Going back to the house, I went with Orsell and Ernest to Tylertown to get some lumber for a table and for screen doors.

Coming back, Orsell worked on the doors for a few hours. He improvised the carpenter's device by which correct angles are sawed, to the great admiration of one or two of my neighbors who had come over to draw water.

As I had to go to Franklinton in the evening, I suggested to Orsell that he knock off and let me drop him by his home. He did so, and on the way we fell into conversation about schools. Orsell, I do not think can write or read. He told me that the schools were very bad. His little boy had gone to school under Miss Dyson at Star Creek, and he considered her a good teacher. He had learned how to recognize all his alphabets, and "he could print his name as pretty as you please." But he was now enrolled at Bethel, and he hadn't learnt anything. "Professor, you know we don't have us any good teachers. The schools ain't much good. Now, they open up school, and they get ready for the Fair. Then they get ready for a big Christmas concert. Then after Christmas they start the children workin' for closin' concerts, and they don't teach 'em anything."

I asked him what sort of a man was Professor Crane. Professor Crane, by the way, had called his class of three little urchins together while I was copying the names from the register. He used the class to recite his own virtues to me and to cast innuendoes at Professor Magee at Black Jack who had displaced him, both for my benefit.

"Now boys, what is a dual purpose chicken?"

One little boy replied, "It's a hen what lays eggs."

"Is that all a dual purpose chicken is?"

Another little boy said brightly, "It lays and can be et, too."

"That's right," said Professor Crane enthusiastically.

(It appears to me that here is precisely the basic problem of vocational agriculture in these schools. The teachers are not intelligent enough to translate the verbiage of the agricultural professors into terms understandable by the children; nor do they have the respect of the community as practical farmers in their own right.)

Professor Crane went on with the lesson.

"Now boys, what can you do with you peanuts? You can plant 'em, can't you? And you can raise you some chickens, and you can raise you some cane, and some peanuts, and you can exhibit 'em at the Fair, and maybe you can win some money. I won six dollars with my Plymouth Rocks at the Fair. Now, you can't expect a man to tell people to raise fine purebred duroc hogs if he ain't got some himself, or some Plymouth Rock hens if he cain't do it hisself, can you?" (This a crack for my benefit at Magee, also a crack at showing me what a fine practical farmer he, Crane, was.)

To continue with Orsell on Crane. "He's just a windbag, professor. Why, some of the young folks got up a petition to get rid of him, but he's in with these white folks—Stringfield and Barker and Bickham are mighty tricky. Whenever Barker and Crane want to put anything over they get Stringfield to write it out here under his name. They're full of tricks."

I asked Orsell about Mr. Barker. "Well," he said, "he's a Barker." I asked him what he meant, family or name. He answered, "Both. His father was a deacon in the church, and one of the biggest rascals around here."

Coming back from town I passed Mr. Bickham—Boy—with Luther Graves, the car stuck with a blowout. Mr. Bickham was gentleman enough to stick with the party in distress. Miss Gabe had gone to town too. Little Oliver Graves was along. Orsell had asked me to carry his little children, a little girl and a boy, up to their grandfather's house, Mr. Monroe.

About 5:30 I went with Mr. Boy Bickham over to see Fletcher Smith, the white school board member for this ward. On the way Mr. Bickham told me about the teachers. "Professor, we have just cheap-grade teachers here." I asked him about the method of appointment. It seems that Mr. Stringfield won't send anybody to Star Creek whom the people don't like. Mr. Bickham was quite frank about Mr. Crane. "Professor, he's just a cheap-grade teacher—about the best we knows about out here. He's in with these white folks. The white folks raised him. He used to pick cotton down in the country with Stringfield and Bateman, and they likes him. He's jus' a good ole nigger, ain't got much sense."

Mr. Bickham on the way also told us about the Cemetery, which is currently reported to be a blaze of color. Mr. Bickham said they plowed it up and sowed flower seed broadcast with the grass seed. "Whatever we has to do, whether the's anything to be done or not, we jus' meets at the Cemetery every second Saturday and works on it iffen there's anything to be done."

I asked Mr. Bickham whose idea the beautifying of the Cemetery was. It was his idea, he said, modestly, quietly, yet proudly.

At Mr. Fletcher Smith's we found Mr. Melton Magee waiting for us. Knowing the expectation of many white men in the South that Negroes should take off their hats when speaking to them, I left my hat in the car and went up bareheaded. I got my first shock when Mr. Melton Magee introduced me to Mr. Smith, not as Professor, not as Doctor, not as Dean, but as "Mister Bond." I do not know of a single Negro principal or teacher in the South who would have done that.

There was no air of deference or slavishness about either Old Man "Boy" Bickham or Melton Magee. They were dignified, self-assured, polite but not to be kidded. Mr. Bickham told Mr. Smith that the school needed "deskes"—that the Star Creek school never had had enough "deskes," although the school board had promised them. He told Mr. Smith that they had some second-hand "deskes" from the white school, and they had always hoped for enough, but they had worked hard for the school, and "they'd wiped their mouths and said nothin," but they knew they ought to have deskes all the time. He told Mr. Smith that the route of the trucks left much to be desired, the children had to walk too far. Mr. Smith told the story about his wife, who had to walk to Warrenton when she was a child, to school. He said that a child who could get to a truck was mighty lucky. Mr. Bickham was supposed to agree, but he said nothing. He maintained an impressive silence that was indubitable evidence that he considered Mr. Smith's illustration beyond the point.

Mr. Smith told one of the familiar jokes I have heard so frequently—he said that "the boys over at Star Creek would come to the school and work and when they went home they would carry a pocket full of nails with them." Mr. Bickham was supposed to laugh. He did not, and it was Mr. Smith and not Mr. Bickham who was obliged to laugh that embarrassed laugh that usually follows on the part of the Negroes.

Mr. Smith told how good the Board had been, and how much he had done for the schools.

"Yassuh, Mr. Smith, but I'se talkin' about what Star Creek needs now."

The manner of both Magee and Bickham was in utter contrast to everything that I have ever experienced so far as the attitude of Negro teachers to superintendents and school board members is concerned.

October 27, Saturday.
Worked on the house.

October 28, Sunday.
Orsell came up to pay me a visit, looking for Ernest. He was all dressed up. He told me of his life as a tenant. The woman for whose husband he works is very fond of his two children, and would like for them to stay at her house. He told me that his wife's sister's husband had suddenly fallen sick, and gone into spasms after a violent headache. He was halfway expected to die, but was better now.

Orsell said that he made it a little better than many of the owners. Jeff Burkhalter, the prosperous Negro tenant, made twenty bales for Mr. Jeff King this year. Orsell works on halves. He made six bales this year. He also works constantly at odd jobs.

(Miz Gabe said that more work could be had on the schools from owners than from tenants, because the white folks said when their tenants came to work on the schoolhouse that "they was just wastin' their times; they calls that idlin.")

Orsell is a carpenter, repairs shoes, drills wells, cuts hair, and has other arts which yield him a steady income.

He ordered a dresser-wardrobe from Sears-Roebuck for $15.51, cash. Both his wife and he have difficulty in writing, so he asked Miz Gabe to write out the order for him. Miz Gabe asked Julia to do it, and Julia asked me to do it.

Orsell says the land now hereabouts is very cheap, the Great Southern now selling some cut-over land for as low as $4.00 per acre.

His wife's sister, Annie Mae Conley, is now at Charity Hospital in New Orleans. Orsell says that it doesn't cost anything to go there, except fare there. His wife was very puny until he carried her there and they operated on her and she came back and she has been fine ever since. The entire cost to Orsell was a round-trip ticket of $1.50 to New Orleans.

Saturday, November 10.
Lotsa folks is a grindin the cane. I went down to Franklinton today and I took with me Mr. Monroe. I went over to the school house when I got up, about seven, and they want [there wasn't] nobody there. I comes on home and carpentered around the house all mornin'. Miz Gabe and the Widow Graves and one of her chillun, a young gal, and one of Luther Graves lil white haired chillun, they come by and picked some cotton outin Miz Gabe's patch for to make some mattresses with.[7]

When I went by the schoolhouse on the way to town, I found seven or eight men helpin Green Bickham finish sealin the schoolhouse and a puttin in the window casins and things. The mostes of us jes sat roun and joreed[8] aw'ile Green was a-finishin the casins, for, like Boy Bickham, he said, "Wesa bout reached the pint where we caint do no more, perfesser, but wese'll have to let Green finish 'er up." They knewed about me a-comin over early like, and Mr. Monroe, he said, "Perfesser, I doan see how you kin lay in bed as late as you does. I couldna no more a do that than I could fly. Me, I allus gits up in the mawnin at fo o'clock."

Then Mr. Griffith a-said, "Monroe, you coulda lie in bed that late iffen you had somebody to lie in bed with." And they all busted out laffin, and they asted me, "What about it, perfesser?" And I saw that Mr. Monroe was a-blushin like, and I said, "I ain't a-goin to say nuthin bout that." And they said, "Perfesser is jist a makin it easy on Monroe."

On the way to Franklinton I picked up a man at Mr. Willie Bickham's store, Mr. Seymour. Mr. Willie's store got robbed t'uther night, so Miz Bickham tole me. They took nigh about a thousand dollar worth of stuff out, so she said. The sheriff is atter em, she said. He thinks its been done by some of these folks that works in cahoots with these peddler folks, that goes aridin aroun the country sayin they sells lower than anybody else. That's how they kin do it, sez Miz Bickham, and they ain't got no license, either.

Mr. Seymour joreed Mr. Monroe about agettin married again, but Mr. Monroe, he never seemed to mind it none atall. He told Seymour, joreein' like, "But you didn't see that woman that a come up here f'om Nawleans to see me, tuther day."

I expecs that Mr. Monroe is agoin to get married real soon, and Julia and I'sa helpin hit along. Now that weve done got the house all sealed, I expecs that Mr. Ernest and Miz Gabe agoin to move into the house as soon as we leave, and Mr. Monroe agoin to take hisself another wife.

Miz Gabe says Mr. Monroe ought to take hisself another wife, acause his nature is agoin to his head iffen he dont.

In Franklinton Mr. Monroe abought hisself fifty syrup cans. Itsa mighty cold today, and Mr. Monroe likely to make syrup any day now. Hes mos got thru strippin the cane, he startin to work at hit early in the mawnin.

When I got home this afternoon, I found that the Graves girl had put on a clean dress and come back to see Julia. She told her all about the killin. There was a preacher a stayin at John Wilson's house, and the white man came and quarrelled with the boys, John Wilson was agone away. The mule already had been dipped at another vat, and the ranger made like he was agoin to go into the pen and git the mule out. And one of the boys cussed him. Alla that trouble came about because that boy cussed that white man. Then the white man went and called up the sheriff, they had been speechless for two weeks, and they wasn't on good terms nohow. Well, the sheriff come, and the shootin began. The gals was so scared that two of em jumped offen the porch and started runnin through the woods. One of em caught her foot in the barbed wire and purty nigh tore her foot off. The white men said, Come back or we'll shoot, and one of the gals was so desprit she jus come on back. When the shootin started, the preacher went out back and he found the sheriff dead and the ranger gettin' ready to kill all of the family, and he went up to him and he said, don't you do that, and he didn't. One of the neighbors awent down to the house, he was a white man, and he asked what was the trouble, and he saw the boy was shot, and he went back to telephone fo a doctor, and the deputy was alyin out kilt, and he didn't see him or know he was kilt.

The gal that ran away kept on arunnin and she got to Mr. Jeff King's place, and Mr. King, he let her stay there all night, and afterward let her stay on his place til things quieted down like.[9] One of the boys, he runned off into the woods behint Mr. Monroe's brother's place and the boy, he slep out in the woods and Mr. Monroe's brother fed him durin the day. When they catched him, they arrested all of Mr. Monroe's brother's folks and took em to jail at Franklinton.

That night, said Oretha Graves, I heerd somethin a stirrin out in the yard, and I went and peeped. They was two white men a sittin out in the yard, a sayin nothin, just a-sittin. They was white men at all the colud folkses house who had cars, and they was a-watchin to see that nobuddy helped this Wilson boy get away in a car. They didn't say nuthin to nobody, excepen one woman's house where they made her make em some coffee.

They was a crowd that acome to the jail at Franklinton that night and wanted to lynch the whole family, and theyda killed everybody in that jailhouse, but they was some white men there that tole em, if you tries to take these folks, we'll shoot. And then they got the soldiers.

(These Negroes are certainly brave people. Imagine feeding a fugitive from justice when you know that detection may mean sudden death, certainly imprisonment! And old John Wilson has moved into a place on the Franklinton black top, and he says, sez Orethia, "they ainta nobuddy agoin to do anythin to me.")

At night I went over to see Mr. Fletcher Smith. He was amilkin cows out in the back, and when I yelled Hello, at the back gate, Miz Smith tole me to go out to the dairy barn and I'da find him there. Mister Smith talked real polite to me, while I stood and watched him milkin. I asted him about the dairy business, and hit want much, to hear him say. It haint been long senct they jus had dairy plants aroun here to handle milk, and most of the folks was too interested in lumberin. Now its acomin.

I asted Mister Smith why the folks roun Star Creek didn't like milk. He said it twas because the run of em never had enny milk. And then there was the way they et the milk, right hot out of the bowl from milkin. Nobuddy'd like milk like that.

"They's a heap a chillen roun here now acomin up with no milk," sez his son, who'se a milkin alongside of 'im. "It sho grieves my heart," sez Mister Smith, "to see chillen acomin up without no milk. My family, why we uses two gallons of milk a day." (Mister Smith mus weigh nigh onto three hundred pound.)

Mister Smith's boy, he starts talkin to Mister Smith about what he's agoin to do tonight. Mister Smith thinks he'll go over and set up with old Mr. King, who's been mighty po'hly of late. Young Mr. Smith thinks he'll be agoin to the show. Tim McCoy is on in a picter. Young Mister Smith told about the way Tim McCoy acted in his last picter.

Atter they got thru milkin, I goes into the yard to talk to Mister Smith. Mister Smith sits down on the runnin board of my car, like he was agoing to talk to me side by side, but w'en I asts him to let me get a book outen the car, he changes his mind and sits down on the runnin board of the milk truck about ten feet away. Mister Smith lights hisself a pipe and sits down. Atter a while, his son acomes out and drives off, and Mister Smith acomes over and sits down besides me. The car rattles all over.

I tells Mister Smith what I'm a tryin to do, and I shows him the book. Mister Smith, he sez that he reads a whole lot, mosly papers, but he sho does appreciate that book and he'll be a lookin at it. He tells me about the way the country used to be, tarnation wild, real desperado country, about thirty years ago. They was some ignormous things done then, sez Mister Smith.

We talks aroun and aroun. Mister Smith tells me about the HOLC.[10] It ain't no good, sez Mr. Smith, because any man that kin git credit from the bank can now get money and get it cheaper than he can git from the scheme. They's too many people alookin for somethin for nuthin. Why, sez Mister Smith, I hadda boy awurkin fer me, and I was a payin him to plow up some land to sow some oats last Fall. He comes to me, and he sez, Mister Smith, I'm agoin to sign up with the relief folks. I tole him, Boy, do you know whut yure doin? And he said, Well, they pays $1.50 a day, and they pays off every night, and I'm a goin to sign up. So I pays him off, and he goes down and signs up. Well, his brother signed up too. He didn't get no card to come to work for about six weeks, and w'en they found out his brother wasa workin too, they laid him off. And he coulda been workin fur me all the time, iffen he had awanted to.

Sunday, November 11, 1934.
Went to Sunday School. Mr. Manning was Superintendent, Mr. Barker secretary. Mr. Bickham asked me to teach the class, but I refused. They are evidently reluctant to expose a supposed ignorance by discussing matters before me. Mr. Bickham then took up the task. He was, evidently, nervous. The lesson was a Peace lesson for Armistice Day. Mr. Bickham skipped, in his reading, Armistice, apparently because he couldn't read it.

The real meaning of the text (if there is any real meaning) eludes these people because of their inability to read. The reading of the Bible yields only the most highly formalized reactions. Key words presenting difficulties in pronunciation are entirely sloughed over. No one seemed to grasp the meaning of the "Peace" lesson. "Peace" was interpreted to mean personal adjustment in the community, with no thought of international conflict. The emphasis in the readings from Galatians was on "morals," witchcraft, idolatry, etc.

When I raised the question of a conflict between pacifism and Law, the interpretation given to Law was the Mosaic Law. No notion seemed to exist of a possible conflict between authority of the State and the Authority of the conscience. The only person who seemed to get my point was one of the Barkers, a bitter faced man very fond of argumentation, more intelligent and better read (or a better reader) than the others, who seems to be heartily disliked by the other men, who, apparently, are more successful farmers, but not as sophisticated. Barker was the only one of the elder men who had on a store suit instead of overalls. He was not the Barker who is the Secretary.

My question about war and the higher law, designed to arouse an argument, succeeded, but the argument was specious in that the other side, composed of Mr. Bickham, Ranse Magee, and others, didn't see the point at all, and were greatly annoyed.

Apparently the only real reason for the Sunday School is that it provides an open forum for debate on topics concerning which there is *some* small fund of information on the part of all concerned. The youngsters take delight in reading verses loudly, showing their superior ability to read as compared to the elders. In last week's Sunday school one young girl, when an argument came up over the difference between charity and kindness, had recourse to a dictionary which she took out of the school bookcase.

The room at the school used for community meetings and for Sunday school is referred to as the "Holy Room." The larger room to which an addition has just been made is the secular room, in which dances, concerts, and affairs of a social nature are held.

This evening I went with my wife to visit Mr. Bickham. Willie Pearl, Mrs. Lu, and Miz Gabe went along. The talk was mostly about old time dancing. Mr. Bickham was quite fond of the idea, and told us about old time fiddlers. The new dances, he said, didn't amount to nothing. But when the old folks useter dance, they just dansted until they was wet all over with sweat. There was old Doc, who could really fiddle a tune. Old Doc, he would come to a frolic, and all the boys and girls they would just about waship old Doc. They'd almost as soon a-spread palm leaves down befo him, alike he was the crowned king. They'd ajus line up befo him, all awaitin to dance, and old Doc, he would ajus take his fiddle and start apattin his foot and play

ta-ta-taroo—lee———

And they would all ajus about start to break down, but old Doc would stop, and he'd start up agin

ta-ta-taroo—lee———

and then he'da stop. And all the boys and gals woulda yell at old Doc, tellin him, Come on, Doc, go on and play, but old Doc woulda jus start up agin

ta-ta-taroo—lee———

and then one of the niggers (Excuse me, perfesser, I jes will say that word) woulda say, I knows w'ats the matter wid old Doc, he ain't had no whiskey—and sure nough, somebody wouda give old Doc the bottle, and he'd up it and drink til it would be mos nigh empty, and then old Doc, he'd start agin—

ta-ta-taroo—lee, ta-ta-taroo,
le-a-di-lee-dee, ta-roo, taroo

and by this time old Doc, he'da been gone. He'da never stop playin the wile the bottle was up to his mouth.

(Miz Gabe told Julia about some woman who had abeen takin too much alum to keep from a-havin any more babies, and she got real puny, the doctors had to give her some body elses blood. Alum, said Miz Gabe, acts jes like persimmons.)

Miz Lu say she don't keer for Jubilees singin in the church. It's alright in the schoolhouse, but it ain't right in the church. Miz Gabe asked her, whyn't it alright in the church? They does it. (Jubilee, these quasi-minstrel troupes with secular songs mixed with others.)

November 14, 1934.
Walked toward the Cemetery today. We were directed to a "cemetery" by several people, walked for miles, and finally reached a white cemetery where a grave was being dug. I asked Jim Burkhalter, Mr. King's tenant, who was there, how far to the colored graveyeard. Both whites and Negroes were digging the grave. We walked on and at the next house found that Mr. Bennie King had died. We walked on to the St. James Cemetery (it proved afterward not to be the cemetery of which Mr. Bickham had spoken, and for which we were looking). From here we walked on to home, by Mr. Bennie King's, and saw a group of white men standing out front talking. A Negro woman crossing the road stopped as we walked up as though to greet us, but when she saw that she did not know us, passed on. All conversation stopped as we walked by the group of white men, who looked at us closely.

Just a little beyond we passed Uncle Dave Griffin, who, in his work-a-day overalls, was on his way to the graveyard, for Mr. King's buryin'. He had been a-shuckin' some cane, and was awful hard rushed, but Mr. King had been a good old man, and he thought'e ought to go down to the buryin. All of them Kings is nice folks.

Passed on. At the school house we met Mr. Monroe on his mule, on the way to the buryin. At one of the houses we had been told that there were some colored folks buried in the white graveyard.

Later in the day, Julia saw Mr. Monroe, and asked him about the colored folks buried in the white folks graveyard. Mr. Monroe was a-sittin on the gallery, Julia and Miz Gabe in the kitchen.

Miz Gabe said, "Mr. Monroe's wife's mother buried there, ain't she, Mr. Monroe?"

"Yes," answered Mr. Monroe, "she's buried there, and a sister of hers is buried there, too." Mr. Monroe did not seem to speak with approval.

"Shure 'nough!" said Julia, animatedly and provocatively.

"Yes," he said, with what seemed like bitterness, but what may have been only hunger, as he had been workin' in the cane patch all afternoon and hadn't had any dinner yet, "but don't nobuddy know where their grave is, though. They weren't never marked."

Mrs. Graves, called a widow-woman, whose husband has deserted her, and who has six girls and numerous boys, was married to a man whom Mr. Monroe constantly berates as a worthless fellow who was doing real good, but never mentions the fact that he, Graves, was Mr. Monroe's first wife's brother. In conversation with Ernest the next day, it develops that Mr. Graves and Mr. Monroe's wife were the children of Mr. Tommie Graves, a white man, still living, now paralytic.[11] It is also Mr. Monroe's wife's mother, by whom Mr. Tommie had a family of mulatto children, who is buried in the white graveyard, and probably her sister had a mulatto family by another or the same white man. Mr. Bennie Graves, whom we met as a caller at the Magee home on the first day of our presence here, and who was "raised up with Mr. Monroe and Mr. Bickham," is related to Mr. Tommie, probably his son. I asked Mr. Ernest if Mr. Tommie looked out for his colored relatives. Mr. Tommie had one boy, he said, who lived out in Texas now, who used to claim Uncle Pete wherever he was. "Sho, Uncle Pete? I know Uncle Pete." He'd do it anywhere, even amongst White folks. You know white folks don't usually like to claim their colored kin." I asked Ernest if Mr. Tommie did anything for his colored kin.

"Sure," said Ernest. "He's known for law, he knows more law than anybuddy in the Parish. Whenever any of em gets in trouble, he goes down to Franklinton and talks around, and pretty soon nuthin is heard about it."

It is also probable that the land of all of these Negroes was acquired by the help of their white relatives. Mr. Monroe for example paid $400 for his place. Mr. Ernest paid $400 for his place. Mr. Graves has a farm next to it. Now, it is quite probable, and will bear investigation, that Mr. Tommie paid the money for Mr. Monroe's farm (his daughter's husband) or for Mr. Graves's farm (his son). Ernest accordingly is his grandson. (Ernest never mentioned the latter.)

There is a Burris family in Franklinton. (White and black.)

Mr. Monroe's father was married three times and had three sets of children. Willie Pearl's father was not Ranse Magee's daughter, although she was Miz Lu's daughter. Willie Pearl is a light mulatto.

Miz Gabe is no relation to Willie Pearl or to Miz Lu, but they call each other "Cousin."

Asking Mr. Ernest about present day relations between white and black women, he says that kind of thing doesn't go on now days. It just happened in the olden time, when the women worked around the white folks and couldn't help themselves. Mr. Ernest's relation to Mr. Tommie was always treated with utter silence, not even implicitly.

Yet, after stating that white women who ran with Negroes in Bogalusa were bad women, Ernest said sadly, here and there there's one who forgets herself,—and Perfesser, a white man and a black woman's the freest thing on earth. They can do what they please.

At the school, Mr. Crane has just got the lumber for a new toilet for the school, and is planning to put it up. The girls and boys were playing basketball. Mr. Sibley refereeing and coaching, not apparently knowing much about anything.

Cane cutting still going on, all day, Miz Gabe helping out in the field. Mr. Monroe has almost finished his patch.

November 15, 1934.
Took Mr. Ranse Magee, Mr. Ernest, Mr. Fletcher Bickham, and Mr. Sibley to town today to see Mr. Greenlaw about the dynamo for the lights for the school. At the schoolhouse, saw Mr. Crane. He reproached me before them all for not having told him that Mr. Lewis was coming next week. Without thinking, I told him that I thought I had told him—and I thought I had. The boys were out working on the steps. He was trying to get the toilets up in preparation for Mr. Lewis' visit. He was also greatly worried about Mr. Lewis' impending visit. I had attached no importance to it, and so told him before the men, that I thought it would be better just to let the school go ahead normally without making any fuss about the visit. The men and Mr. Crane seemed to take this as an affront. It was unfortunate on my part. Sibley took the occasion as a knock at Mr. Crane. I must go over and apologize to Mr. Crane tomorrow.

This evening Miz Gabe, Willie Pearl, and Mr. Ernest came up, Miz Gabe intent on making candy. She brought the cocoa, which she had had Ernest buy in Franklinton, and some lard, in order to get Julia to make the candy, or to show her how it was done. Julia had been making candy, and giving it to them, and their love for sweets led the men to insist that Miz Gabe make some like it. Miz Gabe had told Julia that "I tole him that if I didn't have to spend so much time cookin cornbread and collards I'd have time to make some candy." They had asked Miss Hynaneatha to show them how, but at the school meeting today when the women meet, Miss Hynaneatha said that she had left her recipe book at home and that they would make pine needle baskets again. This they did. Apparently this is the only crafts taught in the normal schools, for I have seen it done everywhere. But the women of the community really imagine these frightful little things to be beautiful.

The candy making went on apace while I filled out the loan blank under the National Housing Act for Mr. Ernest. He wants to borrow the smallest amount, $100. He figured up his income as amounting to $300 a year, the Act calling for loans not in excess of an amount one-fifth the yearly income. He had only the vaguest ideas as to the manner in which he was going to use the money, roofing and fencing being statements of $57 approximately.

This illustrates the bad influence we are on this community. Our few primitive repairs have inspired emulation. There is lime in the privy of Mr. Monroe, imitating the lime on our privy. Now, that lime costs 2 cents a pound, and yearly would total at least $3.00, for the cleansing of a privy for a household of four. That would be one percent of the yearly total income of the family for lime for a privy.

Now, Julia's candy has cost at least 40 cents the batch, using a can of condensed milk (Borden's), about an eighth of a pound of butter, and cocoa, and sugar. Miz Gabe's candy, using plain milk, the rough lard used hereabouts, and sugar, is, of course, much cheaper, but it doesn't taste as well.

Now, should Julia teach the women to sew the simple things she can sew?

That will cost them money for thread and cloth.

Mr. Ernest tells me that they raise all feed for the stock. They feed half rations to the mules after the fields done grazed over. They work a mule on thirty ears of corn when they're working him, and feed him ten a day when not, during the winter. That way, he said, they keep a mule "mud fat."

November 16, 1934.
Went over to school this morning. At 10:30 all of the children out in the yard cleaning up, the steps being repaired, and inside, the rooms being cleaned, Mr. Crane located in his office quite immaculately.

Had a conversation with Mr. Crane. Told him that I was sorry for my rudeness of yesterday. Mr. Crane was handsome about it, (to me, apparently in his old manner of duplicity, still harboring a grudge for not being told of Mr. Lewis' coming, but plying with me the old trade of fooling the white folks, in my case, someone in whom authority was vested. I doing likewise. Our conversation proceeded on this basis.) I told Mr. Crane how deeply appreciative I was of his great services to the school and to the community. I do not think he was fooled. However, it was one of those conversational demands of the situation.

Mr. Crane went on to tell me how deeply he appreciated my giving information about the coming of Mr. Lewis. "You know how it is, professor, somebody always wants to sort of freshen up when anyone is coming to his house." He went on to tell about how he liked to have things spic and span for inspectors. He knew Mr. Lewis. He was raised up with Mr. Jackson, who is in charge of the State Vocational work. One time a Federal man gave Mr. Crane a low rating. At the meeting at Baton Rouge these ratings were announced, and the question was asked if everyone was satisfied with their ratings, to stand up. Everybody stood up but Mr. Crane. He told Mr. Jackson he wasn't satisfied with the ratings for him, that it was unfair and dishonest. Mr. Sargent, the Federal Vocational Supervisor from Washington, was there. But they changed Mr. Crane's rating, and Mr. Jackson took him aside and told him that as long as he, Jackson, had that job, Mr. Crane would have his.

Mr. Crane said that everything he asked from the white folks he got. He had just asked them for three new toilets, and they gave it to them.

I said to Mr. Crane, "These are mighty nice white folks around here, aren't they?"

And Mr. Crane said, "Yes. Man and boy, I was raised up around here, and coming and going I haint never had no trouble with none of 'em. They always treats me as nice and polite as they can. *As long as you know your place*, they treat you fine. Why, I ain't never had no criticism except from among my own race. My race is alright, but they can't do anything for you. When they wanted that extra room, one of the teachers said that she'd give five dollars; I didn't say nothing, but I got up afterward and told them that they didn't have the money to do that. So they didn't. Then they had a meeting one Sunday afternoon, and I had Mr. Bateman out to it, and he give us this extra room, just like that. Now, I'm worked to death doing things for people. I've terraced 1728 acres this year. I had so much to do that I told Mr. Stringfield I couldn't do everything that was asked of me. Of course, there's the school board members. They asks you to do things, and it's right that you should do it. They give you your job. The other night I was got up at 2 o'clock in the morning to doctor on one of the school board member's horses. He was nigh dying, but I just doctored on im with home remedies and reading out of books and I cured him."

"Mr. Crane," I said, "how come all these white and colored folks have the same name, like Bickham, and Magee, and the like? Does it go back to slavery days?"

(It will be remembered that Ernest had been very reluctant to mention this relationship, and that he had never said that he, himself, was related to Mr. Tommie Graves, while saying that his mother was his daughter.)

"Later than that," said Mr. Crane, smiling. "You know, Professor, I says that some day there won't be another black man left in this country."

"I thought," I interrupted, "that kind of thing was just in the olden days."

"It's going on right now, professor." (Ernest had said there wasn't anything like this going on now.) "Why, there's a trustee of the school in Franklinton, John Taylor, and two daughter's of hisn' had white babies in the last three months. It started with one of 'em cookin' for a white man, and now he's jus a keepin' her. John Taylor says that he can't control his daughters, but the scriptures say that a man should rule in his own house before he exercises dominion over other folks.

"Why, my father when he died had eighteen children, and sixteen of em are living now. He died leaving 175 acres of land. He entered, homesteaded, on 104 acres, and bought the rest. When he died, he didn't owe a cent. That's mighty rare, Professor, for a man to die not owing anybody. And all of his children have bought homes of their own.

"My father's father was a white man. There's a whole passel of white Cranes on the other side of town. Professor, folks is getting more and more immoral, all the time. There's as much of that goin on now as there ever was.

"I was wondering," I said, "about the Burrisses in town. Are they any kin?"

"They sure are" said Mr. Crane. "You take John Burris that runs the store, and George Burris works there, and his son, they's half brothers. And they really looks out for 'em. They won't let nobody say anything about George Burris." [12]

(Evidently Professor Crane is a strictly marginal man, living by virtue of his acquaintance with the white folks, by his relationship with them, by the protection they give him, by their patronage. He is "frank," but in the sense of not seeing any lack of virtue in confession, in recognizing that the white folks have made him what he is and are responsible for his well being. Perhaps Ernest's failure to talk as readily about his white kin was due to the fact that he had not profited so directly from his white relations, but was obliged to wring his living from the soil.)

"Saturday night," said Professor Crane, "a white man stobbed a colored man to death in Bogalusa over a colored woman."

In the afternoon I attended a football game between Plaquemine and Franklinton colored schools. Mr. Barker sent us complimentary tickets. The Franklinton team was well coached and put up a good game. The Plaquemine team had decided not to come the night before, and had telephoned; but had been persuaded to come after it was decided by Franklinton to lend them football togs, which they lacked.

The Plaquemine team came in assorted uniforms, some overalls, some plain pants, some the Franklinton cast off togs, which in turn were cast off to the Negroes by the white high school. About fifty whites were present at the beginning of the game, including the brass band from the white school which played marches as the colored football team and rooting section marched in. The Franklinton football team was led in at a run by Miss Burris, Miss Washington Parish Training School, a daughter of the local Burisses, dressed in a yellow football sweater with a blue skirt. I noticed the young white boys critically eyeing the colored girls as they passed them, and the colored girls looking coy. There were a number of white girls in the brass band. All of the colored boys appeared to be on the football squad.

The game was very ragged, the Plaquemine team offering little opposition to the Franklinton team. Most of the white folks left at the end of the first half. As the game started, one of the Plaquemine boys took off his shoes and hurled them to the sidelines. He played the balance of the game barefoot. The boy in overalls was Plaquemine's best player, making innumerable tackles, and viciously.

Mr. Bateman, the superintendent, and others, were out. When Stringfield came, he said, "Barker, Mr. Bateman said for you to come and get him." Principal Barker said, "Yes sir," and left the field to drive after Mr. Bateman. When Mr. Bateman got ready to go, he said, "Barker, take me home." And Barker did.[13]

(I believe that Mrs. Barker takes out Mr. Bateman's washing. One day I picked up the little Barker boy, who said he was going after the clothes. I let him out at Mr. Bateman's house. Or perhaps Mrs. Barker supervises the girls at the training school who take out the washing.)

At the game was Mr. John Taylor, the trustee of the training school, whom, Mr. Crane assured me, had been presented by his daughters within the last three months with two mulatto babies by white men.

November 17, 1934.
Arose at 6:30—bright sunshine. Walked over toward Eulis Warren for eggs. Met Mr. Monroe leading his mules, going toward syrup mill.

Talked. It seems that one man out this way has deserted his wife and four chillun, and they hain't heerd from him since he left about the first of the year. They don't know where he is.

Some folks suspect that he runned away to take up with Linkton Magee's wife, who lives on the next farm. She had a father mighty low over by Picayune, and they wrote for her to come over. She went and staid about a week, and then come back. Then she went back, they writing to her, and she ain't come back yet. Last time they heard from her, she was in Florida.

Mr. Bennie Graves runs the syrup mill. Old Mr. Tommie Graves is a mighty fine man. He's paralyzed, but he gets around in his little cart, he even goes into the woods looking for his cattle. Mr. Tommie is a mighty fine man. Mr. Monroe's brother was in the penitentiary, and they paid several folks to get him out, but none of em did. Mr. Tommie went and got him out, and it didn't cost 'em nothing.

Murdis Magee is the son of a man who was Albert Magee's (white) father. He had lots of land (Murdis's father) and three or four hundred head of sheep. He raised his own stock. There was just two boys, Murdis's father and Murdis's Uncle. Murdis's Uncle was a drunkard, his father a Christian. Murdis Magee's uncle is still living. And fight! He'd fight you for anything, and anybody.[14]

Miss Hynaneatha is Murdis's sister.

Mr. Monroe's wife was half-sister to Mr. Willie Crane's father.

Mr. Monroe is half-brother to Mr. Silas, who lives in Hattiesburg now. Mr. Boy Bickham is half-brother to Mr. Silas. Miz Gabe's mother and Miss Hynaneatha's mother (also Murdis's mother) were full sisters. Both must have been intelligent women. Miz Gabe is very intelligent. Miss Hynaneatha has been to Tuskegee, and Mr. Murdis is Federal Agricultural agent.

Mr. Monroe says he raised Luther Graves' father.

The syrup mill is running full blast, but they won't get around to Mr. Monroe's cane until next week. Mr. Monroe calls Bennie Graves "Bennie" before the white men, in the same manner as when he was calling around to see the other folks.

Went to Franklinton to attend meeting of teachers in Parish. They were concerned first with the election of officers for a parish teachers association. Mr. Barker totally incompetent as acting chairman. Miss Todd prompted him and the assembly. My observation of the community meeting at Star Creek suggests that the Star Creek community conducted their business much more speedily and intelligently than the teachers. The fellow Magee at Blackjack was the most intelligent man there, excepting, perhaps, a young fellow named Johnson who teaches at the Parish training school. Amacker, at Bethel, was pretty intelligent, also a young man.

Stringfield and another white visitor, Weakley, principal at the Mount Hermon School, came in just as they were beginning to discuss the teachers association and representation there. The Negroes wanted permission to get off with pay for the teachers association. They talked around the subject, toyed with it, joking Mr. Stringfield, an elaborate ritual, without asking him directly. It seemed to be a regular pattern of how to get things. I notice that they all refer to each other as Mister and Mrs. before the white people, with no self consciousness.

I was called on to speak, and spoke too long, nine minutes, about nothing. My speech was confused, an illustration of my own confusion. It was not highly appreciated by the teachers. I spoke of how lovely the people at Star Creek were. I don't think the teachers got the point at all.

Mr. Crane was there. After the meeting, he told me that Mr. Weakley was a fine man. Weakley went out with Stringfield without either speaking to me. Weakley came back and told me he wanted to meet me. In his speech to the teachers he had told them the old story of Booker T. Washington and the fact that no Tuskegee student or graduate had ever been indicted (????). The Negroes applauded this statement, again in the pattern.

Weakley told me—it was not a conversation—that he had lived in Louisiana 26 years. He was from Tennessee, Clarksville. He never had been able to understand how they treated Negroes in Louisiana. "Why, in Tennessee they voted all over the State, just like white folks," and he believed they paid the same salaries in the schools (a mistaken belief). "Why, once at Clarksville, a colored boy was working for a white man, and he grabbed the man's wife by the arm. Why, anywhere else they would'a lynched him. But they just called in the doctor and the sheriff, and the doctor said he was crazy, and they sent him on to the asylum, and that's all there was to it. I'm just telling that to show how things are in Clarksville.

"Why, there are wealthy men of your race in Clarksville. There was one man owned nearly two blocks of city property. There never has been a lynching in Montgomery county."

November 18, 1934 (Sunday).
Services were at Jerusalem. Reverend Hawthorne of Hattiesburg preached. Sunday school was not at Star Creek today, but at the church.

Miz Gabe went to church. Neither Mr. Monroe nor Mr. Ernest went. Mr. Monroe has not been to church or to Sunday school that I knows of since we been here.

Mr. Monroe had the picture of a woman which he showed me. She was a large woman with white stockings. Fletcher Bickham was with him. He said to me, "Perfesser, How you like them legs?" I said nothing. Mr. Monroe said, "Her legs is powerful too big, don't you think, perfesser?" I laughed, and he did too.

November 19, 1934.
Ernest, Monroe, and Orsell left at 3 o'clock in the morning in my car to go to Bogalusa to see King Gulley, whose band is to furnish music for the Fair. I told them to be back by noon as I was expecting Mr. Lewis.

In my overalls I walked over to the school. Mr. Crane was just arriving. It was ten o'clock, and he was overdue. A class of children was waiting for him in the newly arranged school house. The yard had been freshly swept. I also understand that a call was sent out to all of the boys of older age to come to school this week. Carl, Mr. Bickham's boy, whose father give him away when didn't nobuddy think he'd live, and who Miz Bickham has raised almost 'til he's a man, is in school this week. (Carl is in the 4th grade, and is in love with Willie Pearl.)

Mr. Crane, explaining his lateness, said that he had vaccinated 65 hogs for cholera this morning. They were white folks hogs, many of them belonging to Mr. Fletcher Smith. He'd have to tell Mr. Stringfield that he had to give up his terracing work, he had so much work to do tending animals. The white folks is what made it possible for him to get a salary, and he was going to help them. Our race don't do no good for you, and they cain't.

Mr. Crane said "I see you're in your overalls. White folks takes to that." (I started to tell him that I wore the overalls because they seemed the most appropriate garb for a country in which everyone wears overalls, but decided not to.) He said, "Mr. Stringfield says you're a mighty fine young man." I thought this was bait, and so I said nothing.

(Ernest told me afterward that Mr. Crane said to him, "Do you know what perfesser's real business is?" and "It's got me right puzzled." Ernest said he didn't tell him nuthin. When Ernest told me this, expectantly, I just laughed.)

At Franklinton, where I went, in the afternoon, all newspapers were sold out. One of the young white men at the filling station, on inquiry, walked to his house three blocks distant and brought me his copy of the *Picayune*, which he gave to me.

The mail man came as I was at the school. An old woman ran up with one of these blue pension blanks. She asked me, as she waited for the mail rider to make out a money order, if it was right that she was to get $30 a month as soon as she sent it in.

I said, "No, that just is an association that's trying to get that to pass, it ain't passed yet," but she said, "It says so right here," and she pointed to her blank, to the line where it referred to the kind of bill the Association was trying to pass. She paid no more attention to me and walked on to the mailrider, who proceeded to make out her money order.

Miz Lu and Willie Pearl had come to the house Saturday night, Miz Lu with one of the blanks. I advised her against doing it. Mr. Bickham was wondering why he hadn't got a blank. I think I persuaded Miz Lu not to send in her dollar. I wondered if I should have.

In the evening J.R., the Widow Graves' young son with a club foot, came up with two tickets for Henrietta for the "Most Populous girl." We bought them. Then we asked J.R. to stay for dinner. He did, and ate heartily, although it appeared later that he had already eaten and had slipped away. Mrs. Graves was down at the surrup mill, helping Mr. Bickham cook syrup at Ernest Warren's mill (white). Soon Henrietta, Oletha, and Marshall, his sisters and brother, came up, looking for J.R. While Julia and Henrietta washed the dishes, Marshall, Oletha, J.R., and myself sat in stony silence in the dining room. Julia suggested riddles. Oletha knew numbers of them. J.R. tried to say some, but he always got mixed up. Then they began to tell stories. They were familiar nursery stories, Lil Red Ridin Hood, Babes in the Woods, etc., but they were told with new diction. They also knew several Brer Rabbitt stories. It appears that Miss Dyson, the teacher, has taught them.

Oletha is black, J.R. is chocolate, Marshall brown with sandy, nappy hair, J.R. with wiry black hair, Henrietta brown with curly brown hair with a glint of bronze. She would be an extremely attractive girl if ever she was clothed and cleaned up just once, and Julia wishes to do it, but I advise against it. Miz Gabe has said, "Willie Pearl's a nice girl, she don't run round like Henrietta."

Oletha is very aggressive. She tells stories beautifully.

Although J.R. (club footed) could never get his stories right, the other children always let him finish. They didn't tease him when he stumbled, although they all knew it. They seemed very good natured together.

As they left, Oletha burst into a "bad" rhyme which she shouted. It was pure deviltry.

A heavy rain come up about nine o'clock. I stayed up late to read, and the kitchen leaks like a sieve.

At the threat of rain in the afternoon, Mr. Ernest harnessed the mules up to the wagon and began to haul in cane shucks from the field. He is through shucking and topping, but neither he nor Mr. Monroe can get their syrup ground until the "big folks" get through. The big folks, it appears, are the white owners. There are two mills in the neighborhood, Mr. Bennie Graves and Ernest Warren's. The Graves mill is powered by a tractor, and has a capacity of 150 or so gallons a day. The Warren mill is a press mule-drawn, with a capacity of only about 50 gallons a day. Mr. Bickham cooks at the Warren mill, Mr. Bennie at his own. In the first conversation I had with Mr. Monroe, he says that Bennie will grind when whoever gets there first. But it really appears that he grinds for the big men first, the men who have from 150 to four hundred gallons of syrup to make. Mr. King has a mill, but he mostly makes for hisself and for his tenants.

November 20, 1934.
Got up, went to school. Still raining. Breakfast cooked in shower in kitchen. Went by Miz Lu's house and got a quart of buttermilk, also a mess of greens. Mr. Crane told me yesterday that he was planning to cut down three oaks in the yard. They made the sheds rot, and they shaded the garden. Neither the garden nor the sheds seem to me to be worth the sacrifice of these oaks, which lend good shade to the yard and add a little of beauty to the grounds. But there does not appear to be in the minds of these people any idea of trees as aesthetic objects. I asked Miss Lu about the trees, and when I saw that it was her idea to cut them down, I desisted.

Going home, I saw Uncle Wade Callahan, he says his name is, but Mr. Monroe says that they jus call him Brumfield. I invited him up to the house. On the way he told me he was looking for Mr. Ranse, because he intended to do some work for him. Mr. Ranse was out by my house, so I told him to come up and wait there, and to sit and talk. Going up the hill we met Mr. Ranse, who was with Fletcher Bickham and Ernest. Mr. Ranse came on down the hill and began to talk to Uncle Wade about work. They were bargaining for the services of Uncle Wade and his wife.

Uncle Wade is an old man. He has two teeth in the front of his mouth, and they project from the receded gums like two denuded gateposts. His hair is peppercorn, and white, and the skin of his skull shows browner above the chocolate black of his face. His eyes are quite brown and bright. He walks with a cane. He asked me, "How old does you think I am?" I inspected him with great dubiousness, seeking to imply that I thought him very young. With great satisfaction, Uncle Wade said, "You wouldn't think I was between seventy and eighty, now would you?" "I sure never would of thought it!"

Mr. Ranse asked him what he'd work for. Well, he'd worked for Bickham, he and his wife, for a gallon and a half of syrup and dinner, a day. (Labor is hired and paid for on such an arrangement. The other day Ernest was complaining that he'd offered two gallons of syrup and dinner for help, but the fellers had rather work over at Bennie's syrup mill for a gallon and a half of syrup a day, and they had to furnish their own eatings. But he guessed the fellers was lookin' at workin a long time at the syrup mill, whereas he would only give em work for a day or so.)

Uncle Wade told Mr. Ranse that he didn't want to work for no syrup, he and his wife had already got twelve gallon of syrup, and that was enough to do for them. He wanted to work for something else. I saw that my presence was interfering with bargaining, and so I walked on.

At the house, I gave Ernest the key to the car. The committee had tentatively come to an arrangement with Mr. Greenlaw by which he was to sell them a second-handed Delco light plant for $60, $30 down and $30 to be paid next harvest time. Now, Mr. Greenlaw wants to change the notes, so that they agree to pay $20 down and $8.00 a month until all is paid. The committee members think this a great injustice, because us farmer folks, we cain't pay like that, we've got to pay when we's got money, and that's jus in the time after layin' by time.

Along came Uncle Wade after the others left. He done made his rangement with Mr. Ranse. (Uncle Wade proves to be a very unreliable witness about rates of pay, either an awful liar or just "weak in de head" as Mr. Monroe said he was.) He said he worked for Mr. Jim King and Mr. King he paid from $1.50 to $2.00 a day. I believe that he must be using "gallons of syrup" interchangeably with "dollars."

Uncle Wade tells me that he's got a "nice wife, she's honest, she's clean, she's hard workin, and she don't never do no wrong. We been married thirty years, and we ain't never had no trouble. We ain't never been parted. My wife, I don't ask her to work. I jus say, 'If you ain't got nuthin to do, you can come along with me, if you can.' She likes to work. We stripped cane for Bickham, and I worked for Mr. Jim King. He's a fine man. He always pays you like he says he will. Now, all folks ain't like dat.

"I strips cane as good as any of em. Some folks uses a knife, but I (looking at his hands) I jus strips it wif my natal hand. Cose, it hurts some, and it burns some, w'en you strips with yo hands, but if you takes and rubs some kerosene on em w'en youse thru, hit don't hurt at all. It burns some in the pan of yo han (indicating palm), but jus rub kerosene, and hit's allright.

"Yessir, I got a good wife. She's honest, she's clean, she's hardworkin, and she works right along wid me. We hain't never been parted but once, and been married thirty year. Dat time, I was wukkin in Columbia, up in Marion county. I wukked up dere for ten, fifteen years. I done good up dere. I used to wuk fo the City of Marion."

"What did you do, Uncle Wade?"

"I'd mow lawns, and I'd cut wood, and I'd do mos anything. I usedter make two and three dollars a day. Then I followed Mr. Brown down near Bogaluse, wid a saw mill. He was a nice man, but he didn' pay his debts. He had a nice wife, a mighty nice woman, and he'd skip behin her to keep fum payin his debts. She had a powerful lot of money. She would tell him, 'Now, Mr. Brown, you ought to treat everybody right, and pay yo debts.' She was a little woman, a spare made woman, but she sure could tell Mr. Brown what to do."

"While we was livin in Columbia, I went to town to get some grocery. I got the grocery, but I didn' go home wid it. I jus fooled around.

"Me and my wife been married thirty year, and we hain't never been separated, cepn one time, and I was de cause of dat. Yessir, *I* was the cause of *that*. We was livin over in Columbia. I went to town to buy de grocery, and I didn't come back. I just fooled around all day, going fum one woman to another. I come home, and my wife, she met me at the door, and she didn' see no grocery. She said, 'Where my grocery?' And I 'menced to look up. And she say, 'You had plenty time to look down; no use lookin' up now. You migha bought my grocery first and then gone back to yo' madam.'

"Then she said, 'Go get yo hat.' That's all she said. 'Go get yo hat.' An I looked at her, and I didn't believe she meant it. But she did.

"Then my nephew spoke up. He's a man like dis. He don't stand fo' nuthin fum nobody. He runs a pressin shop in Columbia for w'ite and black, and he mighty well off. He real independent. He my sister's boy. His daddy R. Warren, and R. Warren thinks a whole lot of that boy. You know R. Warren, what got the big store at Hackley. My nephew bout your color.

" 'Well,' my nephew said, 'Don't you go nowhere, Uncle Wade. Even if you has gone around with some wimmin, you hain't done no more than any other man'd do.'

"Well, things went on. My wife wouldn't talk to me, she wouldn't say nuthin, things was real aggravated. So, on a Saturday I went down to de station, and I got a dray, and I sent it atter my trunk. My wife weren't nowhere to be seen. I sat down in de train, it left Columbia at 1 o'clock, and, I couldn't he'p myself, the tears just come a-runnin down my cheeks, and I jus cried.

"Bout a month later, my brother, Dave, he said, h'aint no use you folks actin like dat. You jus sen her de money and tell her to come on down here. And I did, an we been livin here every since."

Toward the afternoon I walked down to the syrup mill with Mr. Monroe. He told me that Uncle Wade was an old wastrel who had thrown away all of his money when he was young, and now he had to work hard, he and his wife, and they had to stay on Uncle Dave's place, Uncle Wade's half brother. Uncle Dave owns a pretty large place, is a trustee of the school, and a deacon of Jerusalem Church.

On the way to the syrup mill we passed near the Warren house, and near the crossing where Mr. Sam Warren, father of R. Warren, was run over in his buggy by the train. Again Mr. Monroe told me the story. "Perfesser, I really don' believe that old man was in his right mind, or he intended to get kilt. The buggy jus got on top of the crossin and stopped. The train blowed and blowed, but the buggy didn't budge, and old man Warren he didn' try to git out.

"He had jus come from seein a young white woman he was runnin after, lived in the house Mr. Travis lives in now. I expects some other younger man was cuttin him out, and he mus have felt mighty bad about it."

Said I, "Mr. Monroe, was the woman married?"

"Yes," he answered, "but she was separated from her husband. Afore Mr. Sam started runnin around with her, another old man, Mr. Haley's wife's father, Mr. Haley what own the big store at Clifton, he runned around with her, and he kilt hisself."

Said I, "She was death, wasn't she?"

"Yessir," he answered. "After Mr. Sam got kilt, she went off from here with another man, and I hear she's livin down in Bogalusa way now."

At the syrup mill we found Mr. Bickham cooking the syrup. The Widow Graves was helping. A white man, a young man, Ernest Warren, who owns the mill, was sitting by on a log. Andrew Brown was feeding the mill, which was drawn by two mules which are worked with another team in two hour shifts.

The Warren boy's wife sat out in the backyard about fifty yards distance, in a bonnet and gingham dress, nursing a baby. A little boy about three or four years old was playing around the yard. Mr. Monroe and Mr. Bickham called the white boy "Ernie."

I asked what they did with the skimming, which they were careful to take up and save in a barrel. Everyone laughed. It was good for beer, and, added the Warren boy, it was good hog food.

Mr. Monroe and Mr. Boy Bickham began to tease the Warren boy about his little child, which he was now holding up.

"Ernie, do you think you can raise that boy right?" said Mr. Monroe.

"I'm raisin him jus like my daddy raised me," replied Ernest.

"Hits a pity," said Mr. Bickham, "what triflin' boys some good men has. Now yore daddy, he was a mighty good man."

Mr. Monroe joined in. "Yes, if that boy takes after his grand-daddy, he'll be a mighty nice little fellow."

Ernest took the teasing in good spirit. "Well, I don't know how it is with the colored section, but I've known some white preachers had children as bad as any you could find, anywhere. I've been out with preacher's daughters could drink as much whiskey as I could."

"Do tell," said Mr. Bickham.

While we were walking back from the syrup mill, Mr. Monroe told me that R. Warren's daughter had turned out awful bad. She was married, but she run off with a preacher. At least, she didn' exactly run off with him, him going to New Orleans and she following after him soon after. They was livin together down there now, he heeard.

He (Mr. Monroe) got in a fight with that Warren boy's daddy once what owned the syrup mill. It happened like this. He had been working hard for old man Sam, and the boy, he wasn't doing nuthin. "We wuz both boys, I was jus nigh grown. He wanted me to go huntin' with him. I told him I was too tired. He said he was goin to make me. He jumped me. It was right in old Man Sam's house, and when he heeard the scufflin, he come in and cussed his son out. He knowed what I had did that day."

(When we went down to the syrup mill, the Warren boy was sitting there whittling, watching Mr. Bickham and Aunt George cook. The Warren boy had on boots. Mr. Monroe said to him, "I'll rassle you for them boots." The Warren boy got up and said, "Come on, I'll throw you." Mr. Monroe was only joking. He had told me the same thing the other day, when I was wearing my boots.)

Said I, "My father was a preacher!"

They didn't know whether to take it as a joke, as I had intended, or not.

Then Mr. Monroe turned to talking about what a good man Ernest's papa was.

Willie, the hired boy who was helping Mrs. Graves strain syrup through a cloth some little distance away, whispered to her, "Yeah, and if that little boy turns out like old man Sam he'll be a bobcat, too."

Mr. Monroe walked over to the yard and talked some to Mrs. Warren. He had a long private conversation with Andrew Brown.

Coming back, Mr. Monroe said, "That white lady said to me, 'I see you got that great man with you. I hear he's a mighty nice man.'"

We were passing near Andrew Brown's house. The little children playing around had always attracted our attention. One is a very pretty little black girl. They are reputed to have beautiful voices thru the neighborhood.

I said to Mr. Monroe, "Mr. Brown sure has got a lot of lil' uns."

Mr. Monroe said, "They ain't his. They's his daughters."

I asked him, "Whose their daddy?"

He said, "Four or five different men."

I said, "Who were they?"

He said, "I really don't know."

As we passed the house, Mr. Brown's daughter was standing out. She looked like she was pregnant again. Mr. Monroe spoke to her in the manner of a man who would have said more had I not been there. As we had left the lot where they were making syrup, Mr. Brown had yelled to him, "If a rain comes up, *you* could stop by the house, if the perfesser wasn't with you," and laughed. I am wondering if Mr. Monroe hasn't been having something to do with Mr. Brown's daughter, him being a widower for almost two years.

November 21, 1934.
Raining hard all night and this morning, and all day. Mr. Bickham killed hogs, three, today. Mr. Ernest brought us a piece of liver. I went over to the school. Mr. Crane wasn't there, neither was Miss Hynaneatha (Mrs. Vick). She had sent word she was sick. Mrs. Dyson was teaching her class. There were only 15 children present out of an enrollment of more than 100. Mrs. Vick had also been "sick" the day before. It was a rough day and she lives about a mile from the school. It appears that these absences from school on the part of the teachers are not uncommon. Mrs. Dyson and Sibley are a little more faithful to their duties, probably because they do not have the security that is assured Mrs. Vick and Crane. Crane is the white folks friend, and has

white relatives, works for the white folks, and has powerful colored relatives, the Crane family being one of the best off in the parish. Mrs. Vick is the sister of Murdis Magee, the Demonstration agent, and probably has other attachments in and about concerning which I have not yet learned. She is separated from her husband, but they were together during the fair, he teaching in Mississippi.

The widow Graves, Aunt George, helped Mr. Bickham kill hogs today. All of her children were there, too. J.R. was out, as he frequently is. Miz Gabe says the Graves chillun is hard to learn. They ought to be with their frequent absences.

In the school I listened to Mrs. Dyson hear a class in reading in the third grade. None of the children could read, with the exception of a little girl named "Gradure-Lee" (probably for "Gradually"?) Barker. (Was she born "Gradually"?)

The Barker child is the daughter of the Secretary of the Community Association. Evidently her superior reading is due to the family superiority in culture.

In the afternoon, Olee (it is Olee, not Oletha), Henrietta, and Willie Pearl and J.R. came up to the house. Henrietta wore a dress with puffed sleeves (is this one of the rewards of her "running round" in contrast to Willie Pearl's being a nice girl?). Mr. Bickham came up with a piece of meat for us. I notice the children treat him with great familiarity. I said to J.R., "you should have been in school today." Mr. Bickham said, "He wasn't holpin none, he was jus in the way. Aunt George ought to be whipped for that." He said, "J.R., you oughta been in school today," and kicked the boy's club foot significantly. This brutality apparently was apparent only to Julia and myself, certainly not to the good old Uncle Boy. We wondered if the familiarity of the girls with Mr. Bickham was due to their own individual forwardness, or to a general custom of the country.

November 22, 1934.
It "faired off" last night, and the weather turned colder. Mr. Ernest yelled for us to come down, about 7 o'clock, that he was going to

knock one. We went down. Miz Gabe's sister and nephew were there to help. Ernest was trying to shoot the pig with a .32, but missed several shots. He blamed the gun, but I thought he was nervous. Mr. Monroe was disgusted with this slow business, and took an axe to the pig, after which he stobbed it. Another pig was killed soon afterward. There was a fire with two kettles, and a barrel, half sunk into the ground. After dousing the pigs in the barrel, the little one was hung up and Mr. Monroe butchered it while Ernest and his nephew were still cleaning the hair off the big one. Mr. Monroe was very proud over his skill. . . .

Julia went over to Mrs. Bickham's, to get the meat chopper. Mrs. Bickham was rendering the lard. Mr. Bickham had gone back to work on the syrup mill.

The women cleaned the guts, the men cutting the meat up.

While gutting the pig, Mr. Monroe severed a gut. The excrement popped out. "You musta left this pig in the field las' night," said Odell. Miz Gabe produced a string and neatly sutured this opening, later washing off the filth.

Mr. Monroe neatly carried out the work of butchering the hog. Julia said, "It's just like an operation." Apparently no one had ever thought of it in that light. They entered into the idea with great zest. As the larger hog was swung up to a table—he was too big to hand— Ernest said, "Let's put him on the operating table." Odell, Miz Gabe's nephew, said, "He's got an appendix."

Miz Fannie, Miz Gabe's sister, calls Odell her baby. Apparently a grown man, he is to go back to school after the Fair.

While fixing sausage in the kitchen—the guts are cleaned and sticks are pushed through them to turn them inside out, long rods—a conversation came up in the kitchen.

Miz Gabe said, "I didn' know Ermitrude had herself in that shape."

Miz Fannie said, "I knowed it as soon as I sawed her. She came in the house and I gave her some chicken and she et it and she said, 'this chicken sho is good to me.' And I said, 'I guess it is good to you.' And she said, 'Now you're tryin' to start up somethin.'"

Miz Gabe laughed. "No you wasn't. It was already started up, wasn't it? Wonder why they try to keep people from knowin' it? I don't see no reason to keep people from knowin it, especially if you's married."

While they were cleaning the guts, Miz Gabe said, "Those sanctified people tickle me singing that song, 'This thing's gettin better every day.'"

Miz Gabe and Miz Fannie started singing, as they pushed the sticks thru the guts,

"This thing's gettin' better every day
This thing's gettin better every day—"

Then a gut burst, and Miz Gabe said, "*This* thing ain't gettin' no better!" Both laughed merrily.

Mr. Monroe came in fussing. Ernest had gone to town with Horace, and Mr. Monroe wanted to go over to the syrup mill.

Mr. Monroe said, "This ain't none of my work. (He was out in the yard cooking the lard.) I don't generally do this. Gabe ought to be doin' this. I don't want to be out here all the evenin'."

Miz Gabe said, "I don't want to be in this kitchen all the evenin', either. I haven't got but two hands, have I?"

Mr. Monroe came in again and said, "Gabe, I want a bucket and a cloth, and something to dip the lard with."

Miz Gabe said, "Go git 'em, Mr. Monroe. You know where they is."

Mr. Monroe said, "Gabe, you know I don't know where nothing is."

He got the bucket, and went on out. Odell came back in, and Miz Gabe told Julia where to get a cloth.

Then Miz Gabe started fussing about Mr. Monroe. "You know he sho is a lot of trouble. Uncle Boy ain't half the trouble he is."

Said Julia, "Maybe his wife spoiled him."

"No," said Miz Gabe, "he's been used to working, his wife taught him how to work. He needs a wife to look after him. He ought to have that woman with them big fat legs laid out amongst these sausages."

(A notable fact is the reliance that all put on Miz Gabe and her intelligence. With the meat chopper, for example, Mr. Ernest put it together wrong, with the meat screw backward. Miz Gabe had to take it to pieces, wash it, and put it back together right.)

Just before going to town, we went down to Miz Gabe's with the garbage. Julia went in front. As she went up the backsteps, she looked through the kitchen door and there was a white man sitting down across the table from Mr. Monroe, eating some of the newly prepared pork with gusto. He was very taken aback, apparently, to see us. Miz Gabe invited us to come in and eat, but I declined. I first thought it was Mr. Monroe's mulatto boy, but it wasn't. It was a white man from Bogalusa who was trying to sell a Delco light system to the community.

As Ernest and I drove away, he said, "Perfesser, it's funny the way these white folks carry on, and yet, when they comes amongst you, they're just as nice as they can be. Now that feller was jus as nice as he could be."

I asked him, if the man wasn't doing that just because he was away from other white people. His answer did not satisfy me.

"Oh, no. Now, you take Mr. Jim King. He's one of the best-off men there is in this Parish, and he'll come around, and if he's hungry, he'll sit down and eat with us jus like one of the family."

After I had gone, Julia was in the yard turning the sausage grinder. Mr. Monroe and the white man came out. The meat grinder was not grinding well. Miz Gabe said, "Miss Julia, you can't manage that, can you?" Julia answered, "I think the meat's too fat." Mr. Monroe said, "No, it just ain't put up right, but I don't know nothin' about it. Gabe generally does that." The white man chimed in and said something about the grinder not being put up right. He wouldn't agree with Julia. I and (she) have noticed that this is typically true, that white people refuse to agree with you even on minor points like this, from what appears to be a sheer unwillingness to accept the fact that a nigger might be right in an explanation.

But the operation of the grinder did show that it was the meat, and it was very obvious that fat was the cause of its faulty operation.

The white man said, "Maybe it is the meat. You try it, Grand-dad—" (addressing Mr. Monroe). Julia then walked into the house.

Miz Gabe said, volunteering the information without being asked, "I just sat him down to the table just like he was anybody else, because I didn' have no time to fix no extra place for him. And he ate like he enjoyed it, too."

I went on to town and got some groceries. I am now called Bond by the postmaster, Mr. Greenlaw, the salesman in Burris' store, and the drugstore salesman.

I went out to the school to see Mr. Barker. Mr. Barker congratulated me on my speech to the teachers. He told me that it had so inspired the Superintendent that he had come out again Monday and talked to the teachers about morals. (I didn't see the connection, and I thought Mr. Barker was kidding me, but Mr. Barker's life is founded on kidding people, so I didn't mind it.) He also told me that my visit had resulted in getting new locks for the doors. I see Mr. Dyson putting new locks in on the doors at Star Creek, so perhaps my visit was also responsible for that, too. It appears, so says Mr. Barker, that during the time when I was on my feet, the door blew open behind me, and Mr. Stringfield closed it with his foot. After the meeting, said Mr. Barker, he told Mr. Stringfield, "I hated to see you embarrassed before the visitors, having to close that door with your foot after it blew open." And he told Mr. Stringfield what a wonderful evidence of good relations between the races I had thought the turning out of the white band for the colored football game was. Mr. Stringfield just beamed, said Mr. Barker. Right after that, said Barker, Mr. Stringfield said he was going to send over some new locks.

"That's the way you have to get things," said Mr. Barker, "from these white people."

At the filling station, there is a division of labor for servicing my car, when I drive up. Mr. Bickham puts in the gas and even the water, but he calls the colored attendant to check my tires. Never will he stoop so low.

November 23, 1934.
Drove to Baton Rouge. The Delco lights were brought up before we left and installed. The Fair Association was much disappointed when Mr. Greenlaw changed the original terms of sale, which had been that they pay $75, $30 down and the rest payable next harvest time. The members of the community did not want to sign a note for monthly payments, to which Mr. Greenlaw changed the arrangement. Hence the presence of the salesman from Bogalusa. The final arrangement was that there should be paid the sum of $50, $25 down, and $25 borrowed from the bank, a note being signed by the members of the community. It now seems that all the dickering was just that, that both Mr. Greenlaw and the members of the community association knew perfectly well that they intended to get the lights from him.

In Baton Rouge in the afternoon, went to Dr. Felton Brown's office. He insisted we go to his house to stay. We did so, gladly. His wife is a Creole, beautiful. He has a little yellow-haired girl of about two, Joan, who is just learning to talk. She has very fine toys, and is a very intelligent child.

At the teacher's association, saw the Symonds. Felton Clark[15] joked with us outside to the effect that the Association was called a Negro association, but that the entire day had been taken up by calling upon second rate white superintendents to speak. At the invitation of Miss Fannie Williams,[16] I addressed the Parent-Teachers Association briefly on the subject of my Aaron Douglas quilt.

November 24, 1934.
At Southern University, where the last session of the Teachers Association was held. In an open forum on vocational education, at which Felton Clark presided, one lady said with great vigor that she wanted to go home and "do something intangible."

After leaving the Association, we came back to town and dined with the Browns, very satisfyingly. Then on to Natchez. Stopped off at Afton Villa, which is an ante-bellum home so placarded from a highway sign. The owner of the house stepped out as we drove in. The trees, now beautiful, were planted in 1849 when the house was built. The master of the house charged us 0.25 apiece, and conducted us through the house and yards. He was politeness itself. In one of the parlors sat an old woman, a sort of malicious sprite. The owner was telling us of the mistress of the mansion, who sang beautifully. She corrected him with a tinkling, amused laugh—a very devilish, malicious laugh— "That was her daughter, not her." This was the only notice she took of our presence. She was thin, and a perfect picture of decayed, neat gentility.

At Natchez we discovered that Allison and Liddie had gone to Alcorn. Followed them did we. We had a flat tire at Harrison, right in front of the railroad trestle from which three Negroes were hung several years ago. Miss Althea Dumas accompanied us, and told us that the crime of the Negroes had consisted of shooting as many white men as they could before they themselves were captured. A Negro at a neighboring garage fixed the tire. The store in front of which we stopped had one side for Negroes to eat in, and another side in which whites ate. A Negro cooked for all.

Ate largely and to bed.

November 25, 1934.
Up, ate breakfast. We were staying at Mrs. Nelson's house. Mr. Nelson got his M.A. at Iowa State this past summer, in Education, I believe. He talks as though he was an illiterate. Speaking so some woman, he said that "she berthed a baby." He seems to be a good hearted fellow, though.

Inspected the campus. Found out that the new president, William Bell, was an old acquaintance, having taught with him in Oklahoma. He is young, and appears to be more intelligent than when I once knew him. From various reports I understand he got the job through the patronage of a prominent State Senator who lives in Meridian, from which Bell comes.

Inspected the library. It is frightful. I understand that some four or five thousand volumes from an older collection are stored elsewhere in the school buildings, and there are probably many valuable documents in them, considering the origin of the school. I urged the librarian (a woman) not to throw them away. It is doubtful if she understood what I meant.

In afternoon, ate huge meal prepared by Mrs. Nelson, drove back to Natchez, stayed overnight with Allison;[17] went over to call on Dr. and Mrs. Dumas.

November 26, 1934.
Drove to Star Creek. Arrived at dusk.

November 27, 1934, Tuesday.
All is astir in preparation for fair. I went over to the syrup mill with Mr. Ernest. I drove. As I got over there, Mr. Tommie Graves, the old paralytic white man who is Mr. Ernest's grandfather, and the father of Mr. Monroe's first wife, was sitting out by the mill talking to one of his white grandsons. As I came up, he was wheeled in. Mr. Ernest yelled to the man pushing the chair, "Kin I holp you?", and, being answered affirmatively, helped him push Mr. Tommie into the house. A ramp has been constructed for his entry into the house. He has a rubber-tired cart of two-wheels which he drives all around the country.

On the way over to the mill, we passed and picked up Aunt George, who was going to carry some food she had cooked to a woman just delivered of a baby, which Mrs. Graves had delivered. We also passed J.R. and Marshall, Mrs. Graves' boys, who were riding in a two-wheeled cart much like that of Mr. Tommie, who is also their grand-father, since he is the father of Mrs. Graves' husband who deserted her several years ago.

At the mill I talked about one thing and another to one of the Graves boys and to Mr. Jake Jacobs. Mr. Jacobs was very sad over his boys, who, he said, did not take on to all of the things he tried to teach them about doctoring cattle. Why, he said, some folks claimed that there was no such disease as hollow horn, but he knew how to cure it. Why, he had a cow that had been ailing yesterday. He knew it was hollow horn and hollow tail. The cow just wouldn't get up. He got four men, and they lifted the cow plum up, but she wouldn't stand up after they lifted her. So he took a knife, and he just whittled on that cow's horn, right down near the base, and when he had made a hole in it, he poured in some turpentine. The cow just blew stuff out of her nose — but she didn't get up. Next, he cut off her tail. He had already split her tail, and poured turpentine on it, but this time he cut it off, since the place where he had put the bandage, the bandage had come off. So he cut off her tail, and that cow, well, she just got right up from there and ran away like a house on fire. You tell me that you can't cure hollow-tail, concluded Mr. Jacobs triumphantly.

I learned also from Ernest what had happened in our absence. When I had come in, on Monday, Miz Gabe told us that there had been a little trouble, that Luther Graves had hit John, Ernest's cousin, over the head with a piece of stove wood, and that John was in a mighty bad fix.

According to Ernest, what had happened was this: "John and Luther were great friends. You couldn't see one without seeing the other. Well, on Saturday evening they were all over to Luther's place, and they were figuring on sending the electric boy, the boy what been fixing on the lights, back to town. He didn' have no way to go back to Franklinton. Well, I had gone down to Warrenton and got a bottle of beer." (Evidently whiskey, as there is plenty of cane beer around now, much closer than it would be possible to go to Warrenton for made, expensive beer.) "Luther had done told me that he wanted John to go across the creek to a frolic with him, that John had plenty of money, and after John had got two or three drinks that he'd spend all that money. But I told John not to go with him. So Luther came by my house with the electric boy, and he asked John to go with him to town, and then go cross the Creek. But John told him he'd done changed his mind. So Luther went on.

"Then John went over to Luther's store, and he was about to go home, and he bought ten cents worth of candy. Marguerite didn't have no money to change it with, and John said that he'd pay her next day, because his wife knew just how much money he'd left in his pockets with, and he'd better bring every penny home.

"He was just standin' in front of the fireplace, lookin' at the fire, when somebody come up behind him and hit him in the head with a piece of firewood. He never knew who did it, but he knows. One of the boys there said Luther done it.

"When he came to, he run out in the yard—Marguerite had already run out (Marguerite is Luther's wife)—and Luther shot two shots of Buckshot after him.

"He ain't et nothin' for two days since then. He's mighty bad off. Luther claims that John was playin' with his wife. Now, perfesser, that ain't no way to do. He might have protected his wife. He could have taken her outside and talked to her. Now, folks won't know what to think of her, her bein' a school teacher, it's mighty bad for a man to do something like that."

(Piecing the story together from other sources, it appears that John told Luther he was going home, expecting Luther to take the electrician to Franklinton and to go from there to the dance. Apparently John thought it then a convenient way by which he could then slip back by the store. There were a number of "boys" there, but also apparently John was with Marguerite in another room, at the house, which is separate from the store. Luther, instead of going to Franklinton, doubled back to Star Creek, and caught John in the act of "playing with his wife." Whether this implies infidelity on the part of Marguerite, or whether John was bull-dozing her by taking candy without paying for it, I do not yet know. At any rate, John himself confesses it was his fault.)

Ernest continued by telling me that "Marguerite went on off to her mother's people, and Luther didn't know where she was. He didn' find out until Sunday afternoon, and then he went and got her." (Marguerite is a Burris, from Franklinton—the family which is a-kin to the white family from that town.)

November 28, 1934.
Thanksgiving Day. The fair is on. Our oil stove was borrowed for the use of the booth, which is being run by Mr. Monroe's brother-in-law. Mr. Ernest borrowed my car to bring the band from Bogalusa, King Gulley. The band consisted of a violin, a base viol, a cornet, a guitar, a banjo, and an entertainer who dances (with a chair in his mouth) and also plays a guitar, named Smokey. King Gulley plays the Viol.

The principal feature of the afternoon was a basketball game between Star Creek and Bethel. Bethel won by a large margin. Some child from Bethel hit Willie Pearl in the nose, and she cried, then wanted to fight. A teacher from Bethel referred to Willie Pearl as a "cry-baby." Miz Lu went and told Willie Pearl to shut her mouth, and not to fuss. The play was very rough.

There was a great deal of drunkenness. Mr. Burkhalter, the prosperous tenant on the Jim King place, was drunk and bouncing around. Out in a buggy on the seat lay Miz Gabe's brother, dead drunk. He was pointed out to us by Mr. Monroe, who seemed to take a malicious pleasure in it.

In the afternoon, we were called into the assembly room by Mr. Crane, who invited all in who wanted "a little instruction." Many filed sheepishly in. The feature was a speech by Mr. Fletcher Smith, the member of the School Board. In introducing him, Mr. Crane stressed the fact that many were obliged to stand in the auditorium, because there were not enough seats to go around. He also stressed the fact that Mr. Fletcher was a mighty good man, a man that stood for something, a man that everyone respected.

Mr. Smith acknowledged the introduction by sayin, "This Crane fellow is a pretty smart man. He brought me in here so he could tell me about those seats. Well, I pledge to you that by this time next year there will be enough seats in here to accommodate all of the people (applause)." Course, there's lots of things I'd like to know, but when you get in the Board of Education, you've got to use all kinds of ways to get things from them boys.

Mr. Smith went on to give a speech about the origin of Thanksgiving. It was a very good speech. He referred to the church, and to his faith, in God and the church. There was an infidel, he said, that was trying to get him to listen to his *infidelicy*. He told him, "No, I don't want to hear nothing about *infidelicy*. I believe what I believe, and you can believe what you believe, but I don't want to go to hell. If I went to hell, I don't think I'd know what to do, and I don't think they'd know what to do with me there. No sir, I didn't want to listen to any of his infidelicy."

After Mr. Smith spoke, Mr. Crane called on many other people, including numerous local citizens, and the teacher-trainer from Southern, Mr. Clark, who mildly criticized Mr. Crane's management of the fair. The President of the Community Fair Association for this District spoke, also. At the last, Mr. Crane called on me to speak. I believe that he did this because he wanted to show me what a small factor I was in the community and in his eyes. Mr. Crane dislikes me heartily, I am sure. Part of this is due to the fact that he now thinks that I am not as big a man as he once took me for, and regrets having tried to fool me in his class, and to impress me before. I believe that my wearing of overalls declasses me in his, as in other sights. I think also my prestige suffered with Mr. Crane when I suggested that Mr. A. C. Lewis was coming to visit, and Mr. Crane worked himself to death in order to get the school ready for his visit. When Mr. Lewis didn't come, Mr. Crane thought that I was of no import and was probably lying. Then, of course, Mr. Crane can never forget what I told him in the presence of others that day, when Mr. Lewis was expected and Mr. Crane reproached me for not telling him, and I told him that I thought the school should always be ready for inspection.

In the evening was the concert, and afterward the dance. About 6 o'clock a regular typhoon came up, and delayed us so we missed the concert. Our Thanksgiving meal consisted of back-bone given to us by Miz Gabe and sauerkraut. The wind blew so hard that rain was blown all over the kitchen and dining room, and the kitchen was a puddle as it always is when it rains.

The dance was in the auditorium room. The practice was to empty the room after the free concert and then to charge ten cents, two for fifteen, for the dance afterward.

The dancing, to say the least, was spirited. However, it was not graceful, the dances being what Mr. Bickham calls the "new kind of dancing," and with this none were very familiar. Much of it was mere stamping, all rushing. All kinds of dress was worn, from kimonas to evening dresses, from overalls to double breasted pimp suits. The dancing featured much solo work, boys dancing around by themselves, and couples breaking apart to sashay up, and men twirling their pardners around in pirouettes.

The best dancer was a little twelve year old girl who had slipped in. When her mother found out, she sent in and got her.

There were from fifteen to twenty white boys and girls present. Ernest was master of ceremonies. During the intermission, the crowd was entertained by the dancing member of King Gulley's troupe, on the whole a mediocre, but amusing performance if judged by "big-time" standards. His feature was to dance with a chair, and the marks of his teeth were in the chair when he had finished.

Mr. Ernest was very blasé as master of ceremonies. During the intermission, the crowd flocked onto the floor, blocking the view of Smoky's dancing from the young white people at the end of the room. Mr. Ernest asked them to move back several time. None did.

Mr. Andrew Bridges, a stupid, owl-looking white man who was assigned to the Fair as a deputy officer, moved uncertainly up to assist. Ernest, half-drunk, said, "That's right, Mr. Bridges, make 'em move back," in a commanding tone. Mr. Bridges obediently did so. Mr. Bridges conducts himself as though he is afraid that any moment one of these drunks will push him over.

November 29, 1934.
At midnight or afterward Leman Magee, the uncle of John, who was hit over the head with a piece of fire-wood by Luther Graves last week, came to the house and called me out. He wanted me to take John to Charity Hospital when I went to New Orleans Friday. I agreed to do so.

At 1 o'clock in the afternoon, before I had dressed, Leman came by and came in to take a seat. Leman is one-eyed, and unfortunately, not recognizing him, I asked him if he was the man who was going to the hospital.

After dressing, I drove with Leman to the school, where we picked up Tommie Warren, a first-cousin of John. Tommie had been to New Orleans before. They had received the address of a former resident of the community, one Dent Brooks they thought, but neither could read the slip on which the address was written. On looking at it, I found that it was the address of a Mrs. Dubois at 2206 Bienville Avenue.

I drove up the road about a mile and picked John up.

December 3, 1934.

While Ernest and Horace went over to Mr. Bickham's, Julia stayed to talk with Miz Gabe. Miz Gabe told Julia that she knew a girl had a little baby this year, not so long ago. She was havin' pains, and her mother was cookin' dinner. She was walkin' up and down, and her mother didn't pay her no attention. And directly she went inside, in her own room, and shet the door, and in a little while she said, "Mama, come here!" And there laid a little baby on the floor. Yes, she birthed that baby right on the floor. And she holped her mother pick up the baby, and all the stuff that went with it, and her mother told her she'd better get in that bed. And she got in bed, but she tried to holp her mother dress the little baby. Now, wasn't she smart?

'Cose, that was her fo'th child. And she'd worked hard right up to the time the baby came.

Said Julia, "It must be an awful thing, to see a baby born." Miz Gabe had seen three born. Miz Gabe said, "It sho is, the woman's jus' sweatin' like she's doin' hard work in the fields."

Julia and Miz Gabe were talkin' in the kitchen, while they was a-washin' the dishes. Says Julia, "Sugarman sure does love you." "Yes," said Miz Gabe, "he was born right here in this house." "Sure 'nough," said Julia. "Yes," said Miz Gabe. "When he was born, I took care of 'im until his mother was able to, and he loves me most near as much as he do his own mother."

When Miz Gabe and Julia had come into the living room, and Ernest and Horace had gone, Julia asked again, "So Sugarman was born right in this house?" Miz Gabe said, "Yes. He was birthed right here on the floor." And Julia asked her, "Why did they put her on the floor?" And Miz Gabe said, "It seems like she couldn't birth the baby on the bed, coz it was too soft. So they put her on the floor, on her knees, and she birthed the baby without any trouble at all."

And Julia said, "Who else was here besides you?" And she said, "Aunt Dosha Warren, she was the mid-wife. And Mr. Monroe's wife, and Miz Lu." Said Julia, "I bet Miz Lu knows a lot about helpin' with babies." Miz Gabe said, "Yes, she's not no mid-wife, but she's good to have around." Julia said, "You've got to have a lot of women around to keep water hot and all that, haven't you?" And Miz Gabe said, "Yes—you've got to have some little baby things there, right handy."

This morning when I came back from town, I stopped by the syrup mill, to pass the time of day with Mr. Boy Bickham. He told me to pass the word along up on the hill that Green Bickham's little boy had died, sudden, after the fair. I went by the school and told Mr. Sibley that the baby was dead, and to tell the children to tell the folks. It seems like the baby was just walkin', and had been up to the fair, for several days, in the bitterly cold weather.

When Miz Gabe was talking to Julia in the kitchen, Miz Gabe said that a little baby had died. "Yes," said Julia, "I had heard about it. How old was it?" "Oh," said Miz Gabe, "It hadn't been weaned yet." (Children here are weaned very late, nearer two years than one.) "No wonder," said Miz Gabe, "that it died. Its mother had had it out to the fair every night." (When Julia had been walking home with Miz Gabe, Friday night, a bitterly cold night, Miz Gabe had told her, "you know, if I had any little chillun, I'd stay at home with 'em. I wouldn't keep 'em out on a night like this. You know it's too cold for children to be out on a night like this. Those women don't even take their babies to the stove, they just stand out where the wind can blow on 'em. Some of 'em take 'em in them tents (i.e., booths), but you know them tents ain't warm enough for a baby."

(Miz Gabe, a very intelligent woman, must have said this to Allie, her sister-in-law, for Allie's baby is eight months old, and Ella Ruth is four. Allie was doing nothing but standing in the cold, outside, holding the baby. It was bitterly cold. Allie must have been offended, for Miz Gabe referred to her as being "very tender-hearted." Sunday morning, Orsell's wife and children came up to our house and "sat" with us a while; later, she told us, when we were about to go home, that Allie was about to go home. She probably said this about the babies to Allie, and Allie's feelings were hurt.)

The child of Green Bickham probably died of pneumonia. Julia faintly remembered, on Thursday, during the bitter cold, a girl holding a baby, who was crying loudly, and watching the exhibit pieces being held up.

December 6th.

Early this morning a Mr. Johnson, a half-brother to Mr. Monroe's wife, came over, bringing some civil war pension papers belonging to his father; he wished to know if it was possible for him to get the pension. His father had died in 1908. He had taken it to a white lawyer in Franklinton, but this man had said that there was nothing that could be done about it. Neither do I, for that matter. His father, he said, had warned him not to trust the white folks around here, that they wouldn't help him get his money.

I told him that I would ask about it in New Orleans, but that I didn't know. His father had belonged to the Tenth U.S. Heavy Artillery. He had enlisted in 1864, and had been discharged in 1867. The old man, he said, had fought with the Yankees, and that after the War he had got some money, but those niggers who went off with the rebels never got anything.

After some conversation, I arose, and he went out into the yard, where, out of ear-shot of Julia, he told me about another predicament. He said that he had homesteaded forty acres. Then he had bought forty acres, and to buy the addition he had borrowed $600 from Mr. Pearce, a merchant, who took a mortgage on both forty's. About four years ago Mr. Pearce had got in a tight, and had told him he wanted the money. Mr. Pearce had said that anyway he could get his money out, he was willing to do it, if he could put it in the loan, alright, if he could put it in the government loan, alright. But, he told Johnson that if he sold the land back to him, he would give it back to him whenever he wanted it, just this time he wanted to get some ready money. So Johnson made over his money to him.

Now, there had been a strange man out with some papers yesterday, and Mr. Johnson was afraid that Mr. Pearce intended to get rid of the land. He had come to me, because he knew I would give him a true answer. Was there anything I could tell him?

Nothing. Even if Johnson's story is true, which may be doubtful, Mr. Pearce seems perfectly within his rights. Furthermore, Johnson's only hope seems to lie in the belief that, since his wife, who quit him, after 32 years of married life, didn't sign no papers, the forty home-steaded acres are not rightfully Mr. Pearce's.

I drove with Julia over to see Aunt Julie Brock. On the way, Mr. Monroe wanted to go to town to buy a cement sack. I told him I wasn't going there, and asked if he knew Aunt Julie. He said, "No." I thought he must be lying (and he was).[18]

Aunt Julie is an old woman, somewhere in her eighties. Her mother had six children, all by different men. Aunt Julie was the oldest, by a white man named Perry. Her sister Ellen was by Tom Burch, another white man, who lived on a nearby place. Adeline was by Clowers, a colored man. Jack was by Sam Thomas, a colored man. Fleet was by George Dillon, a colored man, and Baily Miller was by Lewis Miller.

Aunt Julie is wrinkled, brown, like an Indian, with black hair of which she tells us she was once very proud, that she could tell any girls they might be lighter than she was, but didn't none of em have hair as straight as hers. She has an extremely pleasant face and smile. In talking of one of her sons, Ned, it seems that he killed a white man, and, she said, they got him away through the woods, don't no one know where he is now. Don't no one know if he got away.

(Mr. Monroe the next day told me that the white folks, the Burches, had slipped him away through the woods. All this took place across the river.)

Going back home by the syrup mill, Mr. Monroe was there. We brought him home. There was some teasing about him stopping by the way. Evidently there must be an affair between Mr. Monroe and Andrew Brown's daughter. Probably he is the father of some of the children.

The Lynching

On January 11, 1935, Horace Mann Bond learned that Jerome Wilson had been lynched. "He was found Friday morning at the crossroad going from Bethel to Frank-linton," wrote Ernest Magee, "dead lying in the ditch." Bond, then in New Orleans, could not bear to tell his wife the news over the telephone. He sent her a letter—she was in Nashville visiting her family—and enclosed two newspaper clippings.[1]

Julia was shocked and fearful. "We cannot go back and live there," she wrote back. "We are so unprotected. . . . That little community is at the mercy of whatever impulse may come over these white people." She tried to dissuade Horace from visiting Franklinton with Robert Park, who was visiting him from Chicago. "Coming back so soon after the lynching with what are obviously northern white men will make you an object of suspicion more than ever."[2]

In Washington Parish blacks felt scared; whites feared black retalia-tion. Rumors abounded: black teachers had fled; black schools were closed; black maids had quit working for white people. Leo M. Favrot, an official of the General Education Board based in Baton Rouge, re-ported that whites in Washington Parish suspected that "Reds, the NAACP, or some other organization" was stirring up "an organized spirit of opposition" among the black population.

From New Orleans, Bond wrote to the superintendent of schools. "While I was out there at Star Creek," he explained, "I was always afraid that I might do something that would bring harm or suspicion directed at the Negroes with whom I dealt." Was it safe for him to **77**

*return? Did any whites suspect him of being connected with the
Wilsons? Was there "any feeling that I was a spy or something of that
sort?" A letter from Franklinton telling him that his car insurance had
been canceled added to Bond's unease.*

*Not surprisingly, the Bonds had serious qualms about going back to
Washington Parish. Despite assurances as to their safety from white
friends there, a visit to Franklinton on February 8 settled the question:
they decided not to return to Star Creek. The following accounts of
their brief trip explain why.*[3]

February 8, 1935. Julia Bond's account.
Horace and I announced our plan of going back to Star Creek for the
day at the breakfast table. Dr. [Burbridge] told very lugubrious tales of
what would happen to us if we did go. He repeated the story of his being run out of Monroe, Louisiana, many years ago and told us many
discouraging anecdotes.[4] I was not afraid at all (so I thought) but these
stories made me a little nervous. We drove through town and got presents for our friends in Star Creek. These consisted of a bed-spread for
Miss Gabe, cigars for Mr. Ernest and Mr. Bickham, and a bracelet for
Thelma and a hammer for Orsell and candy for the family. The day was
pretty and we were very merry at the beginning of the drive. As we approached Franklinton we became a little constrained. We drove into the
town and saw very few people—only one Negro. Perhaps there were as
many people on the streets as ever, but they seemed deserted to me.

We drove to the Ford agency to see Mr. Greenlaw, the Ford dealer.
He was not in but would be back at one o'clock. He was attending a
meeting of the Chamber of Commerce. His son-in-law was there and
returned a flashlight of ours that had been there for some time. (We
had lost it some time in October.) Then we drove over to the Washington Parish Training School. I got out at Mrs. Barker's. (She is the
wife of the principal.)

She seemed very glad to see me. We talked for some time without
mentioning the lynching. She told me of her uncle's death and of the
children's Christmas presents. Finally she referred to the "trouble."

She said that she was tempted to write me and to tell me if I had any fears about coming back, not to worry.

"They ain't bother you. Mr. Barker says they can't be too nice in the stores. They jump around trying to wait on you. I don't ever go to town. I buy just what I have to have and don't waste no time with them. I don't go down there cause if they say any thing to me I sho' am going to talk back. Mr. Barker says that I talk too much. My mother said to me 'Daughter, you must be careful. You know that is a back-woods community and not like home (New Orleans) where it is a blow for a blow.' But since this trouble I'd just like to go home to live. If Mr. Barker could get a job I'd move right away. I'd like to send the children away to school. Blanche wants to come and live with you. We're so glad you've come back. We thought that you weren't coming. But you needn't be afraid. Nobody ain't going to hurt you."

She prepared lunch for us and I helped her to churn. Miss Todd came in. She is one of the teachers at the training school. She told us that she went home Friday night after the lynching, as did all of the teachers, but she and the others returned Sunday night. She said that she went to see Mr. Lewis's assistant while she was in Baton Rouge and she brought in the subject of the lynching very nicely. She said, "You know that we are going through a pretty bad time now, Mr. Rogers."

He replied, "Yes, Ella, I know about that."

This was Field Day at the school and they assumed that we had come for this occasion. All of the teachers from Star Creek with the exception of Mr. Crane were there. Willie Pearl, Henrietta and Olee were playing on the basketball team. I walked over to the field with Miss Todd and spoke to all I knew. The teachers were not too glad to see me.

Mr. Amacker said in a loud voice, "Did you bring your pistol, Mrs. Bond?"

Surprised, I replied that I had not.

"Well," said he, "You need it up here."

Miss Gabe told me about going to see Jerome's body the night after the mobbing. "He was washed and dressed and laid out but it was awful the way they beat that boy. One side of his face was mashed in, and you could see the hole in his head. You couldn't tell that it was him except for his mouth. It makes me so nervous whenever I think about it. His po' mother is speechless."

(Mrs. Barker said, "An old man around here told me that if these colored newspapers wouldn't print so much about this trouble that it'd be easier on us. But I told him they were saying things that we couldn't say. We're here and can't help ourselves, but they can talk for us. I just want to have 'em go on and do everything they can. Whoever wrote that up about Mr. Wilson she told it straight!" And she looked meaningly at me. I told her that I hadn't seen that copy yet but I'd try to look it up.)

After leaving Julia with Mrs. Barker, Horace stopped by Washington Parish Training School.

A field meet for all parish schools was going on. A group of the teachers were standing on the school house steps. None were very cordial. I had to ask Barker to let me speak to him. He agreed, but first walked me over to his office where he locked the door. Whenever he heard the outside door creak, he would talk loudly about school records or some such nonsense having nothing to do with our real conversation.

I asked him if he thought it would be alright to come back. He did not answer me directly. He had talked to Stringfield and to Greenlaw, he said, and they had wondered why I had been so nervous; wondered if anybody there had warned me not to come back. And Dr. Brock, the sheriff,[5] had been in Baton Rouge, and some Negro who had known him before, but whom he did not know, asked him what was going on at Franklinton—to what extent it was true that the teachers had been asked to leave, as it was reported.

Dr. Brock had come back, and gone out to see Barker. "Barker," he said, "you know that we've been treating all of you folks right. Now, it ain't fair that these stories should be circulating in these nigger newspapers. Now, some of you fellows ought to go down there and make them take that back."

Hence the letter from the teachers stating that it had all been a mistake that they had been asked to go away.

Barker would not commit himself as to the wisdom of my return. "You know, I think you'd be safer out there at Star Creek than I am here. It would be alright, anyway, except for these colored pimps. They're likely to go to the white man, and tell him you said something that you never did say."

I interrupted him.

"I have heard that there were some Negroes mixed up in that lynching. Is that so?"

"Yes," he replied. "And that's what makes it so bad. If you could only trust your own color, you could feel alright. Of course, you could stay up there in the country, among the home folks at Star Creek, and you'd be alright."

"But," I said, "I'd have to come to town to get something to eat."

"That is true."

Mr. Barker also told me that the leading men of the town disapproved of the lynching, but that lawless elements had done it.

I left him with thanks.

Returned to town, I saw Mr. Greenlaw, after a wait of some few minutes. Meanwhile, I talked about the weather with one of his partners who was in the sales room.

Mr. Greenlaw, when he saw me, immediately plunged into an excited defense of the community. All of the old settlers, he said, disapproved of the lawless action of a few hot headed men. But it was over, and there was no use stirring things up. "Why, Bond, these nigger newspapers are doing an awful lot of harm to your people. They're just agitating, agitating, agitating. If they let the thing drop everything would be alright."

(I started to tell him that the Negro newspapers had suppressed news of the affair in the fear that they might cause the lynching of Jerome. Now Jerome was lynched, and there was nothing to do about it.)

Mr. Greenlaw gave me assurances as to his guarantee of my safety. As I was ready to leave, I told him that my insurance on the car had been canceled.

He seemed dumbfounded at the news. Disclaiming any knowledge of it, he assured me that it could be renewed in some other company.

From Greenlaw's we went up in the country. At Star Creek, coming in by the sand bed, we were nearly stuck. We stopped at Miz Fannie Bickham's first. Mr. Boy was not at home. Miz Fannie was glad to see us, and we, to see her. "Somebody loves us, anyway." Her joy was genuine.

We talked to her for a little while. She said for us to go on, that she would come on over later. As we passed Seymour's lane leading down to Miz Gabe's, we stopped, and got out to walk up to Miz Lu's house. Miz Lu had heard the car and come to the door. She, too, was glad to see us. She took us in and introduced us to her mother, an old black woman who is almost completely paralyzed. Miz Lu is obviously a mulatto. Her mother can hear still, but she cannot talk. We spoke to her, and Miz Lu said, "Ma, these is mighty fine folks."

We had seen Willie Pearl in town, playing basketball. Mr. Ranse was off ploughing.

From there we went on toward Miz Gabe's. We could see Thelma and Sugarman playing in the yard, with some other children we could not recognize. As we approached, Thelma broke off from the group and ran into the house. Just as we drove up, Miz Gabe came out through the gallery.

Thelma and Sugarman told us how they appreciated the books we had sent to them. Thelma repeated "Little Boy Blue," which she had learned from one of them.

We went on up to the house. Here we sat down and talked a while. I waited until the children had gone out to play in the yard, and I asked Miz Gabe about the trouble, and about our safety. Miz Gabe said that it was bad enough about the white folks, but when there was colored pimps joinin' in, too, that made it downright dangerous.

Miz Fannie chimed in. Yes, she had heard that there were some colored pimps in the killing. One of 'em she knew. He had a nub for a hand. (I wondered if this could be the Dillon boy, from Franklinton, who does drive a truck and has associated with the white men as companion in crime for a number of years. He has several fingers cut off. He is the cousin to Mr. Ernest.)

(Mr. Barker had told me that one of his students had found a wrench near the place where Jerome Wilson's body was dumped out of the car. The wrench, he said, was identified as the property of the electric light plant, and it was suspected that the Negro mechanic who works there was also in the gang. The hammer which was found in the jail was identified, as belonging to this same man.

One wonders whether the Negroes were actually in the lynching, either as a result of blackmail or having been paid; or whether it is a tale told by the white men responsible who have actually convinced the Negroes.)

Miz Gabe also said the mob was led by the son of Deputy Sheriff Woods, who was killed last August, and over whose death the entire case had raged. The boy, she said, had come from New Jersey for Christmas, and had stayed over for the lynching.

Miz Gabe and Miz Fannie urged us not to come back. They actually suggested that we should be out of the community by nightfall.

I found that there was a bottle of grape-juice in the kitchen. I opened this, and brought in three fingers of whiskey which I had brought up from New Orleans. Miz Gabe and Miz Fannie drank with enthusiasm. I was sorry that I had not brought more than just enough to "wet their whistles."

After hearing the discouraging accounts given by these two, women, I decided not to come back. I immediately began to pack up my books, leaving the furniture and the bed linen and the food and other stuff in the house.

We said goodbye to them. Before we left, they insisted that we accept presents; Miz Gabe gave us a half-dozen eggs, and Miss Fannie gave us about a peck of peanuts.

Leaving there about four, we were back in New Orleans before six.

Bond settled into his post as dean of Dillard University. But although New Orleans was now their home, the Bonds were concerned about the fate of the Wilson family. Luther was still in jail. His mother,

Tempie, had been freed on bond but the shock of events had unhinged her mind and she was committed to a psychiatric ward at New Orleans Charity Hospital. John Wilson had been forced to sell half his land and mortgage the rest. "I am ruin[ed]," he wrote Walter White of the NAACP. "Please help." But the NAACP, struggling to stay afloat in the depths of the Depression, had no money to assist the families of lynching victims.[6]

Horace and Julia Bond tried to help. They knew that Tempie Wilson had relatives in the North, but tried to dissuade the family from moving to Chicago. It would much better, they thought, if the Wilsons could be set up on a farm somewhere outside Washington Parish, even if only as tenants. Horace appealed to friends, acquaintances, private foundations, and government agencies. Revealing some of his own feelings about the matter, he wrote to one friend: "It is a little bit of hell to think of this man working all his life according to all of the conventional virtues, and then at this late date forced to give it all up."[7]

Bond started writing "Forty Acres and a Mule" with a view to helping the Wilsons. Offering the partially completed manuscript to Harper and Brothers, he explained that John Wilson should receive half of the royalties, and that a further quarter would be given to the Rosenwald School in Bethel—a memorial to Jerome Wilson.[8]

Forty Acres and a Mule

Chapter One

FREEDOM COMES TO ISOM WILSON

som Wilson was just a shirt-tailed boy when they brought him to Washington Parish. The year must have been close to 1835, for Isom was a grown man when the surrender came in 1865. His father's real name, if he had one, was Will Ward, because Ward was the name of the Virginia planter who started out from St. James County, Virginia, with Will, and Martha, and their child Isom.[1]

Will Ward, so Isom's mother told him later, was a native African. Perhaps that was why he was so stubborn about leaving Virginia for Louisiana, when his master decided to sell them all down in the Southwest. Will couldn't have known that his master had to sell his slaves or his land, on account of the Tidewater land being worn out from planting tobacco and corn year in and year out for two hundred years. At any rate, Will didn't want to leave Virginia, and he sulked. Mas'r Ward paid no attention to his sulking, aside from giving him twenty lashes the second day out from Richmond.

The third day out Will acted particularly stubborn. So Mas'r Ward staked him out, spreadeagling both legs, his head, and one arm. Mercifully they left one arm free so that he could keep the steel collar from choking him to death in the night. They brought him food in a wooden bowl, and water in a blue glass jug.

It rained all that night. The next morning, when Mas'r Ward went to unchain Will, he found that he had broken the blue glass jug into little pieces. He kicked and beat Will, but Will didn't say a thing. They chained him by his collar to the end of the wagon where little Isom and his mother were riding. Mas'r Ward was careful about the slaves **87** while he was taking them overland; Martha was going to have another baby, and little Isom rode in the wagon with her because Mas'r Ward didn't want him to look puny from walking two thousand miles when they go to Louisiana. Every now and then he would make little Isom get out and walk alongside the wagon for exercise.

On the day after the night when they had staked Will out, the slave caravan had gone about ten miles when Will fell down behind the wagon. Mas'r Ward let the wagon drag him a little while, and then he rode back behind the wagon to see what was the matter with Will. He thought he was malingering again, but when he looked at his face, he saw that something was really the matter with Will. Will was worth fifteen hundred dollars in Louisiana, and so Mas'r Ward put him in the wagon with Martha and little Isom and let him ride.

Will wouldn't eat anything, and he wouldn't say anything. Mas'r Ward thought he was just another surly black brute. Louisiana would take that out of him.

Louisiana never had the chance. By the time Will died, in a day or so, Mas'r Ward discovered that Will had broken that blue glass jug on purpose, and ground up some of the pieces against his steel fetters. Then he had swallowed a handful or so of the blue glass powder.

When Mas'r Ward finally got to Louisiana, he sold Martha and her expectant baby and Isom to a planter who had two plantations, one on the Bogue Chitto River, just across the state line from Mississippi, and the other up on the Red River in North Louisiana. Martha and Isom were sent to the place on the Bogue Chitto. In 1859, when Isom was about eighteen years old, one of his master's relatives bought him for $1500.00, and gave him to Hezekiah Magee for a wedding present.[2]

Hezekiah Magee was one of a number of planters who lived along the river valley of the Bogue Chitto. The plantation was located in Washington Parish. Washington Parish is one of the sub-divisions of the old Spanish province of West Florida, and the entire section of Louisiana east of the Mississippi is included in what were once known as "The Florida Parishes."

The Florida parishes were just across Lake Ponchartrain from the City of New Orleans, but they might just as well have been a thousand miles away. Commerce and civilization were water borne, and they flowed down the Mississippi, and over the lakes and bayous that linked Latin Louisiana to the East by means of the Old Spanish Trail. The Florida Parishes remained, for the most part, unsettled stretches of virgin pine forests, with settlement taking root only along the rivers. The settlers came from Georgia, from the Carolinas, from Virginia, by way of the central Mississippi plateau. Louisiana west of the river bears the mark of the Latin; the Florida Parishes are Scotch-Irish, except where immigration since the Civil War has brought in colonies of Italians, Hungarians, Germans, and the Jew.

There are three rivers flowing down from Mississippi through Washington Parish to the gulf. The Pearl River on the east separates Louisiana from Mississippi. The Bogue Chitto runs right down through the middle of the Parish. On the West the Tchefuncta River divides Washington from Tangipahoa Parish. Plantation settlement followed these three rivers. In the backwoods were the poor whites, principally squatters, "sand hogs" in the vernacular of the country. In 1860 Isom Wilson was one of a thousand slaves reported by the census of that year for Washington Parish. There were two thousand white persons listed in 1860; less than one hundred and fifty of five hundred white families were slave-owners. Title to the land, aside from the plantation, remained with the Federal Government. Homesteading became possible only after the Civil War, and the piney woods were too inaccessible and too difficult of clearance at a time when a man of capital could pay for a bottom land plantation in one year with a good cotton crop.

Up in Pike County, Mississippi, there lived a planter named Daniels. He had a likely male slave called Wiley, who was the son of a half-Indian Negro woman and a full blooded Choctaw brave. Wiley had learned how to tan leather from his Indian folk, and he was handy with it all of his life. Mas'r Daniels claimed that he looked too much like an Indian, and was afraid that he might run away with them some day. So he sold Wiley down the Bogue Chitto to a Magee who lived across the river from Hezekiah.

Wiley already had children who were almost grown in Mississippi, but he raised another family on the Bogue Chitto. On account of his great skill with leather he was never obliged to do any hard work. He was a great one to make chairs, curing a cow hide and stretching it to make the seat. When he died, he left each one of his children a chair, made by himself. Wiley Daniels' grandchildren still treasure those chairs, and the leather is just as tight as the day he tied the thongs together, more than seventy years ago.[3]

Wiley's favorite child in his new Louisiana home was Mandy. Mandy grew up with the white folks; as they say when a distinction is to be made between a field hand and a house servant, she belonged to the latter class "who was raised by the white folks." Isom Wilson didn't do any field labor for Hezekiah, on the other side of the river, other than that of directing the other slaves what to do. It was natural that Isom finally started crossing the river to see Mandy, and finally they were married in the year before the big house. That is, they jumped over the broom, with Hezekiah and all of the other white folks looking on as their favorite servants were wed.[4]

By that time the big War was going on. It made no difference to the people living up and down the Bogue Chitto. Toward the end of the war the poor white folks back in the woods started bushwhacking and assassinating, and every now and then you would hear of some freighter being robbed on the way from Franklinton to Mandeville, or New Orleans. They raised enough cotton and wool, and they could spin it, right on the place, for clothes, and food was more plentiful than ever because the big planters didn't raise as much cotton as before the war.

Along about the end of the war the rebels came first, and they took all of the horses and mules they could find, which was not many. Hezekiah Magee sent Isom back into the woods with a drove of stock and cattle, and he stayed there until he got word to come back.

One day the Federals came. The old Missis got the news that they were coming before they got there. The big house was built out of logs, hewn on the sides to make them rest flat against one another. There were clapboards nailed along joinings. The old lady made Isom and another boy take down the facing off the door. She had a carpetbag full of greenbacks. They took long sticks and poked money back between the logs; and then they put the facing back on the door frame.

The Federals came just a little before sundown. Isom remembered the Captain riding up into the front yard, where Hezekiah and the old Missus were standing.

The Captain took off his hat and asked them if they had any stock. Mr. Hezekiah told him to go to Hell. The Captain made some of his men take the old man and lock him up in a room. Then they swept that farm clean as a whistle; all but the stock, which was hidden away in the woods, and the greenbacks, which were stuck back behind the door facing.[5]

Isom Wilson was a faithful servant to Hezekiah Magee, and Hezekiah thought the world of all of Isom. When they got the news that Freedom had been declared, Hezekiah called Isom to him. Isom told the story later.

He said, "They just turned the people loose, like you'd open the stock gate and turn the stock loose. My master said to me, he said, 'Well, Isom, you're free—you're just as free as I am. Your are free to go where you want to go.' "

And Isom just looked at his master. "Mas'r," he said, "I ain't got nowhere to go, ain't nothing to go nowhere with, Mas'r." And his mas'r said, "You can stay here with us. We'll pay you the best way we can, until you get yourself started."

Said Isom, "When the niggers got free, we all got notice that they was going to give us all forty acres and a mule. They was to be furnished until they made a crop. Didn't nobody get a mule; the mule come in parts of the country, but the niggers had to buy 'em. By my mas'r give me an ole wore out plough-horse. The old horse died of old age; I kep' him until he died."[6]

Isom stayed there on the place, and he worked on the share. When Hezekiah died he was still living with him. Isom raised Ferdie and Andrew Magee; they were just lads of boys when Hezekiah died. They called him their colored father. There were other children: Roscoe, Tessie, and Jennie I. Many years later Ferdie Magee sold the property he had fallen heir to through Hezekiah Magee to John Wilson, the son of Isom.[7]

After Isom had raised Hezekiah's children, Andrew Magee told Isom about a quarter section that could be homesteaded, laying right next to Hezekiah's old home place. Andrew put Isom on this land, and he showed him how to prove it, and how to take possession. When he had proved it up, Andrew got one hundred acres, and a fraction, and Isom got sixty acres and a fraction. That is where Isom Wilson raised all of his children, and where he lived until he died, an old man.

After he got his own land, Isom Wilson never travelled far. There was no railroad in the parish, and all of the goods brought in to the stores had to be freighted in. Almost until the day of his death, Isom Wilson was a freighter. The railroad came through in 1912, and Isom died in 1911. Until that time, they would load up at Franklinton with cotton, or corn, or some such truck. The freighters usually travelled together, and principally in the time just before Christmas when the traces were still dry and the crops had been laid by for the year, and settlement had been made and tenants were beginning to figure where they would be next year and who would furnish them.

The freight wagons were long and narrow, high wheeled, to pass along the narrow traces and through the deep bogs along the way. They used two yoke of oxen to the wagon, and the trip to Mandeville took two days and a night. It was forty miles from Franklinton to Mandeville.

When the drovers got to Mandeville, the boss man usually gave them a dollar or so to enjoy themselves, during the night before they loaded up from the barges which brought the goods across Lake Ponchartrain from New Orleans. The drovers were mostly young men, and they would all get drunk and gamble in Mandeville on the night they spent in camp on the way back.

Once Isom Wilson took his little boy John with him to Mandeville. Isom came back with another wagon and left John to come back with a white man who was driving two wagons. The white man started drinking as soon as he got to Mandeville, and by the time they started back he was dead drunk, lying on the wagon seat with his head resting on a barrel of flour that was behind him.

When they go out to camp, that night, he just rolled out of the wagon. John Wilson tucked him in, and he took his wallet from him for safe keeping. The white man sobered up when they were nearly back to Franklinton. He was ashamed of himself, and he knew John had the wallet. But he never asked him for it—he knew it was in good hands. John carried the wallet on home with him, and gave it to his mother.

Several days afterward, the white man came by the house for his wallet. John wasn't at home, but his mother, Mandy, gave the man the wallet. The story got around through the country, and from then on people knew that John Wilson was an honest lad, although he was just a lad of a boy.

Isom Wilson was a man like this: If you'd treat him right, he'd treat you right; if you didn't treat him right, he wouldn't have anything to do with you any more. He was well respected in the neighborhood, and he raised his boys and girls to be honest, dependable, shifty men and women. One by one they married off, and Isom helped them buy land and settle down on their own little places. Isom always told his boys that they should never take their wives to some white man's place, for to be a tenant too; and he wouldn't let none of his girls marry any man who wasn't shifty like himself, and gave good promise. He and Mandy were mighty strict on their children, not like the careless way people let their children run around these days, like calves in the woods. He taught his girls to respect themselves, and he wouldn't let anybody else not respect them.

One day Ophelia was ploughing in the field that lay next to the road. Isom didn't often let his girls work in the fields, but it just happened he was hard up for a force, the boys being off cutting ties or something, and this ploughing had to be done. So he set Ophelia at it. She had just turned a furrow at one end of the fence when along came a white drummer, driving a buggy. He stopped in the road across from where Ophelia was turning the plough, and he called out to her. "Say, gal, you want to do a little business?" All Ophelia could think of was to scream, and she screamed way out loud. Isom was back of the house, patching on a pig pen that needed mending. He heard her yell, and he ran through the house and got his shot gun down off the peg as he ran. When the drummer saw the old man flying out to the fence with the gun in his hand, he lashed his horse, and away he went. Old Isom saw what was happening, and Ophelia just stood there, yelling at the top of her voice. Isom took out after the drummer on foot, down the road, hoping to catch a pot shot at him before he turned the bend in the road a mile away. He couldn't catch up, and the drummer got away.

News of that got around, too, and didn't anybody try to joree with any of Isom's girls after that.

The little shirt tailed boy who came from Virginia before the war was an old man when he died. He had raised eleven children by the time he died, he and Mandy together on the old home place they had got through the help of Andrew Magee. Minnie was the oldest, and after her came Simon, Laura, Cornelia, Ada, Ida, Ella, John, William, Samuel, and Ophelia. All of the children, like their father Isom and their mother Mandy, were real shifty folks, and they married into good families and accumulated.

Isom died in 1911. It was forty six years after he had told Hezekiah, "Mas'r, I ain't got nowhere to go, ain't got nothin' to go nowhere with," and Hezekiah had told him, "You can stay here with us, until you can get yourself started."

Isom's children had seen him get himself pretty well started, and he had seen them pretty well started off on the land. The Wilson children owned more than a thousand acres of good land when Isom died. He died on the gallery of the little old house he had built on the part of the section he had got through the help of Andrew Magee. They were all sitting out on the gallery, just before first-dark—old Isom was dozing away in a chair, and nobody said anything, because the old man had been right puny of late and they wanted him to take his rest.

John was there, and Minnie, and Simon, and Samuel. All at once John heard a dove singing nearby, and then he saw a dove light on the railing of the gallery, right close to where Isom Wilson was dozing away. Then the dove flew away. John saw it, and so did Minnie and Simon and Samuel. They didn't say anything for a while. Then Simon got up and went over to Isom and put his hand on his shoulder. "Pa!" he said.

Isom never stirred a bit. He must have died there, peaceful like, while he was sitting there, just about the time the dove flew down and settled on the railing for a minute before flying away again.

Chapter Two

THE HALF-WHITE FOLKS WHO
GREW UP WITH ISOM

It is a hard thing to understand how all of the people in Washington Parish, white and black, are related to each other. It is also a hard thing to know how Isom managed to get ahead so far, and why so many other people of his time didn't get ahead. The people in those times lived like Barbarians, both the white people and the colored people. It is mighty hard to try to untangle where all of the cousins and uncles and nephews and nieces come in—because nearly everyone up there is a cousin, or an uncle, or a niece, to everybody else.

Suppose we think of the white men who owned slaves in those times, and the colored people they owned, people of the same age of Isom Wilson, or maybe a little older. There were two brothers who lived on the river near where Clifton is now, named Jake Magee and Fleet Magee. They were kin to all of the other Magees who had settled up and down the river from Mississippi on down. Jake and Fleet were nephews to Hezekiah Magee, who owned Isom Wilson.[8]

Another white man was named old Jeff Miller.[9] He owned two or three plantations in Mississippi, and one on the Louisiana side. Then there were Bill and Jim Burris. They lived around Franklinton, and the family had always run a big plantation and a big store there. It was said that the Burrises were white Indians, and they laid claim to being part Choctaw. Bill and Jim Burris were young men when the surrender came.[10]

Another white man, prominent at the time of the surrender, was
Dr. Amacker. Dr. Amacker was a foreigner to those parts, having

come in from somewhere else. He soon fitted into the life, and became very prominent. During the Reconstruction time he fought the Republicans mighty hard. When Grant ran for President in 1868 against Seymour, Dr. Amacker was given the credit for returning 638 votes in Washington Parish for Seymour to none for Grant.

Then there was John Magee, a brother to Hezekiah. He had a plantation on the Bayou Sara, and he finally sold out in Washington Parish and moved over there.

Then there was Mr. Tommie Graves, who was just a lad of a boy when the surrender came, but whose family had been considerable before the War. Mr. Tommie always lived on the Creek, where he had a mill and a lot of property until they built the railroad through Clifton and all of the stores moved over to that town. Mr. Tommie was known far and wide as one of the best lawyers throughout the section.[11]

Then there were the Cranes, a mighty respectable family in the olden times.[12] They lived principally across the river from Franklinton, but they owned land North of the town as well. Tom Trigger Bickham was a white man who owned a little water mill halfway between Clifton and Hackley. Tom Trigger got his name from being known as a dead shot, and a ready shot, in the olden times. Tom Trigger went to the War, and when he came back he had a pistol with fifteen scratches on it. He said that each scratch stood for a Yankee he had killed with that pistol. They do say that when Tom Trigger died he had five more scratches on the trigger of that old horse pistol.[13]

If you look at the map, you will see that all of these white men lived along the rivers and creeks. That is where the white people who had any money or property settled in the early days. They did that both because it brought them near to water, and because the land was better. Bored wells were not known in those days, and if you lived back in the hills you had to go down fifty or more feet for water. So the prosperous white people settled in the flats.

The hills were left to the poor white trash, and were used to range stock through. In all of that section South of Franklinton, and over to where Bogalusa is now and below, there was scarcely a Negro slave in the whole section. The white people there were wild ones, sand flies, "hoogins," as they were often called.

There were mighty few regular families during slavery, and right after. All of the marrying was done by jumping over the broom, as Isom and Mandy were wed. Right after the War it was even worse than that. People just took up with whomever they wanted to.

During slavery, of course, it was hard to tell just who was who. About the only time you could tell who was the father of a child was when a white baby was born. That was because the white men wouldn't let anybody else fool with a black woman when they were having her, and you could be pretty sure whose baby it was when it turned up.[14]

Jake and Fleet Magee were good for that. They are two reasons why it is so hard now to separate between who are cousins and not among the colored people in Washington Parish. You remember that they were white, two brothers.

Well, Jake had children by several different colored women. He would have them for a time, and then he would get another. The only time he had any trouble was with a slave named Tom. Tom was reputed to be an African nigger—people said he was a "two headed nigger" because he could tell fortunes and fates. He was slave to Jake Magee, and he had been slying up to Minerva for some little time. Jake didn't know that. Minerva had her first baby by Jake Magee, and she called him Green Magee.

Minerva was working around the big house, and they say that one day old man Jake Magee noticed that she was in a family way again. So he asked her when the baby was coming. The way she answered him, he knew it wasn't going to be his. He was terrible angry, and he got his rifle down and went out to the field where old Tom was chopping cotton with the gang.

Jake Magee wanted to whoop Tom, and he told Tom to put his hoe down and come up to the barn. Tom wouldn't put his hoe down. Then Jake Magee told some of the other slaves to catch him. Tom was stubborn, and he said to the other slaves, "If you put your hands on me I'll break your head with this hoe—I'll bust your brains out." None of the slaves would advance on him, for they knew Tom was a surly nigger, and would do what he said.

Jake Magee just stood there, getting madder and madder. Tom was just as stubborn as ever. He backed away from the gang and vaulted a fence, and started walking backward, facing the gang and Jake Magee as he went. They knew he was making for the Spring next to the Creek, where the swamps began.

Then Jake called out, "By God, Tom, if you don't stop, I'm going to shoot holes through your stubborn black hide." And Tom yelled back at him, "Mas'r Jake, you'll have to shoot me 'cause I ain't goin' to stop." So Jake Magee raised his rifle and he shot Tom down. He fell forward on the ground, just where the spring curbing was. The old folks used to say that the spring never was good any more, that it bubbled red with Tom's blood, and Mas'r Jake had to move it somewhere else to get water fit for man or beast.

Tom's baby was a boy, and he was named Tom Barker, because after Tom was killed, Jake sold Minerva to old man Barker.

As he had Minerva, Jake Magee had Dorcas. His baby by her was called Bill Doc Magee, the middle name for Dorcas. By Ellen Robinson, Jake Magee had George Magee. By Sarah, Jake Magee had a baby named Mary Magee.[15] The family names of these women came after slavery; before emancipation they were just called Ellen, and Dorcas, and Sarah, and Minerva.

While he was having these colored women, Jake Magee had four boys and three girls by a white woman he had married. They didn't always recognize it, but it makes all of Jake Magee's children by the colored women half-brothers and sisters to his children by the white woman. Then, all of the colored women Jake Magee had later had children by other white men, and by other colored men. You can see how that would mix all of the relations up to begin with.

Now, Fleet Magee was almost as bad after colored women as his brother, Jake. After the war, Fleet had a colored baby by Harriet; he was named Eldridge Magee. Fleet also had three colored children by

Harriet's sister, Sarah, another daughter of old man Eli Magee. They were called Will, Lee and George Magee. They were raised by their grandparents, Eli and Minerva.[16]

Fleet Magee had another baby by Cindie Bell. Cindie was a shifty old woman who never married, but she had a houseful of shifty children, all by different men. They always wanted to get Cindie to tenant for them, both the white and the colored farmers, because they said that, "When you get Cindie, you get a laborer and a woman, too." Strange as it may sound, all of Cindie's children turned out well. She would move from plantation to plantation, and wherever she went she had another baby by the man who owned the plantation or the farm. Fleet Magee's baby by Cindie was named Alice Magee.[17] That made Jake Magee uncle to Alice, through his brother Fleet. It also made Alice double cousins with Harriet's child by Jake Magee. There are many other relations you can figure out that will show you how these families came to be so mixed up in the end.

Fleet Magee raised a white family by his proper wife. There were three boys and two girls in this family. The boys moved away, but the girls stayed behind and married men from the Parish. Jacob is dead now, and so is Noel. Silas is living in San Antonio, Texas, now. Minnie married a Babington in the parish, and Emma married a Bateman in the parish. The same thing happened in many of the other white families. Most of the wealthy families had boys, and the boys would move off to the city, or go far away to places like Texas or North Louisiana or even to California. The girls would stay at home, usually. There wouldn't be any one for them to marry, often, in their own set, and so they'd marry some white boy who didn't have anything but who was just coming up in the world. Some of these poor white boys were industrious, and with the help of their wives' inheritance have made it real well. Others were just as trifling now as they ever were.

In the neighborhood of the Bethel community, where the children of Isom Wilson now live, there are other families besides the children of Jake and Fleet Magee that are half-white, or used to be before those mulatto children began to marry black men.

Near Clifton lives old Aunt Julie Brock. Aunt Julie says that she is ninety, although she really doesn't know.[18] She can remember well when the white caps[19] used to beat the colored people for registering, right after the Civil War. That was the time when most of the colored people got their names. They had been Magee's Sam, or Bickham's Harry, until the Yankees came around to let the colored people vote. They had to register up to vote, and they had to have names to register by in the books. So they took names for themselves; sometimes they would call themselves after their masters, such as Sam Magee, or Harry Bickham. Sometimes they would take brand new names, like Washington, or Jefferson, or by most any other name that seemed to strike their fancy.

Aunt Julie used to live across the river up near the Mississippi line. The Brocks and the Burches owned most of the land in that direction, and up into Mississippi from there. They didn't have much dealing with anyone else, anywhere else, because it was so far from every place, and hard to get at. Aunt Julie's father was said to have been an overseer named Perry. She was her mother's first child. Her mother was a half-white woman, who was part Indian with only a little colored blood, if any at all. She was reputed in that country to have been the prettiest little piece there ever was. Aunt Julie even now has long, straight black hair, and when she smiles you could think that she was almost a young girl. When she was young, she says, all of the other girls used to envy her hair, and she was awful proud of it. One of her sons bought her a new set of teeth, several years ago, and when she smiles you don't even see any wrinkles around her mouth.

After Aunt Julie's mother had her by this poor white man Perry, she lived with Tom Burch. Tom Burch owned a plantation across the river, and all of his people were well off. Aunt Julie's mother, Pennie, had a baby by Tom Burch who was named Ellen. Pennie had another baby by George Dillon, a half-white man from near Warnerton. She had another baby after that by Sam Thompson, a black man. The last two children, Fleet Dillon and Jack Thompson, were born after the Surrender.[20] Pennie was like most half-white women—when she was young and real pretty, she had children by white men. Then she had children by a half-white man; and finally she took up with a black man, and had a baby by him.

Just after slavery times, when her mother Pennie was well near middle age, and Julie herself was a very pretty girl, old man Tom Burch, who was nearly sixty years old, took a fancy to the girl—as he had twenty years or so before to the mother. He put Julie into a little cabin just beyond a clump of trees from the big house, and he kept her there for two or three years. She had one baby by him, and she named him Ned.[21] That made Ned her son, but he was also her brother, or at least her half-brother. It made Pennie the baby's grandmother, but she was also something like his aunt. That sounds strange, but it's true, and it is just another way of saying that the families were all mixed up in those early days.

Ned grew up with the white boys on the old Burch place. That crowd across the river was a wild lot, and Ned was as wild as any of them. The white boys treated him just like one of them. One day they were making a shivaree,[22] Ned along with the white Burch boys, and the Pinkstons, and the Brocks. They were rattling chains, and shooting guns, and blowing horns around the lot. One of the cousins to the man who had just been married came out of the house and told them to go away. The boys sassed him back. Ned was a big fellow, and this cousin picked him out and said, "By God, you big yellow nigger, I want you to get off this lot!" Ned was quick-tempered, and he was more than half-drunk. He called the man a son-of-a-bitch, and the man picked up a axe that was leaning against the wall and started out to hit him with it. Ned pulled out a pocket gun and shot him dead.

When the news of that got around, they formed a posse to get Ned, and they fetched some dogs from Kentwood to chase him. The white Burch boys sent word that if anybody came on their land looking for Ned they would blow their damned heads off. The posse looked everywhere except on the Burch plantation. They set a guard on all of the roads and byways, and they were just waiting for the sheriff to come so he could go on the Burch land and bring Ned out to them.

Night came before the sheriff, and the Burch boys took Ned and carried him through the swamps to Mississippi. He looked like a white man anyway, and they gave him money to help him get away. Get away he did, and he's never been heard of since he left. Some say that he was seen in Oklahoma once, and someone else said that he had been seen in Texas. But Ned never wrote back, and right now old Aunt Julie won't talk to a stranger about her son and half-brother Ned, for fear that the stranger is a detective trying to find out where her boy is who left those parts fifty years ago.

Ned was married himself when he went away, although he was just a young man, hardly more than a lad of a boy. He had married Jennie Brumfield. Ned hadn't been gone more than two years before Jennie took up with a man named Allen. They had a house full of children after that.

Franklinton isn't much of a town now, and it never was any bigger or smaller than it is today. Before Bogalusa was built, though, Franklinton was more important than it is now. Before and after the Surrender the Burrises had the biggest store in town. There were two Burrises, Bill and Jim, who were young men who went off to the war and came back full of devilment and mischief. They hated Yankees and were death on the colored people who tried to register and vote. It was said that they, together with a Babington, led the white caps in those parts.[23]

After the Surrender another young man came to town to practice medicine. His name was Dr. Amacker, and he had fought in the war against the Yankees, and he had been wounded. Dr. Amacker was particularly friendly with the two Burris brothers, and they shared and shared alike in almost everything they had.

That went for the colored girls, too. There were some pretty half-white colored girls around Franklinton after the surrender, and they had all been raised gentle by their white fathers. There were some young black girls too who had been raised by the white folks, and now that slavery was over they had nothing to do in Franklinton. Bill Burris had two children by a half-white girl named Margaret Graves. They were called John and Wes Burris.[24]

Margaret Graves was the daughter of a colored woman by old man Nat Graves. Old man Nat was a wealthy plantation owner around where Clifton used to be—before they built the railroad and moved the town five miles to the west so it would be on the railroad. Nat Graves' colored children were Margaret, Samantha, and Ephraim.[25]

After he had the colored children, he had five white children by his proper wife. They were named Tommie, Willie, Mortelia, Eliza, and Harriet. All of the white children grew up with the colored children, and you could hardly tell the difference between them. Perhaps that is why Nat's son Tommie took to Hannah as he did.

Bill Burris also had two children by Puss Crane, another half-white girl. Puss was almost a common woman, even for those days. One of his children by Puss, a boy, died a young man. The other was a girl, Candace.[26]

After he had lived with Margaret, Bill Burris married a young white girl from New Orleans. He never had much luck with his white children, and it was said that he and his wife could never agree on anything. She was reputed to be well learned in that country. Perhaps his troubles with her are why he took up with Puss Crane. The oldest boy, Byron, is dead now. Edward makes a fair living with the contract to feed the prisoners at the jail. Robert got killed, and a girl died a few years ago.[27]

Bill's brother Jim had one colored baby, George Burris, by Lucy Ellis.[28] Lucy was just a girl when the Surrender came, and it was said that the only trouble that ever rose between Jim Burris and young Dr. Amacker was over Lucy. Jim had set her up in a little place just three miles south of Franklinton, and it was said she was his sweetheart as well as his woman. He would come down there from Franklinton, and he would bring his friends down, and Lucy would cook for them and give them refreshments during the long, hot afternoons in the summer while they'd sit on the gallery and swap stories with one another.

Lucy's first baby was named George Burris. Lucy was puny, and Jim had Dr. Amacker to attend to her. Then Lucy turned up with another baby. Jim thought, of course, that it was his, until one night when there was a number of men sitting around talking in Charley Woods' saloon, drinking and chaffing with each other. They were talking about their colored women, for most of them had special colored women, and all of them had been with colored women at one time or another.

They do say that Jim was bragging about Lucy, how smart she was, and how she ran a better house than a white woman could, she was so shifty. Now, this Dr. Amacker had come there from foreign parts, and he didn't like to hear Jim Burris bragging about a nigger wench and making comparisons between her and white women. So he up and told, as a big joke, that the baby Lucy was carrying then was started up by him.

They say that Jim Burris tried to kill Dr. Amacker, right then and there. Anyway, Dr. Amacker didn't stay in those parts much longer after that night. He moved away, and the only Amackers around Franklinton right now are the colored Amackers that came out of that baby that Jim Burris thought was his, at first.[29]

But he didn't turn Lucy out of the house he had fixed up for her, and when she died a few years later, he provided for his boy George. By that time Jim had married a white woman, and he had just one boy by her, as he had just one by pretty little Lucy Ellis who was dead. They say that when Jim Burris was dying, he called his white son and his half-white son in to the room where he was lying close to death. He took their hands, and he joined them across the quilt as best he could, and he made his white son swear to regard George Burris as his true and lawful brother until the end of his living days.

That white Burris boy kept that promise, as you shall learn if you follow the story of these half-white children who grew up alongsides of Isom Wilson.

John Magee was full brother to Hezekiah Magee, who helped Isom Wilson to make a start after the Surrender. Before that time John Magee moved away to the plantation on the Bayou Sara that the family owned. But before he moved he had one baby by Keziah, a half-white girl who belonged to his daddy. She died before the War, soon after she had birthed her baby who was named Wade Magee. Wade was a full grown man at the time of the Surrender. The white folks raised him, and he was always smart.

There was only one white Crane who had any mulatto children. That was Samuel Crane, a minister in those parts, who rode the circuit. Long before the surrender he had two children, Irve and Frank, by a part Indian, part white, part colored woman named Maria.[30] It was said that the preacher taught Maria how to read the Bible, and the folks used to joke Irve and Frank about the parts of the Bible that he particularly took pains to teach her. Anyway, she was a shifty woman, and she was uncommon smart. She raised her children strict and they turned out well.

In the younger generation old Tom Trigger Bickham had a baby by Hannah. Hannah was a half-white woman who was almost grown when the surrender came. She had been a slave to old man Nat Graves before the War, as a youngster, and she worked for him afterward. Hannah was a favorite with Nat's white wife, and she grew up along with old man Nat's white and colored children.

Hannah's first baby was by Tom Trigger. Later on, when he was almost an old man, Tom Trigger had another baby by Cindie Bell, one year after he got her to make a crop, and, as the folks said, to make a baby for him, as Cindie could be depended on to do for whoever she worked for. Tom Trigger's child by Hannah was Jack Bickham.[31] He is living in the Hackley community, on a place he homesteaded with the help of old man Tom Trigger Bickham. Cindie's baby by Tom Trigger was named Mary. The old man died before he could help her, but she grew up decent and married well.

Hannah was one black woman who, instead of beginning babies with the white folks and then taking up the colored, began with black folks and ended her life living in a white man's house with her black children helping her half-white children and their daddy cry for her when she died. Besides the baby by Tom Trigger, Hannah had three children by colored men. She lived in a cabin a stone's throw from Mr. Nat's house, and, along with her babies, she helped take care of his house and his children.

Tommie was just about five years old when Hannah was fifteen, and started helping with the house work. By the time Tommie was eighteen,

Hannah already had four babies at twenty-eight. Tommie was raised by her.

Old man Nat died when Tommie was seventeen. His white wife was already dead. Margaret helped out around the house, and Hannah came over and cooked. Within a year after old man Nat was dead and buried, Hannah had her first baby by young Tommie. It was a pretty little blue eyed girl, and Mr. Tommie named her Inez. He named all of his colored children, personally. There was a custom in those days for the old people to send out word, asking advice as to what name they should give the babies. The half-white babies and the outside black babies usually got their family name from their daddies, and that is why an old woman like Cindie Bell would have eight different children with eight different family names, the father of each being different. But Mr. Tommie personally named his own children, and they lived in a house on the same lot, for after Inez was born Mr. Tommie just moved Hannah into the yard in a little Cabin he built specially for her.

Mr. Tommie had got a right good education before old man Nat died. After then he read law, and he was considered one of the most knowing attorneys that ever argued a case in those parts. He had much property from his father, and he increased it by smart trading. He was not one of these small farmers who had to take a turn in the fields with his help; he supervised the work, and he got people to help him supervise the work.

Mr. Tommie would have made a great man in those parts, but he never got far in politics, and that is how the lawyers got ahead. The white people objected to Mr. Tommie keeping that colored woman in his house. More than that, they objected to Mr. Tommie keeping a colored woman who already had children by colored men, and they thought it outrageous that Mr. Tommie should suffer those black children of nigger men just as he suffered his own half-white children.

Well, Hannah died, and left Mr. Tommie with a houseful of children, him still a strong man in middle age, Hannah having been older than he was. After Inez he had by Hannah Mary, Noonie, and Pete. He was particularly fond of Pete, and he would ride him around on the saddle with him, Pete holding on to the horn of the saddle, and Mr. Tommie speaking to white and black just as proud as could be, him not giving a damn, and acting like it, at what they might think about him and his little nigger boy.

After two or three years Mr. Tommie got lonely for a woman. Times had changed since the old days, and Mr. Tommie didn't want to take up with another colored woman like he had with Hannah. He tried here, and he tried there, to get him a wife; but the young white girls in that community wouldn't have anything to do with him. His reputation was too well known, and none of them would agree to come to his house while all of those black and half-white children were still around. And Mr. Tommie wouldn't agree to get shut of them.

At last Mr. Tommie got him a wife. She was just a little girl, like, and she came from way down in the other end of the Parish, from near Covington or Slidell or one of those places. They do say that she was a free-jack. The free-jacks were a colony of half-white colored people who lived around Slidell and Lacombe, and who wouldn't associate with the colored people, or be classed with them. But the white people wouldn't accept the Free-Jacks as white people, nor let them go to the white schools.

At any rate, they say that Mr. Tommie's white wife that he brought in was either a Free-Jack or had a touch of it in her. Some said that Mr. Tommie got her to show the white girls around there how independent he was. Others said that Mr. Tommie knew that no real white woman would be kind to those children, and he got a woman whose blood would help her be kind to his black and half-white children.

Mr. Tommie's white wife was a kind woman to the children, alright. She had three white children by Mr. Tommie, and they were called Tommie after his daddy, Joseph, and Martha. When Mr. Tommie's white wife came to live with him, Hannah's oldest child, Jack, son to Tom Trigger Bickham, was almost as old as she was. Hannah's oldest girl, Ella, daughter to a half-white man named Irve Crane, was a teenage girl when Mr. Tommie married after Hannah died. Ella worked right well along with Mrs. Graves, and they raised all of Hannah's young children and Mrs. Graves' little white babies together, like they were sisters. Mr. Tommie's white children never forgot Ella, and they loved her as much as she deserved, her being their sister and serving to them as a mother too. They always recognized her and treated her and her relatives as fine as they could.[32] And Mr. Tommie looked after each of Hannah's children, whether they were his or not. The boys he set up on their own forty's; and gave each of them a mule and other necessaries with which to start farming. If any of his children, or his children's wives or husbands, ever got in trouble, Mr. Tommie would be the first to get them out.

There were other half-white children scattered around in the country places, but these are the ones who stayed in the country and had children, either outside or lawful, and who gave their names to the people you meet there now. Many of the white fathers were very particular who their half-white children married, and they made sure that they would marry black men or women they knew, and had confidence in as shifty people. Because of that there was a lot of marrying into the same families, and the relationships have been getting more and more confused every since. It has come to be a disrespectful thing for a girl to have a white baby, or for a white man in the country to live with a colored woman. It has even become a disrespectful thing to have an outside baby, and most of the half-white children and the black folks that the white people raised have become particular about the way their children carried on. A woman like Cindie Bell could have eight children by eight different men, and yet everyone recognized her as a shifty woman and a good hand. Now, the colored farmers and the white farmers wouldn't stand for a woman like Cindie Bell traipsing around the country having babies, while she worked on the share.

There is still a lot of wickedness around the towns, like Franklinton; maybe more there than ever. But out in the country the barbarian ways of the olden times have just about disappeared. They have real families now, and they respect themselves and demand that a woman be self-respecting. They are even getting to be ashamed of the outside children, and all of the mixed relations that they used to take as a matter of course.

Chapter Three

THE BLACK CHILDREN WHO
GREW UP WITH ISOM

Real families among the colored people in Washington Parish didn't start until after the Civil War. Even then it took thirty or forty years for the early habits of promiscuity to disappear, and for the children born in slavery and right afterward to settle down with one woman, in a recognized family where he laid claim to all of the children there. In some cases it took up until a few years ago for that to happen. In some other cases that hasn't happened yet.

Because their mothers were likely to have had so many children by so many different men, the colored people in Washington Parish usually claim kin to each other through their mothers, and not through their daddies. The half-white men and women usually knew who their daddy was supposed to be, and their white fathers recognized them and helped them get ahead in such a way that it was remembered and remarked upon, and so well known throughout the community. But it was rare that a black man could do anything remarkable for his children, and so the name of a black father was not as important to remember, and was not actually so important, as was the name and the remembrance of the mother.

In considering the beginning of families, then, you must remember in the first few years after the Surrender that the women were most important in determining relationships. Now, many of these same women, as they grew older, would have children by half-white or black men who later would establish regular families of their own. It was in this later time that the head of the family became a man.

Isom Wilson and his wife, Mandy Daniels, were unusual in that they made a start on establishing a regular family right after the Surrender. In that way they and their children had the advantage over most of the other colored families in that part of the community. Isom Wilson did have one or two outside children, but Mandy Daniels never lived with any other man than Isom. That was a strange thing at the time they started together; it was not until thirty and forty years later that the same thing could be said of most of the other colored people in the Parish. Perhaps that is why their children had such an advantage over all of the other families, except the half-white ones, among the black people around them.

Minerva's baby by the slave Tom, born after Jake Magee killed Tom for starting it up, was named Thomas Barker. Thomas was a smart man, and a shifty one, through his mother Minerva, and they also said that he got a lot of fire from his stubborn father whom Jake Magee killed. His first child was by Ludie Bell, sister to Cindie, and was named Henry Barker. Henry got killed when still a young man. He was shot by Alex Burton in a crap game. Alex was sent to the penitentiary for it, and he died there. They said of pneumonia, but someone else who was there at the time said that they whipped him so hard he died of poisoning when the skin peeled off his back and the flies laid maggots in the creases where the strap had gulled him.

Thomas Barker had a reputation for being a smart man, but he was also a rascal. He was deacon of Jerusalem Church for forty years, but he was known far and wide to be a rascal as well. He married Nannie Magee. Nannie was daughter to old man Harry Hop and Maria, from Mississippi. It was said that Maria was the daughter of old Wiley Daniels, born to him before he was sold down into Louisiana from Pike County. You remember it was Wiley's daughter, Mandy, who married Isom Wilson; so Mandy was half sister to Nannie Magee, who married Thomas Barker.

Old man Harry Hop and Maria were known as two-headed niggers. They could see visions and dream dreams, and they knew how to hoodoo people. The old man died believing that someone had put a spell on him. Neither he nor Maria ever learned how to read or write, but they were reputed far and wide to know more about the past and the future than anyone else, black or white, in that section of Mississippi. Nannie, their daughter, was a smart women. All of her children by Thomas Barker were smart, and some people lay it to Minerva, the mother of Thomas Barker, and other people lay it to the fact that Harry Hop and Maria were so smart. Nannie was one of the few people in her time who could read and write; they said that she taught herself when she was a young one, out of a Bible that old man Harry Hop had. At any rate, the children of Thomas Barker and Nannie Magee went farther in schooling than anyone else among the colored people in those parts, and it is not strange when you consider that their grandparents were Minerva and the slave Tom, and Harry Hop and Maria, all still reputed above all of the other colored people back in those times of slavery for shiftiness and wisdom.[33]

When you consider that Minerva's son by Jake Magee, Green, was another smart one, and that his children all were easy to learn and got far ahead; and when you remember that the other prominent family, the Wilsons, partly came out of the same stock through Mandy Daniels, it is a hard thing to decide as to whether these colored people got their sense from their white grandparents, from Minerva, from the old stubborn slave Tom, or from Wiley Daniels through Maria, and Mandy.

Sarah Magee—no kin to the Sarah who was old Eli's Magee's daughter—had a half-white girl named Mary by Jake Magee.[34] After having Mary, Sarah had another baby by Tom Greenback Magee, a black man. This child was named Sam Magee.[35] He married Minnie Wilson, Isom Wilson's first-born child. Sarah's sister Harriet, who had Eldridge by Fleet Magee, also had a baby by Tom Greenback, the same who was father to her sister's baby Sam.

Tom Greenback got his name from the war times, when Greenbacks were circulating around. He was known as a good hand, and when he was sold his master claimed he was worth his weight in gold. Just before the surrender his master sold him, and the price was $25,000 in greenbacks.[36] It took so many to pay for him that after that they always called him Tom Greenback.

You will recall Pennie Brock, who lived across the river up near the Mississippi state line. She had Aunt Julie, called Julie Brock, by Perry, a white Overseer. She had Ellen by Tom Burch. She had Fleet Dillon by George Dillon, a half-white man; and Jack Thompson by Sam Thompson, a black man. Jack Thompson was her last baby. The next to the last was Bailey Miller, who was born to her by Lewis Miller.

Lewis Miller was a half-white man, the son of old man Jep Miller and a colored woman whose name I do not at present recall. When he had this baby by Pennie Brook he was a very young man, and she was almost an old lady. Lewis Miller homesteaded, with the help of his white daddy, a quarter section of land on the old Columbia road, North of Franklinton. He was a shifty man, and even went for a big preacher in those parts; but he was recognized far and wide as a grand rascal, to his dying day.

You can hardly count up the number of children which were put on Lewis Miller as their father. If he had been living in slavery times, they say that he would have been a famous breeder. He had women all through the parish, and up in Mississippi. He would preach down at a woman, sitting beside her husband and her children in the congregation; and he would wink at her while he preached. Now, no matter how good that woman was, Lewis Miller was known to have a charm for the best of them; and that husband had better look out if he wanted to keep Lewis Miller from riding up to his lot one day while he was off ploughing in the far field, or gone to town on business. Young or old, married or unmarried, he took them all.

He was conscientious about his outside children, and he recognized them. Whenever one of them got married, old Lewis would start them off with something. If it was a boy, he would give him a mule; if it was a girl, he would give the couple a heifer. He increased his substance, and added to his land, and was a good farmer. They said that Lewis Miller must have given away a drove of mules and a herd of cattle to his outside children, during his day.

The baby he started up with Pennie Brock was his first. His second was by Julie, Pennie's daughter. There were three men who had children by Julie after having had babies by her mother, Pennie. Tom Burch had Julie after he had Pennie, and George Dillon had Julie after he had a baby by Pennie. Lewis Miller had a boy baby by Julie about five years after he had Bailey by Pennie.

Then Lewis Miller had a baby by a woman who was known in the community only as Lilly Potlicker. Lilly was almost a half-wit woman, and it was a great shame to Lewis for having this baby by her. The child turned out right intelligent, however, and afterward married well. Lewis' next baby was by Zilphy. The child was named Ash, and is a fine carpenter and machinist in Franklinton now, although he is well advanced in age.

It would tax my mind to tell you all of the outside children Lewis Miller had. After he got married to Tempie Magee, it is said that he had at least four other outside children. One was by Sookie, and was named Matt. Matt is living in Bogalusa now; she married a half-white man from Mississippi named Blackwell. Blackwell was brother to a woman by whom Lewis Miller had three children. Two of them were girls, and one a boy, named Ott. One of the girls is dead, and the other lives in Bogalusa now. The boy married one of Deacon Fortinberry's children, and lives with her in Bogalusa now.

Lewis Miller's regular wife was Tempie Magee. Tempie was a half white woman, who had one whole sister named Margaret. She also had two black half-sisters, Sarah and Harriet. Sarah was wife to Tom Greenback, and had a baby by Jake Magee; Harriet is the one who had a baby by Fleet Magee, Jake's brother, regular.

One of Lewis Miller's daughters, Mary, married Simon Wilson, son of Isom. Mary was extra intelligent, and she was a school teacher and a nurse for many years. She was also very accomplished when it came to sewing, and embroidery work. Even now she occasionally sells her quilts to the rich white people in Bogalusa. The people keep her so busy now, mid-wifing, that it is hard to find her at home.

Simon accumulated several thousand dollars. He is reputed to be a shifty man and a stingy man. Many of his accumulations come from the thrift of his wife Mary, the daughter of old Lewis. To show you how families grew up in that country, take the case of Simon and Mary. Simon came from a good family that was already well set up, both Isom and Mandy being people of good reputation, and respectable. Mary came from a family where they were respectable, alright, but old Lewis Miller had all of these outside children, and was himself a half-white man all mixed up.

Simon and Mary have ten living children. None of them are disreputable, and all of them have their own little places and are doing well. You might say that there are ten decent families who came out of one child of Lewis Miller, and one child of Isom Wilson. It goes to show how things have changed since the time when customs were very barbarous in that country.

All of Lewis Miller's regular children married well, and did well afterward. Margaret married Walter Crane; Marcus had three wives, but it was no fault of his, the first two dying in his hands. His third wife was Alice Magee, Cindie Bell's child by Fleet Magee.

Sarah Miller married Green Magee. Green, you will remember, was son to Jake Magee by Minerva. Green had three children by Ardell, a half-white woman from above the State Line, before he had Sarah. By Sarah he had eight children, and all of them turned out exceptionally well. Green had one outside child by Ella Graves, who was the daughter by Irve Crane of the Hannah who lived with Mr. Tommie Graves.

Janie Miller married a Jack Thompson, who was the son of Aunt Julie Brock's mother, Pennie, by Sam Thompson. It is interesting here to recall that Jerome Wilson, Isom's grandson, was lynched by a mob that included a colored Thompson, who was the son to Jack.

Lewis Miller was one of the few colored men among the old timers to establish a regular family, in addition to all of his carryings-on with other women beside the one he hit on at last as his lawful wife. Eli Graves was another. Eli was slave to old man Nat Graves. After the Surrender old man Nat set Eli up on a forty acre tract, and he married Margaret. Margaret had already had two children by Bill Burris, the white man of whom I've told you.

Eli's children by Margaret who lived to be grown were Jesse, George, Andrew, Ophelia, and Zadie. Jesse was an idiot kind of fellow, but he always had sense enough to protect his own business. It was a marvel to all of the people how he could manage, and he acted so idiot, like. His head jerked all the time, and he couldn't walk straight. But he could plough, and he could chop cotton, and when he chopped cotton or hoed corn he'd never so much as chop a sprout.

George Graves killed a colored man, and ran away to Mississippi. He was never heard of since. The other children were not much, but at the same time they weren't disreputable. The family has lost the old forty acres that Eli had, and Andrew lives on land that his wife fell heir to through her daddy. Ophelia and Zadie married owners, and live on their farms now.

After the Surrender Eli Magee also settled down. He married Minerva, and the couple lived together into old age. At the time of their marriage, Minerva was already the mother of Green Magee (her child by the slaveholder Jake Magee) and Thomas Barker, her son by slave Tom. Eli already had one son, Abe, by another woman, as well as three daughters, Julia, Sarah, and Kissie. After the three girls left home, Eli and Minerva raised a son of their own, Wiley. They also brought up three grandchildren, George, Will and Lee, who were the mulatto children of Eli's daughter Sarah and the former slaveholder Fleet Magee.[37]

By 1880 Eli Magee's eldest daughter, Julia, had married a man called Wade Magee and given birth to a son and a daughter. Wade Magee was a shifty old half-white man. His father was slaveholder John Magee and his mother a slave called Keziah. After the Surrender he became involved in the Republican Party, and he stayed in politics long after the end of Reconstruction, for Negroes in Washington Parish voted and served on juries until the turn of the century. Wade Magee used to own the post offices in the Parish. He was on the Republican Committee. When the white folks wanted a post office, they had to come to him to get them. Sometimes they got awful mad about it. John Wilson remembers one time hearing a white man say, "We're getting in an awful fix when we have to see a nigger about a post office." The other white man, who had got the post office, answered him, "Well, he's got 'em, and he's got 'em fair." Old man Wade Magee handled the post offices until he died.

Like most other black folks in Washington Parish, Wade Magee tried his hand at farming and became a pretty good one too. In 1902 he took a notion to go to Arkansas, thinking the land there was more fertile and that times would be better. But he only moved as far as Mc-Comb, Mississippi, just north of the state line. He stayed there until he spent everything he had and then began to rent land up there. He was well thought of in that section. After a while he came back on down to Tylertown, and lived there about three years. Then he moved out in the country and farmed again. After a while he moved to Bogalusa, with a view to working for the paper company, but his health failed him. His wife Julia, and daughters Bessie, Inez and Kezie, moved to Chicago. But Wade spent his twilight years in Louisiana, living on the farm of John Wilson, who had married his daughter Tempie. Another of Wade's daughters, Ophelia, lived in Franklinton, where her husband, Rev. A. J. Scarborough, taught school and was pastor of a Holiness Church.

Old Wade Magee was a restless, ambitious man. And like many of the family heads at that time, he was a strong disciplinarian. While he was living in Bogalusa, one of his sons left home with a gun that belonged to someone else. When the theft was discovered, Wade Magee followed his son to Franklinton, gave him a good whopping, and took the gun back. That was Wade Magee all over. Even when he was an old man in his seventies, living with the Wilson family, he still worked. For a while he had a cobbler's shop in Franklinton, right opposite the Post Office on Main Street. Nobody knew how he made any money, but rumor had it that his white relatives helped out with the rent.[38]

Wade and Julia Magee raised fourteen children. Most of them drifted off to other places. One lives in Franklinton, one in Florida, one is in Biloxi, four are in Chicago, and the last time one was heard from, he was in Kansas City. There has been a lot of trouble in that family. But all the children were talented, one way or another. All of them were good cooks, and all of the girls were good seamstresses. John Wilson's wife Tempie has a talent for sewing from that side of the family. Time was when she sewed for all of the white people around where they lived.

All Wade Magee's children were light-skinned, and it was well-known that Wade himself was half-white. In marrying Tempie Magee, in fact, John Wilson was marrying the granddaughter of one of the largest slaveholders in Washington Parish, John Magee, whose family had once owned his own parents.

Chapter Four

THE LYNCHING OF JEROME WILSON

Like their father, all of Isom Wilson's children were real shifty folks, and they married into good families and accumulated. Old Man Isom Wilson was mighty particular about the way his children behaved, and the way they married. One time he chased a white drummer for a mile, with his shotgun, for saying something out of the way to one of his daughters. The girl was ploughing along the fence when this drummer drove by. Isom would have shot him, too, if he could have caught up with him. Simon was extra shifty. He had 320 acres now. He homesteaded a quarter section and bought the rest. He had $2200.00 in the bank when the bank failed. He got 80 percent of that back. Then he had $1709.00 in a trunk in his house, and somebody broke in and stole it.

All of Isom's boys bought land, and own it now. All of the Wilson girls married men who had land, or who bought it after they were married. Altogether Isom's children own more than two thousand acres in Washington Parish today. The old man only left that sixty acres he raised all of the children on. None of the Wilsons was ever in any kind of trouble. The white folks and the colored folks all gave them a good reputation in that country.

Isom's favorite boy was John. John was shifty like the rest of them. He bought a place of fifty acres when he was eighteen years old. The next year he married Tempie Magee. He had been going to see Tempie for about four years before he married her. Then one night he asked her to marry him. She was tickled to death, but she said, "You'll have to ask my father and mother." So John went to old man Wade Magee

119

one night and asked him. It was pitch dark, and John couldn't see the old man's face, and the old man couldn't see his face. That was the only way he could get up the nerve to ask him. But the old man was willing; he just said, "If it's alright with Tempie, it's alright with me. but you'll have to ask her mother, Julie." John never asked her mother—he could never get up enough nerve to ask her. So they just set a date, and then they were married. Isom gave them a little old mule, and Wade Magee gave Tempie a little old heifer. The land John Wilson had bought was just woods; he planted his first crop in pine weeds. He built a house himself, cutting trees and hauling them to the saw mill, where he had them sawed into lumber. Then he hauled the lumber back to his place and built himself a house. That is how he started, with just a little old mule, a heifer and a wife.

John and Tempie worked hard for a long time. Cotton was only four and five cents a pound, and Tempie was puny. John Wilson never let her, or any of his girls work in the fields. But they paid off the notes on their fifty acres, and John was a shifty man. He would make money doing extra things. He would cut stove wood, and for years he made money buying cattle for two white men. It was a marvel to the big white farmers around him how he managed to make as much as he did on his fifty acres. When his boys started growing up, so they could help him make a crop, he would rent other land and make good on it. He took short courses in Agriculture at the local Bethel School, and even at Southern University, the state school for Negroes at Baton Rouge. He followed all of the advanced methods, like the agents told him to do. He was a Deacon of the Bethel Holiness Church, a trustee of the Bethel Rosenwald School, the building of which he supervised, and a trustee of the Washington Parish Training School for Negroes at Franklinton. He had helped form the Bethel Holiness Church, which split off from the Jerusalem Baptist Church. They wanted the ministers to set a better example for the young people, and so they started a church where they could be satisfied. One of the foundations of the church was that young people should not smoke or drink. John Wilson never smoked in all of his life; he hated to see his money going up in smoke.

John Wilson's name was good at the bank and anywhere else. One time, after the war, when the farmers had been buying at war prices, and selling at peace prices, he got way down in the hole. He owed over three thousand dollars at the bank. Cotton went up to 27 cents, and he sold one load of cotton for $2200.00. He got a check for it. With another check, he went into the bank, and he gave those checks to the banker. The banker just stared at it. "Well, John," he said, "I thought I had you hooked that time. It's about the third time I thought I had you, but you've skinned through every time."

John Wilson and Tempie Magee had eleven children. Roy was a talented boy, who could make almost anything he'd see. He made a steam engine once that would blow out of an old syrup can. He died when he was sixteen. Two girls died when they were babies. The children living in the early Summer of 1934 were Luther, Jerome, Moise, Bruce, Felton, Alexzine, Burnell, and Onshell. Luther had spent four years at Southern University, where he learned the trade of blacksmithing. Jerome, Moise and Bruce were grown. They had been through the eighth grade. Jerome was a cook. He had worked in New Orleans for a man, and he had worked in a restaurant in Tylertown. He had come home to help make the crop. He was going to leave for another job the week after the time the trouble happened. Moise and Bruce were boys that didn't want to go anywhere. They were shifty, and they liked to stay at home and work on the farm.

Alexzine and Burnell were going to the Parish Training School at Franklinton. Alexzine was a tenth-grade scholar, and she was talented in home economics. Felton and Onshell were going to school at the Bethel Rosenwald School.

The older boys were thinking about getting married. One of them had said, "Pa, I'd like to get married, but I don't have no place to take my wife. I'm not going to take my wife to some white man's place." So John Wilson, just before Christmas of 1933, had bought another plantation. This new place had 172 acres. He was going to run an eight mule farm. He didn't intend to put tenants on the place; he wanted to put his boys on it, and he was going to direct them and settle them on the land with their families. The notes were to run ten years. The Government cotton rent would pay about one-fourth of each year's notes, and John Wilson was sure that he wouldn't have any trouble paying for the place.

With all of the boys at home during the Spring of 1934, they put in a good crop. They had taken part of it off by the end of July. While times were slack, they mostly laid around the house, chatting and talking, mending harness, sharpening plough points, and such things that occupy a farmer's time when the crop is partly laid by.

John Wilson had a good house. It was so good that one day, when John Wilson was ploughing in the front garden, a white man going by in a buggy spied him. He stopped and said, "John, is that your house?" John told him, "Yes sir, that's my house. I been living in it now almost ten years." The white man said, "Well, I'll be damned! You got a house as good as a white man's. I didn't know a nigger live in that house." The house had six rooms. A gallery ran down the middle of the house, with rooms on either side. It was sealed against the weather, and it was painted a pretty gray. The house was higher in the back than it was in the front, and in the morning the family would sit out on the back to escape the morning sun. In the afternoon, when the sun came around to the back, they would move up to the front of the house. The dining room table had been moved out, part in the gallery, and part on the back porch, so they could get the cool breezes when they ate. When people came to the house, they just came on around to the back to visit.

On the morning of July 21st John Wilson went off to town about nine o'clock to attend to some business. Franklinton was five miles from the home place. The boys were going to bring the wagon to town later in the day, and they were going to stay overnight while John Wilson brought the wagon back. They didn't have an automobile, and never did. Tenants could buy cars, because they didn't have anything, and if they fell behind on the notes the man would take the car back. But if an owner bought a car, and couldn't meet the notes, the man wouldn't take the car back; he'd take the land. So none of the colored farmers who owned their land bought automobiles.

Not long after John Wilson left the house, the range rider, Joe Magee, rode up. There was a cattle dipping ordinance in the parish, and Joe Magee had come to see about an old mule that hadn't been dipped. All of the children were sitting down on the back porch when this range rider came up, and hitched his horse and started into the stock lot. One of the boys asked him, "Mister, what's your business, what do you want?" The range rider turned around and said, "I can't go in the lot?" One of the boys said, "Tell us your business."[39]

The range rider said again, "You mean I can't go in the lot?"

And then Jerome said, "Hell no, you can't go in there if you can't tell your business."

Then the range rider turned to Jerome and said, "What is your name, boy?" And Jerome said, "You didn't tell me yours—I ain't goin' to tell you mine." Then the range rider left, and he went on up to Clifton. Clifton is just one mile up the road.

John Wilson's brother Sammy was at the house. After the range rider left, he said, "Do you all know who that was?" And one of the boys said, "No, I didn't know who that was. I ain't never seen him before." Then Tempie said, "Well, he sure did act funny. It look like he would have told his business." Then Sammy said, "That was the range rider. I bet he was hunting old Emma, that wasn't dipped yesterday." Then Tempie said, "One of you boys better get on one of those mules, and go overtake your papa, and tell him to come on back here." Sammy said, "Well, the ranger will be back here directly. We'll see what he's got to say."

When the range rider came back, he came back with help. He rang up the sheriff and the deputy came and brought two others. They met up at John Wilson's house. There was Joe Magee, and Deputy Sheriff Delos Wood, and Deputy McCauley McCain, and one other. They got out the car and came around to the back of the house. The folks were still sitting there. Moise was sitting down with his back to a post and so to the men in the yard. He didn't get up.

The ranger began to point them out. "There's one, and there's one, and there's one." Mr. Wood said, "Alright, boys, come and go with me." They knew Mr. Wood, and Mr. Wood knew them good. Jerome said, "Go with you for what, Mr. Wood? We haven't done anything. We're home. Show us your authority." And Mr. Wood said, "We don't have to have no authority to take you God Damned niggers to jail."

Then Mr. Wood drew his gun and, opening the gate, began to come in. Tempie yelled, "Ooh, Men, don't come in here with all them guns!" Then the shooting started. Moise jumped up from the porch and grabbed Wood's hand as he came up the steps. The other men participated. Moise was shot through the stomach, twice. Moise just laid down where he was. Then Jerome was shot, then Felton. Then Jerome ran into the gallery, and came around into the room where the guns were kept. You could track him by the blood. He picked up a shotgun and fired out the window.[40] Then he came on out to his brother Moise and laid down by him. Deputy Wood was shot, and laying on the ground. He was shot facing the house, but the ball went in the back of his head. None of the boys had pistols, only shotguns.[41]

After Mr. Wood was shot, Joe Magee picked up his pistol and began to shoot Luther. One bullet went through his hand, another gulled him across the back, and the third skipped him across the head.

John Wilson, plodding along on his mule, began to meet numbers of cars coming from Franklinton, but nobody told him anything. He was almost to Franklinton when a white man told him, "John, I heard one of your boys done killed Delos Wood." So he came on back, hippity-hop on his mule as fast as he could come.

He found the yard crowded with people. In the back yard, a white friend told him about the shooting. A crowd of men were standing on the back gallery. While he was talking to this man, the baby boy, Felton, crawled out from under the bed where he had been hiding. He had been shot through the hip. John Wilson went up to the gallery where the boy was squatting, crying. A deputy sheriff from Bogalusa came running up and tried to talk to the boy. The boy wouldn't talk to him, and started crying. John Wilson said to the deputy, "Let me talk to him, and he'll talk." The deputy said, "You hush!" John Wilson replied, "Well, he isn't going to talk to you. If you let me talk to him, he'll talk." The deputy jumped up and said, "I told you to hush, damn you"—and he struck John Wilson over the left eye with his pistol. You can see the scar now. "You ought to have been dead" said the deputy "forty years ago."

They carried all of the children, with Tempie and John Wilson, to the jail at Franklinton; that is, all but Luther and Alexzine. They got away through the woods. They caught Luther the next day or so. Alexzine was in the woods, and a white neighbor went and got her, and carried her to his house, where they took care of her for several days. Then some colored man told the law where she was, and the officers came and got her.[42]

Moise died in the jail that night. They gave him no medical attention. One old lawyer came in, before he died, and kicked him in the mouth as he lay on the floor. It knocked out several teeth. That lawyer died a few days afterward, of a stroke.[43]

The Wilsons got a lawyer on Friday, July 27th. The trial was called on the morning of July 30th, the following Monday. The case was in the hands of the jury by the afternoon of the next day. Jerome had to be carried into court on a chair. While he was being carried back to the jail to await the verdict of the jury, a mob tried to take him away from the officers. There were some Negro men carrying the chair. They dropped Jerome and fled. The sheriff stopped the mob. He made a little speech. "Boys, you ought to give the jury a chance."

The boys gave the jury a chance, and the next morning they brought in a verdict against Jerome of murder in the first degree.

The lawyer asked for a new trial, but the Judge denied it. The lawyer then took an appeal to the Louisiana Supreme Court. In a short time all of the Wilsons were let out of jail, except Luther and Jerome. All of the colored folks believed that they would get out in time, but they wondered why they kept them in the jail at Franklinton. It is not much of a jail anyway.

Just before Christmas a son of the dead Deputy Sheriff returned from New Jersey.

Somebody started sending Mrs. Delos Wood, the widow of the dead deputy, copies of a Negro newspaper which printed occasional accounts of the killing and the trouble in general. The white people didn't like that. The Negro newspaper in New Orleans suppressed a lot of news. They were afraid that they might cause Luther and Jerome to be lynched by enraging the white people at Franklinton.

On the eighth of January, 1935, the Supreme Court of Louisiana handed down a decision in the case of the *State* v. *Jerome Wilson*. The Court set aside the conviction of Jerome by the lower court on the ground that he had been denied a "fair and impartial" trial.[44]

On the eleventh day of January, early in the morning before first dawn, eight or nine men unlocked the doors of the jail and came up-stairs to the cell where Luther and Jerome were, with two other fellows. Afterwards Luther said that he couldn't recognize any of the men. Jerome began to scream. He knew they had come for him. There was a little stable lock on the door, and it seems that the men didn't have the keys to that door. While they were breaking the lock, someone shot Jerome. Jerome kept on screaming. When the men finally broke down the door, one of them bashed in Jerome's head with a hammer. They took him by the heels and dragged him down the stairs. The other prisoners could hear his head hitting the steps—"thump, thump, thump"—as they dragged him down.

Outside the jail they put Jerome's body in an automobile. They drove out on the road toward John Wilson's home, and near there they threw the body—naked—into a ditch. When Alexzine was starting to catch the school bus next morning she saw a crowd at the cross-roads. Two white men stopped her. "Don't go over there," they told her. "Your brother is lying over there, dead."

That day hundreds of people, white and black, came up to the Wilson house while they laid Jerome out. They stood in little knots around the house, talking. When a certain Negro man drove up and came into the yard, they all stopped talking. They said he was a pimp for the white people. They knew what he wanted. They even said that some Negro pimps, some trifling fellows who worked for some white people in Franklinton, had helped the white folks lynch Jerome Wilson; and they believed this particular fellow was trying to find out what everyone was saying. It was hard enough when the white folks would take a boy out and kill him like a dog, after the High Law had given him another chance; but when you couldn't trust your own color, it seemed like the end of the world had come.

Sheriff Brock brought a coroner's jury out, and they found that Jerome Wilson had come to his death at the hands of a person or persons unknown. Sheriff Brock told the New Orleans *Times-Picayune*, "There wasn't any lynching; there wasn't any mob, either. There was just about six or eight men who were going about their business."

All of the leading white farmers felt very sorry for John Wilson. They all told him not to move, that he was just as safe in Washington Parish as anybody else. They told the colored people that, too.

Yet the colored people were all very afraid. Some other white men had said that they were going to massacre all of the colored people, and they didn't want to see so many Negroes on the streets at Franklinton. If they hadn't said that, the Negroes heard that they had. The Negroes who worked for the white folks were afraid to cross the railroad tracks into the white section to go to work, for they thought if Jerome Wilson could be killed so easily, they might be killed too, and nothing would be done about it. The white people said that the Negro newspapers, and the National Association for the Advancement of Colored People, and the Communists, were agitating among the Negroes.

The National Association for the Advancement of Colored People did send a telegram to President Roosevelt protesting against the lynching, from their New York office. The Negroes had never heard of the communists before.

Senator Huey Long, when asked about the lynching, said that "It just slipped up on us, but I am sure he (Jerome Wilson) was guilty as hell."

You might think that was the end of the first lynching of 1935. But the Negroes remained afraid. The white folks said that everything was over, but they claimed the Negro newspapers and the NAACP and the Communists were agitating among their help, and making them surly. The white people couldn't see why the Negroes should be afraid just because there were still a dozen or so men roaming around in the parish who had recently taken a boy from jail and killed him, when those men knew that nothing would be done about it regardless of what the Supreme Court of Louisiana had said about his guilt.

On Saturday night, February 9th, a white man named C. Booty crossed the railroad tracks into the Negro quarter to have a little fun. One or two of his friends were with him. They had guns, and they had been drinking. They went into a Negro barber shop, and chased all of the Negroes there into a restaurant next door. They followed the Negroes next door, where somebody shot C. Booty through the head. They arrested all of the Negroes they could find, and then turned them loose, except Gene Clark. Gene Clark was a first cousin to Jerome Wilson, the son of Ella Wilson and John Clark. They took Gene over to Baton Rouge for safe-keeping. C. Booty was the son of Dyson Booty. Dyson Booty was the night jailer, and he had been on duty the night that Jerome Wilson was taken out of the jail. C. Booty had just got out of the penitentiary, and had not been long back in Franklinton.

John Wilson had to sell his old home place to pay for the expenses of the first trial, and for the appeal. He had moved his family to the new place where he had expected to settle his boys so they could raise a family, like Isom and John had done before them. But now Moise was dead, Jerome was dead, and Luther was still in jail. Tempie was always puny, and she had nearly gone crazy during the trouble. Tempie didn't want to go back to Washington Parish to live; John Wilson did.

If you talk to John Wilson, even now, with two of his boys dead, one in jail, and his old home place gone, you might be surprised to find out how much he still believes in his white friends. Didn't those friends of his know that Jerome was going to be lynched? "Yes, but. . . ." Couldn't they have kept Jerome from being lynched if they had wanted to? "Yes, but. . . ."

He was sure that none of his trouble came about from any of the white people who knew him, or who lived near the Bethel community. This man, and that man, and the other—one after one, as he names them—they are mighty fine men, they are real nice white folks, they always treat you honest. The white folks who did the lynching, why, they must have been some white folks from another part of the parish, where they don't have any colored people. Then you begin to wonder just why Jerome Wilson was lynched, anyway.

Well, one old Negro man told me that "It was 'cause them boys cussed that white man. That started all of the trouble." You can run it back like this: If John Wilson hadn't picked the morning to go to town when the range rider was coming, he would have been at home when Joe Magee came by. If he had been at home, no one would have had a quarrel with the range rider; Deputy Sheriff Wood would never have come out from Franklinton; there would have been no shooting; there would have been no trial; and there would have been no lynching.

Old Isom Wilson, who got his land through the help of Andrew Magee, would never have cursed that range rider; nor would his son John. But you can figure it out another way. If there had been no Isom Wilson to get land, or John Wilson to start off with "a little old mule, a heifer, and a wife," there would have been no Jerome Wilson who could think that he was at home and could ask a white man what he wanted in his stock lot. There might have been a Jerome Wilson, but he wouldn't have had a stock lot, and his landlord would have attended to the dipping of a mule.

After all, there is one reason that everybody will agree with. Isom Wilson, who got his land through the help of Andrew Magee, was not just a good old man; he was a "good ole nigger." And John Wilson was not just a good farmer; he was the "best nigger farmer" in those parts. And cursing the range rider, taken by itself, is not so terrible; it was terrible, and had terrible consequences, when "them nigger boys cussed that white man." That was the thing that Jerome forgot when he made his big mistake.

The sons and daughters and grandchildren of men like Isom Wilson own more than fifteen thousand acres in the Negro communities neighboring upon the town of Franklinton. I know a white man who knows his Louisiana. He told me, "Well, I guess that will break up that community. I've never seen it fail yet; a lynching always breaks up a Negro owner community."

Isom Wilson was one of Jerome Wilson's grandfathers, and Wade Magee was the other. Isom's children stayed on the land, and they and their children never had much trouble. They all turned out like John Wilson. Wade Magee's children, except Tempie, the mother of Jerome, wandered around a lot. Some are in Chicago, some in New Orleans, and some in other places unknown to their relatives. The city Magees haven't done as well as the Wilsons who stayed on the farm, at least up to the last year. Some of them have separated from their first wives, or husbands, and taken others. One or two have been in the penitentiary; two have been killed in brawls, one place or another. Others are on relief rolls throughout the country. A sociologist might write an essay on it and call it "The Pathology of Urbanization."

John Wilson still has six children. He doesn't know anything about the "Pathology of Urbanization." All he knows is that he is a good farmer and that he wants to farm and raise his family in Washington Parish. But, although he is shifty, he doesn't know how farming will be somewhere else. He wants Alexzine, and Burnell, and Onshell to finish school, and study home economics in college. He wants Bruce and Felton to establish themselves as shifty men. Above all, he wants to get Luther out of jail. When he does that, (if he does), he will probably have to start in farming somewhere else, or go to the city to get a job, where some of his wife's relatives live.

So the story of the first lynching of 1935, begun in 1865 by Isom Wilson and Hezekiah Magee, has a few more chapters coming. You can say one thing for old Isom; he had a shifty lot of children, and they all make good home owning, "nigger farmers."

EPILOGUE

While John Wilson was in New Orleans, visiting his wife in Charity Hospital and talking with Horace Mann Bond at Dillard University, he left Alexzine, the eldest daughter, in charge of the younger children.[1]

The day soon came, however, when a white neighbor, Jim King—the man who had bought the old Wilson farm—told Alexzine that according to rumor a mob was planning to lynch the rest of the Wilson family. It would be best, he told her, if they left Washington Parish at once. A cousin hastened to New Orleans to warn John Wilson not to return.

In the early hours of a March morning, a school bus drew up outside the Wilson farm and Alexzine shepherded her drowsy siblings on board. Clutching mattresses and bundles of clothes, the children were driven west through the dark countryside. Their journey ended in the Negro township of Scotlandville, now part of Baton Rouge, then outside the city boundary. There, Aunt "Babe"—Ophelia Scarborough, Tempie's sister—was living with two of her daughters, Irma Dean and Freddye, who attended Southern University.

Crammed into a three-room "shotgun" house that usually accommodated three people, the six Wilsons doubled up in bed, with John and little Onshell sleeping head-to-toe on a cot in the kitchen. It could only be a temporary refuge, of course, and the Wilsons were soon looking for other shelter. They found a roof a few miles away in Baton Rouge, at the home of a schoolteacher (a distant cousin) and her husband.

The Wilsons had a wretched time. John Wilson sold his remaining property in Washington Parish, but for much less than he had paid for it. With six mouths to feed and with escalating lawyer's bills for Luther's defense, his money soon ran out. Accustomed to the economic security and self-respect that came with ownership of land, John Wilson had to look for a job in the middle of the Great Depression. He was reduced to sweeping floors at a grocery store.

Bond drew the plight of the Wilson family to the attention of Will Alexander, head of the Farm Security Administration. "Doctor Will" was the leading figure in the interracial movement of the interwar era: director of the Commission on Interracial Cooperation, trustee of the Rosenwald Fund, and the first president of Dillard University. But all Alexander offered was a modest donation, in the name of the CIC, toward the NAACP's defense of Luther Wilson. Should Wilson's lawyers choose to forgo his fee, Alexander noted, the money saved could be used "in helping Mr. [John] Wilson to get started elsewhere."[2]

In June 1935, after almost a year in jail, Luther Wilson was finally released; five months later, the prosecutors quietly dropped their cases against Luther and his mother. Luther's white lawyer, needless to say, billed the NAACP in full. The Wilson family never received a penny in material assistance from the NAACP, the CIC, the Rosenwald Fund, or any other organization. Once the family had broken up, with Tempie and the children in Chicago, Horace Mann Bond abandoned his attempt to find them another farm.[3]

Bond also set aside the manuscript of "Forty Acres and a Mule" and never returned to it. He had received a discouraging response from Harper and Brothers, who declined to offer him a book contract on the basis of an unfinished manuscript. It seems unlikely, in any case, that a white publishing house in the 1930s would have touched an account of miscegenation so detailed and explicit as that contained in "Forty Acres and a Mule." To this day, miscegenation is an extremely sensitive topic for whites. While elderly blacks in Louisiana still chuckle over a quip they attribute to Huey Long—"You could feed all the pure whites in Louisiana with a nickel's worth of red beans and a dime's worth of rice"—whites are still horrified by suggestions that they might have black ancestors, however distant, or black cousins, however far removed.[4]

As lynching declined in the late 1930s, Bond had a diminishing incentive to complete his manuscript. Although southern senators successfully defeated antilynching bills in Congress, the threat of federal intervention, and the pressure of public opinion, encouraged state and local authorities to curb lynching. Doing so was a relatively straightforward matter, for most lynchings occurred after law enforcement officials surrendered black prisoners to lynching parties. When governors, judges, prosecutors, and sheriffs decided to put a stop to lynching, lynching stopped. After the death of W. C. Williams near Ruston in 1938, Louisiana saw no more lynchings for eight years. The lynching of John C. Jones near Minden in 1946 was the state's last, according to the standard definition of the term. The lynch mobs that had terrorized blacks from the time of Reconstruction to the Second War passed from the scene. Sooner, perhaps, than he could have anticipated, Bond's manuscript became dated.[5]

All the efforts of Horace Mann Bond to help the Wilsons proved unavailing, and after 1935 he lost touch with the family. Some twenty years later, however, after they had moved to Atlanta, the Bonds became friendly with Mrs. Freddye Henderson, who ran a successful travel agency that pioneered tours to Africa. More years passed before Julia, now widowed, discovered that Mrs. Henderson had grown up in Franklinton and was a first cousin of Jerome Wilson. With Mrs. Henderson's help, it became possible to locate John Wilson's surviving children and trace the history of the Wilson family since 1935.

After a short time in Baton Rouge, the Wilsons began to split up. Over her husband's entreaties, Tempie Wilson left for Chicago, carrying their youngest daughter, Onshell, with her. There they joined Tempie's mother, Julia Magee, and her sisters, Kezie and Inez. Alexzine and the two other children were forced to fend for themselves. Fortunately, their mother had taught the girls to sew, and they earned money by taking in clothes. And every two weeks or so Uncle Sammy, John Wilson's brother, drove up from Washington Parish with provisions donated by friends and relatives. Uncle Sammy also helped to raise money to send the Wilson children to Chicago. One by one, they left Louisiana and joined their mother, until only Alexzine was left. Eventually Alexzine, too, boarded a Chicago-bound train, arriving on Easter Sunday, 1936. The children never saw their father again.

One can only imagine John Wilson's feelings as he saw his wife and children depart. He had lost his land, and now he lost his family. Staying in Louisiana, he eventually "took up" with another woman, reportedly one much younger than himself. His children learned of the relationship and were pained by it, but they could not condemn their father. What hurt most was losing contact with him. Felton recalls writing to him and waiting in vain for a reply.

John Wilson died in April 1945 at the age of sixty-four. Alexzine returned to Washington Parish to bury him in the same community cemetery where Moise and Jerome were interred. At the graveside Alexzine met the woman who had been John Wilson's partner; she felt grateful that someone had looked after her father in his declining years. Felton, however, only learned of his father's death when he returned from overseas service with the navy, long after the funeral.

Although they never lived together again as a family, the surviving Wilson children looked after their mother and kept in touch with each other. They quickly sank roots in the North and settled down to stable, hardworking lives.

Their initial destination in Chicago was Aunt Kezie's house on Forty-ninth Street and Indiana Avenue. Within three or four years all the girls had married and set up house with their husbands. Aunt Kezie taught Alexzine how to use an electric sewing-machine, and she helped her to find a job with an upholstery firm. Alexzine worked in Chicago for nineteen years; after moving to New York she found a similar job in Manhattan's garment district. The other daughters stayed in Chicago and became wives and mothers. Burnell married a businessman. Onshell married twice; her second husband is a minister.

The three surviving Wilson boys, Luther, Bruce, and Felton, all found work in Chicago. Luther, the oldest child in the family, worked in the stockyards. Bruce, after drifting around the country for a time, got a job in a steel mill. Felton, the youngest son, became a union plasterer, a skill he practiced throughout Chicago for the next forty years, with a five-year interruption for wartime service in the U.S. Navy.

All the Wilson children, except for Luther, married and had children, although in contrast to the custom in the rural South, they kept their families small. Luther, who had one "outside" child, a daughter, back in Washington Parish, died at the relatively young age of forty. All the other children lived into old age. When Bruce died in 1987 at the age of seventy-five, he left a daughter, four grandchildren, and three great-grandchildren.[6]

Burnell Wilson spent her twilight years in a Chicago nursing-home; she passed away in 1996. Onshell, the youngest sister, does not wish to talk about the painful memories of sixty years ago. Felton, now in frail health but of sound mind, states that he was too young to remember much of what happened. "It was just like a dream."

But Alexzine, the eldest surviving child, remembers everything. Living alone in a simply furnished apartment on the nineteenth floor of a senior citizens' center in Brooklyn, she can still feel the pain, terror, grief, and humiliation that accompanied the events of 1934–35. But she also recalls the kindness of Uncle Sammy and the other relatives who helped her. She has warm memories, too, of her white neighbors, the King family, who helped protect the Wilsons when they were threatened by a lynch mob. She and Burnell made a point of stopping by the King farm when they drove through Washington Parish in 1950. Although Alexzine professes a grim satisfaction in believing that the men who lynched her brother all met untimely deaths, she does not nurture bitterness or hatred.

Tempie Wilson, a diminutive, light-skinned woman whose physiognomy attested to African, Indian, and European blood, died in a Chicago nursing-home in 1975 at age ninety-three. She left five children, ten grandchildren, sixteen great-grandchildren, and two great-great-grandchildren. Frail, and nervous, she had always needed looking after, and had lived, at various times, with her son Luther, her sister Ophelia, her niece Johnnie, and her other son Felton. Despite her longevity, she never fully recovered from the nervous breakdown she suffered forty years earlier after the lynching of her son Jerome.

The Wilsons in Chicago lost touch with nearly all of their friends and relatives in Washington Parish. But Franklinton has altered little in sixty years, and the area is still full of people, blacks and whites, called Bickham, Crane, Graves, and Magee. Delos Wood is buried in the Magee family cemetery, not far from the graves of the two Hezekiah Magees. His wife and children, including Joe Wood, who died soon after the lynching, are now buried beside him.[7]

In the Wilson family cemetery the paint on the wooden crosses has faded; few of the graves can be identified. But in the Bethel community that straddles the Old Columbia Road, black families bearing the Wilson name—descendants of Isom Wilson and Mandy Daniels—still farm, worship at the same churches, and send their children to Franklinton High School (now integrated). The Wilsons and Magees of Washington Parish have now been on the same land for six generations and more. With relatives across the South and the North, they defy easy generalizations about the "black family." Their story is a complex record of achievement, tragedy, and endurance.

NOTES

Introduction

1. Horace Mann Bond to I. J. K. Welles, May 15, 1936, part 1, reel 5, and "Memorandum for the Rosenwald Fund Explorers to be Used as an Incomplete Guide for the Research Part of Their Activities," 1934, part 2, reel 29, both in Horace Mann Bond Papers, microfilm, Duke University (original at University of Massachussetts, Amherst); "News Letter to Rural School Explorers," November 1934, in Julia W. Bond Papers, private collection. For Bond's biography, see Wayne J. Urban, *Black Scholar: Horace Mann Bond, 1904–1972* (Athens: University of Georgia Press, 1992).

2. Julia W. Bond, interviewed by Adam Fairclough, April 9, 1995, Atlanta, Georgia.

3. Bond to I. J. K. Welles, May 15, 1956, Bond Papers.

4. It is likely that Bond, at the suggestion of Robert Park, kept the diary with a view to eventual publication in some form; Park to Bond, October 19, 1934, part 2, reel 29, Bond Papers.

5. Horace Mann Bond, "A New Kind of Social History," speech at Bogalusa, February 15, 1935, part 4, reel 10, and Bond to J. J. Coss, February 15, 1937, part 1, reel 5, Bond Papers. It is worth noting that Robert Park, Bond's mentor at the University of Chicago, was not only an admirer of Washington but had also acted as his principal ghostwriter between 1905 and 1912. Park travelled with Washington extensively, accompanying him to Europe in 1910. "I think I probably learned more about human nature and society, in the South under Washington, than I had previously learned in all my previous studies." See Louis R. Harlan, *Booker T. Washington: The Wizard of Tuskegee, 1901–1915* (New York: Oxford University Press, 1983), 290–91.

6. James D. Anderson, *The Education of Blacks in the South, 1860–1935* (Chapel Hill: University of North Carolina Press, 1988), 153–76. "The fact that these schools were called 'Rosenwald Schools' and the belief that they were paid for mainly by the Julius Rosenwald Fund, kept down [white] criticism of the school officials. In actual practice the Fund never gave even half the cost of a building and generally contributed an average of about one-sixth the total cost of the building, grounds and equipment"; S. L. Smith, *Builders of Goodwill: The Story of the State Agents of Negro Education in the South, 1910 to 1950* (Nashville: Tennessee Book Company, 1950), 119–20. Bond was ideally qualified to study the results of the Rosenwald school-building program. In 1929–31 he had received Rosenwald funding to conduct a survey of black schools in Alabama, Louisiana, and North Carolina, research that provided useful material for his first book. A Rosenwald fellowship then enabled him to work on a doctoral dissertation, a study of black education in Alabama, at the University of Chicago. When the Rosenwald Fund financed the birth of Dillard University, a merger of two ailing black colleges in New Orleans, Bond was offered, and accepted, the position of academic dean. Before taking up his new job, however, he agreed to participate in the "School Exploration Group"; Julia was also employed on the project.

7. Horace and Julia Bond, "A Description of Washington Parish," n.d., part 2, reel 29, Bond Papers.

8. Gilbert C. Fite, *Cotton Fields No More: Southern Agriculture, 1865–1980* (Lexington: University Press of Kentucky, 1984), 208.

9. New Orleans *Times-Picayune*, July 31, August 3, 7, 1934.

10. Somewhat disingenuously, Bond later told the superintendent of schools that "I did not discuss the trouble either with Negroes or with white people, but tried to keep entirely out of it." Bond to D. H. Stringfield, January 19, 1935, part 2, reel 30, Bond Papers.

11. Bond to Robert M. Labaree, March 20, 1935, Julia W. Bond Papers; Bond to Frederick L. Allen, March 13, 1935, part 2, reel 30, Bond Papers.

12. Bond to Robert E. Park, April 2, 1935, part 1, reel 5, Bond Papers.

13. E. Franklin Frazier, *The Negro Family in Chicago* (Chicago: University of Chicago Press, 1932); *The Negro Family in the United States* (Chicago: University of Chicago Press, 1939); Bond, *A Study of Factors Involved in the Identification and Encouragement of Unusual Academic Talent Among Underprivileged Populations* (Washington, D.C.: Office of Education, 1967), 43.

14. Lee Rainwater and William L. Yancey, *The Moynihan Report and the Politics of Controversy* (Cambridge, Mass.: M.I.T. Press, 1967); Andrew Billingsley, *Black Families in White America* (Englewood Cliffs, N.J.: Prentice-Hall, 1968); Carol B. Stack, *All Our Kin: Strategies for Survival in a Black Community* (New York: Harper and Row, 1974); Joyce Aschenbrenner, *Lifelines: Black Families in Chicago* (Prospect Heights, Ill.: Waveland Press, 1975); Harriette Pipes McAdoo, ed., *Black Families* (Beverly Hills, Calif.: Sage, 1981); Orville Vernon Burton, *In My Father's House Are Many Mansions: Family and Community in Edgefield, South Carolina* (Chapel Hill: University of North Carolina Press, 1985); Herbert G. Gutman, *The Black Family in Slavery and Freedom, 1750–1925* (New York: Pantheon, 1976). See also, however, Ann Patton Malone, *Sweet Chariot: Slave Family and Household Structure in Nineteenth-Century Louisiana* (Chapel Hill: University of North Carolina Press, 1992), which argues that although the slave family household "appears not to have been matriarchal . . . it was not clearly patriarchal either." Malone believes that "overzealousness in revising earlier misconceptions concerning the composition of the slave family and community has led some recent historians or their popularizers to exaggerate the stability of the slave family, to overemphasize the patriarchal features, and to overestimate the incidence of two-parent family households" (257–58). Burton warns about the pitfalls of generalizing about the slave family from inadequate data: the federal census listed slaves "only by age and sex (not by name), under the name of the owner," and while some enumerators listed slaves in family groups, "slaves were often arranged in groups from eldest to youngest" (Burton, *In My Father's House*, 168). For a reasoned defense of Frazier's ideas on the black family, see Anthony M. Platt, *E. Franklin Frazier Reconsidered* (New Brunswick, N.J.: Rutgers University Press, 1991), 115–43.

15. Bond to Robert M. Labaree, March 20, 1935, Bond Papers.

16. Two of Horace Mann Bond's grandparents were white men; Urban, *Black Scholar*, 1–2.

17. Horace Mann Bond, "Two Racial Islands in Alabama," *American Journal of Sociology* 36 (January 1931): 552–67. In 1910 Governor James K. Vardaman of Mississippi expressed the typical white view when he opined that "while a few mixed breeds and freaks of the race may possess qualities which justify them to aspire to above that station [of servant and menial], the fact still remains that the race is fit for that and nothing more" (quoted in

Horace Mann Bond, *The Education of the Negro in the American Social Order*, [New York: Prentice Hall, 1934], 102). In 1938, delivering a marathon filibuster against an antilynching bill, Senator Allen J. Ellender of Louisiana flatly stated that "any 'Negro' of notable ability owes success to white blood"; see speech outlines, box 1280, Ellender Papers, Nicholls State University, Thibodaux, Louisiana.

18. Mark R. Schulz, "Interracial Kinship Ties and the Emergence of a Rural Black Middle-Class: Hancock County, Georgia, 1865–1950," *Georgia in Black and White: Explorations in the Race Relations of a Southern State, 1865–1950* (Athens: University of Georgia Press, 1994), ed. John C. Insoce, 141–72.

19. Arthur F. Raper, *Preface to Peasantry: A Tale of Two Black Belt Counties* (Chapel Hill: University of North Carolina Press, 1936), 138–39; Elizabeth Rauh Bethel, *Promiseland: A Century of Life in a Negro Community* (Philadelphia: Temple University Press, 1981), 96–97.

20. Thomas Dixon, Jr., *The Clansman: An Historical Romance of the Ku Klux Klan* (New York: Doubleday, Page, 1905), 238–43. On the enormous influence of Dixon, via Griffith, see John Hope Franklin, "*The Birth of a Nation*: Propaganda as History," in *Race and History: Selected Essays, 1938–1988* (Baton Rouge: Louisiana State University Press, 1989), 10–23.

21. Horace Mann Bond, "Forty Acres and a Mule," *Opportunity* 13 (May 1935): 140–41, 151.

22. Bond, *Education of the Negro in the American Social Order*, 414; Bond to W. P. Dabney, March 20, 1935, part 2, reel 30, Bond Papers. See also Loren Schweninger, *Black Property Owners in the South, 1790–1915* (Urbana: University of Illinois Press, 1990), 134–84. The Wilsons were "shifty" in the sense of hard-working and resourceful, as the word was used by blacks in Washington Parish.

23. A. P. Tureaud to Georgia M. Johnson, August 3, 1943, box 8, folder 17, A. P. Tureaud Papers, Amistad Research Center, Tulane University.

24. Walter White, *Rope and Faggot: A Biography of Judge Lynch* (New York: Alfred A. Knopf, 1929); Arthur F. Raper, *The Tragedy of Lynching* (Chapel Hill: University of North Carolina Press, 1933); Jacquelyn Dowd Hall, *Revolt Against Chivalry: Jesse Daniel Ames and the Women's Campaign Against Lynching* (New York: Columbia University Press, 1979, 1993); Robert L. Zangrando, *The NAACP Crusade Against Lynching, 1909–1950* (Philadelphia: Temple University Press, 1980); James R. McGovern, *Anatomy*

of a Lynching: The Killing of Claude Neal (Baton Rouge: Louisiana State University Press, 1982); George C. Wright, *Racial Violence in Kentucky, 1865–1940: Lynchings, Mob Rule, and "Legal Lynchings"* (Baton Rouge: Louisiana State University Press, 1990); W. Fitzhugh Brundage, *Lynching in the New South: Georgia and Virginia, 1880–1930* (Urbana: University of Illinois Press, 1993), 138; Terence R. Finnegan, "At the Hands of Parties Unknown: Lynching in Mississippi and South Carolina, 1881–1940," Ph.D. dissertation, University of Illinois at Urbana-Champaign, 1993.

25. Brundage, *Lynching in the New South*, 138. A few days before I visited Washington Parish in May 1995 a minister had referred to Jerome Wilson's lynching in his Sunday sermon.

Portrait of Washington Parish

1. The other family names were Bickham and Magee.
2. Pronounced "mo-ease."
3. Farmers had been suffering a recent outbreak of Texas fever tick.
4. The whites included storeowner Willie Bickham and farmer Jim King.
5. John Wilson's recollection of the "Balltown Riot" was rather different. "More white people were killed than colored," he told Bond, "but they did not make it known. . . . Old Man Creole Lott killed about six. His wife hid his ammunition—that's the reason he did not kill more"; in transcript of Bond's interviews with John Wilson, reels 29–30, Horace Mann Bond Papers. On the Balltown Riot, see also "Causes of the Balltown Riot," Bond Papers; E. Russ Williams, Jr., *History of Washington Parish, Louisiana, 1798–1992* (Monroe, La.: Williams Genealogical and Historical Publications, 1994), 291–92. According to a newspaper account in the [New York?] *Record-Herald*, November [?], 1901, three whites and as many as fifteen blacks were killed (Tuskegee Institute clippings file, microfilm, Perkins Library, Duke University).
6. On the Bogalusa strike of 1919, see James Francis Fouché, "The Bogalusa Quasi-Riot of 1919: A Microcosm of National and Regional Hysteria," M.A. thesis, Louisiana State University at New Orleans, 1972; Bernard A. Cook and James R. Watson, *Louisiana Labor: From Slavery to "Right-To-Work"* (Lanham, Md.: University Press of America, 1985), 168–72.
7. As a reading of the Star Creek Diary reveals, the individuals Bond describes here are composite characters drawn from several people; "Jessie Bent" is based on Tommy Graves. The family names are pseudonyms for Magee,

Bickham, Crane, and Graves, surnames that many whites and blacks shared. Curiously, there were few white Wilsons, suggesting that Wilson was one of the few black surnames that was *not* derived from the name of a local slave-holder. Blacks and whites also to a large extent shared the same personal names. Names such as "Fleet Magee," "Monroe Magee," and "Green Magee," for example, can be encountered in every generation among both blacks and whites. There were, however, three distinctive names, of probable African origin, that persisted among local black families: Tempie, Keziah (or Kissie), and Vanda (or Vander). For their derivation and meaning, see Newbell Niles Puckett, *Black Names in America: Origins and Usage* (Boston: G. K. Hall, 1975), 83–91, 402–5, 460.

8. Willie Bickham.

Star Creek Diary

1. Monroe Magee (b. 1871), father of Ernest Magee (b. 1895).
2. A. C. Lewis, state superintendent of Negro schools (a white man), 1923–40.
3. Melton Magee (b. 1882), son of George Boone Anders Magee (b. 1851) and Hannah Graves Magee (b. 1850).
4. Ed Magee (b. 1891), son of Ella B. Graves (1874–1932) and Green Magee.
5. Orsell Magee (b. 1902), son of Monroe Magee and Ella B. Graves Magee.
6. Willie Crain (b. 1884).
7. Bond lapses into local dialect when writing in the first person, but not consistently.
8. Chatted; joshed (from jaw?).
9. Alexzine Wilson, the oldest daughter.
10. Home Owners Loan Corporation.
11. Thomas J. Graves (b. 1856), son of Nathaniel Graves and Arcadia Graves. Although Hannah Graves had children by Tommie Graves, it is probable that Ella Graves, who married Monroe Magee ("Uncle Monroe"), was Hannah's daughter by mulatto Irvin Crane. Andrew Graves, husband of "widow Graves" (Hettie, b. 1894), was the son of Eli Graves (b. 1846) and Margaret Graves (b. 1852), and hence the cousin, rather than brother, of Ella Graves Magee.
12. John Burris (b. 1864), son of James M. Burris (white, b. 1826) and his

wife Sarah (b. 1837); George Burris (b. 1862), son of James M. Burris and slave Lucy Ellis (b. 1840).

13. Thomas Barker (b. 1882), son of Thomas Barker (b. 1860) and Nannie Magee Barker (b. 1860).

14. Murdis Magee (b. 1891), son of Green Magee (b. 1855) and Sarah Miller Magee (b. 1870); Albert Magee (b. 1892), son of Eldridge Magee (b. 1866) and Sarah Bickham Magee (b. 1874).

15. Felton Grandison Clark, president of Southern University, 1938–68. Son of Joseph S. Clark, president of Southern University, 1915–38.

16. Fannie C. Williams, principal of Valena C. Jones High School, New Orleans, and recent president of the American Teachers Association.

17. Allison Davis, anthropologist and author of *Deep South* (1941).

18. Julia A. Brock (b. 1854), widow of Andrew Brock (b. 1846).

The Lynching

1. The Bonds had left Star Creek to spend Christmas in Nashville with Julia's family. After attending a three-day conference in Atlanta devoted to the Rosenwald project, Julia returned to Nashville, planning to stay there until the end of January. Horace drove to New Orleans, and eked out his meager savings by boarding with a black physician and his wife while waiting for his first paycheck from Dillard University. The Bonds were to be reunited on February 1 and planned on returning to Star Creek a week later.

2. Ernest Magee to Horace Bond, January 14(?), 1935, Horace Bond to Julia Bond, January 13, 1935, and Julia Bond to Horace Bond, January 15, 1935, all in Julia W. Bond Papers. Horace Bond decided not to visit Franklinton with Park. Instead, accompanied by Alvin Jones of Xavier University, New Orleans' Catholic University for blacks, he drove the eminent sociologist to Mobile on a hectic three-day trip that took the trio to Creole and mixed-race communities along the Gulf Coast. Racial violence later touched Alvin Jones directly. In June 1950, while accompanying a group of prospective black voters to the registrar's office in Opelousas, St. Landry Parish, he was assaulted by sheriff's deputies who were awaiting the group's arrival. Jones was employed at the time by the Louisiana Progressive Voters League, and he was encouraging black registration in a parish where no blacks voted. Badly beaten about the head, Jones sustained injuries that contributed to his early death in 1951.

3. Bond to Ambrose Calliver, January 9, 1935; Bond to Robert Redfield, January 17, 1935, part 1, reel 5; Bond to Mr. Stringfield et al., January 19, 1935; Leo M. Favrot to Will W. Alexander, February 12, 1935; Bond to W. P. Dabney, March 20, 1935, part 2, reel 30, all in Bond Papers. Horace Bond to Julia Bond, January 20, 1935, and J. E. Bateman to Bond, February 2, 1935, both Julia W. Bond Papers.

4. In 1908 the journalist Ray Stannard Baker referred to this doctor when he wrote: "I visited Monroe, La., where two Negro doctors had been forced to leave town because they were taking the practice of white physicians." He added, "In the same town a Negro grocer was burned out, because he was encroaching on the trade of white grocers"; Ray S. Baker, *Following the Color Line* (New York: Harper and Row, 1908, 1964), 250.

5. Jeptha Latimer Brock (1879–1949) was a graduate of Tulane Medical School who, following in the footsteps of his father, Jeptha S. Brock, practiced as a doctor in Washington Parish. He served as sheriff between 1932 and 1940. (E. Russ Williams, Jr., *History of Washington Parish, Louisiana, 1798–1992* [Monroe, La.: Williams Genealogical and Historical Publications, 1994], 406.) According to Alexzine Wilson, Brock attended the births of the Wilson children; he may have delivered Jerome.

6. John Wilson to Walter White, August 27, 1934, NAACP Papers.

7. Mrs. Freddye E. Henderson, interviewed by Adam Fairclough, April 10, 1995, Atlanta; Bond to W. P. Dabney, March 20, 1935, and Edwin Embree to Bond, June 20, 1935, part 2, reel 30, Bond Papers. He mailed similar pleas to W. R. Banks, president of Prairie View College in Texas; Estelle Massey Riddle, president of the National Association of Colored Graduate Nurses and a Rosenwald "Explorer" in Calhoun, Louisiana; Edwin Embree, president of the Rosenwald Fund; and Will Alexander, head of the Farm Security Administration.

8. Bond to Frederick Lewis Allen, March 13, 1935, series 2, reel 30, Bond Papers.

Forty Acres and a Mule

1. Isom Wilson (mispelled "Isum" and "Isham" in the U.S. Census) was born in 1833. All dates of birth are calculated from the censuses of 1870, 1880, 1900, and 1910. They are, however, approximate at best, especially in the case of former slaves.

2. There were two Hezekiah Magees. Bond was probably referring to Hezekiah Magee (1834–88), who married Harriet Bickham (1842–1908) in 1859. He was one of several sons (all of whom owned slaves in 1860) of Hezekiah Magee (1796–1870) and Dicey Magee (1800–1878).

3. Wiley (Wiley Daniels, b. 1824) was the slave of Robert Daniel (sometimes spelled Daniels). In 1849, upon Daniel's death, he became the property of his widow, Sarah Marrow. In 1861, after Sarah Marrow's own death, her estate was divided and Wiley became the property of Sarah Ann Daniel. See "Inventory of Robert Daniels," March 29, 1849, and "Robert Daniels, et als (Act of Partition)," October 21, 1861, both reprinted in E. Russ Williams, Jr., *History of Washington Parish, Louisiana, 1798–1992* (Monroe, La.: Williams Genealogical and Historical Publications, 1994), 143–46. As Williams notes, because the court house burned down in 1897, and because documents relating to local slaveholders are scarce, these are two of the very few records that list slaves by name.

4. Amanda Daniels (b. 1845) was the daughter of Wiley and Minnie. She was also the property of Robert Daniel and then Sarah Marrow. In 1861 she passed into the ownership of Mary Ann Daniel, the wife of Jacob Magee. According to John Wilson, "She was their housemaid when the soldiers came."

5. On the impact of the Civil War on Washington Parish, see Williams, *History of Washington Parish*, 181–211.

6. According to the U.S. Census of Agriculture, in 1870 Isom Wilson cultivated fourteen acres of land, which he owned, and produced two bales of cotton. He owned no mules or other livestock. By 1880 he owned eighteen acres of tilled land, sixty-two acres of woodland and forest, and livestock valued at $75.

7. John Wilson was probably referring to Andrew Magee (b. 1850), the son of Pleasant Magee (b. 1819), who was the elder brother of Hezekiah Magee, Jr. Roscoe (b. 1871), Ferdie (b. 1874), and Jennie (b. 1877) were Pleasant Magee's children by Margaret Magee (b. 1835), his second wife. According to John Wilson, "My father raised Ferdie and Andrew because he was living with them at the time of the death of their parents."

8. Jacob Magee (1818–1901) and Fleet Magee (b. 1835) were sons of John Magee (1792–1877) and Sarah Magee (b. 1792). John Magee was the brother of Hezekiah Magee, Sr. Thus the probable owner of Isom Wilson, the *younger* Hezekiah Magee, was a cousin of Jacob and Fleet.

9. Probably Jeptha Miller.

10. William Addison Burris (1835–1906) and James Madison Burris (1828–1908) owned seventeen slaves between them in 1860. William briefly served as clerk of court after the war. James served as parish judge, parish superintendent of education, and mayor of Franklinton (Williams, *History of Washington Parish*, 361, 364–65).

11. Thomas J. Graves (b. in 1856) was the son of Arcada and Nathaniel Graves. In 1860 Nathaniel Graves owned eight slaves, one of whom, a twenty-one-year-old woman, was described as mulatto.

12. Also spelled Crain.

13. I have been unable to locate Bond's source for this information. John Wilson told him, "I don't know why he is called 'Trigger.'" I have also been unable to positively identify "Tom Trigger" Bickham. The most likely candidate is Thomas Dolphus Bickham (1844–1904), who served in the Confederate army and after the war became a prominent businessman and civic leader in Franklinton. He served as sheriff of Washington Parish, 1878–84. See Williams, *History of Washington Parish*, 294, 399. His father, Thomas C. Bickham (1818–71), served as sheriff before the war.

14. It should be emphasized that this is Horace Mann Bond speaking, not John Wilson.

15. Mary Magee, born in 1854, perhaps was the sister rather than the daughter of Sarah Magee, for the latter was born no earlier than 1841. (Sarah Magee was listed as twenty years old in the 1870 census but thirty-eight years old in the census of 1880.)

16. In 1870 Harriet Magee (22) was living with her son Eldridge (2), described as mulatto, in the household of Albert and Charlotte Carter. She was described as a domestic servant. In 1880 Sarah Magee and Daniel Carter (probably Albert Carter's son) had a nine-month-old baby, George, described as mulatto and listed as a step-son. Her other sons Will (5) and Lee (4), both described as mulatto, were included in the household of their grandparents, Eli and Minerva Magee.

17. In 1880 Sinda (or Lucinda) Bell (25), lived in the household of her brother, Alex Bell. Her three children included Alice, age five (1880 census).

18. The 1880 census lists Julia A. Brock (20), described as mulatto, as the wife of Andrew Brock (45).

19. Ku Klux Klan.

20. In 1880 Fleet Dillon (15) was living in the household of George Dillon

(22), described as mulatto, and Amanda Dillon (21). George was probably the man Bond referred to as the son of George Dillon (40) and Pennie Brock.

21. In the 1900 census Ned Brock (b. 1881) is listed as one of five children of Andrew Brock (b. 1846) and Julia Brock (b. 1854).

22. A variant of charivari, "a mock serenade of discordant noises, made with kettles, tin horns, etc.," often after weddings.

23. Probably Robert Babington (1820–1906). Babington was an Irish immigrant who opened a mercantile store in Franklinton. In December 1864 Babington, in charge of Confederate supplies in Washington Parish, was arrested by a Union raiding party for his Confederate sympathies. After the 1868 election, when questioned by a congressional committee, Babington denied threatening or refusing to supply blacks unless they voted Democrat. See Williams, *History of Washington Parish*, 204–9, 232.

24. In 1880 Wesley Burris (12) and John Burris (9), both described as mulatto, were living with Eli and Margaret Graves (1880 census).

25. According to the U.S. Census (1870 and 1880), Ephraim Magee was the husband, not the brother, of Samantha Graves. It seems likely, however, that Margaret and Samantha, both decribed as mulattoes, were indeed sisters.

26. In 1880 the household of Ervin Crane (25) and Mary Crane (18) included Candacy (9), described as a sister (1880 census). In 1900 a "Candasia" (probably the same person) was the wife of George Burris.

27. The 1880 census describes William Burris (35) as Washington Parish clerk of court. His household included his wife, Flora (32), and three children, James (14), Byron (13) and Edward (6).

28. In 1870 Lucy Ellis (30) headed a household that included five children, among them George (8), described as mulatto, and later known by the name George Burris (1870 census). In 1880 an "L. Ellis," described as a black servant, age twelve, was living in the James M. Burris household.

29. In 1870 Lucy Ellis had a nine-month-old baby, Almo, later known by the name Almo Amacker. The 1880 census included Lucy (36, described as a servant) and Almo (9) in the household of Lewis and Tempie Miller.

30. In the 1870 census Maria Crane (40) headed a household consisting of herself and two sons, Ervin (18) and Frank (14), both described as mulatto.

31. Probably Jack Bickham (b. 1870), who had a large family by Mary; or possibly John W. Bickham (b. 1867), who married Kissie, the sister or half-sister of Wade Magee.

32. Ella B. Graves (1874–1932) was the daughter of Emily Graves/Magee. She later married Monroe Magee, the "Uncle Monroe" of Bond's "Star Creek Diary."

33. In 1900 Thomas and Nannie Barker had ten children, one of whom, Lucius Barker (b. 1879) became the first black doctor in Washington Parish.

34. Probably Jeptha Miller.

35. In 1870 Sarah, wife of Thomas Magee ("Tom Greenback"?), had a nine-year-old son named Sam (1870 census).

36. Presumably Confederate dollars.

37. This paragraph has been added by the editor to replace a section of the original manuscript in which Bond confuses Eli Magee with Eli Graves. The transcript of Bond's interviews with John Wilson, and information obtained from the U.S. Census, both indicate that Julia Magee, Tempie Wilson's mother, was the daughter of Eli Magee, not Eli Graves.

38. The two preceding paragraphs have been added to Bond's narrative. They are based on the transcript of Bond's interviews with John Wilson, Wade Magee's son-in-law, and the editor's interviews with Alexzine Wilson and Freddye Henderson, Wade Magee's grandchildren. According to family tradition, Magee's full name was Wade Hampton Magee.

39. The county agent of the U.S. Department of Agriculture mentioned that a recent outbreak of Texas Fever Tick had been virtually eradicated; D. L. Bornman, "Narrative Summary of Parish Agricultural Agent, Washington Parish, 1935," reel 41, Agricultural Extension Service Records, National Archives, College Park, Maryland.

40. Jerome told the coroner's jury: "My brother, Moise, got up and came to where I was and asked what I was wanted for, and grabbed at Mr. Wood. Mr. Wood shoved him back, and Moise grabbed at him again and tussled with him. Mr. Wood pulled his pistol and shot Moise. I ran into the room and was shot in the leg by someone, I don't know who. I reached in the next room and grabbed the . . . shotgun and shot out the door one time. I must have shot Mr. Wood" (*Franklinton Era-Leader*, July 26, 1934).

41. The implication, of course, is that Wood was killed not by Jerome Wilson, but accidentally by one of the whites. Delos C. Wood was also a Magee. He and Jerome Wilson were, probably unknown to each other, distant cousins. Wood was the son of Thomas J. Wood and Louisa Margaret Magee, the daughter of David Magee and Elizabeth Magee. After his parents died, Delos

Wood was raised by his grandmother, Elizabeth, David Magee's widow. David Magee was a son of the elder Hezekiah Magee, hence nephew to John Magee, who was Hezekiah's brother and Wade Magee's father. Thus Delos Wood and Jerome Wilson shared two great-great-grandparents, and were therefore third cousins (Information about Wood from "Delos C. Wood," entry in Minute Record, August 6, 1934, Washington Parish court records, Washington Parish Court House, Franklinton, Louisiana).

42. According to John Wilson the white neighbors, Mr. and Mrs. Jim King, sheltered Alexzine at the home of their black tenants, Alfred and Melissa Magee. This accords with Alexzine Wilson's own recollection sixty years later.

43. Prentiss B. Carter, a former district court judge. The *Franklinton Era Leader* of July 26, 1934, reported that "a crowd of 500 or more miltant citizens" gathered outside the court house after the Wilsons were taken to jail. According to Alexzine Wilson, a number of whites, including neighbor Jim King, helped to keep the mob at bay until it calmed down. The crowd eventually dispersed about 2 A.M.

44. *State v. Wilson*, 181 La. 62, 158 So. 621 (1935).

Epilogue

1. Unless otherwise noted, the following account is taken from editor's interviews with Julia W. Bond, Freddye S. Henderson, Alexzine Wilson Young, and Felton Wilson.

2. Will W. Alexander to Bond, April 15, 1935, series 1, reel 9, Commission on Interracial Equality Papers, microfilm, Hill Library, Atlanta University.

3. Minute Record, district court, Washington Parish Court House, entries for June 7 and November 4, 1935.

4. Eugene F. Saxton to Bond, May 15, 1935, part 2, reel 30, Bond Papers.

5. One needs to be careful about stating that lynching "ended." Many racial murders—especially the killing of blacks by policemen—were lynchings in all but name. Even when the law took its course, moreover, the quality of justice that blacks received in southern courts was so defective that many executions merited the term "legal lynchings." See the discussion of this point in George C. Wright, *Racial Violence in Kentucky, 1865–1940: Lynchings, Mob Rule, and "Legal Lynchings"* (Baton Rouge: Louisiana State University Press, 1990), 251–305.

6. The surviving siblings cannot recall the exact year of Luther Wilson's death.

7. Joe Wood was electrocuted, while working for a power company, shortly after the lynching. Blacks in Washington Parish believed that he had returned to Louisiana from New Jersey in December 1934 seeking revenge for his father's death.

BIBLIOGRAPHY

Manuscript Sources

Horace Mann Bond Papers, University of Massachusetts, Amherst (microfilm in Perkins Library, Duke University, Durham, North Carolina)

Julia W. Bond Papers, private collection

Commission on Interracial Cooperation Papers, Hill Library, Atlanta University (microfilm)

Ellender Papers, Nicholls State University, Thibodaux, Louisiana

Magee-McGehee File, compiled by Leonardo Andrea, 1951, Franklinton Public Library, Franklinton, Louisiana

National Archives, RG28, Record of Appointments of Postmasters, 1832–1971

National Association for the Advancement of Colored People (NAACP) Papers, Library of Congress (microfilm in Alderman Library, University of Virginia, Charlottesville)

A. P. Tureaud Papers, Amistad Research Center, Tulane University, New Orleans

U.S. Census Population Schedules, Washington Parish, Louisiana, 1820, 1830, 1840, 1850, 1860 (free), 1860 (slave), 1870, 1880, 1900, 1910, 1920

U.S. Census of Agriculture and Manufactures, Washington Parish, Louisiana, 1850, 1860, 1870, 1880

Washington Parish Community Family Histories, compiled by Bonnie Dyer, n.d., Franklinton Public Library

Washington Parish Court House, minute records

Published Sources

Anderson, James D. *The Education of Blacks in the South, 1860–1935.* Chapel Hill: University of North Carolina Press, 1988.   **151**

Aschenbrenner, Joyce. *Lifelines: Black Families in Chicago.* Prospect Heights, Ill.: Waveland Press, 1975.

Baker, Ray S. *Following the Color Line.* New York: Harper and Row, 1908, 1964.

Beck, E. M., and Stewart E. Tolnay. "The Killing Fields of the Deep South: The Market for Cotton and the Lynching of Blacks, 1882–1930." *American Sociological Review* 55 (August 1990): 526–39.

Bethel, Elizabeth Rauh. *Promiseland: A Century of Life in a Negro Community.* Philadelphia: Temple University Press, 1981.

Billingsley, Andrew. *Black Families in White America.* Englewood Cliffs, N.J.: Prentice-Hall, 1968.

Bond, Horace Mann. "Two Racial Islands in Alabama." *American Journal of Sociology* 36 (January 1931): 552–67.

———. "A Negro Looks at His South." *Harper's Magazine* 163 (June 1931): 98–108.

———. *The Education of the Negro in the American Social Order.* New York: Prentice Hall, 1934.

———. "Forty Acres and a Mule." *Opportunity* 13 (May 1935): 140–41, 151.

Negro Education in Alabama: A Study in Cotton and Steel. Washington, D.C.: Associated Publishers, 1939.

———. *A Study of Factors Involved in the Identification and Encouragement of Unusual Academic Talent among Underprivileged Populations.* Washington, D.C.: Office of Education, 1967.

Brundage, W. Fitzhugh. *Lynching in the New South: Georgia and Virginia, 1880–1930.* Urbana: University of Illinois Press, 1993.

Burton, Orville Vernon. *In My Father's House Are Many Mansions: Family and Community in Edgefield, South Carolina.* Chapel Hill: University of North Carolina Press, 1985.

Carter, Prentiss B. "The History of Washington Parish, Louisiana, as Compiled from the Records and Traditions." *Louisiana Historical Quarterly* 14 (1931): 36–59.

Cook, Bernard A., and James R. Watson. *Louisiana Labor: From Slavery to "Right-to-Work."* Lanham, Md.: University Press of America, 1985.

Dixon, Thomas, Jr. *The Clansman: An Historical Romance of the Ku Klux Klan.* New York: Doubleday, Page, 1905.

Fairclough, Adam. *Race and Democracy: The Civil Rights Struggle in Louisiana, 1915–1972.* Athens: University of Georgia Press, 1995.

Fite, Gilbert C. *Cotton Fields No More: Southern Agriculture, 1865–1980.* Lexington: University Press of Kentucky, 1984.

Franklin, John Hope. "*The Birth of a Nation*: Propaganda as History." In *Race and History: Selected Essays, 1938–1988.* Baton Rouge: Louisiana State University Press, 1989.

Franklinton Era-Leader. Franklinton Public Library, Louisiana.

Frazier, E. Franklin. *The Negro Family in Chicago.* Chicago: University of Chicago Press, 1932.

———. *The Negro Family in the United States.* Chicago: University of Chicago Press, 1939.

Gutman, Herbert G. *The Black Family in Slavery and Freedom, 1750–1925.* New York: Pantheon, 1976.

Hall, Jacquelyn Dowd. *Revolt Against Chivalry: Jesse Daniel Ames and the Women's Campaign Against Lynching.* New York: Columbia University Press, 1979, 1993.

Harlan, Louis R. *Booker T. Washington: The Wizard of Tuskegee, 1901–1915.* New York: Oxford University Press, 1983.

McAdoo, Harriette Pipes, ed. *Black Families.* Beverly Hills, Calif.: Sage, 1981.

McGovern, James R. *Anatomy of a Lynching: The Killing of Claude Neal.* Baton Rouge: Louisiana State University Press, 1982.

Malone, Ann Patton. *Sweet Chariot: Slave Family and Household Structure in Nineteenth-Century Louisiana.* Chapel Hill: University of North Carolina Press, 1992.

Platt, Anthony M. *E. Franklin Frazier Reconsidered.* New Brunswick: Rutgers University Press, 1991.

Puckett, Newbell Niles. *Black Names in America: Origins and Usage.* Boston: G. K. Hall, 1975.

Rainwater, Lee, and William L. Yancey. *The Moynihan Report and the Politics of Controversy.* Cambridge, Mass.: M.I.T. Press, 1967.

Raper, Arthur F. *The Tragedy of Lynching.* Chapel Hill: University of North Carolina Press, 1933.

———. *Preface to Peasantry: A Tale of Two Black Belt Counties.* Chapel Hill: University of North Carolina Press, 1936.

Schulz, Mark R. "Interracial Kinship Ties and the Emergence of a Rural Black Middle-Class: Hancock County, Georgia, 1865–1950." In *Georgia in Black and White: Explorations in the Race Relations of a Southern State, 1865–1950,* ed. John C. Inscoe, 141–72. Athens: University of Georgia Press, 1994.

Schweninger, Loren. *Black Property Owners in the South, 1790–1915*. Urbana: University of Illinois Press, 1990.

Urban, Wayne J. *Black Scholar: Horace Mann Bond, 1904–1972*. Athens: University of Georgia Press, 1992.

White, Walter. *Rope and Faggot: A Biography of Judge Lynch*. New York: Alfred A. Knopf, 1929.

Wilkins, Roy. "Huey Long Says—An Interview with Louisiana's Kingfish." *Crisis* (February 1935): 41–42.

Williams, E. Russ, Jr. *History of Washington Parish, Louisiana, 1798–1992*. Monroe, La.: Williams Genealogical and Historical Publications, 1994.

Wright, George C. *Racial Violence in Kentucky, 1865–1940: Lynchings, Mob Rule, and "Legal Lynchings."* Baton Rouge: Louisiana State University Press, 1990.

Zangrando, Robert L. *The NAACP Crusade Against Lynching, 1909–1950*. Philadelphia: Temple University Press, 1980.

Theses and Dissertations

Finnegan, Terence R. "At the Hands of Parties Unknown: Lynching in Mississippi and South Carolina, 1881–1940." Ph.D. dissertation, University of Illinois at Urbana-Champaign, 1993.

Fouché, James Francis. "The Bogalusa Quasi-Riot of 1919: A Microcosm of National and Regional Hysteria." M.A. thesis, Louisiana State University at New Orleans, 1972.

Interviews

Bond, Julia W., April 9, 1995.

Henderson, Freddye S., April 10, 1995.

Wilson, Felton, June 28, 1995 (telephone).

Young, Alexzine Wilson, July 18, 1995.

INDEX

A Loose Game

A Loose Game
The Sport and Business
of Basketball
by Lewis Cole

The Bobbs-Merrill Company, Inc.
Indianapolis / New York

Library of Congress Cataloging in Publication Data

Cole, Lewis.
  A loose game.

  1. Basketball.   I. Title.
GV885.5.C64   796.32'3   78-55649
ISBN 0-672-52303-5

For Bernard Cole

Contents

Apologies and Acknowledgments

This book is bound by the present. In it, the past appears as history—facts, photos, recollections—the way I have experienced it; the future doesn't figure at all. In years to come, basketball may be an entirely amateur sport, or it may be played by teams with members from both sexes; European franchises may compete with American ones for top stars, and women's games may fill Madison Square Garden and the Hemisfair Arena in San Antonio. A bad prognosticator, I haven't concerned myself with such predictions. My intent has been to look at basketball as a peculiarly American institution and to view it in the present, from the vantage point of a privileged fan, drawing attention to its unique and determining features. To their pleasure or unhappiness, most of the people who helped me fulfill this self-appointed task appear by name in the following pages, and I take this opportunity to extend a general and sincere thanks to them all. Some don't get credit in the text and deserve special mention here: Stefanie Tashjian-Woodbridge, V. J. Picarillo—Pic, Rafael Yglesias, Cathy Wein, and also my niece, Kristina, who sat patiently with me through one long afternoon of endless high school contests though the games bored her stiff. In their own ways, both immediate and remote, and sometimes quite maddening, they all contributed to the writing of this volume.

"I had in mind the tall, agile, graceful, and expert athlete . . ."
—James Naismith
on the invention of basketball

1. Playing Ball

I have always been taller than average—shoulders straight, I stand close to 6′ 6″—and because of my height people have generally assumed that I'm a good basketball player. To my embarrassment, old gentlemen I meet in elevators often ask me what college I played for, and kids on the playground are dismayed when I tell them I can't dunk. As a child I suffered whenever two schoolyard captains chose players for their teams. If one of them didn't know me, he picked me first and was disgusted by my performance. If I had previously ruined his hopes to win, he selected me last—only when there was no chance that the competition would stick themselves with this turkey. "Come on," he would order me grudgingly, and the game would begin—for me, an unrelenting contest of indecision, awkwardness and ignorance, during which I had little idea of what to do and was hopelessly incapable of executing those feats I happened to know I should perform. Other sports I played rarely. In fourth grade I once hit a triple, and I recall running across a field as part of a football team just twice in my adolescence and never since. But to the public school gym in winter and the playground in spring I constantly returned, my desire to play ball, like my height, an inexplicable fact of my constitution. One of my father's favorite stories is how he watched me miss basket after basket while visiting me one day in summer camp. The ball finally, accidentally, fell through the net. "Another one for Cole," he claims I announced proudly to myself, and if I scored on a nice shot this very afternoon, I would feel the same flush of victory. The game ceaselessly inspires me with its quickness, intelligence, grace and strength, and I must have felt this even when I was a child and basketball was a mystery, because

1

otherwise why would I have suffered so through those hapless, luckless contests of my youth? To be able to play basketball well and confidently seems to me to be a singular blessing in the world, and it is only now, when as a thirty-year-old man I don't have to suffer the slings and arrows of schoolyard mockery—or, at least, don't have to suffer them silently—that I have started to put my height to advantage and have tried to become the basketball player everyone has always imagined me to be.

In this contest I'm not alone. During the winter editors and lawyers rent school gyms and play with a frenzy for two hours, and in the spring doctors and teachers chase kids off the playground. A friend of mine who lives in Cambridge is a typical case. An expert in child education, he flies around the country advising universities and is expert enough in his field to earn a decent living working only half-time. The rest of his days, he spends playing or talking basketball; and, for all his achievements, his greatest pleasure comes during the hours he dribbles and shoots with the local boys at the YMCA. Short and stocky, he wears steel-rimmed granny glasses and looks nothing like the perfectly proportioned, stately players whose names he calls out as he tries to imitate their moves on the court. We discuss our progress as players when we meet—"They call me roadrunner," he told me excitedly a year ago, referring to his teammates, immensely proud of their approbation—and the game possesses for both of us a power over our imaginations that I would have considered unlikely and unfortunate just a few years ago. Now the sport is a not inconsiderable part of our lives, and the story of my own experience with the game is a study in how this transformation happens and also an introduction to the world of the fans—both players and observers—of which I'm now a part.

For years after graduating from junior high school, I rarely touched a ball. I went to the High School of Performing Arts, a public school that had neither team nor gym; and though my college, Columbia, had a championship squad the year I graduated, my sole interest in sports while an undergraduate was a vain attempt to make the administration waive my physical education requirement. Eventually, Columbia used my perpetual absence from their gym as a reason not to grant my degree, a commitment to athletics on their part that seems bizarre and excessive, except that I had participated in the '68 strike and threatened to return to their graduate school unless they proved I wasn't qualified. (Six years later, they surrendered it to me.) Certainly, my reluctance to pick up a ball didn't spring from political principles. One long summer afternoon my SDS friends and I, all of us about to go to jail for a month, played ball down in Riverside Park. Once again, I had to apologize for the uselessness of my height, and it was only to save myself from the sure humiliation of this experience that I had assiduously drawn the administration's attentions to all my physical maladies.

Three years later, I was staying out on Long Island, and one overcast day a friend insisted I accompany him to an outdoor court. In junior high school, my first black friend once promised to teach me how to play ball—"You should be a giant on the court, Lew," he told me—but he gave up in despair after an hour. My present friend had less ability than my childhood companion and, perhaps consequently, more patience. Over several hours, he advised me to arch the ball higher, dribble it lower, aim over the front rim of the basket, pass when I couldn't shoot. "Go inside," he kept insisting when we played one-on-one, meaning I should dribble the ball as closely as possible to the basket before shooting, rather than heaving it up from far away. Following his commands, I won my first game and felt—foolishly, wonderfully—like a champ.

The court we used was a tar platform in a corner of a long green lawn where schoolkids were playing football. Their shouts floated over the field to us in the late afternoon, and the next summer the memory of this scene, made verdant and idyllic by my sense of accomplishment, persuaded me to return to the game for my second adult try. Ten of us met regularly every Saturday morning, and I anticipated our contests with increasing pleasure, until one day I found myself suddenly back in my childhood nightmare. I was chosen first, not by my friend who knew and tolerated my limitations, but by a complete stranger who, I imagined, considered me a natural winner at the game. As in my childhood, I felt condemned throughout the contest, and kept apologizing for my failures. A ball bounced off my hands out-of-bounds—"Sorry about that," I said; a member of the opposing team intercepted a pass I should have caught—"My fault," I told my teammate. One of life's most galling experiences is to play with others at a game one hardly knows; and even after our team had somehow managed to win, I felt obliged to excuse myself again to our captain. "You played all right," he cheered me. "You just should go closer to the basket."

His comment was my first hint that playing basketball as an adult would be considerably different from my childhood experiences with the game. When you're a kid, people are either good at something or they're not, and you don't expect them to change much. I remember Stevie Zimmerman, a round-headed friend of mine who was a brilliant student; I always felt hopeless when his mother asked me why he didn't play ball with all the other boys. Stanley Bardax was a joking fat kid who took off all Christian, Jewish and Greek Orthodox holidays; and ten years after junior high school I was amazed to discover he had turned into a dazzling pre-med, considered quite a catch by all the girls in his class. And, nostalgically, I recall the shock I experienced when an older friend of mine informed me that Harvey—dark, straight-haired, good-looking, and the best white athlete in the neighborhood—would never make it in the pros. "Are you kidding?" my friend asked me. "Every block has its Harvey. They're all over the place. He probably couldn't even get into the minors." Not only couldn't I imagine a more natural athlete than Harvey—who was my friend to boot, and who played basketball with me in his house, using a Spalding and a wastepaper basket—but if Harvey wasn't going to be a ballplayer, then what would he become?

With adults the opposite is true. When you play ball in a pickup game, the one thing you can be sure of is that no one on the court who is over twenty-one is a professional or ever will be. These men's lives are invariably different from the ones suggested by their bodies and individual prowess. A blond-haired jock is a radical economist who works as a night watchman for a living; a wiry-haired short fellow is a mechanic; a burly black man, a literary editor. One strong, seemingly vain young man played regularly in a brutally competitive game in Amagansett, Long Island. He turned out to be a remedial reading teacher working in Ocean Hill–Brownsville.

The game he played was the adult version of my childhood fears. Men gathered for it every Sunday, fiercely determined to play. After a rain one morning, they doused the court with kerosene and set a match to it to burn off the dampness. Fifty players participated in this weekly contest, and only the winners stayed on the court. Each game was short, and if your team lost, you sometimes had to wait for an hour before enjoying another try at two games in a row. Only the very best players were picked from the losing team, and consequently the pressure to win was enormous. A friend once played there, falsely imagining the game would be a pleasant way to kill some time. He dropped one pass and never felt the ball again. "You should learn how to play ball, fella," one of his teammates remarked scathingly while the game was still in progress. Except for occasional criticisms, he then ignored him for the rest of the contest.

The one player who did see regular action here was a seventeen-year-old senior from the local high school. A neighborhood rich kid who owned his own car, he was a natural athlete who outplayed all the other men on the court. Of all the contestants, only he seemed to enjoy the game, since he was always assured of being picked for a team. Yet for all his ability, the older men still coached him, yelling at him not to shoot, or shouting at him to pass the ball while he dribbled into a pack of defenders, faking and coasting his way up to the basket, his movements a series of instinctive responses and gestures that successfully guided him through the human wall of his opponents and were too quick to be studied or learned. After the games, he hung out with the other players, meeting young single New York women through them, and his social adventures seemed to please the older men as much as his athletic feats, as though through him they were experiencing the youth they had always dreamed about for themselves, though none of them were over thirty-five. To me he was another Harvey, and it shocked me (again) when another neighborhood kid let me know that the champ really didn't like basketball all that much. "He calls that the old man's game," my informant told me. "He just plays with them to get their girls. Golf is his real sport. He says that's where all the money is."

The unpredictable mix of characters you find on any basketball court is one of the joys of the game. Basketball was invented by a Canadian Protestant minister and promoted by the YMCA, but now it is called "the city game" and has been thoroughly appropriated by the mix of ethnic groups and sprinkling of intellectuals that make up the populations of our large cities. Downstairs from the tenement in which I live is a corner lot that Robert Moses converted to a playground in the thirties, and on practically any afternoon I can meet there a constantly amusing cast of national and social types playing against one another: ten-year-old black kids dribbling through the legs of middle-aged artists; fifteen-year-old Asian-Americans shooting over the outstretched hands of Irish garage mechanics; Italian high school seniors aspiring to be starters on their college teams, trying out their newly coined fakes and steps against kids wearing yarmulkes.

I was fearful when I first approached these courts after my summer dabblings in the game, because they had been the settings for all my childhood anxieties. Even now my nightmares often take place in a schoolyard where shadows chase me and from which there is no escape; and I knew I had passed a stage in my psychic development when one night, in my usual dream, I discovered a pair of tiny jets sticking out from the backs of my shoes, and flew triumphantly away over the heads of my assailants.

Concrete and vast, these playgrounds and lots were the arenas for all adolescent tests, and during the fifties, when gangs started roaming the streets, parents and cops periodically warned us not to gather there. One night a kid was stabbed to death in a gang fight. The next day the rumor started that the killers planned to attack our public school, and we were released early under the protection of a police guard. The gang, the Fordham Baldies—gangs were white then, not black—were said to shave their heads and carve *x*'s into the cheeks of young girls. For my neighborhood, Washington Heights, a residential community of European immigrants, these tantalizing and disquieting events proved that the city was going to pot, but these fears exaggerated the actual danger. Certainly, the number of frightful encounters I suffered growing up in the city were quite few. Indeed, the worst occurred in Belleview, New Jersey, then a suburban retreat, where one afternoon a group of older boys cornered my cousin and me in the town's new schoolyard, forcing us to stand with our backs against a wall and not duck as they tossed small pebbles at our heads. I now suppose that this mild torture had been suggested to them by countless execution scenes they had watched in Hollywood movies, and they must have had some idea that our agony would give them enjoyment. "You're bullies!" my cousin bravely shouted to them as we ran away, and I was swamped by the same wave of outrage, fear, humiliation and hopelessness that had propelled me from that schoolyard then when I walked back onto a city court for the first time as an adult.

I won the first five games I played, my body responding to my psychological need to win, since I never would have dribbled on the concrete again if I had lost. Instead, with victories under my belt, I didn't feel so low losing the next ten games I played, and told myself that "my game" had fallen off rather than admit the hard truth that I had had no "game" to begin with. "No consistency," I complained with the self-indulgence of the essentially satisfied person as I missed several shots in a row, having just hit six straight from all over the court. My younger brother cut through my pose impatiently. "Lew," he told me, "if you had any consistency you'd be in the pros."

The games I played in enjoyed a normal city cast. There were many Italians, kinky-haired and uncommunicative; numerous intellectuals; and solitary blacks. The Italians sat on a bench, talking to their girls while my friends and I took shots around the basket. They ignored us completely, and only grudgingly accepted our invitations to play, trooping onto the court in their Saturday-league baseball uniforms. They performed with ease and daring, the best of them a tiny kid named Nicky who could hit nine out of ten shots from mid-court and who dribbled with absolute control while running with great speed. He was a wonder to me, and I suffered what I hoped to be my last loss of innocence in these matters when I spoke about him to a fourteen-year-old neighbor of his who was tall and agile and who practiced every day to get into shape for his coming two-week stay at Bob Cousy's summer basketball camp. "He's through," he told me about my small star. "He's too small to make it in college, and besides, he never passes you the ball." This criticism had never occurred to me, because I had always been relieved to let Nicky take his accurate shots when he played with me; but I could see his rival's point. "His glory days are over," the fourteen-year-old finished, taking a jump shot. The ball fell through the hoop, and another kid grabbed it. "Next week he starts working for his uncle."

No blacks played regularly on the court. A young black boy had been knifed to death there the year before, and although many residents of the block had witnessed his murder, no one would identify the killers. During those moments of heavy breathing between games, I often wondered whether the local guys we played with had seen or even participated in the crime, and every time a black kid entered the game, my own sense of unease heightened. They drifted onto the court singly, some playing in elevator shoes and others just coming from work. All approached the contest with the attitude that it was theirs by right and immediately became the man to beat, exhibiting a high level of performance and a singular confidence in their abilities, requisites for meeting the challenge of playing on an unfriendly court.

It was on this court, while playing with a black friend, that I first realized I had become a regular ballplayer. A man my age, he loved basketball and performed extraordinary feats, continually displaying the combination of agility and command that marks a talented athlete. We had matched ourselves against two other playground hang-outs, one of them a sculptor who had played on his college team and was built like a bulldog. I had played with him once before, a dismal, humiliating performance, and now his side was winning as my friend missed all his shots. I approached the rest of the game with hopelessness and despair. "You're rushing your shots," my friend whispered to me in an aside. "Take your good one. The soft jumper." I wondered at his remark. Until then, I had believed it was simply in the cards for us to lose, and not a matter subject to either reason or energy. That's the way ball was when I was a kid, and I still looked at the game with a child's wonder, even viewing my own occasional successes as inexplicable happenings. The concept that I had enough practical knowledge of the game to change the course of this contest was entirely foreign to me, and I skeptically listened to my friend's advice. We set up the play, the ball fell through the hoop; and with the enthusiasm that follows the successful resolution of a problem, we went on a tear, keeping the other side from making a point. "Good game," the sculptor told me at the end, the traditional playground salute; in turn, I complimented him with a champion's grace. "You'll get us next time," I answered, knowing that I had become his equal in some way, and not simply because of my performance.

We normally attribute magic to athletes—amazing is the word most often used to describe their actions; awesome, incredible and fantastic, running a close second and third—and basketball seems to demand the intervention of the supernatural because of the variety and difficulty of the game. You must run forever and quickly, jump and catch, shoot, pass, push and shove, and master the thoroughly unnatural act of bouncing a ball bigger than your head on the floor as you maneuver quickly past opponents who have both hands free and are possessed with the idea of taking the ball away from you. Besides, it is a notoriously loose game—you can't play it well if your body and mind don't enjoy the agility that comes with relaxation—and this quality sometimes makes the most incomprehensible athletic feats appear to be matters of ease. Players who are under six feet float through the air and dunk the ball, literally putting it into the basket; giants dribble it with speed and dexterity down the court; otherwise ordinary men shoot apparently blindly and are already running backwards downcourt before the ball finishes falling through the net. Even professionals sometimes resort to a sort of fatalistic belief in the irrational in order to explain triumphs and disasters in a game. "You can't do anything against him when he gets like that," one player remarked about another who had just scored forty points. "It's like he's unconscious."

The careers of professional basketball players encourage this abandonment of logic. American sports today, both professional and amateur, are a vastly profitable and wildly speculative business, and the amounts of money won and lost in basketball by players, investors and teams challenge the imagination as powerfully as any moves you see performed on the court. A world of princes, thieves, lawsuits, unions, vendettas and gambles, it calls upon myths and dreams to describe it, just as Hollywood did in its golden youth. "I knew another zero went off my contract with every shot I missed," said one once highly regarded college player after suffering a series of embarrassing games on national television; and three years ago a tall and talented eighteen-year-old named Moses Malone graduated from high school into the pros with a three-million-dollar contract. Such split-second transformations—like that of the fairy-tale frog who turns into a prince—don't yield easily to the logic of most people's everyday lives, and it isn't surprising that the protagonists of these dramas are talked about as heroes, and the stories of their professional careers are molded into modern folktales, complete with obscure beginnings, early prophecies, and dramatic announcements of their unusual talents. The coach of the Knicks leads the team on to victory after a sudden promotion from scout in mid-season; Red Auerbach (the general manager of the Boston Celtics) makes an extraordinary trade; one of the players executes a legendary debut—Spencer Haywood, who, it is said, caused his first college game to end early by accidentally busting the backboard with a literally shattering slam-dunk; or George McGinnis, who, one is told, wore out seven pairs of brand-new sneakers during a forty-minute high school contest that he wanted badly to win.

On the playground, these matters of business and prowess are the gossip that passes for conversation. During summer camp once, my boys' bunk went on a hike, and we passed the time by saying whatever words entered our minds. The object was to see how long it would be before one of us mentioned sex; the record was forty-eight seconds. It's the same playing ball. As you hang around the basket and practice your shots, you talk about any number of passing matters—Patty Hearst, the latest variety of flu, the warmth in the air and the slowly lengthening days that presage the arrival of spring—but invariably your talk returns to the game and its details.

When I first found myself indulging in these sessions of exchanging information and admiration, I considered them mere time-killing, a sort of social formality. I had shunned them as a kid, and certainly had never considered them the equal of the ceaseless discussions my friends and I had engaged in at Columbia. While the jukebox played Dylan or the Rolling Stones, we sat around large tables in the student cafeteria, sharing opinions and stories about Joyce and Lenin. Our talk was intellectual exercise by which we created new attitudes and judgments; it brought life to subjects we cared for. We injected our passions and preoccupations into events and works that were presented to us with a coolness and objectivity that we considered antithetical to the texts themselves.

Now, it seems to me, playground gossip serves the same function, perhaps an even more necessary one. I know a woman who runs the local general store of a small Maine community; she can tell you pretty much anything you want to know about the town's inhabitants or history, pulling up meaningful statements and incidents from the deep well of her memory and offering you a narrative on her native land that is fresh with insight and intimacy. "Now Charity," a mutual friend of ours once remarked to me about her, "is a *serious* gossip," and the same must be said for that community of people who yak about basketball. The game is one of the great pleasures of their lives, and while gossiping about it they judge and analyze performances, determine standards, fix categories, and explain events. In sports, it is physical actions—the curl of your fingers as you drop the ball into the basket, the timing of a jump, the strength and accuracy of a throw—through which reason and intent are made manifest; but it is only in the distinctions and categories of gossip that one can share and prize these otherwise ephemeral acts.

"Serious gossips" on the playground are those who have something original to say, whether or not they've seen the latest game on television or read the most recent sports story in the newspaper; and age doesn't determine their status. The man, for instance, who tells you that Denver won't win the championship is not worth listening to, because everyone has been saying that for the last two years. But the kid who tells you casually that you don't leap strongly enough toward the basket when you take a lay-up demands your attention. It doesn't matter whether or not he's right; he has thought about the game with reason and judgment.

The more you watch basketball, the more you realize how vast are the possible topics of conversation. In the course of a game, nothing happens which you can't detail or analyze, and the best fans of the sport are those who guide you lovingly through the maze of people, rules, tactics and strategy that make up a contest. Then the game, like a new land, invites you to explore it, and you discover tracts of anatomy, skill, class, race, religion, age, finance, history, psychology and fans. There is pro-ball, college ball, high school ball and playground ball; one-on-one, two-on-two, three-on-three, four-on-four, and full court games—five-on-five; sharp elbows, large hands, strong fingers, thick ankles, massive torsos and extended Achilles tendons—the secret to 5'10" youngsters who dunk the ball; there are players who stand strong, accelerate quickly, move to the basket, dominate the boards, shuffle-step past their opponents, shake and bake, shovel-pass, trigger the fast break, and choke in the clutch; there are forwards, guards and centers, play-makers and prima donnas, chuckers and gym shooters; there is white ball and black ball, Catholic school ball and public school ball; coaches, managers, trainers, physicians, announcers, reporters, agents, scalpers, bird dogs, flesh peddlers and investors; and there are fans—bettors, groupies, kids, businessmen, intellectuals, has-beens and never-weres, workers and professional players; there are leagues, divisions, records and play-offs; champions and losers, teams that are profit-makers or fortune-breakers and that run clinics, play a patterned offense, keep coming at you, run and gun, blow you off the court; and ones with deep benches, a strong forward line, a Rolls-Royce backcourt, and swarming defenses that never give you a break; and there are games, blow-outs and heart-breakers, laughers and yawners, and the most classic basketball contest of them all, the game that is an even match of skill and strength, which either team can win, and which is decided only in the final seconds when the last pass is intercepted, the last rebound is grabbed by a member of the opposing team, or the last shot simply doesn't fall through the net.

Fans live for that sort of game, whether it takes place in a schoolyard, a gym or an arena. Games create their own magic and suspense, each match-up, team and player possessing a character distinctly its own—and I've spent many hours looking through the chicken-wire fence that surrounds city courts, postponing all appointments and duties until a game is finally decided. I am fickle with the pro teams—I root, of course, for my home team, the Knicks, whose predicaments are a compendium of all the aspects of the game and its business—and no event of such essentially unimportant consequence can provoke as much anxiety as a close game played by my favorite. But for refreshment on worried days, I attend my neighborhood playground. The players run back and forth, a man leaps and shoots, I stand in the warming sun, observers comment around me, the game's won or lost, and I'm ready to take on the world. "Basketball junkies," people call my type, but the phrase has always struck me as a misnomer: I leave such contests with my senses quickened to all the possibilities of the day that lies before me, and the humanity that surrounds the game has often blessed an otherwise unmemorable evening.

Recently my brother and I got some free tickets to the Garden. The game was an uninspired contest, and toward the end I noticed a familiar-looking old gentleman sitting in front of me. He was a New Jersey high school coach who had once asked me directions to the City College gymnasium where a summer tournament was being held. "He coached John Shumate," a friend who accompanied him and his wife had informed me, referring to a young black star. I thought the remark an excusable exaggeration—the old man looked to be in his seventies, and who could blame his friend for wanting him to gain a little glory?—but before the game began, the old man did indeed walk up to the mountainous player on the court, and the two shook hands warmly. Now he calmed his wife, who threw her coat down on the floor, exasperated at what she imagined was a Knick coaching error that lost the team the game, and they argued all the way down the five flights of escalators. They were still debating the point when my brother and I got into a taxi. "They lose again, eh, man," the middle-aged driver said in the soft tones of a West Indian accent. My brother and I gestured disgustedly, and the three of us were off on a nonstop talk about all the possible remedies for the troubles of the team. "Do you play ball?" I asked him as we arrived. "Oh, man," he answered, shutting off the meter, "I've played ball all my life. Jamaica, England, Italy. There is nothing like ball." I tipped him and wished him a good evening. "You too, man," he said. "I'll see you on the court."

2. The Rules of the Game

I'm shooting baskets on the playground. It's a dog day and I haven't run in weeks. My breath is scant, my legs already aching. A neighborhood kid wanders toward me, asks if I want to go one-on-one. "Too hot," I say, and invite the kid to shoot with me. Several minutes later, we're fooling around and he tries to block my shot. I reproach myself: Who knows? Maybe I'll win. "All right, let's play to eleven," I tell him. "Everything back?" he asks. "Winner's out?" I nod my head. "Make your own calls," I answer. He bounces the ball twice while I tie my sneaker. "Hit or miss from here," he announces, and shoots as I wave my hand in assent. The ball falls through the basket, and I retrieve it while he waits beyond the foul line. I pass the ball to him; he tosses it back to me. I turn to look at the basket, checking my position, and bounce it back to him. The game begins.

This moment fascinates me. Many people believe that only the final minutes of a basketball game matter because of the frequent reversals of fortune and startling individual performances that attend such climaxes. When I was a new fan, end-of-the-game displays thrilled and mystified me; now, seasoned with experience, I regard them coolly. As a fan, of course, I gratefully accept whatever quirks of fate bless my favorite team. But few games present me with the surprises that greeted my first ventures into the sport. Those ultimate two minutes of disorder and excitement—the coaches summoning plagues of time-outs and intentional fouls, the clock relentlessly stalking possibility, the fans insisting on improbable luck—now appear to me the dramatic summation of the themes and principles that presented themselves at the start of the contest. With false pride perhaps, I believe that their inexorable logic carries me away, not their madcap chance.

But I still wonder about the beginnings of games. At seventeen, I started working in a ramshackle bookstore on West Forty-third Street. The boss told me my work began at ten, and on the first day of my employment I left my house at a quarter past nine, with plenty of time to arrive punctually, except that the subway was delayed. I opened the bookshop's door five minutes late. Not imagining the fractional difference would matter, I apologized perfunctorily to my boss, and he chewed me out. Ten meant ten, not five or four or three or two or even one minute later, and I couldn't work for him if I didn't obey that rule. Until then I had considered the job part of the general adventure I imagined my life to be—working in a bookstore was romantic. From then on, my employment became an unnatural duty. The last steps I took toward the store in the morning belonged to a universe different from the one I inhabited once I entered the shop; at the end of the day, the clatter of heels I heard over my head when I packed mail-order books announced the end of my imprisonment.

Basketball games have a similar mystery. You're standing around the court, taking shots, feeling long and strong, loose, without care. Then two people choose up sides. Within moments you're running up and down, calling to your teammates, dribbling, guarding and shooting, your mind repeating commands and curses. The court becomes an arena for an arbitrary conflict between people, the game a drama of their humors and furies. Make me a malted, my friends and I used to joke. All right. Poof! You're a malted. The beginnings of games are equally capricious, and also irrevocable and complete—transformations as sudden and commanding as the instant in which I became my boss's vassal.

The ritual of suggestion and agreement practiced by my challenger and me orders this change. Basketball is an elastic sport; you can stretch it to twelve men or reduce it to three, narrow a contest to five minutes or spread it out over two hours. Few baskets meet the required height of 10 feet—I cherish one set at 9'6" because it lets me dunk—and people play the game in gyms, alleyways and open fields. In the twenties and thirties, pro games were performed in dance halls; after the contest, the baskets were dismantled, a big band filled the stage, and couples Charlestoned where the players had run. Some college teams, Long Island University and Seton Hall, for example, still play in auditorium pits, and I've seen at least one game performed on a stage. NBA courts uniformly measure 94' x 50', but the game's tradition of versatile dimensions is so fixed that the collegiate and high school rules state only a court's maximum size, letting school budgets and the predilections of coaches determine the final boundaries. Coaches and players often complain about this chaos, but the makeshift nature of basketball is a glory of the game; the sport is accessible to all who wish to play it.

This flexibility isn't accidental. Unlike all other major sports, basketball is an invention, a form of athletic exercise and competition that didn't exist before December 1891, when it was created by one man, James Naismith. Naismith intended to fashion a sport that people would enjoy and from which they could profit physically. The proof of his design's brilliance is basketball's universal success. Less than a century after its creation, basketball enjoys Olympic recognition and worldwide attention. With the possible exception of soccer, it is played by more people than any other sport. (The Chinese favor it especially, and their women's team performs with balletic flair. I saw one of their athletes sink a behind-the-back hook while floating in air, a shot I've never witnessed any other time.)

Naismith himself seems an unlikely discoverer of this strange new world. A Canadian minister, he was born poor, orphaned at nine, and lived with a bachelor uncle until the age of sixteen, when he quit school to work in logging camps. He appears to have considered life a sort of combat: as a child, he had to make his first pair of ice skates by hand; as an old man, he stated that aging's chief effect was to compel him to win battles in a shorter period of time. One story relates his meeting with Amos Alonzo Stagg, a football great and Naismith's contemporary. When Stagg gripped Naismith's hand as though it were a football, Naismith responded with a wrestling hold. The two remained friends through life, and Stagg once complimented Naismith as a competitor for "doing the meanest things in the most gentlemanly manner." Naismith's son describes nighttime storytelling sessions in the kitchen with his father, and other incidents betray an almost hurtful innocence about the man—once Naismith marked his son with crayons while using the child as an exhibit in a physical education class. But his son's portrait of Naismith ultimately suggests a dogged, cramped person with a stiff Puritanical mien that is very different from the burlesque sport he fathered.

Naismith invented basketball when he was still young. After working as a logger, he decided to become a minister. In the seminary at McGill University, he began to play rugby and pursued the game so enthusiastically that fellow seminarians reportedly stayed up nights praying for his soul. Their devotion was but partly rewarded; on graduation, Naismith enrolled at the International Training School of the Young Men's Christian Association in Springfield, Massachusetts, a training academy for future YMCA leaders.

A photo of Naismith with his first basketball squad shows nine handsomely proportioned young men, thick-shouldered, black-haired, several sporting full mustaches, all of them looking like leads from a Hollywood musical about the Gay Nineties. As part of their courses, these men played football and baseball in summer, spring and fall; winters, they practiced calisthenics, tumbling, Indian ball and gymnastics, and the boring training irritated them. "What this generation wanted," Naismith later wrote, "was pleasure and thrill rather than physical benefit only. . . ." By the time Naismith was promoted to a teaching position in the academy, two instructors of the winter classes had quit, unable to curb the incorrigible behavior of their students. A year before, Naismith had boasted to the Y's chief instructor that a winter sport could be invented to fulfill both the desires of the students and the academy's requirements. At the time, the instructor, Dr. Luther Gulick, hadn't challenged Naismith to make good his boast; now he appointed Naismith to quell the rebellion and create such a game.

For Naismith, the test had moral and personal consequences, as well as practical ones. "The problem," he wrote gravely, "seemed to threaten the whole subject of physical activity, especially in the YMCA." Gulick's personal opinion of him mattered deeply to Naismith. "I hated the thought of going back and admitting that after all my theories, I too had failed to hold the interest of the class," he wrote. "All the stubbornness of my Scottish ancestry was aroused; all my pride of achievement urged me on; I would not go back and admit that I had failed." Still, after two weeks, he could neither interest nor discipline the class. Basketball was his last resort.

He conceived the game overnight, or rather puzzled it out, applying the principles of other sports to the problem of fashioning a civil active indoor form of athletic competition. "My first generalization," he stated in an essay describing his invention of the game, "was that all team games used a ball of some kind; therefore, any new game must have a ball." He ruled out small balls because they required the use of sticks. This left rugby and soccer balls, and Naismith chose the first—the ball of the game he loved—until he realized that the new sport's indoor setting precluded players from running with the ball or tackling one another and that the round soccer ball better suited his purpose. "So far," he continued, "I had a game that was played with a large light ball; the players could not run with the ball, but must pass it or bat it with their hands; and the pass could be made in any direction." He modified this concept, prohibiting a player from striking the ball with his fist, but encountered another problem. What would the players compete for? He concluded that "in all existing games there was some kind of goal," and proceeded to "devise some objective for the player." He considered the different sorts of goals used in hockey, lacrosse, tennis and football, and decided to place his goal posts at the end of the field, their usual position in running games. However, he couldn't allow goals "into which the ball must be driven," because players would throw the ball into the mark, and play would become rough. Therefore, he set the goals on a horizontal plane, "[compelling] . . . the players . . . to throw the ball in an arc" and making force, the source of rough play, "of no value." Again, this decision raised a problem. Naismith's class consisted of eighteen men, and "if nine men formed a defense around the goal, it would be impossible for the ball to enter it." Consequently, he decided to raise the goal, making it higher than any player. Finally, he wondered about the best way to start the game. In rugby, the referee threw the ball into the field between two lines of opposing players. This was too langerous for an indoor sport, but, Naismith reasoned, "if I picked only one player from each team and threw the ball up between them, there would be little chance for roughness."

The next day Naismith translated his theoretical concepts into thirteen practical rules, adding referees, the number of points per goal, and the crucial injunction that players could not "shoulder, hold, push, trip, or strike in any way the person of their opponent." Naismith had envisioned boxes as the goals, but the janitor of the academy could supply him only with two peach baskets. Naismith fastened these to the lower rail of a balcony that overlooked the gymnasium floor and introduced his class to the game. "All the players wanted to shoot," one of the participants later remarked, and within months basketball was a new attraction at Y's and other sports centers throughout the country.

Naismith's description of how he invented the game always reminds me of a narrative detailing the birth of another American institution, an essay by Edgar Allan Poe on the writing of his poem "The Raven." Like Naismith's work, Poe's essay is a fill-in-the-blanks account of ingenuity answering need. "It is my design," Poe wrote, "to render it manifest that no one point in its [the poem's] composition is referrable either to accident or intuition—that the work proceeded, step by step, to its completion with the precision and rigid consequence of a mathematical problem." This is a more sumptuous version of Naismith's original boast that he could construct a game by following sound principles, and Poe painstakingly proves his point. A poem should elevate the soul, he writes; all excitement, by necessity, is brief; therefore, he decided his poem should be one hundred lines. Beauty is the province of poetry; sadness its most powerful manifestation; therefore, he decided his work should communicate a melancholic tone. A poem could not achieve its desired effect without a refrain; the refrain must be brief; therefore, he decided the refrain should be one word. The refrain would close each stanza; it must be "sonorous and susceptible of protracted emphasis"; therefore, he decided he needed a word containing o's, "the most sonorous sound," and r's, "the most pronounceable consonant." The word had to embody this sound; the word also had to be melancholic; therefore, he decided on the lament, "nevermore." The entire fifteen-page essay continues in this elaborate fashion, drawing, like Naismith's, a classic design of American pragmatism.

Poe of course intended his essay as an argument against prevailing Romantic theories; his spiteful piece wants to teach his audience how they are tricked (no discredit to his genius, since he practiced the craft among the best). But this aspect also compares to Naismith's moment of genius. Naismith wished to prove that athletic training at the Y could answer his generation's need for enjoyment and that he was equal to the task. Indeed, both men's works are studies in the manipulation of pleasure, and the true difference between the two is the reflection they cast on their authors. Poe's essay is merely perversely clever in the end: as in most of his writing, his genius seems to lie outside it, beckoning us to imagine what uncompromised achievements this mind might have fashioned. Contrarily, Naismith's essay captures his creative spirit entirely: the light of that inspired moment never brightened his life again.

In this respect, Naismith's career parallels that of many athletes. He was a creator who commanded the world's attention but couldn't hold it, a victim of ephemeral genius. Shortly after the premiere of his invention, he met his future wife, a secretary who was watching an exhibition game. They moved first to Denver, then to Kansas, where Naismith coached the university's first basketball squad to a mediocre record. He became a father, a minister, a professor of physical education, and eventually an ancient accessory of campus life, a somewhat touchingly remote old man who mattered to people mostly for his past achievements and whose present opinions earned only obligatory respect.

His views on basketball were considered particularly anachronistic because he so firmly resisted the game's success as a spectator sport. In 1937 he attended a doubleheader at Madison Square Garden and expressed astonishment at the large audience. For him, sports wasn't business, and basketball was just a rest stop on the serious journey of building a sound body. "It is peculiarly adapted," he wrote in 1894, "for giving health without involving severe mental strain." He never parted from this opinion. His constant comment about the game was that it didn't require a coach; he instructed both his sons in tumbling rather than in shooting baskets, and considered fencing a more valuable exercise than running up and down the court. His son remarked that Naismith was prouder of inventing the first football helmet, a chamois cap Naismith designed to protect his own cauliflower ears, than of creating basketball.

Naismith's modest comments on his one great achievement are reminiscent of the common complaints by athletes that they are honored for the wrong reasons. Supremely willful individuals, they resent that their greatness rests on those magical moments when all circumstances conspired to their advantage and they effortlessly produced the answer to every problem. They would rather be remembered for the hard times when they struggled for points and only succeeded by using the store of craft and determination they had gained through years of work. Like Job's, their complaint is understandable; but also like Job, their unique individual quality is that they can surrender to such moments and fulfill their special promise. Naismith also did this. Fusty, bull-natured, tutorial, he nonetheless let his spirited genius guide him for at least one night and created a game that belonged, for once, solely to the players, not to the difficulty of scoring, the demands of a special athletic skill, or the brute force of play. "I had in mind," he wrote, describing the ideal player for whom he had designed the game, "the tall, agile, graceful, and expert athlete." Put anybody on a court, let him score a goal, and the "tall, agile, graceful, and expert athlete" is who he secretly believes he is.

From the first, players and coaches tinkered with Naismith's model. His invention was part of a general discovery of sports—the popular acceptance of both football and baseball came about during the same period—and one player even claims that the first professional basketball contest was played in 1893 at Herkimer, New York, hardly two years after Naismith had first demonstrated the game. By the turn of the century professional leagues existed, and the Y's that had introduced basketball to the country now banished the game from their gyms because of its frivolous and commercial nature. "When men commence to make money out of a sport," Naismith's tutor, Dr. Gulick, waspishly wrote, "it [the sport] degenerates with more tremendous speed. . . . It has inevitably resulted in men of lower character going into the game."

Nonetheless, these men dominated the exploration of this new world and mapped out its limits, seeking to discover within its confines the El Dorado of a perfect game, a combination of speed, stars and skill that would keep the customers coming.

Sometimes they changed rules to keep the game active and fair, one of Naismith's first intentions. One of the game's original thirteen rules reads that "when the ball goes out-of-bounds, it shall be thrown onto the field of play by the person first touching it." This led to wild melees. One recorded instance tells of the ball bouncing high into a gym's balcony. One team rushed up the stairs to retrieve it; the other formed a human ladder. The rule was soon reversed; the team last touching the ball before it went out-of-bounds lost possession of it. Players still tricked their opponents, but less dangerously. For a decade after its invention, basketball was often played on courts surrounded by wire fencing, the origin of the appellation "cagers," the word newspapers still use for the sport's players. Competitors sometimes took advantage of the cage by trapping their opponents against it or pulling out the flexible wire and creating arbitrary boundaries on the court. Now the cages have come down, but the tactics remain. A player runs after a ball with an adversary at his heels. While grabbing the ball, he realizes that his momentum will carry him out-of-bounds, off the court. Jumping into the air, he slams the ball off his opponent's leg and keeps possession. It's a playground ruse, but you'll see pros do it and win applause.

Rules about the basket were also changed to keep the game competitive. Naismith had forbidden any tricks with the goal. "If the ball rests on the edge [of the goal]," he instructed, "and the opponent moves the basket, it shall count as a goal." Doubtlessly, he didn't mention touching the ball in this injunction because the athletes of his day couldn't leap ten feet into the air. Thirty-five years later, however, players had overcome the impediment of the basket's height; they blocked airborne shots, dunked balls, tipped them into the basket while they bounced around the rim. The game's Rules Committee, representatives of the various amateur organizations playing the game, declared that no player could touch the ball when it was inside the basket's cylinder; then, ten years later, that no defensive player could interrupt the ball's downward flight; ten years later again, that no offensive player could do the same.

Sometimes players promoted changes in the rules. Naismith's laws didn't include the peculiar act of dribbling. He merely required the player "to throw the ball [in any direction and with either one or both hands] from the spot on which he catches it." Players threw the ball repeatedly over their heads while standing still; they bounced the ball while moving; they dribbled, stopped, and dribbled again. This last maneuver—now a violation called the "double dribble"—was used particularly by the pros to free themselves from the man guarding them, and crowds enjoyed the displays. But the Rules Committee presiding over the amateur game believed the dribble reduced team play. For twenty years they tried to define and limit the dribble, and ultimately ruled that a player could dribble but once. The only result of this edict was a rebellion among the college coaches who immediately declared their independence from the Rules Committee, set up their own organization, and let the dribbler roam.

The most important rule change, however, directly contravened Naismith's intentions for the sport. He had asked one question of his rules: were they fair? His followers wanted to know something else: was the game exciting? By the thirties, they had agreed that basketball failed this test. Inevitably, some tactic or player dominated the game—teams stalled the ball to preserve tiny leads, big men stood near the basket—and audiences were bored. The game needed some standard of skill, some absolute that couldn't be manipulated, the equivalent of football's fourth down and baseball's three strikes. Modern sorts, the entrepreneurs of the game decided that their answer was time. In 1932 they introduced this new factor into the game, stating that once a team in-bounded a ball, the offensive players had but ten seconds to dribble or pass it over the half-court line. Since then every player's progress is measured by the clock. You have five seconds to throw the ball onto the court, three seconds to stay near the basket if your team's playing offense, and twenty-four seconds to shoot—a decree issued by the pros in 1954 and mimicked sloppily in amateur play by a series of complicated rules.

All these rules of conduct vary at different levels of play; like the church, basketball is eager for converts. High school games are shorter than college ones—four eight-minute quarters compared to two twenty-minute halves—and college contests are less frenetic than professional ones. Occasionally, these differences cause substantial changes in a player's style. When Kareem Abdul-Jabbar entered UCLA, the National Collegiate Athletic Association ruled all dunking illegal. Ten years before, Wilt Chamberlain's collegiate debut had inspired changes intended to offset the man's height and strength; but the dunking rule was seen simply as a way of keeping Jabbar—and black players generally—in their place. However, the prohibition helped Jabbar develop a soft jump shot close to the basket. Sometimes rule changes simply cause confusion. In all kinds of organized American basketball, a player has ten seconds to shoot a free throw from the foul line: fouls were intended as penalties and the rule wants to make the shot count. In Olympic competition, however, the player must shoot his free throw in five seconds. Once I observed a contest between American and Soviet high school all-stars. An American player was fouled and stepped to the line, bouncing the ball and concentrating on the basket. "Five seconds, five, five!" his coach yelled from the sidelines, trying to remind the player of the change in rules. Distracted by the coach's command, sure that he enjoyed a good ten seconds to shoot, the player turned to the coach and asked what he wanted. "Shoot!" the exasperated coach cried to the befuddled player as the referee blew his whistle. "Five-second violation," he announced, and the player and coach traded nasty glances the rest of the half.

In unorganized playground ball, the sport's most versatile and popular form, you agree on the rules before you play, a nip-and-tuck exchange that previews the competition of the game. In my contest with the kid, we decided first on the length of the contest. I suggested eleven because my legs wouldn't last any longer. He countered by proposing that the player who grabbed a rebound off the other's shot had to dribble the ball behind the foul line before he could shoot. This rule minimized the advantage of my height. I would probably control more rebounds than the kid; he would probably shoot better than I. His chance to win was to score from outside, and the rule made this neither more nor less difficult. My chance was to collect more rebounds and consequently take more shots, but the rule prohibited me from putting the ball immediately into the basket and scoring. It also meant that I had to dribble the ball a lot if I wanted to get near the basket, giving the kid an opportunity to steal it, another plus for his side, since he was smaller and faster than I.

Our next agreement, "winners out," is a rule of thumb on New York playgrounds. In all kinds of basketball games, the action stops after a goal is scored. Who gets the ball? Originally, Naismith used the same device that started the game; the referee simply threw the ball straight up at center court, one player from each side trying to grab it or tap it back to a teammate. Few players or coaches liked this. It slowed the game, and a team blessed with one exceedingly tall player easily dominated the contest. (Or a clever one. Eddie Gottlieb, who coached the Philadelphia SPHAS, a victorious team of the twenties, told me his team always controlled the jump ball. "We didn't have a big man," he said, "but we had our ways." He still refuses to disclose them.)

Over the years, the Rules Committee continually modified the center jump. A player had to jump with a hand placed behind his back; he was prohibited from catching the ball until another player had touched it; he could tap the ball but once; he could tap the ball twice but not touch it a third time. Even with these modifications of the rule, teams and audiences continued to complain. I like to think that part of their dissatisfaction was aesthetic. Center jumps provide terrific photos—the players tensed and extended in the air, their faces set—but as a dramatic moment the center jump is generally an anticlimax to the psychological tension preceding it. A player tips the ball out-of-bounds, the ball bumps off a player's ankle and rolls on the floor, a player leaps precipitously, and the whole episode must be repeated. It's an unstately maneuver that serves only to show fans what a chaotic display lies in store for them, and it's best to keep it at a minimum. In 1935 the Rules Committee began to do this. Trying out a new rule, the West Coast schools kept the center jump at the start of each half, but eliminated it after every basket, simply awarding the ball instead to the team that hadn't scored. At the season's end, the schools reported the experiment a success, and the Rules Committee

voted the change into law against Naismith's advice. It ha
remained in effect ever since. (The NBA used to stage cente.
jumps at the start of each quarter; now the team that controls th
tap at the beginning of the game automatically takes the ball out ir
the fourth quarter also, the other team enjoying this advantag
during the second and third quarters.) In full-court playground bal
the rule also applies. But in half-court games, one-on-one or any o
its many variations, the player or team scoring the basket gains th
privilege. In my experience, this rule is universally accepted. Th
only game I've ever played without it was a one-on-one match
sometimes engaged in with a fellow writer from Ithaca, New York
He insisted losers take out the ball and swore he had always playe
the game that way in Ithaca. He was shorter and older than I, an
although I have never visited the schoolyards of that town, I stil
believe that his timeless tradition was mere spur-of-the-momen
opportunism.

The last point in the contract negotiations between the kid an
me—"call your own"—is the most crucial. Ensuring against an
roughness in the game, Naismith created fouls, penalties suffere
by teams and players for disobeying his injunction "not t
shoulder, hold, push, trip or strike in any way the person of thei
opponent." He appointed three referees, one more than are use
today, to monitor the behavior of the players. If a player foule
twice, he left the game until a goal had been scored. If the refere
decided a player had fouled his opponent intentionally, th
offender was disqualified with "no substitutes allowed." If on
team committed three consecutive fouls and their opponent
none, the referees immediately awarded the guiltless party a goal
Naismith imagined that these fines would prevent muggings on th
court, but the first exhibition game proved him wrong. The facult
played the students, and Amos Stagg, Naismith's good friend
shocked the inventor with his unsportsmanlike tactics. (Stagg als
scored the faculty's one goal to the students' five.) Naismit
remonstrated with Stagg, but his pleas were bootless: basketball i
still a contact sport in which advantage is gained not simply by guil
and speed but also by brute force.

A player I'm guarding leaps to shoot and I push him. I'v
committed a defensive foul. My victim shoots two free throws fron

he foul line for a point apiece. While dribbling the ball, I slam into an opponent who was standing still. I've committed an offensive foul. The other team gains possession of the ball. Jumping for a rebound, I reach over my opponent's shoulder and cuff him on the head. I've committed a loose-ball foul. The other team gets possession again. I'm permitted but six fouls (five in college basketball) before I must leave the game, and the penalties increase as both teams commit more infractions—"the bonus situation," when players who are fouled take an extra free throw. If I get mad at the referee for calling all these fouls on me and tell him he's a dumb motherfucker—a common occurrence—I've committed a technical foul. The other team's best shooter takes a foul shot for one point. If I'm still mad at the referee and impugn his honesty, punch another player, throw the ball into the stands, swing from the basket rim, or paint my hands with glue, I've committed another technical. The referee jerks his thumb, ordering me out of the game. The crowd cheers or boos; I glower; my coach complains; the referee runs downcourt; the game continues, and if I'm a professional player, I'll be fined anything from fifty dollars to ten thousand dollars.

Other detours from the rules are labeled violations, class-A misdemeanors punishable only by surrendering the ball. A player can't grab his own pass, move more than a full step and a half while holding the ball, jump up and down while holding the ball, or perform a "double dribble." You also lose the ball if you break any of the rules about time, or—maddeningly—go out-of-bounds.

Referees maintain these codes of conduct, an onerous and impossible duty. In any game you'll see players fouling their opponents, stepping on the boundary lines, traveling, using more than their allotted time. Cheating to gain the advantage of a foothold or a second is part of their craft, and referees either simply don't see these violations or disregard them. But occasionally they see too much. Phil Sellers, a strong, small (6'5") forward who played for Rutgers two years ago, led the team to an undefeated regular season. He played close to the basket, shouldering his way around opponents who moved to intercept him or clobbering those who stood their ground. During the regular season, referees tended to call fouls in his favor. In the national championships, they changed, calling the fouls against him. Sellers was playing under pressure; a senior, he wanted to impress the pro teams which would soon be drafting him. He had become notorious as a complainer and hot-shot, and he knew he had to replace this image with the picture of a calm, confident team player. The series presented him with a perfect display case, but he was undone as the calls continued to penalize him. He took bad shots and complained about the referees; by the end of the tournament, his market value as a ballplayer was minimal.

Some coaches bait referees continually. The foulest language I've ever heard was uttered by Cotton Fitzsimmons, a peripatetic character who travels from one team to another. At the time, he was coaching the Atlanta Hawks, a perennially ragtag bunch who had begun the year with a string of surprising wins. I observed him at a game in Boston which the Celtics commanded from the start, and the only performance that kept the contest from becoming unendurably tedious was Fitzsimmons's ceaseless invention of obscenities and expletives. But, however much players and coaches revile them, referees still listen to the men on the court when they point out violations or suggest calls. If a player complains that his adversary elbowed him or positioned himself illegally, the referee cuts him off sharply, telling him to play ball; but the next time the opponent nudges his man or comes downcourt, the referee blows his whistle. Whatever the referee may believe, no player or coach thinks that a single man can spot all infractions, so their test for a good official is not the justice of his decisions, but whether or not he distributes evenly between the two contestants the benefits and disadvantages gained from his oversights, mistakes and hesitancies.

Complaining about referees is, of course, a favorite pastime of basketball fans, and it's hard not to find some games in any season when referees have given decisive advantages to one team. In the '77 college semi-finals, Marquette won over North Carolina at Charlotte with a last-second play. The Charlotte team insisted that the final shot had been launched after the buzzer and that the game should go into overtime. The referee disagreed. He was right in the instance, but wrong about the game; the final shot scored only because one of the players broke the injunction not to touch the ball when it's on the rim of the basket. Leonard Koppett—the wittiest, most knowledgeable of basketball writers—claims that referees have become more inconsistent, vituperative and personally biased in their decisions since the forties. But complaining about referees generally gives them an importance they don't possess, because they play no truly independent role in the game. I'm reminded of this every time I watch a basketball game. I'm not a good judge of umpires, and the present crop may all be hacks, but umpires perform a qualitatively different function from that of referees. Their duty is to determine not simply whether a player comports himself correctly, but how well he performs: Does he pitch a strike or a ball? Does he beat the throw to first or run too slowly? This appointment gives the umpire's position an aesthetic dignity and power altogether lacking in the job of referee. Indeed, you can't play baseball without an umpire; it becomes another game, softball or batting practice. But full-court basketball games are played daily without the presence of the men in striped shirts. Players like the kid and me "call their own" fouls, traveling, up and down, double dribble and out-of-bounds; and court etiquette decrees that you respect the other player's judgment.

Usually players maintain this politeness through the first half of a contest but when the score is close, they forget about it. They put down the ball, stalk off the court, or threaten to crush their opponent the next time he shoots. "Choose it up," the other players suggest, but the two combatants won't let a show of fingers decide the issue. One makes the other surrender by refusing to give up. Insulted, injured, they finally both return to play; a moment later, two others start arguing. Players will even invent rules when they get riled. In one full-court game, an opponent suddenly complained that I was violating the three-second rule. Did he have a clock? my teammates asked. But our accuser, a lawyer, was adamant, and our only recourse was revenge. We surrendered the ball, but as soon as they threw it in, we insisted that they had violated the five-second limit.

Sometimes the rules confuse even players who have dedicated their lives to the sport. Watching one summer league game, I sat near Floyd Lane, a player and coach for nearly forty years. A player, dribbling the ball, stepped over the half-court line and inadvertently lost control of the ball. When he grabbed it he was in the backcourt, and he lost possession—once you cross half-court on offense, you must keep the ball in the front court until an opponent touches it. Floyd asked a companion who was a referee if the player's move was always illegal, and the two speculated for a moment. "There is no instance," his friend finally decided. "In this game, you never move back."

Is it any wonder that players enter warily into such an unnatural state? My favorite outdoor court is a corner lot at Fourth Street and Sixth Avenue. It's known throughout New York as a show-off place where many men who once played college or semi-professional ball still stand and wait for a game. The kid and I started our game when he shot the ball—"hit or miss from here"—but the preparations for these more elaborate contests often take a quarter of an hour, and you're never sure if the game will actually get off the ground.

A lot of time is spent negotiating who will play. Did Kenny or Bishop have the next game? Bishop claims it's his, but Timmie, who doesn't like Bishop, insists it belongs to Kenny. There was a dude from Brooklyn in a red shirt, and Bishop agreed with him that he had the next game; but where is he now? Bishop looks around for his witness while kids run onto the court and heave balls at the basket. The players who have just exhausted themselves in the previous contest drink water, chat with friends while leaning on cars, hang on the wire fence and breathe deeply. One player flirts with a girl: Where do you live? Albany. Where do *you* live? Bed-Stuy. Players who have just won their first game of the afternoon and are anxious to run start needling Bishop, "Come on, man, let's play."

They reach a compromise: Bishop and Kenny will play on the same team twice. Timmie doesn't really care, because he's a member of the winning team anyway and plays no matter what. But a newcomer to the court—a large fit-looking white man wearing an Ohio State University sweat shirt—complains that the agreement freezes him out of the next two games. Everyone ignores him. "Shit!" he explodes, planting himself at center court. "I'm standing right here!" He looks for an audience and seizes on Mike. "I had the game after next, Mike, you know that, goddamnit!" Mike shrugs. He has played on the court for several years and, like most ballplayers, understands that you must suffer small injustices if you love the game. What does it matter if the white guy plays in the second or third game? "No harm—no foul" is the rule and the only reasonable way to behave on the court. "Don't be stupid, man," he advises. "You'll have the game after Kenny's. Come on, Bishop, man," he calls, "let's start."

Bishop stalks the court, marshaling his forces. He's large and rangy, with thin muscular arms, and he must command. He picks his players as though he's a general manager and acts as though the delay of the game is everyone's fault but his own. "You playing, Donald?" he asks one forward who is stuffing some pants into his clothes bag. Donald doesn't really want to run, because Bishop leads games into disastrous childish arguments, takes bad shots, harasses his teammates. Still, it's early to quit. "One," Donald replies, meaning Bishop must replace him if their team wins. "All right," Bishop agrees and bounces the ball hard against the concrete, catching it with two hands as he goes off to round up some guards.

"You ready yet, man?" Kenny asks Timmie as he saunters toward mid-court with the ball. Timmie shrugs his shoulders and gestures toward Mike. The arrangements are not his affair. He positions himself under the basket near five or six other players. Kenny shoots the ball from thirty feet, and everyone grabs for it as it falls through the net. "Three points, three points," a player announces as he dribbles out to center court and takes a jumper. A friend laughs at his egotism and lackadaisically sticks his hands in the air to block the shot. Someone asks Timmie if he's playing in the next game. He catches the ball and dribbles to the foul line; shrugging his shoulder in answer, he rises in the air and shoots.

A quarter of an hour has passed since the end of the last game, a tied-score affair that took as long to finish as this one takes to begin, and the spectators on the other side of the fence, businessmen and passersby, wait patiently. Occasionally a viewer remarks that he saw one of the men on the court play in college. "He used to know how to play some ball." They laugh at the inane negotiations taking place on the other side only when the participants do. They never complain. Unlike spectators in an arena, they haven't paid for that luxury.

"Bishop," Mike demands, "goddamnit, let's go!" At the other end of the court, Bishop turns and faces him, outraged. "You always bitching. Get your own goddamn men ready. We set to run." On the street, he's an entirely friendly fellow, collecting funds for some day-care center I doubt exists. He never threatens anyone and suffers the considerable disappointments of his life gracefully. Once I found him in a fast-food joint, a dime shy of a hamburger, pretending to the counterman that he had accidentally left his wallet at home. "My man," he asked boldly, "what am I to do?" But on the court he becomes hysterical, a tight ball of fury and competition, exerting himself in hopeless situations and blaming his teammates constantly, coaching them to wait for a good shot while he takes errant ones, encouraging them only after he scores a basket. It's an eccentricity his companions accept, hoping in every game they play with him that he'll resist the temptation of craziness and display his better self. The one time I ever saw him fight, Mike pulled him away. It was an end-of-the-game affair; someone had called a foul, and Bishop refused to accept it. He held onto the ball—this adult, capable man—and refused to start playing, taunting the other men and threatening them. "Bishop," Mike insisted, "you act like an animal! Stop it, man! You make yourself into an animal!"

Now he stands with Kenny and the rest of his team on their side of the court, indignantly shooing away kids and hangers-on who try to take one last shot. Mike's team wanders onto the court, loose limbed and ready for the contest. "We only got four, Mike," Timmie informs him at the last moment as Bishop looks disgustedly at the sky. "Come on!" Donald cries. "Pick someone else." Mike turns distractedly and finds an eleven-year-old trying to dribble the ball through his legs. "Come on, come on," he insists. Bishop throws up his hands in despair; Timmie shrugs.

At the moment when you're certain no game will happen, Mike bounces the ball to his man—one hop into the other guard's hands. They exchange some words, and Mike struts down a side of the court, positioning himself while the man with the ball dribbles it across center court, bouncing the ball with one hand, his eyes set ahead of him, the other arm free to wave and signal as the player guarding him advances to within a few inches of his body. There is an anticipatory instant. The players set themselves, readying themselves to execute again the plays and moves they have perfected. "Watch the center, center," someone calls, meaning the area, not the player. The game begins.

3. The Pyramid of Success: Basketball as a Business

MEMORANDUM

January 1, 1977

Re: Basketball as a Business

I. Background

1. Basketball is a business, a part of the entertainment industry. It has vast financial dimensions. During the season, 20,300 high schools, 630 junior colleges and 1,014 senior colleges hold games. Every week 700,000 high school students play in approximately 15,000 contests. Each season 25,000 four-year college students perform in 12,500 games. The National Basketball Association (NBA), the professional league, stages 902 matches a year in twenty-two cities, and a series of play-off contests in twelve cities that extend through early June. People pay to see all these games: fifty cents at local high schools and up to twelve dollars for a good seat at Madison Square Garden. This money adds up. Several years ago, the total assets of sixteen NBA teams exceeded 140 million dollars; the total revenues from seventeen NBA teams reached 90 million dollars. The figures have only risen since.

2. These relatively new fortunes mark the climax of a remarkable success story. Commerce has always accompanied basketball; players charged spectators to see them perform within a few years of the game's invention. But the game didn't enjoy the traditional prestige of baseball or the intense local loyalties claimed by football or hockey. While the sport produced some stars in the

34

twenties—Nat Holman, Joe Lapchick, Dutch Dehnert—professional teams couldn't sustain any large fan support. They toured the country: traveling road shows playing (and usually winning) against local favorites. In the thirties, college basketball won national attention with a series of doubleheaders at Madison Square Garden, but this triumph didn't help the professional game. Throughout the war, regional leagues struggled to survive, and when a group of arena owners decided to start the Basketball Association of America in 1946, they were skeptical about the wisdom of the venture. They risked the investment only because basketball teams cost relatively little to manage and the owners needed regular attractions to fill their stadiums on the nights hockey wasn't played. The association expanded to include the strongest teams of the other professional leagues, driving these competitors out of business, and in 1949 became the NBA. They fielded seventeen teams, organized into three divisions representing the eastern, central and western areas of the country, the last a short-lived amalgam of backwater towns such as Waterloo, Iowa, and Sheboygan, Wisconsin. They also featured the prodigious talents of George Mikan, the period's top basketball star. Still, the owners figured they'd be lucky if they broke even.

3. Instead they discovered a gold mine. In 1950 a scandal ruined college basketball as a big-city attraction. Professional basketball quickly took its place. By the end of the decade, the NBA was recognized as a member of the professional sports family. Ten years after that, it was a multi-million-dollar business. Players were national stars, television rights worth fortunes, franchises valuable properties. In 1967 businessmen paid the NBA $1,750,000 to start a team in San Diego; four years later, they sold the same team for $5,700,000. Boston, an historic franchise that changes hands repeatedly, was sold in 1965 for 2.9 million dollars and again for 3.6 million dollars three years later, and an even 6 million one year after that. In 1973 the Detroit Pistons were owned by Fred Zollner, who had started the team in Fort Wayne, Indiana, after the war. (Originally, he had wanted to call the team the Fort Wayne Zollners—an act of egotism even George Steinbrenner hasn't considered—but the league prevailed against him.) The squad had several good players and one great one—its

center, Bob Lanier—but the team wasn't a champion and often even failed to qualify for the play-offs. They played in Cobo Hall, an unattractive location in downtown Detroit, and commanded an average audience of eight thousand fans, two thousand fewer than they needed to break even for a night. When some garment manufacturers asked Zollner to sell the team to them, he said the price was 5 million dollars. They considered the figure ridiculously high and waited for Zollner to come down. Instead, several months later, the NBA sold a newly created franchise in New Orleans for 6 million. Zollner raised his price from the steep 5 million to a soaring 7 million and promptly found a group of investors willing to pay it.

4. In 1967 a group of young businessmen decided to take advantage of the game's popularity. They founded another professional league, calling it the American Basketball Association (ABA). Their goal was to force a merger with the NBA and realize large profits on originally small investments. They competed for top stars, making the salaries of athletes in both leagues rise, and within three years the NBA sued for peace. But during the sixties the players had founded a union, the National Basketball Players Association; this organization opposed the merger, charging the leagues with violations of the antitrust law. For six years the three sides maneuvered to gain their own interests. Finally the court arranged a truce. The NBA paid 4.3 million dollars in damages to the players and approximately 1 million for court costs; they also granted the players certain contractual rights. At the cost of about 16 million dollars, four ABA teams joined the NBA, and the NBA emerged as the sole major professional league in the country, the emperor of the sport.

II. Organization

1. These fortunes are produced by competitive contests performed by teams of skilled athletes. The teams are called franchises; the organization managing the collective body of the individual franchises is the league. If someone wants to own a team, he buys a franchise; for a large sum of money, the league grants him the right to share in their distribution of players, play against other teams, participate in their play-offs, and keep a

percentage of any subsidiary income such as television money; in exchange for these privileges, the buyer agrees to abide by the league's rules, or constitution. The same type of organization exists on all levels of the game—high school, college, semi-professional —the only difference being the amount of money a team costs and earns.

2. The franchise is limited to a geographical area and is comprised of the players and the people responsible for presenting the contests. Trainers, scouts, equipment managers, ball boys and team physicians help the athletes to prepare for games. Press relations people, secretaries, the team comptroller, ticket managers, announcers and advertising executives work to make sure people attend the games; they do everything from distributing schedules and posters to staging half-time shows to running summer camps where the players are the coaches.

3. Only the coaches, general managers and owners combine both these functions in their duties. Usually they divide responsibilities among them. Many coaches don't like to negotiate contracts with players, because they feel their behavior in the bargaining session might undercut their command of the athlete on the court. General managers refuse to criticize the work of their coaches. Occasionally, though, one assumes the duties of the other. In 1970 Eddie Donovan, the general manager of the New York Knickerbockers, joined the new Buffalo franchise; and Red Holzman, coach of the Knicks, filled his place. Similarly, a general manager is sometimes appointed coach when the commander of the team fails to perform satisfactorily. Generally, one man can't discharge these double duties successfully; after several years of Holzman's rule, the team had lost valuable players without gaining new ones. The dreams of glory imagined by general managers when they first become coaches usually turn into nightmares of defeat.

4. In any situation, neither general managers nor coaches are successful without a command of both the business and the sport. Pat Williams, the general manager of the Philadelphia 76ers, is famous for his ingenious promotional campaigns, but he wouldn't keep his job without signing major athletic talents; and Al Attles, the coach of the Golden State Warriors, led his team to a

championship through a series of clever business decisions. Ineptitude in either sphere of activity dooms a coach or general manager to failure, turning him into a juggler who catches only one ball. Clair Bee was a living legend as a college coach; as a professional he invested in a hopeless team and lost a small fortune. Roy Boe, the owner of the New Jersey Nets, made millions as a shirt manufacturer, but his capricious attitude toward his team impoverished his franchise's value. Even geniuses can foul up. Paul Silas was a forward for the Boston Celtics, and his talents had been shaped to fit the team's needs perfectly. When he demanded a larger salary, Red Auerbach, master coach and brilliant general manager, refused the request. Auerbach peevishly traded Silas, and with the loss of the player the team started to fall apart. Players must enjoy a good business sense also, taking care not to sell themselves too cheaply or price their services too high. After selling Julius Erving, the Nets ballyhooed a guard named Bubbles Hawkins whom they had signed in mid-season; they even devoted a promotional night to him, handing out bubble blowers to the audience. The team's executives never considered Hawkins more than a decent substitute, but they didn't tell Hawkins this, figuring that the knowledge would destroy his performances; as a result, he believed himself invaluable to the team. The next season he demanded a large salary. The team balked; Hawkins held out. The team picked up some other guards eager for even minimum contracts, and Hawkins's career as the team's star was finished.

5. The league watches over the activities of the individual teams. It manages their collective business—hiring referees, negotiating television contracts, bargaining with the Players Association—and arbitrates conflicts between teams. Its titular head is the commissioner, presently Larry O'Brien, the old Democratic Party politician who, it is rumored, sees the position as a stepping-stone to an eventual appointment as a Federal Commissioner of Sports. The commissioner is presumably the chief executive of the business. His actual power is debatable, and although the league office publicly tries to present itself as an independent body, it makes no unilateral decisions. The commissioner's actions are overseen by the Board of Governors,

the congress of owners that meets several times each year, and the owners can fire him when they please. O'Brien is credited with leading the league to an era of industrial peace, but one league official stated that the merger would never have been approved without a committee of owners convincing their colleagues of the deal's merits. O'Brien—and people throughout the league—evidently disapproved of the sale of Julius Erving to the 76ers but kept quiet during the transaction, and league officials voice private criticisms of Bowie Kuhn, the baseball commissioner who has recently gained fame by interfering with deals between teams: basketball owners, league officials say, wouldn't tolerate such behavior. Sometimes the owners themselves are so at odds with one another that the league office claims power by default, and, as the representative of all the teams, it occasionally keeps the parts from murdering the whole. The commissioner penalized New York and Atlanta for breaking league rules, saving several franchises from embarking on a fratricidal legal conflict. But league officials more frequently describe their employers' relationship to them as a sort of benign neglect—occasionally, teams even forget to notify the league of game scores. One league official searched his memory for some contact with an owner; all he came up with was a telephone call from Fritz Dixon, the multi-millionaire new owner of the Philadelphia 76ers. Dixon had contacted the league to suggest that it commission a new trophy for the national championship.

III. Basketball as a Hierarchy

1. Every aspect of the basketball business is organized hierarchically. On the team there are rookies, subs, starters and stars; the front office is ruled by a chain of command that runs from the lowly secretary to the omnipotent owner; and decisions that affect the entire business must theoretically pass the examinations of the individual team, the commissioner's office and the Board of Governors.

2. In all of these hierarchies, money indicates station. A star earns more than a rookie; an owner possesses more wealth than a general manager. The television contract for the NBA is worth more than the one for college ball, and tickets for a championship

college contest cost more than those for front-row seats at a high school game. The rank to which one is appointed is a reward for excellence and signifies one's power. Stars' past performances earn them the right to determine the play of their team, and the same logic presumably applies to owners, even if they made their fortune in real estate and know nothing about the game they finance.

3. Similarly, there are different levels of play. High school ball lies at the bottom of the slope, underneath the high plateau of college competition, a steep incline that climbs from NCAA Division III schools to the western junior colleges to the high commanding ground of the big state universities—UCLA, Michigan, North Carolina. Above them all stands the summit of achievement, the NBA, an Everest surrounded by the lesser heights of the game—the semi-professional leagues that pay players one hundred dollars a night and provide entertainment in out-of-the-way towns; the industrial leagues bankrolled by companies; the European franchises where a player can earn an honest living, and the ubiquitous summer leagues which provide a home for players exiled from the fame, glamour and money at the top.

4. For fans, these distinctions help order the experience of watching games. Educated viewers are gourmets who enjoy a wide variety of tastes, but most spectators can't judge the contests they watch. They can't tell whether a match between two doormats of the NBA demonstrates a better quality of performance than one between two college teams. They know only their feelings; the game left them bored, irritated, thrilled, confused. The labels attached to performers or teams give the fans a standard by which they can judge what they see and make an instant drama out of an otherwise routine event. They can say a team "let down" or another "played above its game," and the anticipation of watching masters provides an additional excitement to a contest: Will Houston and Elvin Hayes beat UCLA and Kareem Abdul-Jabbar? Will Bill Walton and the world champion Portland Trailblazers triumph over Julius Erving and the all-star Philadelphia 76ers?

5. Professional basketball especially needs this attraction, because the primary reason people attend these games is to

experience the thrill of the contest. The football team in Tampa, Florida, continued to lure fans even though it had lost twenty consecutive games. People go to baseball parks not only to watch great pitchers and hitters, but also because the tickets are cheap, the air is warm, and the kids can buy peanuts and popcorn and crackerjacks. Alumni and students support their college basketball teams; and for many the games are a social outing and spectacle, complete with a big band, cheerleaders, and the inevitable fraternity pranksters. Hockey fans are addicts and get high off any junk. But professional basketball enjoys none of these margins. Badly played professional basketball games are uniquely dispiriting events; the arenas are claustrophobic barns, the tickets too expensive, the 7:30 tip-off time inconvenient. Even when the Boston Celtics were a masterpiece, during the sixties, you could buy seats for play-off games at the Boston Garden just hours before the contest began; and the average audience for the New York Knickerbockers fell by several thousand just a season after the team failed to post a winning record.

6. Professional basketball tries to overcome these limitations with two enticements. The first is individual talent. Undeveloped teams in particular use this ploy. When Kansas City hadn't a chance of posting a winning season, Coach Bob Cousy decided to highlight the play-making and scoring talents of Nate Archibald; when a franchise began in New Orleans, the team, the New Orleans Jazz, featured the exploits of Pete Maravich, a local favorite who had played at Louisiana State University. Before Philadelphia became a powerhouse, it suffered through several dreadful losing seasons and offered to trade George McGinnis and a good shooting guard, Fred ("Mad Dog") Carter, for the sole services of Earl Monroe and a first-round draft choice. Monroe's considerable abilities wouldn't have helped to build the team for the future, but he would have won them a respectable number of games; and, most importantly, his name was a box-office draw in Philly because he grew up there.

7. The attraction of these individual stars, however, quickly loses its power. The feat of putting a basketball through a hoop, no matter how acrobatically it's performed, simply lacks the drama of hitting a home run or catching a touchdown pass. The thrill that

ensures continued fan support is the promise of competition between evenly matched teams. Indeed, without exciting collective talent, leagues can't sustain themselves. There were lots of reasons why fans didn't regularly attend the New York Nets' games at the Nassau Coliseum when Julius Erving led the team—including an antipathy among the largely white local population for a predominantly black team. The main one, however, was that other ABA teams simply didn't provide the Nets with sufficient challenge to persuade fans to pay eight dollars a ticket on forty-odd nights of the year.

8. Basketball men call the need to present tight contests "competitive balance." The main mechanism they use to preserve competitive balance is the college draft. At the end of each season, each team selects several college players who are leaving their schools and claims the right to sign contracts with these athletes. The athletes, of course, have the option to refuse the offers; but they can only negotiate with the franchise that has selected them. The team with the worst record picks first, getting the cream of the crop and presumably enjoying the maximum opportunity to improve their future prospects. Sometimes the device works: Milwaukee won only twenty-seven games in the '68–'69 season and took Kareem Abdul-Jabbar as their first-round draft choice at the end of the year; they triumphed in fifty-six games the next season and twelve months later became national champions. Frequently it doesn't work, poor teams staying poor while rich ones thrive. Most players consider competitive balance a mere blind. For them the draft, and the other machinery created to maintain competitive balance, serves another purpose altogether: it keeps their salaries down.

9. But even if all professional teams were evenly matched, fans still wouldn't attend games regularly unless they believed they were watching something special, an entertainment they couldn't see elsewhere, superior performances worth the costly tickets. For many years, professional basketball didn't enjoy this preeminence. People considered college ball better than the professional variety of the sport, and although players just as skilled as today's performed in paid competitions, their displays didn't attract regular fans. Nowadays, people consider professional ball the

highest expression of the game; this notion is so widespread that it has become an assumption. Many fans prefer to watch college games, and some even enjoy high school contests best of all; but common opinion holds that the professional players have mastered the most demanding form of the sport. Occasionally, some college coaches complain about the professional rules; but in practice they follow the NBA's lead, emphasizing speed, strength, and scoring in contests, and, like the pros, they highlight individual stars.

IV. The Pyramid of Success

1. The general theory justifying the hierarchy of money and quality is that fortune rewards excellence and money accompanies mastery. Certainly the men who helped transform the game into a financial success believe their prosperous condition is well deserved, the result of courage, foresight and ingenuity. The stories they tell of their good fortune are unique in the world of team sports. Each part of the entertainment industry converts its quest for riches into a moral tale—the competitive striving of ballet, the open road of the circus, the gambles of Broadway. Sports manage this same trick. People imagine the baseball business to be a pastoral romance; football is pictured as a spartan one. Basketball makes an obeisance to these popular American ideals; throughout the history of the game, there has existed a minor, but powerful, tradition of straitlaced Puritan fellows from the Midwest who strive for sound bodies and Christian souls—Naismith's descendants. The classic example of the strain is John Wooden, ex-coach of the UCLA basketball team, who led his squads to ten national championships and is considered by many to be the greatest coach in the sport's history. In the sixties, UCLA won so consistently that people tuned in games just to see if a miracle would strike and the wonder team would lose. Wooden's great genius was for recognizing talent—his winning record wouldn't have been so spectacular without Gail Goodrich, Walt Hazzard, Kareem Abdul-Jabbar, Curtis Rowe, Sidney Wicks and Bill Walton on his teams—but he acted as though his self-effacing manner and homely pieties were responsible for his success. He invented a diagram called the Pyramid of Success, a triangle comprised of building blocks representing different personal

qualities such as loyalty and self-control, each square containing an aphoristic definition. Presumably these qualities were reflected in his on-court instructions. He was famous for inventing the full-court zone press, an athletic representation of religious diligence and discipline; and he never countenanced flashy behind-the-back passes: to him, they always proved the wisdom of the maxim that pride goeth before a fall. His role as a minister to the body and mind was remarkably consistent throughout his career, and his example has even influenced coaches in the professional game. Dick Motta, ex-coach of the Chicago Bulls and presently of Washington, is a short, intense native of Wyoming who was raised in a stern impoverished Mormon household. For him, as for Wooden, the game is almost a religious exercise; and he says he prays before every contest, asking God to help the team perform to the best of its ability and entertain the audience.

2. But these types are rare in the sport. Basketball is the unique sport of urban America, and the heroes who have truly stamped its character are peculiar to the myths of immigrant city life, not the fables of Indiana pastures. The game is the vaudeville of professional athletics, the business of *gonifs* out to make a buck. Its managers are distinctly ethnic types—one of the first professional teams called itself the Buffalo Germans—and the game's roll call of great men reads like a graph charting the flow of immigrants to the country's large industrial cities: Jews, Irishmen, Italians, and, presently, young blacks whose families came north at the end of the Second World War.

3. In this community, the heroes are men such as Abe Saperstein and Red Auerbach, self-made figures whose knowledge of the game made them rich. Saperstein, the son of a London tailor, grew up in Chicago. Too small ever to realize his own athletic ambitions, he worked at a neighborhood athletic center, coaching one of the city's all-black teams, and attempted to showcase his squad in a newly opened nightclub on game-and-dance nights. He failed but tried another scheme: he scheduled his players to perform in small midwestern towns, billing them as the Harlem Globetrotters to let everyone know they featured an all-black cast. By the forties, his act was the most famous basketball team in the world, and Saperstein was a millionaire. Auerbach was also short,

also the son of an immigrant—this one a dry cleaner. He was a better athlete than Saperstein, but couldn't make the grade either. After the war, he landed a job as the coach of the Washington Capitols, one of the teams in the league that later became the NBA. He won lots of games, fought with his bosses, and in 1950 negotiated for a position as coach of the Boston Celtics, a team that was losing an inordinate amount of money. "If you don't get us a winner, you won't be in Boston next year, because there won't be a team here," his boss told him. All right, said Auerbach, and signed a contract guaranteeing him ten thousand dollars and a share of the profits for one year. He wheeled and dealed for players, argued with referees, by a stroke of fortune captured Bob Cousy, and in 1956 risked his future by trading two proven stars for an untested college center named Bill Russell. The Celtics won the national championship, missing the prize only once again in the next decade. In 1966 Auerbach retired, the greatest professional coach of the game, part-owner of the club, a millionaire. Like Saperstein, he was the success story of the urban working class, a penniless Jew (or Irish or Italian) who made it big.

4. The myths such men made of their lives differ from those created by people like Wooden. If Charlie Finley hadn't existed, baseball would have had to invent him—his cynical business maneuvers make the other owners look like paragons of virtue. But John Wooden is the anomaly in basketball, the man privileged enough to worry about something other than the dollar. Auerbach and Saperstein can't enjoy the luxury of such margins. "A huddle," Auerbach writes, "is a one-minute summit conference when a coach and his athletes get together to talk about the way they're making a living." They are aliens, isolated by their desire for power, their heritage denying them social success, their ambitions obliterating their heritage. For them, the peaceful Sunday outing at the ballpark, the demanding combat of the football field are ideals coined by satisfied people, the prosperous farmers of the Midwest, the golden-haired boys of the Ivy League. Their romance, the romance of the game they created, is the only one poor people can afford, the conquest of money. Certainly they try to invest meaning into this struggle, puffing it up with the values of comradeship, integrity and bravery, shaping it into their own

moralistic pyramids of success, like Wooden, making a mystery out of their fortune, turning the betrayals and compromises of their careers into an allegory entitled Virtue Rewarded. Who doesn't want to feel good about his social triumphs? Still, in basketball at least, history proves them wrong. The men who made the sport into a business didn't win fortunes by traveling the path of merit; rather they achieved their successes by following one route: the track of the dollar. The power of riches and the desire for wealth shaped the career of their enterprise, and the magnetic influence money exerted on the game can be seen in the two formative events of basketball's development as a business—the college scandal of 1951 and the struggle over merger that ended in 1976.

V. The Scandal

1. In February 1951 the New York District Attorney's office, then headed by Frank Hogan, informed Nat Holman, the coach of City College's basketball team, that three of his players were about to be arrested for fixing games. In basketball you don't bet on which team will win; you wager on the margin of points by which a team will triumph or lose. This is called "the spread," and bookies establish one for each game with the intent of collecting as many bets as possible. If a winning squad plays a mediocre team on the favorite's home court, the bookies give the probable victors, say, an eleven-point margin. If you bet with the spread, you wager the favorites will triumph by eleven points or more; if you risk your money the other way, you're figuring that somehow the underdogs will keep the score closer than that. Although this device wasn't invented for the purpose of fixing games, it does allow a team to throw a contest without losing it, and this is what Hogan's office said the CCNY players had been doing. The D.A. claimed that the players had accepted bribes from a man named Salvatore Sollazo, a forty-five-year-old jewelry manufacturer with a long criminal record. Sollazo had bet approximately thirty thousand on each game and almost twice that amount on one. His contact with the players was a young athlete named Eddie Gard, an ex-star of Long Island University's basketball team, which, coached by Clair Bee, was nationally recognized for its excellence. The players involved had received minimal amounts for their services, the sum of all the

bribe money barely equaling the total of just one of Sollazo's bets. Shortly after the first arrests, other players from the CCNY team were also charged, and during the next half-year, athletes were arrested for similar offenses at six other schools: Bradley, Toledo and Kentucky in the Midwest, and Long Island University, New York University and Manhattan in the East. Eventually four players were sentenced to jail for up to a year, and Sollazo was punished with eight to sixteen years in the state penitentiary. In total, thirty-two players were implicated in Hogan's investigation, and eighty-six games held between 1947 and 1950 were proven to have been fixed; the facts suggested that these figures were but a part of the actual sum.

2. These revelations caused one of the worst traumas in the history of American sports. Like Watergate, they were a public drama and followed a turbulent course, erupting again just when they finally seemed to have subsided. One terrible incident was the arrest of Floyd Lane, a CCNY player. Lane, who wasn't arrested with the first three offenders, gave a public speech defending the team at a mass rally on the CCNY campus. An attractive fellow, he became a hero overnight and led his depleted squad to a victory in Madison Square Garden several nights later. Five days after that, the police arrested him, too. The mighty also suffered. Upon hearing of the first arrests, Adolf Rupp, the coach of the Kentucky team, said that gamblers couldn't touch his players with a ten-foot pole. Several months later, players from his team pleaded guilty to throwing games, including one in a tournament for the national championship. Rupp promptly changed his attitude. He compared the events to the 1919 fixing of the World Series and said, "The Chicago Black Sox threw games, but these kids only shaved points."

3. Stories like these aroused the public imagination, and the scandal took on the form of a morality play. The *New York Post* even ran a poll to see how people felt the players should be punished. In a year filled with ugly pageants—the Rosenberg trial, MacArthur's man-on-horseback return to America, the Hollywood witch hunt conducted by the House Un-American Activities Committee, the Kefauver investigation of organized crime—the basketball scandal remained top news. It provided the public with

a subject for outrage, and inspired editorials that sounded every chord of American social relations—urban low-life versus small-town morality, black versus white, youth versus experience, the values of education versus material success. It was alternately considered an attack on American virtue by mobsters, a vengeful display of anti-black and anti-Jewish sentiment, a condemnation of commercialism in amateur athletics, a proof that democracy acts justly. Its only tangible effects were on its participants: it ruined the players, wrecking their careers; and blessed the business, turning professional basketball into an established sport and allowing the collegiate game to develop into a financially successful national institution.

4. This double coup was achieved by the upsetting of New York's long preeminence in the world of college basketball. Soon after its invention, basketball left its eastern home and settled the West. In 1906 the University of Texas won a string of forty-four games—a record only broken more than fifty years later by UCLA—and the national champions of the game during those early years included representatives from every part of the country: Wisconsin, Illinois, Virginia, Oregon and Montana. As early as the twenties, Iowa played games in a new field house that held up to twenty thousand spectators. Still, the game lacked the glamor of a national reputation until 1934, when a sportswriter named Ned Irish arranged a doubleheader at Madison Square Garden. The games were played to a full house, and the next day the New York papers declared college basketball a national attraction. (The same sort of metamorphosis transformed soccer only a few years ago when, after many seasons of playing to a largely empty stadium, the New York Cosmos—the city's representative in the North American Soccer League—suddenly attracted seventy thousand fans to a Sunday game held in Giant Stadium. The crowd stamped the game as publicly approved.) Irish quit his job as a sportswriter, became a professional sports promoter, and for eighteen years was the kingpin of college basketball. Players liked the recognition they received playing at the Garden, and schools enjoyed the large profits from the arena's box office. Irish arranged whole schedules for teams, booking them into arenas in other cities as they traveled east; the climax of their journeys was

always the match in the Garden. In 1938 Irish held the first National Invitational Tournament, the NIT, and until the scandals, this competition provided the country with its annual champion. At the same time, New York basketball flourished; small city schools such as Long Island University and St. John's were producing wondrous court combinations. Their regular games with out-of-town powers were considered premier events, the audiences cheering the locals coached by men such as Nat Holman and Joe Lapchick, who had been stars in their own playing days. After the war, these teams became national powers. The LIU team later implicated in the scandals is still considered by some to be one of the greatest quintets ever to play the game, and the CCNY team in 1950 performed a remarkable feat, winning both the NIT and the tourney conducted by the National Collegiate Athletic Association, a "grand slam" without precedent.

5. The scandal changed all this. When the first arrests were announced, the New York coaches and Irish acted as though the charges concerned only individual cases. But this ruse didn't work. On February 22 the City team played Lafayette in the Garden to a crowd that numbered fewer than eight thousand, and shortly after, City had to cancel the rest of its schedule. The arrests mounted, and the disgrace of cheating stigmatized both the New York schools and the Garden. Irish's power disappeared. The NIT was discredited and performing in the Garden became a source of embarrassment, not pride. Schools from outside the city began to attract the best players produced in New York; the large field houses of state universities became the arenas for the top college contests, and the rule of college basketball came to rest securely in the hands of coaches and physical education departments. The National Collegiate Athletic Association grew to be an increasingly powerful institution, funded substantially by the revenues collected at college games, and its tournament became a celebrated event, earning close to two million dollars net profit in 1975. Already established, college basketball no longer needed New York to help it gather prestige; within twenty years, it bowed only to football as a profit-maker for academic institutions.

6. At the same time, the scandals helped promote professional

basketball. After the war, Max Kase, another sportswriter, had suggested to several owners of arenas located in big cities that they start a major professional league for the sport. Kase was to receive the New York franchise; indeed, he had already selected Nat Holman as his team's coach. But the plan needed the prestige of the Garden to succeed, and Irish refused to let the new league play there unless he owned the New York franchise. For eleven thousand dollars, he bought the rights to the New York team from Kase and started the Knickerbockers, a property now worth more than ten million.*

7. Irish had only a limited interest in the Knicks; he bought the team primarily because he didn't want any competitors. His real profits came from the college games, and throughout their first seasons the Knicks played more frequently at the 167th Armory than at the Garden. A sign of the disparity in the popular appeal of college and professional ball is that games against such otherwise obscure schools as Bradley were sellouts in the Garden, while Irish considered professional matches against the teams from Sheboygan and Waterloo such losers that he refused to suffer the embarrassment of announcing them on the Garden marquee, and held them in the Armory instead. The most dramatic example of the difference is the coverage in the New York press of the 1951 NBA championship series. The Knicks entered the play-offs as decided underdogs, possessing only the third-best record in their division. But they won their first round against Boston and, after matching triumphs with Syracuse in the second tourney, emerged victorious from the decisive game. The Minneapolis Lakers with George Mikan were the usual winners of the Western Conference and the national championship in those days, by Mikan had been injured that season, and Rochester, a fast, clever team that used the talents of Red Holzman, future coach of the Knicks, took the

---

*Irish's maneuvers displeased some of his colleagues in the league. "He knew nothing about basketball," says Haskell Cohen, the NBA publicity director until the sixties, his animus perhaps partly inspired by Irish's reputed anti-Semitic attitudes. "I remember when I first proposed the all-star game. Irish said it would never work. He told me so on the corner of Fiftieth and Eighth Avenue. He ran the Knicks terribly; as soon as they got rid of him, they became champions."

Lakers' place. New York promptly lost the first three games in the best-of-seven series. Then, in a remarkable comeback, the Knicks won the next three contests, running the tourney to its final match. Playing in Rochester, they finally surrendered the rights to the crown. The drama qualifies as one of the classics in New York sports history. Yet none of these games ever reached the front pages of either the austere *New York Times* or the blabbering *New York Post*; none was played at the Garden; and interested readers couldn't even discover the final outcome of the championship match until a full day after the game, when a story finally appeared on the fourth page of the *Times*'s sports section.

8. The scandal was developing when the Knicks entered the play-offs, and the Garden's schedule probably couldn't be changed at such a late date; but even then the public's preference for college ball was changing, and the dollar signs pointed to the professional game. Late in February, after the first CCNY players had been arrested, the Knicks played a game at the Garden and drew a crowd of thirteen thousand; this was nine thousand more than their average audience. During the play-offs, turnaway crowds appeared at the Armory. When the season ended, Maurice Podoloff, the NBA commissioner, announced that the Knicks would play most if not all of their games at the Garden the following year; and Nat Holman, coach of the ravaged CCNY team, told the press that professional basketball was the game's only hope in the city. Other major changes accompanied the NBA's conquest of the country's wealthiest and most powerful city. At the start of the season, the league had rid itself of the smaller midwestern franchises to cut its traveling costs and make its image more respectable; the Boston Celtics had drafted the first black player into the league; the league had staged its first all-star game in Boston only a month before the scandals broke, and it had signed its first television contract, a deal with Channel Five in New York which stipulated that the network would broadcast up to thirteen games for three thousand dollars a contest. It also enjoyed the talents of Bob Cousy—its first great superstar. The only major change still to be effected was the introduction in 1954 of the twenty-four-second clock, the rule ensuring speedy, exciting contests. Other than that, the league

was set to take off as a business, and they blasted into the void created by the scandals in New York.

9. The coincidence of these events—the demise and startling resurrection of college ball and the rise of the professional game—is remarkable, and certain peculiarities of the story suggest that the scandal was a partly manipulated affair. The most suspicious element is its timing. The scandal came to light at the exact moment when professional ball could best take advantage of the revelations. Possibly this was a fortuitous accident, but people from those times insist that long before the scandal actually broke, everyone knew that players were throwing games. During the scandal, Jimmy Cannon, the *New York Post*'s great sportswriter, said that his affection for the sport had ended "when it became a national lottery," and a well-known bookie testified after the scandal that games in the Garden had long been so notorious for being fixed that he never placed a bet on a match held there. And only a month before the first arrests, Stan Isaacs, a sportswriter for the *New York Daily Compass,* had hinted that the LIU team was dumping games. In those days, many college players worked summers at Catskill resorts such as Kutscher's, and Hogan charged that Sollazo had first contacted Gard, his pimp for the players, at one of them. At the time, Haskell Cohen and Red Auerbach managed Kutscher's athletic program, and Cohen claims that they did not hire a single one of the players later charged with accepting bribes; they simply knew which players were on the take. Even if half these claims can be dismissed as hindsight, there remains an impressive body of evidence proving that lots of people in the business knew that games were being fixed.

10. The fact that nobody acted on this knowledge before February 1951 is even more interesting because of the D.A.'s history with the case. Hogan helped build his reputation with the scandals, presenting himself as a remorseless prosecutor. The record indicates otherwise. Several attempted bribes at the Garden had been reported before the scandal started, and Hogan's office had dismissed all but one of these cases. The exception ended with an indictment, but also a statement from an investigator from Hogan's Racket Bureau saying that the incident was an isolated event. A month before the arrests of the CCNY

players, Junius Kellogg, a black player for Manhattan, reported a bribe to Hogan, and two fixers were jailed. Presumably it was this case that spurred the D.A. to seek out the gamblers indicted in the scandals. But even this explanation shows a wrinkle. Shortly after the Kellogg case came into the open, Max Kase, the same sportswriter done out of the Knicks, told Hogan that he knew that games were being fixed; he also said he knew the name of the go-between who had shuttled the players to Sollazo. The story goes that Hogan thanked Kase for the information and asked him to keep it private until he had made some arrests, and Kase agreed. Kase was the first newsman to write the story, a feat for which he won that year's Pulitzer Prize. Kase never said that his informant was a participant in the scandal itself, and presumably he got his information from a disgruntled bookie. There is reason to doubt this tale, but the story can't be discredited, because Kase never identified his source. Still, whoever the source was, he must have supplied Kase with convincing information, more than names or the scores of thrown games. All accounts leave unanswered the question of whether or not Hogan knew Kase's facts before the reporter presented them to him. It's a mystery—or a testament to Hogan's incompetence—how a newspaperman could have amassed information that equaled or surpassed the facts gathered by the D.A. on a case which he was presumably investigating. And if Hogan was preparing the case before Kase came to see him, why did the D.A. need an extra month to begin arrests? Certainly Hogan didn't have facts proving the full scope of the conspiracy when he did make his first arrests; his main source of information was the testimony of the players who implicated others in their confessions. When Kase gave his scoop, it was public knowledge that Hogan was looking into the gambling on college games. Perhaps Kase's source only wanted to perform a favor for his friend and give him the credit for a big story that was about to break; but, given Hogan's track record of never finishing investigations, his almost willful blindness toward a commonly witnessed and talked about affair, it's also possible that Kase's informant gave the reporter the story to make sure that the D.A.'s office would continue its work. The information he handed Kase was an insurance policy against Hogan's rectitude; it assured someone that, with or without Hogan's agreement, there would be a scandal that could wreck the prestige of college ball in New York.

11. Whether or not individuals manipulated the scandals, a natural conspiracy of interests controlled them. In every instance, the charge only affected those without power. A notorious example is that Hogan never indicted players from Catholic schools—the D.A. was a devout Catholic—though it's still widely believed in the trade that members of the St. John's team dumped as many games as the CCNY players. Hogan maintained that Sollazo, the fixer, was an independent, free-floating sort. He never offered proof that Sollazo wasn't connected to the mob, a conclusion that is still prompted by the circumstantial evidence. Sollazo lived in the same building as Frank Costello, used Louis Lepke's lawyer, had been convicted of a series of major felonies, owed the government $1,128,493.37 in back taxes, bet grand amounts of money—once approximately $100,000 within forty-eight hours—and, not the least, inspired such fear in people that even today informants won't talk about his activities because they are scared of reprisals. Fifty percent of the players who served time for their criminal activities were black, although the great majority of the athletes indicted were white, and one of the blacks, Sherman White, a nationally recognized star, was sentenced to a longer imprisonment than five of the men who actually fixed the games. Some assistant coaches were sacked, but no head coaches suffered unduly. Holman was brought up on disciplinary charges by the Board of Education, but he fought and beat them; Clair Bee wrote an article for the *Saturday Evening Post;* Adolf Rupp continued in his position for some twenty-odd more years. There's no suspicion that they were in on the gambling; they made good livings at their jobs, Bee's salary increasing three hundred percent during his tenure at LIU, including an appointment as the school's vice-president. But their innocence was willful; they were family members who refused to recognize an evil or unhappiness residing in their house. Only the poorest schools implicated in the scandals lost future revenues from their teams. CCNY and LIU disbanded their athletic programs, but Kentucky, with a new four-million-dollar gym, didn't interrupt its schedule. Judge Streit, who presided over the case, noted in a statement he read before sentencing the players

that Clair Bee "considered basketball just a business venture," but Bee's profits hardly matched the fortunes earned by the football coaches of big southern and midwestern universities. Streit excoriated the practices by which schools recruited athletes and paid for their services, singling out LIU and Kentucky especially, and the *New York Times* reported that "the scramble among some colleges for athletic victories and big gate receipts has afflicted higher education in the U.S. with several evils having wider implications than the 'dumping' of games by schoolboys, bribed by professional gamblers." These same charges could be lodged against any number of schools today. People didn't stop gambling on college games either. At the height of the scandals, some students pretended to place bets at the Garden during a game, testing the diligence of the police. No one stopped them. Today, the spread for college games appears regularly in the papers, and you can use your credit card to rent a service giving you the latest information on teams, players and the best long shots. The sanctimoniousness of Hogan, the judge, newspaper editorials, and college coaches is appalling. Minnows were caught in the scandals; the sharks swam free.

VI. The Merger

1. The struggle over merger—the war between the leagues —started in the late sixties, when the ABA was formed. At the time, sports were enjoying a boom, and investors tried to cash in on their popularity. The era was the Mississippi Bubble of the athletic world. Spending relatively small amounts of cash, promoters created new leagues which they hoped would eventually merge with already established ones. If the scheme failed, the loss was written off; if it succeeded, properties that had cost little suddenly became valuable franchises.

2. In its past history, the NBA had overcome challenges similar to the one posed by the ABA. Six years earlier, Abe Saperstein had started a new league called the ABL (American Basketball League). Saperstein believed that the NBA had promised him their first West Coast franchise; instead the league awarded it to Bob Short, the owner of the Minneapolis Lakers, who moved his team to Los Angeles. Saperstein hoped his new creation would

cramp the profits of his betrayers, but his instrument of revenge fell apart. Its memorable contributions to the game were some rule changes; hiring the first black coach in professional ball, John McLendon; beginning the first franchise in Hawaii (the travel costs were prohibitive and the site was dropped); and employing Connie Hawkins, the great forward who had been banned from the NBA. (It also let George Steinbrenner, owner of the Cleveland team, enter the world of sports.) But the ABL never enjoyed much chance of success; two years after he had created it, Abe Saperstein was bankrolling the league, and he soon called it quits.

3. The ABA was more determined than the ABL. It relied on more investors than Saperstein's league, and it lived in flusher times, when cities were eager to support new franchises. Its owners convinced George Mikan that he should serve as commissioner, giving the league a public hero. The league also introduced three changes into the game: it allowed teams thirty seconds to shoot the ball, credited baskets shot from more than twenty-five feet with three points rather than two, and played the game using a red, white and blue ball. This ball, Mikan's idea, became the symbol of the league; it is the only campy artifact in the history of the sport, an item conceived in such truly bad taste that people have come to love it.

4. The investors in the ABA always planned to make their fortunes with a merger. During the early days of the upstart league's career, its strategist, Robert Carlson, wrote an article for the *New York Law Forum* saying that the ABA "from the outset . . . conceived and designed a strategy of conflict . . . to force a merger with the NBA." The key elements of the plan were signing players from the NBA (and college superstars) and "a frontal attack on the NBA by an action in which the ABA alleged numerous violations of the anti-trust laws, including a claim that the NBA had unlawfully perpetrated a monopoly on 'super-stars.' " The ABA filed this suit in 1969 and aggressively sought NBA and college stars, signing Rick Barry, Spencer Haywood and Billy Cunningham. Because NBA owners had to bribe their players to stay home, salaries jumped. John Havlicek's earnings went from $15,000 a year in the '62–'63 season to $250,000 in the '72–'73 season. In '68, a year after the ABA had begun its operations, his salary increased

$85,000. Oscar Robertson's fortunes had a similar rise. In 1960 the Big "O" signed a three-year contract for $100,000 and a percentage of the gate receipts; in the '74–'75 season, he received $250,000 plus another $20,000 for the play-offs. These figures are reflected in the median salary for NBA players: $35,000 in '69–'70, $55,000 in '71–'72, and approximately $142,000 at present. Afraid of these rising costs, the NBA owners agreed to discuss merger with the ABA, and by April 9, 1970, the *Washington Post* reported that there was but one "major stumbling block" to consolidating the leagues; the rest was settled. For a cost of eleven million dollars and some superstars, the ABA could join the NBA; during the first three years of the projected merger, the two leagues planned to draft players collectively and follow the same rules, but not share television money. After that, they would operate as one business.

5. The NBA players interrupted this wedding just before the ceremony. On April 16 they filed a court order asking for a temporary restraining order against a merger, alleging that "the defendants [the NBA and the ABA] are combining and conspiring to restrain trade in professional league basketball." The next morning the protagonists battled in court. The players argued that the merger would create a monopoly, illegally restricting their right to sell their services to the highest bidder. The owners answered that basketball wasn't really a business; as NBA commissioner Walter Kennedy later explained to Congress, "I think that all professional sports people would contend that sports isn't a business in the accepted sense of the word. It is an entirely different activity." The Supreme Court had created the precedent for this response, because it had once granted baseball a special status as a business, allowing it to disregard anti-trust measures. The basketball owners referred to this and claimed that the plans for merger were really nothing more than preparations to petition Congress to grant basketball the same exemptions baseball enjoyed. This assertion was pure flummery. On April 18 Ned Irish, a member of the NBA committee negotiating the merger, told the *New York Daily News* that the NBA Board of Governors had passed a resolution favoring merger "several weeks before" and that he believed that the committee's recommended plan would have met with the board's approval. Still, the NBA lawyers said those news

stories were wrong. "I might as well tell your honor right now," one defense attorney argued disarmingly, "and I am sure you know, that newspaper articles rarely have an enormous amount of truth to them, particularly in the sports field." The NBA lawyers insisted that a restraining order would limit the leagues' First Amendment rights to petition Congress for a redress of grievances. The judge couldn't deny this, but he remembered a similar case on which one of the NBA lawyers had served. Two banks had planned to merge; plaintiffs had asked for a temporary restraining order. The lawyers for the banks had stated that their clients merely planned to consolidate, and the judge had refused the injunction. Over the weekend, the banks went ahead with their plans, and it took years to untangle the joint accounts when the action was finally ruled illegal. "Having once been burned, I am twice shy," the judge now declared, and ordered the leagues to remain separate, reserving for them the right to meet and discuss lobbying Congress if they desired. Thinking the decision only a temporary setback, the owners persuaded twenty-six senators to support a bill for merger, telling them that the players also wanted only one professional league. The players retaliated. They told the senators that the owners were liars, lobbied members of the Congressional committee handling the bill, and sought and received the support of the Black Congressional Caucus. By the time the hearings on the bill began, it no longer seemed likely that Congress would ratify the plan of the owners. Senator Ervin chaired the hearings, opening them sternly. "Many years ago," he said, "the term chattel was used to denote the legal status of slaves. That is, they were considered a type of chattel which was used as a piece of furniture or livestock. This use of the term chattel applied to human beings, and the condition it stands for are so abhorrent that we don't even like to acknowledge that they ever existed. Yet in a real sense, that is what these hearings are about—modern peonage and the giant sports trusts." The committee's final bill was thoroughly anti-owner. It allowed a merger, but only with a major re-organization of the basketball industry: it granted the players many contractual rights; prohibited any NBA teams from profiting directly from the merger (indemnity money had to come from television revenues); and, to ensure that professional basketball didn't run college and high school contests off the court, insisted that no professional games held within seventy-five miles of amateur contests could be broadcast on any Tuesday or Friday night after six or on any Saturday from November 1 through March 15. The owners of course wanted no part of this—at least the NBA owners; the ABA jumped at any deal—and for five more years all sides battled in and out of court, a struggle so unexpectedly protracted and costly that some participants compared it to Vietnam. The legal record of the suit is thirty-eight volumes long, a total of two hundred thousand documents and forty-five thousand pages of transcripts; and the fortunes gambled on the outcome were so large that the ABA pledged a $100,000 retainer fee to its lawyer, plus 3 million if he forced a merger within six months, 1.5 million if the goal took him a year, and a paltry $750,000 for any time after that. In the end, the case never came to trial. None of the participants had ever really wanted it to. The courtroom sessions were their equivalent of the Vietnam peace negotiations, attempts to win at the bargaining table what could not be won on the battlefield. When the judge ordered that the case had to be either dropped or adjudicated, all those involved agreed to settle it out of court under his guidance. The players received rights allowing them greater negotiating freedom with the teams and five million dollars in damages from the NBA. For the rest, the agreement didn't differ substantially from the original one that had provoked the court battle. Four ABA teams joined the NBA; the other ABA franchises were dissolved. The new members paid approximately sixteen million dollars in entrance fees, surrendered the rights to some of their league's superstars, and agreed not to share television revenues for the first several years. As a matter of pride, they referred to this unconditional surrender as a merger; the NBA called it an expansion.

6. This struggle produced no heroes. All the actors in the drama considered their roles virtuous ones: the NBA imagined it fought for tradition; the ABA pictured itself as an underdog; the players presented themselves as guerrillas in the battle for civil liberties. Some truth exists in these self-characterizations. The players certainly were misused by owners—they still are—and they did gamble their careers, investments that, unlike the monies invested

by ABA and NBA owners, couldn't be written off on their tax statements. Most owners now are essentially businessmen, many of whom have made their fortunes in real estate or the media, and they're used to negotiating with their workers, however unpleasant the task might seem to them. But the old NBA owners who originally resisted the Players Association and merger really were antediluvian types. When Tommy Heinsohn, then a forward on the Celtics and head of the Players Association, threatened to call a strike at the 1964 All-Star game unless the owners agreed to a pension plan, Walter Brown, the owner of the team, took the demand as a personal betrayal and labeled him "the number one heel in sports." Fred Zollner, the owner of the Detroit Pistons, flatly refused to recognize the Association. "I have no union in my other businesses," Larry Fleischer, the head of the Players Association, says Zollner once told him, "and I'll have none here." Fleischer describes Abe Pollin, the owner of the Washington Bullets, as a self-conceived "great liberal rabbi" and claims Pollin once expressed disbelief when negotiating a point with the Association. "I don't understand you," Fleischer says Pollin complained sincerely. "I'm absolutely convinced that this is fair." Still, the players' revolt was fundamentally a bourgeois revolution; one NBA lawyer called them, not unfairly, "the highest paid enslaved group that ever walked into court," and when the battle was finally joined, the Players Association opted for money, not civil rights. Indeed their legal fight was as much a decoy as the ABA or NBA suits. Their legal assault on the contractual relations between owner and player merely countered the plans for merger: Larry Fleischer says that 1973 "was the best of both worlds for the players," because both leagues were competing heavily for their services, even though the contracts the athletes signed contained the noxious clauses they were protesting in court. And when the final agreements were reached, the Association showed no more sympathy for the athletes on the ABA teams driven out of business than the NBA owners did toward their defeated competitors.

7. The compromised gestures of the players are slight, however, compared to the grand proportions of the owners' cynicism. Some ABA men speak movingly of their struggle with the NBA, coloring their memories with a sort of adolescent glow,

highlighting moments of comradeship, just as old-timers in the NBA relate fond remembrances of their struggle for economic survival. But in the end, men in the ABA betrayed even their most minimal principle of loyalty: to make money together. In the war between the leagues, the signing of superstars was the most important battlefield (the two minor fronts were control of geographical areas and getting television contracts). The signing or losing of important individual talents marked the leagues' journeys toward success, like stops on a board game. In spring 1975 the two college prizes were David Thompson, an acrobatic forward from North Carolina State, and Marvin Webster, a seven-footer from Morgan State, dubbed the "Human Eraser" for his shot-blocking abilities. It seemed that both would play in the NBA, and their loss to the ABA followed another major blow to the red, white and blue league. A few weeks before, the New York Knickerbockers had signed a contract with George McGinnis, a player for the Indiana Pacers and one of the ABA's top superstars. McGinnis's deal with New York fell through, but he remained in the NBA, leaving the ABA with only one national attraction, Julius Erving, and a dim future. Then the Denver ABA franchise announced that it had signed not only the promising Webster but Thompson also, and the league's coming season suddenly appeared brighter. It started some new franchises and renewed attempts to secure a television contract. Now, surely, the ABA men thought, the NBA would come to its senses and sue for peace, and men in the ABA league office even began figuring which NBA divisions ABA teams would play in and planning a new schedule, imagining that a merger was but a month away. Instead, on September 25 Denver and New York unilaterally applied for membership in the NBA. Two of the new ABA franchises collapsed immediately, and a third followed quickly. The thin unity that had bound the owners together broke, and after stumbling through a fratricidal season, the survivors bought their way into the older league.

8. Men who worked in the ABA league office still refer melodramatically to the Denver–New York action; one called it the "most infamous day in the history of basketball." But the betrayal shouldn't have been a surprise. The ABA owners had rarely acted honorably. The case of one ex-ABA owner is an example. Rep-

resenting some millionaires, he bought a franchise for the '74 season. The other ABA owners flimflammed him from the start. The league representatives promised him the services of an NBA superstar who had recently jumped to the ABA, a top college player and a negotiable price of 1.5 million dollars for the team. When the buyer tried to bring the price down, the league officials told him they had to make the deal first; then they would bargain. The buyer agreed. The league officials thereupon reneged on every aspect of the deal. The NBA player, it turned out, was set on returning to his old league; the price for the team was never reduced; and the college player had already been drafted by another ABA team. Since neither the buyer nor the player knew this, the two negotiated a contract, and when the buyer entered his first meeting with the other ABA owners, he was immediately brought up on charges of tampering. His entrepreneurial brothers never did teach him the league rules; they repeatedly tried to force him to sign players they didn't want, and they didn't even have the courtesy to give him a complete constitution of the league. The copy they handed him was outdated, and one page was repeated four times; like a character in a Kafka story, he couldn't have played by the rules even if he had wanted to. The league meetings were "cesspools," the owners of strong franchises merely wanting to soak new investors, and within a year the buyer's sole desire was to leave the league, even if it meant losing some of the millions he had invested in the enterprise.

9. NBA owners refer to such shenanigans as "bush-league," citing them as proof of the ABA's corruption. But no higher morality ruled their behavior. All along they had wanted to run the ABA out of business and maintain their control over players, and the twists and turns of their public positions were only maneuvers to gain these goals. NBA owners told the senators that the players supported a merger when the athletes didn't; the owners argued in court that they had no plans to consolidate the leagues when in fact they did. They constantly disobeyed court orders, trying to drive a wedge between the Players Association and individual athletes, not responding to interrogatories, missing dates on which they were supposed to give depositions. The ABA's lawyer was Frederick Furth, a tall, blond, flashy type from San Francisco who

introduced himself to the judge with the announcement that he was one of the top antitrust barristers in the country; and once he walked into court and asked for a postponement because he was running for office in San Francisco. The NBA lawyers weren't such adventurers, but the difference was a stylistic one. They used every possible legal argument to delay a judgment while their clients wheeled and dealed. The NBA owners, for instance, claimed in court that each franchise was a separate business; yet the owners each contributed to a pool of funds to help pay the salaries of superstars, an insurance policy protecting the league's talents. They publicly discredited the ABA even while negotiating with it—in one instance not even letting ABA players perform in a charity game—and they undoubtedly enticed the Denver and New York owners to help destroy their own league. In the winter of '75, the NBA believed that the players would win their suit if the case came to trial, a possibility that made a merger seem attractive. But in July the judge, who often appeared lost during the legal proceedings, seemed to reverse his stand, allowing the NBA a slight but arguable legal defense. The judge's ruling followed the signing of McGinnis, and shortly thereafter Denver and New York applied for membership. It's hard to believe that representatives from the NBA didn't suggest the sudden move. Carl Scheer, the Denver owner, had long-standing personal ties with NBA men, and he is generally credited with masterminding the maneuver, dragging Roy Boe, owner of the New York team, along behind him. Certainly these two businessmen would have surveyed the NBA's probable response before risking the gamble: if the NBA voted no, they might have been owners of teams without leagues to play in. Scheer denies ever meeting with NBA representatives before applying for ownership in the league, but most queries about a meeting are met with more ambiguous answers. People say that they don't know about such an encounter, not that it never happened. And some witnesses are less circumspect. One general manager of an ex-ABA team said he was "sure" that representatives from Denver and New York had discussed the applications with members of the NBA before filing them, and an owner of an ex-ABA team stated that he had been informed that a meeting of two to six representatives from both leagues had taken place, including Scheer and Joe Axelson, the president and the general manager of the NBA Kansas City Kings.

10. Not surprisingly, these combatants have no kind words for one another, each accusing the other of greed and duplicity. NBA owners call their ABA counterparts pirates and the players ingrates and mercenaries. The ABA players think the NBA players sold them out; the NBA players think the ABA players are scabs and incompetents. The NBA players dislike their owners, and the ABA owners are a nest of vipers so intent on attacking one another that they can barely spare the time to snap at their NBA enemies. They especially revile Angelo Drossos, the owner of the San Antonio Spurs, one of the ABA teams that joined the NBA. Drossos was selected to negotiate the final merger plans with the NBA and carried several suggestions into the meeting. The maximum option was for six ABA teams to join; four was the minimum. Drossos was supposed to fight for the first. Instead, the story goes, he immediately agreed to the second. "He just lay back on the table and spread his legs," one ex-member of the league office says, using the gutter jargon common in the business. And the agreement between the players and the owners met with no greater approval. Fleischer says he had to convince himself to sign it, and Paul Snyder, then the owner of the Buffalo Braves, called it "the worst deal in the history of sports." Yet all this ill-feeling has little effect. In the end, Fleischer did accept the agreement and did get the players to ratify the proposals; and for all the owners' blustering, they also voted affirmatively. The same men who complain about Drossos won't refuse to answer his phone calls. Their moanings are an expression of almost theoretical emotions, the way they would feel if they were something other than businessmen; their complaints have no relation to their actions, because finally money is the only object that commands their mutual respect.

VII.   The Modern Game

1. In a sense, the struggle over merger marked the entrance of basketball into the modern financial world. It helped spread the game even more thoroughly around the country and witnessed the coming to power of new owners, highly paid players and the agents

who represent the stars. But its effects on the basketball contest itself weren't so beneficial. For a variety of reasons, it helped change the game into more of a spectacle than it had ever been. People generally critical of sports believe all fans are simply eager to enjoy sudden vicarious thrills. But pure excitement and spectacular feats are hardly the sum of the common fan's interest. Part of the fan's traditional enjoyment has been observing the slow process by which a team develops—the particular contributions and careers of individual players, the peculiarities of the hometown arena, the history of struggles with specific teams, the entire drama of a franchise's failure or success. During the struggle over merger, this long-standing relationship weakened; the game became a seemingly arbitrary collision of athletic talents in a neutral location, an isolated curious object for marvel and admiration. This was caused, in part, by purely financial factors; for example, players left a team, or a franchise quit a city; and many fans simply didn't and still don't extend the same concern they feel for an underpaid rookie to a player making millions. The change was also partly caused by the kind of athletic talent coming out of the schools: superb individual performers who dominated games, players such as McGinnis, Erving, McAdoo, Thompson, Barry. But overriding these reasons was a general tendency, encouraged by the merger, to promote and present the game as a spectacle.

2. An instance of this is the new schedule used by the league. In the past, one of a season's dramas arose from the contests between teams in the same conference who played each other more frequently than they played teams in different divisions. This schedule meant that a team had to best its immediate competitor, and it allowed squads to develop complicated, enjoyable strategies for beating one another. The teams played as many road games as they do presently, but the trips were shorter, and because the journeys were in the team's geographical neighborhood, squads didn't have to endure the staggering amount of time they now spend in planes. After the merger, the owners chucked this tradition, much to the annoyance of some coaches and general managers. Since '76 every team simply plays the other squads in the league four times a season, regardless of their conference. The reason given for the change was money; the owners believed that

more people would attend games to see individual superstars than to see teams, and what would teams in the Southwest do if Julius Erving graced their arenas only twice a year while appearing four times in Madison Square Garden? Perhaps this is so, though it argues against the owners' claim of competitive balance. Certainly the effects of the schedule aren't questionable. It severely increased the amount of road travel. In the '76 season, Kansas City spent two weeks in planes: on a Sunday they performed in Omaha; on Tuesday they flew to New Orleans, Wednesday to Washington, Thursday back to Missouri to play a home game; and finally they enjoyed one day off before starting another three-day trip from Phoenix to Los Angeles to Portland. The new schedule also diminished the quality of play. In the '76 season, home teams won more than two-thirds of all contests, and in '77 only Portland, the champions, had a winning record on the road. The predominant style of play became a run-and-gun game, the home team, physically more alert than their weary combatants, simply exhausting their competitors; and without previous intimate knowledge of the other team's style of play, squads couldn't organize to defeat their opponents strategically. Individual efforts captured the game.

3. But the most powerful influence that turns the game into a spectacle is television. Television dollars matter to every level of the game; for college teams a contract with a local station can transform the squad into a profit-making enterprise overnight. During its struggle for success, the ABA ranked a national television contract second in importance only to signing superstars. (Men from the league insist that the NBA kept them from getting one at this time. The ABA was negotiating with NBC; Ted Munchak, the ABA man conducting the meetings, told the ABA owners that the network was 99.4 percent committed to a deal. Then NBC suddenly ended the discussions, buying instead the rights to the National Collegiate Athletic Association games—a change of heart, ABA men claim, that was instigated by the NBA. The network was also instrumental in persuading the NBA to accept the four ABA teams into the league; at the last minute, NBA owners balked at the arrangement, but CBS sweetened the pot,

promising them an extra four million if they welcomed the renegade franchises.) The biggest television contract for basketball was CBS's recent multi-year agreement with the NBA to pay the league seventy-nine million dollars for the right to broadcast games regularly from the end of December through the final rounds of the play-offs in early June. Money from CBS is the league's main financial support; without it as many as half the teams in the league might collapse immediately. This influence has been unhealthy. A welfare program for capitalists, it allows franchises to remain in business while fielding continually weak teams, almost encouraging owners not to invest in their squads, since they are ensured a paycheck from the network anyway.*

4. Presentation of the games is part of the CBS sports package, its weekly collection of athletic events. Sports are among television's mainstays, and CBS wanted the NBA because of the success ABC had enjoyed presenting them several years before. The ABC productions are justly famous. At that time the league hosted a number of well-balanced teams, and the play-offs during those years were an almost ritualistic exercise, a drama highlighted by the excellent ABC announcers, including Bill Russell. Presently, the league is more of a mishmash, teams changing in nature seemingly overnight. The way CBS presents the games only adds to this confusion. They care nothing for the particulars of the sport or the slow drama a season creates. For them the games merely fill a slot in the time they allot to sports broadcasts; and while this is an understandable attitude for a television executive to take, it tends to homogenize all sporting events presented on the air. They lose their individual natures, becoming a ceaseless display of individual derring-do and collective hysteria, an

---

*The other part of this welfare system is the tax write-off, a government subsidy provided to owners, allowing for the depreciation of the team they buy. That is, they can subtract a substantial percentage of the total salaries they pay their athletes over the first five years of their ownership. Owners manipulate this allowance to their advantage. One tax lawyer testified that a partnership of two owners, showing a loss from operations of six million dollars, could manipulate write-offs worth about two million dollars cash, an investment realizing a 132.5 percent return averaged over five years.

essentially bland product. Basketball probably enjoys a larger
audience now than ever before, but what these viewers see is a
confusion of bodies and styles beyond normal human understanding. For the network producers, excitement is everything, and
they fill the screen with so many fireworks that the bright colors
cancel one another out. In the last two years, their mania for
busyness has even led them to switching from one contest to
another in the midst of matches, offering the viewer an
inexplicable fifteen seconds of San Antonio versus Golden State
before returning to Buffalo against Portland; by the time the
announcers finish the line-ups, the viewer is watching two entirely
different sets of players. The producers insist on spotlighting stars.
Knowledgeable basketball fans pride themselves on admiring a
team sport in which collective abilities triumph over individual
performances, and they will watch any contest, no matter how
obscure its participants, as long as the game is close. For them the
drama comes from the even balance between teams, a quality not
difficult to explain to a novice, either in the sport generally or in a
particular game. But the television producers, like the owners,
evidently believe it is an insufficient enticement for a large
audience and offer them single stellar talents instead. If the star
doesn't dominate the match, the announcers naturally instruct the
viewers that the other squad's superior teamwork triumphed, but
this caution is merely an afterthought; their constant references are
to the acrobatics of individual performers, not to a team's record,
its collective defensive ability, or its unique use of an athlete's
particular talents. Often their highlighting of individual stars
makes a game anticlimactic, because many superb basketball
players are simply not always exciting to watch. Julius Erving and
George Gervin fly through the air, but a large part of their
greatness is the consistency with which they shoot thoroughly
routine fifteen-foot jump shots. New viewers, anticipating extraordinary feats, wonder why the stars are so prized, and are
even given a cause to complain that the players are "off their game"
and a chance to berate them for not earning their huge salaries.
They're also confused by the seeming irrelevance of single heroic
acts to a game. They're shown Erving dunking the ball five times
on slow motion, but then the Doctor's team loses the game, and the

viewer rightly wonders why the moment was so important. During the '77 championship series, Portland clearly dominated one game. In the middle of the contest, Erving performed an inspired dunk, and the announcer exploded with a babble of words predicting the feat would cause a turnaround. It didn't. Instead, the moment dramatized Philadelphia's reliance on Erving (or Doug Collins) to carry their offense, a strategy causing their eventual failure in the series. The announcers help brew this pot of steaming chaos. Those who work regularly with teams develop relationships with the players and the squad; in their broadcasts they reveal these feelings in their voices and comments, becoming the representatives of the fans absent from the game and letting these viewers experience the athletic contest through their spoken narrative, including moments of boredom, disappointment and frustration. The CBS announcers, on the contrary, enjoy no special feeling for any team; such emotions are prohibited because they would demonstrate favoritism. They experience the game merely as an isolated event, and their commentary mirrors this. They manage to convert any movement on the court into a cause for anxiety, exclaiming that Randy Smith is open under the basket, dramatically whispering that Bobby Jones moves well without the ball. The need they feel to provide drama lifts them to occasionally extraordinary tautological heights: "That's Jimmy McMillian's first point," commented one during a Knick-Washington game broadcast on CBS. "His main ability is scoring, and when he's not scoring it probably means he's not doing what he's best at." Later in the same contest, he offered this analysis after the referees had hit the Washington team with a technical foul. "Well, this may be the thing to fire up the Bullets, or it may give New York the break they need." They use nicknames appallingly—not the special intimate words players call one another, images suggesting their peculiarities or special talents ("Butterbean," "Ack-ack," even "the Dipper"), but clunky dog tags used to identify athletes for the presumably uneducated watching the tube: moody, determined Bill Walton becomes "the mountain man"; the gifted genius of Kareem Abdul-Jabbar is diminished into "the franchise." (Walton was a special target for these pot-shots. "Call it vegetable power," Brent Mussberger, one of the CBS announcers, exclaimed after

Walton dunked a ball in one contest, referring to the center's culinary preferences. Much to his credit, Walton protested the use of these dumdum monikers.) Occasionally their sober neutrality makes them sound like reporters analyzing election returns: "An interesting statistic here, Brent," one informs the other. Words always seem to fail them. "I like to think that the word intensity is used an awful lot on basketball telecasts," one said to the other during a contest. "But not in this game." His partner agreed. "Absolutely not," he replied. "Especially in a game of this magnitude." Their search for instant thrills leads them into a maze of contradictions; within minutes, they tell the viewer to watch Sidney Wicks's "awesome" first step, the team play of the Celtics, and the battle under the boards between Curtis Rowe and Marques Johnson, commenting parenthetically that the last two were both coached by John Wooden, and praising the referees for running a tight game and prohibiting any violence, though their voices indicate that they'd be excited if a fight broke out. Not trusting the eloquence of pictures, they ruin the normally sensitive camerawork of the crew. The viewer watches George Gervin sweating on the bench, his face somber, anxious. Suddenly the announcer's voice pipes up: "There he is, folks. They call him the Ice Man. He's sweating now." The words diminish the image instead of heightening it with additional understanding. The viewer doesn't believe the announcer's excitement, and this suspicion is confirmed by the capricious manner of the broadcast. The game isn't allowed to develop suspense and tension; the strange excitement that commands an arena is lost during the commercial breaks, the constant commentary. Instead of letting the viewer experience the moment in which the coach calls a time-out and the players regroup and plan for victory, the screen is filled with a slow-motion shot of the last basket. Without some hiatus, how can the viewer enjoy the true excitement of the minute, the question of whether the players' meeting will result in failure or success? The broadcasts are so cynically shaped that CBS didn't even go into the locker rooms to share the celebration of the players after the final game of the '77 championship series. Instead, they held those shots for another show and switched to the last minutes of an obscure golf tournament, a mere switch of the camera managing to convert two moments of truth into one meaningless instant.

VIII. Reactions of Fans

1. Fans understandably resent such manipulations of their sport. They gripe about players' salaries and the quality of contests, and owners opportunistically refer to these comments as reasons for paying players less. But these are natural dissatisfactions, part of the pleasure of being a fan; some even take the high salaries of players to mean not that the athletes get paid too well, but rather that they, their admirers, receive too little for their own labor. Indeed, the sadness with which fans now frequently view the game isn't caused by any particular change in the sport. It is rather a reaction to a truth they don't wish to recognize: that basketball is a business, a product ruled by the laws of the marketplace.

2. The reluctance to see basketball—or any sport—as a business is so powerful that even men who make their living from the sport are affected by it. They are amazed when the happy world of comradeship and athletic striving they had imagined they were inhabiting collapses around them and financial decisions affect their lives. The president of a great automobile company doesn't explain unpopular management decisions by answering that his company is a business. That truth is self-evident, so he finds other dodges, such as rates of profit, labor troubles or vanishing markets. But people in basketball always ask who's there when money knocks on the door. A local favorite is traded—well, he says, I didn't want to go, but, you know, sports is a business. A franchise moves to another city—well, says the general manager, we just couldn't attract enough fans and, you know, sports is a business. An arena announces a rise in ticket prices—well, says the owner, you know, sports is a business. Not since Sherman's "War is hell" has such a simple declarative sentence been employed to explain so many complicated, unpleasant deeds. Deep down, people simply don't believe that sports is a business; they consider it a fraternity, a calling, an institution; and they pursue this illusion until events they experience personally deny it. Even the detailed knowledge possessed by many fans about the business of sports doesn't

convince them. People know a lot about sports, partly because they read the sports page with the regularity of a broker studying the business section. But sports are also reported in greater detail than other businesses, especially other elements of the entertainment industry. In the past, sports pages limited their news to reports of athletic performances; now they normally include items concerning contracts, disputes among management, television ratings, and the personalities of owners. A sample of stories from the past weeks includes an analysis of a secret funding agreement between the new owners of the Boston Red Sox and a local bank; endless speculations over the sale of the Oakland A's, including demographic studies of the Bay Area; the hiring of Sonny Werblin to head Madison Square Garden Corporation; a contractual dispute between Brian Taylor and the Denver Nuggets; and a Congressional investigation of the National Collegiate Athletic Association. The mechanisms that run the business are second-hand knowledge to a large audience. Ask a plumber whether or not Simon and Schuster should pay a hundred-thousand-dollar advance for a sequel to *Looking for Mr. Goodbar* (guaranteed movie sale, hard-soft distribution), and he'll hem and haw, wondering what you're talking about; the same man will give you an instant opinion on whether or not Milwaukee got rooked when it traded Kareem Adbul-Jabbar for six rookies. If all the moviegoers in America studied *Variety,* their knowledge of Hollywood might begin to approximate the vast scope of facts and figures sports fans possess about the objects of their devotion.

3. Much of this information fans simply don't see as the mundane profit and loss calculations they truly are; the facts come wrapped in the tinsel of professionalism and entertainment lore, scenes from fairy tales. The awards presented at the season's end—Most Valuable Player, in the All-Star team—are the league's Oscars, the endless struggle to field a winning squad, the glorious toil of producing a box-office smash. The spoofing puns on the sports pages—McAdoo? or McAdon't? asked one—are the bizarre headlines in *Variety.* "Bankable" stars become "franchise" players, performers so skilled and popular that their presence alone ensures crowds at the gate. The hundreds of unpleasant but funny stories about the hard-nosed movie moguls of the past, such as Jack

Warner and Harry Cohn, are the many tales of the league's early *machers*—Red Auerbach, Abe Saperstein, Eddie Gottlieb, Ben Kerner, Walter Brown—fables good for laughs, though the listener is thankful not to be part of them. Even the myths are similar. The old actor, past his prime, returns for a command performance. The star battles through a personal tragedy and reclaims fame. The girl in the chorus line replaces the leading lady and becomes an overnight hit. In basketball, these heroes are John Havlicek beating the Phoenix Suns for the NBA championship at age thirty-six, Connie Hawkins banned from the league for a crime he didn't commit and finally recognized as a superstar, Randy Smith drafted by Buffalo on the seventh round and now one of the sport's great guards. Rich with money, talent, greed and desire, sports provides popular exemplary tales, and its business details encourage fantasy, not betray it.

4. But the fundamental reason fans resist seeing basketball (and other sports) as a business is that they don't want to know that the game is a profit-making venture. They view the increasingly public, nasty details of the financial and managerial activities of the game as a kind of betrayal. They want to keep basketball out of the world they inhabit, away from dollars and cents, interoffice memos, unfair promotions, unions, lawsuits and unrequited loyalties. For them, basketball and sports present an idealized mirror of the world, a standard by which one can measure one's behavior and worth. It's a source of comradeship and courage one can't find elsewhere, and it supplies moral precepts and examples for their daily encounters—someone is a money player, a choker or a team man. They like to identify with the progress of players and teams because in some way they see their own development reflected in these contests. The competitions on the court make heroic the successes and failures of their own lives, and provide a poetic mode to describe the social relations, work, and needs that rule their days. The quest for money alone—the search that describes the game—can't do this, and the recognition that money, whether the dollars of gamblers or of CBS, controls the game destroys the illusion. It denies fans one of the great gifts of sports, the possibility of picturing our lives as a romance, even the immigrant romance of money. Instead, it presents our lives in an

unpleasant fashion, shattering what was once a golden mirror and reflecting back to us a world of sordid motives and compromised decisions, the commonplace, unheroic, self-interested, brutal life captured in the phrase spoken daily that basketball—this inspiration, this source of joy, this arena of beauty—is "just a business."

4. Shooting

Shooting is basketball's unique invention, and is the breath of the game. A ball falls through the net, and the players halt, becoming momentary statues while one forward glides past the basketball, his empty hands opened wide. A rookie savors the second, holding his shooting hand motionless, wrist bent, palm flat, the stretched fingers forming a broken curve, an exaggerated, harmlessly vain gesture pointing toward the basket, a still photo of success. An old-timer checks the court immediately; he has just scored his 8,280th point, and where is the man he must guard? The crowd cheers and the tableau comes to life—the ref bouncing the ball once and tossing it to a player waiting out-of-bounds, the men running downcourt, the shooter trotting toward his own territory. "You, you," he gestures, pointing his finger at the man who passed him the ball, and another teammate salutes him with a clenched fist while passing him on the run. In a few moments, their opponents will be celebrating.

Putting the ball into the basket is a theme with endless variation. When I was in the fourth grade, my favorite player was Bob Cousy. He heaved the ball from mid-court at the game's end, a gesture immortalized in photos: the little man pauses in air, one leg straight, the other bent at the knee, a racehorse leaping, the arm preparing to chuck the oversized beach ball fifty feet. Our court was the school gym; our referee was Mr. O'Brien, an affable giant who taught sixth grade, cursed out loud—a habit that won him my affection—and kidded us when we complained about our teachers. He had played in college and occasionally coached us, instructing us to shoot only two-handed set shots, the stylish version of the way children naturally toss the ball. "Jesus Christ," he shouted every time one of us threw up Cousy's shot, "you've gotta have brains in your ass to shoot like that! Don't ever take that shot!" His admonition was useless; even six years later, we periodically returned to our old gym and irked Mr. O'Brien with our capricious tosses. "You guys are totally undisciplined; you don't know how to play ball," he dismissed us. I'm sure he tells the same thing to his current students when they practice the game's present styles: a Julius Erving slam-dunk from the foul line or DT's (David Thompson's) jump shot, three feet in the air and thirty-nine-inch arms stretched to heaven.

The development of shooting is a triumph of individual style over subject matter, because scoring in basketball is an essentially undignified act. Physically, it requires neither great strength nor coordination. You stand squarely toward the basket, your fingers firmly stretched over the ball, resting comfortably on the rubber's grooved seams. You raise your arms, aim to put the ball over the bucket's front rim, and release it, the three-fingered web of your thumb, index and middle fingers steadying, pushing and guiding the ball's flight into the basket.

The object you shoot, the basketball, is an inescapably absurd figure. The hardball, Roger Angell writes, is designed perfectly to be thrown; a football's appearance shows that its nature is to be kicked, caught and safely tucked away; the soccer ball is a classic sphere of handsome patched leather, and even the pelote in jai-alai claims centuries of tradition. Compared to these distinguished relatives, the basketball is a cumbersome mutant. It inherits its pebbled skin from the original pigskin models and its seams from the soccer ball. It wears garish colors—yellow, bright tan, even red, white and blue—and its history is a joke: its middle-age crisis concerned whether it should be sewn together or molded into one piece. For an object created solely to be thrown and caught, its dimensions are vast: a portly thirty-inch belly, a weight of twenty-two ounces, and an athletic bounce of not less than forty-eight inches when dropped from a height of six feet. Unlike its legitimate brothers, the basketball commands neither fear nor respect. Accidentally hit someone in the head with a hardball and the victim suffers a concussion; bounce a basketball off a player's skull and you're part of a vaudeville act. Clumsy, wide of girth, foolishly predictable, the basketball announces its nature with the immediacy of a stereotyped Dickens character: it exists for play.

When you're young, the basketball challenges you. Your hands can't grasp it, and you're too short to dribble it through your legs. You must shoot it using both hands, and your entire body lurches forward at the strain. The ball seems to enjoy pestering you. It slams off the backboard and bounces beyond your reach or rolls playfully downhill, where you must trudge to retrieve it. Often you spend more time chasing it around the playground than watching it fall through the hoop. When you're older, the basketball becomes an object of pleasure and derision and the more skill you enjoy as a player, the more contemptuously you treat it. Players palm it; dunk it; slap it around; toss, throw, chuck it; spin it on one finger; roll it over their shoulders, up their arms, down their legs; and kick it into the stands. They slam it against the backboard and push it through the hoop, bounce it high and stuff it over their heads, dribble it behind their backs and through their legs, and make it perform every conceivable trick, humiliating it unrelentingly and proving to this rotund nemesis of their youth that they are its masters, not its slaves, and can make it (literally) jump through hoops.

This ease and playfulness in scoring contributes to basketball's popularity and low estate. When a small guard scores with a jumper from the side, my father calls it a miracle. When a giant dunks the ball, he complains that the basket should be higher. His attitude of alternating awe and disrespect is typical. Most kids playing sports still imagine careers as shooters when they have already surrendered their desires to throw touchdown passes or regularly hit the ball beyond the park fence; and, because anyone can throw the ball once into the basket without trying, the shooter and his skill attract a mix of contempt and esteem from their fans. Practicing an art everyone believes is distributed democratically, the shooter suffers the fate of writers: everyone believes he could become one. Not one of my friends—teachers, lawyers, therapists, magazine editors, Hollywood agents, photographers, political organizers—doubts his or her ability to sit right down and write a novel, but none of them imagines he or she could paint a mural. Literature excites and moves them more than any other art, and, perhaps consequently, they also believe deep down that, essentially, writing is easy. They believe writers lack unique talents and consider authors unduly privileged, whiners and pests. Most fans hold similar opinions of shooters.

With their exorbitant salaries, all athletes, of course, have become objects of resentment for fans, but high scorers in basketball, such as Walt Frazier, Sidney Wicks, Nate Archibald, Phil Smith and Kareem Abdul-Jabbar, occupy a special villains' niche in this hall of antipathy because of the game's peculiar nature. In other sports, scoring is the mark of triumph and, appropriately, the goal is hard-won; a home run is always a wonder, and a touchdown is either a miracle of speed and cunning or a victory of brutal determination. The harder the labor, the bigger the goal, and the winner deserves the trophy because he or she has endured more difficulties than his opponent, a Protestant ethic for the playground. The fan's quintessential hero is a hustler, an athlete presumably without talent who fights his way to championships with determination and guts.

From the time basketball became a popular sport, it countered this romantic notion, because scoring is simple in this game. Most great athletes are physical geniuses—their bodies are different from ours; they possess greater strength, speed, coordination, stamina—and basketball irrepressibly announces this truth. Commentators, of course, like to speak of the game's physical abuse, and a few baskets are won in any contest because of sheer force, but in general basketball awards its goals to mastery and style—consistency, range, adaptable grace, intelligence. If you possess these virtues, the game rewards you with points; without them, you finish a contest frustrated and annoyed, not understanding why the smaller guy won against you; and if the spectator doesn't appreciate these talents or the game does not evidence them, the sport ultimately becomes a boring and insipid spectacle.

Many crusty fans don't like admitting this truth about the game; they love it, but have been taught to revere the Puritan attitudes of other sports and seek to nurture them in basketball, singling out for special praise their favorite team's version of the presumably untalented, hustling ballplayer (usually white, coincidentally) whose luster doesn't claim the attention commanded by brighter stars. Steve Mix plays forward alongside George McGinnis and ulius Erving for the Philadelphia 76ers. McGinnis and Erving receive millionaires' salaries, and the team would win considerably fewer games each season without their formidable talents. Mix struggled to get hired—for three summers he wrote teams innumerable letters asking permission to attend their tryout camps, and worked winters in the ABA, European and Eastern leagues and every available paid pick-up tournament—and his reliable performances have only occasionally led the squad to triumph. When McGinnis and Erving joined the team, the news was front-page headlines, and fans count on them to score, the ticket holders feeling cheated if the two don't perform brilliantly. Mix's arrival was hardly noticed, and fans urge him to score. He's their true favorite. Why? Do they like Mix for his limitations or because he overcomes them? Is he proof for them of the possible greatness in us all or of our essential mediocrity? Do they sympathize with him for his career's hard labor, see his limited team role as an example of self-awareness, or do they relish these facts simply as a rebuke to the easy dollars and instant gratification they imagine his superstar teammates demand as a right?

Certainly athletes such as Mix don't conceive of their abilities and careers in the same way their fans do. When athletes are winning, they often present themselves as dedicated fellows happily taking advantage of some good luck; but even superstars always believe they can accomplish more with a new coach, team or mental attitude, and they actively despise the idea that they have reached the full limits of their success. Average players don't consider their periodic superlative performances as flukes. The nights they score forty points instead of eight serve as examples to them: if they enjoyed more playing time, if the team used a different offense, if the coach didn't exhort them so insistently, they would blow their opponents off the court every night. Unlike their admiring fans, they can't enjoy the privilege of believing their dedication is a virtue or their humility a social grace. These qualities are necessities of survival for them, unpleasant, immitigable facts of their existence. The broken bones, the years spent trekking from one tryout to another, the humiliation of playing in Europe or in the semi-professional leagues, the long night drives to and from games played in ancient small-town arenas, the limited time on the court, all the stories and truths that charm the fans are misery and gall to the player. They bespeak the one fact he can't admit: unlike the star who scores, he is not great.

Masterful scorers are called "percentage shooters." Basketball fans often comment, justifiably, that statistics don't accurately reflect a player's performance, because individual efforts result in collective success. If I box out my opponent, my teammate may rebound the ball; if I distract an opposing player, my teammate may make his shot. Scorekeepers record blocked shots only when an opposing player touches a ball in flight, but a player who continually jumps with his opponent and obstructs his view of the basket invariably succeeds in preventing numerous goals. Scoring isn't affected by such metaphysical quandaries. Once a play is executed, the player either hits or misses his shot, and the statistical mirror is exact. If he scores, the record book shows 1 under "Field Goals Attempted," and 1 under "Field Goals Made," and the player is shooting one thousand percent; if he misses, he's shooting zero.

Every player enjoys greater accuracy from particular areas on the court. The shooter claiming the highest ratio of successes to attempts, Kareem Abdul-Jabbar, usually positions himself at the basket's left side, ten feet from the hoop—the "low-post"—and drops in a hook: it's one of his percentage shots. Every player works to develop these. Elvin Hayes favors the same side of the court as Kareem, a few paces farther back; his back facing the basket, he turns as he raises his arms and rises in the air. Nine times out of twenty, the ball bounces off the glass backboard and falls smoothly through the net. Some players shoot accurately from a long distance; Pete Maravich, Lloyd Free, Nate Archibald and Calvin Murphy regularly chuck up balls from thirty feet without damaging their averages, and Jerry Lucas was famous for his far-traveling bomb. Others are quirky. My favorite is Freddy Brown, a guard for the Seattle Supersonics. An idiosyncratic master of offense, he shoots anything from anywhere—hooks, jumps, scooping lay-ups that bounce once on the rim and fall in. He boasts a solid forty-seven percent shooting accuracy from the field.

Players know the floor intimately; just as buoys guide fishermen, the court's painted markings signal to players their distance from and angle to the basket. On lucky nights, every shot falls, and the player leaves his safe haven, releasing the ball confidently from improbable positions and ranges; when he slumps and the ball repeatedly spins out of the basket, hits the front rim or bounces off the back one, he retreats to the places and devices that have ensured his past successes.

In professional basketball, no player hits less than forty percent of his shots. Excellent marksmen—Frazier, Tomjanovich—make nearly half of their attempts. Jabbar occupies a special class: he scores five and a half out of every ten times, the best record for accuracy in statistical history. High averages don't necessarily accompany good shooters, or low ratings bad ones. Dave Twardzik, play-making guard for the Portland Trailblazers, scores sixty percent of the time, but limits himself primarily to lay-ups; his record indicates speed, anticipation and cleverness more than faultless aim. On the contrary, Pete Maravich, the league's leading scorer, ended one year with a forty-three percent average but had played on a poor team that relied on his scoring. If his talents were joined with those of better players, he would take fewer shots—during the season he tried to score more than twice as many times as any other player on his team, a startling twenty-eight attempts per contest—and hit more baskets.

Theoretically, everyone has a percentage shot. My eight-year-old niece Kristina enjoys riding horses more than playing basketball, but she aims the ball truly when she stands near the basket; and one day my brother invented a turnaround jump shot with which he scored regularly. I can predict that the ball will pass through the net once out of every five times I hook from the side, and a forty-year-old English teacher friend of mine will hit twenty consecutive shots from the right-hand corner. Unfortunately, such performances are meaningless, because shooting differs dramatically between practice and a game. If Tom Seever and I were friends and occasionally played ball together, I would experience the same difficulty in hitting one of his pitches whether he threw it to me in Central Park or Shea Stadium. It is similarly impossible for me to kick a fifty-yard field goal. But on a basketball court during a pleasant afternoon, I'll make a good percentage of my shots; if I play in an actual game an hour later, however, my average will sink lamentably.

The critical difference between the two circumstances is tha during a game I am perpetually hounded by players who try t make me miss. If they have played against me previously, the know my shooting preferences; if they're fresh acquaintances, the learn my tendencies within the contest's first minutes. Either way by the time the score is tied, they can anticipate my moves. I rais the ball too slowly when I take a jump shot, lift it from my wais when I drive for a lay-up, beat them to the basket only when I firs enjoy the shelter of a teammate's screen. Consequently, m opponents try to bat the ball out of my hands, slap it away from th backboard, limit my movements to areas where they can see me. I they realize I'm terrified of approaching the basket from the left they work hard to keep me there; if they determine tha periodically I move unstoppably down the middle aisle, they force me toward the side. A player who is considerably smaller than will of course experience difficulty in guarding me; but I am such predictably mediocre performer that any halfway decent court antagonist can successfully badger and thwart my winning designs.

Some players shoot more accurately when they're guarded tightly. Another actor friend of mine continually reminds me of the night he shot fourteen times and scored twenty-eight points. He's twenty-five, and the feat was one of his most memorable performances. "Fourteen for fourteen, Lew," he says whenever we meet. I remember the scene. He likes to shoot off-balance from a distance, and his teammates thought his first tries were lucky hits. My team, his opponents, swarmed around him. Alan (Rosenberg; I've promised to mention his name) kept scoring. He's not particularly tall or strong, so he couldn't jump higher or fight clear of his tormentors. He just dribbled into our pack, jumped, tilted back a few inches, and pushed the ball off his fingers. At the time I wasn't aware of his secret. Taller players normally guard him, and when they position themselves between him and the basket, he uses their bodies or outstretched hands as a sort of sight aimed toward the basket; he actually depends on this helpful opposition, and without it he shoots erratically, the ball falling short or hitting too high on the backboard.

Percentage shooters are unlike either Alan or me. Their skills create conditions, not vary with them. The mark of their talent is

ot the release of the ball but the movement that precedes it.
.very center knows that Abdul-Jabbar rarely scores when he's
wenty-five feet from the basket or when he finds himself on the
asket's right side; so his opponents elbow, push and shove him
·om his favorite spot. Jabbar's insistence on maintaining his
·osition, and his ability to turn toward the basket and raise his
hooting hand without fouling a player or losing the ball, make him
xceptional. His wondrous aim ensures the success of his shot, but
t doesn't account for his average. Without his determination and
lexterity, he would never enjoy the opportunity of shooting; his
elease of the ball is merely landing the fish.

Jabbar's height helps his shot, of course. Baskets hang ten feet
bove the court floor, and obviously a seven-footer such as Kareem
loesn't encounter the same difficulties in shooting as a smaller
nan; Kareem is so tall that even when he hooks eighteen feet from
he basket, the ball starts its flight toward the goal at a downward
ingle. Tall players like to say that their size causes them other
problems, that they are clumsier than shorter players or foul more
requently, and they can prove their point with sufficient examples
of towering players who hardly score. But height remains an
nvaluable asset; only three players are listed on the NBA's rosters
of both top scorers and percentage shooters, and all are centers
—Jabbar; Walt Bellamy, an ex-Knick who ended his career in
Detroit; and Wilt Chamberlain.

This statistic isn't surprising. Critics of basketball argue that the
sport is an unfair game because big men dominate it. Their point is
evident but meaningless, because physical gifts partly determine
the nature and outcome of any athletic competition. Strength aids a
boxer, and a batter needs excellent eyesight to hit a hardball
consistently. Tall basketball players simply display their physical
advantages more openly than athletes in other sports. The sole
complaint against their presence in the game that merits discussion
is a purely hedonistic one: tall players dull a contest's excitement
because they score points so predictably.

Fans don't like to admit to this shallow concern. A female friend
of mine couldn't watch a game in which Chamberlain appeared
without expressing her annoyance. "He's a real dumb-dumb
moron," she used to say while the Dipper repeated his moves,

stepping toward the basket and plunging the ball into the net, or jumping slightly and releasing the ball as he leaned backward. Other friends disagreed; they argued that Chamberlain was the victim of his size and times. "How can you say that?" she would counter, sharing the tendency of many fans to find disagreement unbelievable. "He's just a robot. I can't sympathize with him." Invariably, these discussions ended with detailed examinations of Chamberlain's personality—not only did he try to beat the Knicks, he also campaigned for Nixon!—and attempts to determine which position was racist, and whether or not it was sensible, fair and correct to judge a performer by his or her character. The fundamental issue always remained unresolved: Chamberlain's height and strength—in his prime, he was reputed to be one of the strongest men in the world—disgusted her and excited them. She named her antipathy boredom, and they called their enjoyment an appreciation of the sport.

My friend's contempt for Chamberlain wasn't uncommon; disrespect dogged his career; and when Jabbar entered the league ten years after Chamberlain's debut, he met the same unsympathetic attitude. Although he scored as methodically as Chamberlain and his physical gifts were as prodigious as the older man's, he silenced his critics by the end of his rookie year. He accomplished this rout because he used his physical equipment more masterfully than his predecessor had. He manufactured a greater variety of shots than Chamberlain, shot accurately from more positions, and created more opportunities to score; and these talents declared him the superior entertainer of the two. He is capable of superb gestures. Several seconds short of his team's losing the '74 championship by a point, Jabbar found himself holding the ball, stranded in the left-hand corner eighteen feet from the basket. He bounced the ball, readying himself, and raised his arm in a wide arch, his head turned toward the hoop, his other arm bent at the elbow—an impossibly long, lean Etruscan warrior in flight. The ball passed through the net, and his team won. The attempt was lucky only in the sense that such a shot enjoyed fewer chances for success than one taken closer to the basket. The hook was the best percentage shot available—the least likely to be blocked and Jabbar's most effective weapon—and the game-winning goal testified to Kareem's talents, not to his accidental good fortune. Given the same situation, Chamberlain would have been helpless because of his limited repertoire. He would have lacked the athletic mastery to score the point, and the thrilling moment would have been a dud.

Jabbar's advance beyond Chamberlain as a player reflects a general movement in the game. Basketball's basic theory is that the closer you are to the goal, the more you score, and originally the sport was a passing game; shooting was only the denouement to the climactic tosses that preceded it, and the strategy of all basic plays was to free a player and let him shoot a lay-up. Coaches still cling to this theory, and some teams actually practice it—Princeton, St. John's, and the NBA Chicago squad coached by Dick Motta—but players have continuously expanded their frontiers on the court floor. Ironically, their innovations in this most inventive game have been uniformly resisted. "You see," one old coach once explained to me, "the moves players make today were once unthinkable to us. We dribbled facing forward; they dribble backwards. We went into our defensive stance"—he assumed the posture: a low crouch, one arm stretched forward; a short, aging man with a determined look—"and no one ever got by us. Now they all get by. Who would have thought you could do that? No one. It was unthinkable. It was the same with one-handed shots —you just didn't think it could be done!"

The one-handed shot he mentions has been credited to Hank Luisetti, a Stanford University forward of the thirties. Basketball is so thoroughly a playground sport that most of its creations, like cooking recipes, are anonymous. Eventually, when one player demonstrates the invention in a dramatic situation, he becomes a Homer, a man associated with years of unrecorded creativity. Luisetti won recognition because of a single game played in Madison Square Garden. His team opposed LIU, then a national power coached by Clair Bee. Bee spoke condescendingly of Luisetti's shot before the game—the player's curious release of the ball preceded his arrival in New York—and the contest was a match between a controlled eastern quintet and an anarchic cowboy. Stanford won, and although Bee later said he had lost the game because of a coaching error, people interpreted the victory as a success for Luisetti's unconventional form. If Stanford had lost coaches would have benched players who shot with one hand Luisetti's triumph deprived them of any argument against it.

Luisetti's shot helped basketball change into the speedy game we see today. Before the Stanford-LIU game, players relied on the two-handed set shot, the ball held at chest height, the knees bent Coaches claimed that this method ensured accuracy, but the form was also peculiarly suited for their type of play. It necessitated the passing displays which the coaches valued so highly, because you can't launch the ball from this position unless no one is guarding you closely. Running in patterns around the court, the players passed the ball to one another until their best marksman was free to shoot. He set himself into position, crouched, bent his arms, and released the ball in a high arch that occasionally touched the low roofs of old gyms. You can still observe this style in playgrounds next to large suburban communities of self-exiled middle-aged New Yorkers. Three baggy men challenge the young hot-shots; the kids run and rebound, but whenever the ancient mariners hold the ball, they pass it unerringly, quick salvos preceded by slight fakes. Eventually the kids gang up on one of their opponents, leaving another old codger free, and he shoots, an effortless toss that scores.

By itself, the one-handed shot didn't threaten this slow offense. Luisetti released the ball with stunning quickness, but most players freeze momentarily before they try a set shot. If you watch Paul Silas, you'll sometimes see him attempt a goal from twenty feet. He's a decent but slow shooter; he positions himself, raises his arm, steadies the ball, and checks his aim. By the time he has finished his preparations, an opponent has blocked his view of the basket, and Silas either passes or throws an errant shot. But Luisetti's invention resulted in the one-handed jump shot, and this technique, which combines accuracy, quickness and versatile range, uncontestably secured the court as the shooter's domain.

I saw a dramatic instance of the jump shot's importance once in a college game involving the University of Houston. Houston's star was Otis Birdsong, a tall, strong guard with a shot as fine as his name; he fakes quickly and jumps straight up, his body a stretched muscular line that ends in a perfect balletic point. Birdsong's usually accurate shooting had deserted him in the second half of this game, and the other team led by a point, with a few seconds remaining. Otis dribbled upcourt, halting shortly before he reached the foul line. An opposing guard greeted him immediately. Without the invention of the jump shot, Birdsong would have contemplated three equally disagreeable options: he could have passed, a dereliction of duty as the team's best shooter; he could have driven to the basket, where four opponents waited for him; he could have shot the slow two-handed push which his foe could have easily anticipated. In short, he would probably have lost the game. Using the jump shot, he managed to win. He held the ball, crouched low, gestured left and right, and jumped. His opponent helplessly mirrored Otis's moves. If he touched Otis, the referee would call a foul; his one chance to stop the goal was to block the ball in its flight, an unlikely possibility, since he was neither taller than Otis nor an exceptional leaper. He gamely stretched his arm above him. Birdsong muttered some unintelligible insult to his foe and flicked the ball; as he landed, the buzzer announced the game's end; the ball flew through the net, and Houston won.

Coaches react ambivalently to great jump-shot artists such as Otis. After the game, the Houston coach—Guy Lewis, who sometimes covers his face with a towel during a contest's climactic moments—commented that he knew Otis would score. "I saw him coming down the court, and I told my assistants, 'Otis is going to win this one for us.' " But three days later when the situation repeated itself and Otis missed, Lewis didn't say a word. Throughout his second year on the Philadelphia 76ers, Lloyd Free was criticized for his long-distance jump shots. When the team entered the play-offs, Free's audacious attempts won several games, and his coach, Gene Shue, suddenly explained that he wanted Lloyd to shoot from thirty feet: the same form that had earlier been castigated as undisciplined and erratic was now a high percentage shot delivered on demand.

There are hundreds of tales reporting such dramatic shifts in judgment. What else can the coach do? He's paid to win games, and the natural genius of the shooter brings him a winning record.

The same physical brilliance demands autonomy during the game. The coach is at the mercy of his player. My English-teacher friend relates a tale from his high school career. A gifted athlete with long, tapered fingers, he was the team's scoring star. The coach had always insisted that David didn't hustle enough, and in a fit of resentment one night David decided to prove his worth. He shot the ball every time he held it and scored some forty points in the first half, giving his team a commanding lead. Glorying in his success, he returned to the bench, where his coach ordered him into the locker room: he swore he'd never let David play for him again. His rebuke is a coach's dream. They'd all like to make their hot-shots fizzle under the cold water of their discipline, but they can't, because any cooling of their stars threatens to dim the bright light of their own success.

David was the type of player called a "pure shooter." Like Rick Barry or Bill Bradley, he possessed neither great speed nor finesse, nor was he particularly strong. Consequently, he couldn't charge to the basket (unless the area wasn't guarded) or shoot dunks, double pumps or oop-de-doops from the foul line. His talent was aiming and releasing the ball, taking advantage of those moments when he was free, and trying to create such situations by running constantly in an attempt to lose the man who guarded him, moving—as they say—without the ball.

The complimentary opposites of pure shooters like David are players such as Elgin Baylor, Earl Monroe and Julius Erving, the heroes of the playgrounds who are called one-on-one men, athletes with exceptional control of their bodies who score by outmaneuvering their opponents. A photo of Baylor shooting while Bill Russell guards him is an example. The two are in the air, a foot under the basket; Russell has tangled his hand on the net trying to stop Baylor's shot; Baylor's arms—leather sinews—are outstretched, his neck craned backwards; and his hand is about to flick the ball over his head into the hoop. With such defiant improvisations he scored seventy-one points one night and is the league's third highest scorer, his record bested only by Chamberlain and Jabbar. Monroe offers different specialties; because he is shorter than Baylor, his game is earth-bound. His most imitated move is to spin while dribbling, an exciting moment partly because he bounces the ball spasmodically and you fear he'll lose it. Only 6'1" as an adult, Monroe was tall when he was younger. He used to play center; there he began his shot with his back facing the basket. When he increased in years but not in height, he translated this movement into a guard's gesture, and no matter how tightly an opponent shadows him, Monroe manages by the subtlest combination of feints and pushes to spring himself free to take a shot—his patented oop-de-doop, an underhanded toss with his legs tucked at the knees, as though he were skipping rope, or his jumper, a clean snap of his wrists. He also displays an endless variety of slithery, jerky lay-ups—twists, false gestures, nods and twitches—and shoots the ball using either hand, banking it off the backboard, or hooking it over his head while standing under-neath the basket, on all occasions releasing it so softly and truly that if it bounces on the rim, it invariably falls through the net.

Erving has transferred many of these motions to the air, and his movements near and under the basket particularly are inspired by Monroe. His body performs the most versatile acts; approaching the basket in the air, he finds an opponent blocking his path and stretches his arm around his foe to bounce the ball off the backboard. He presents the most complete development of any offensive player yet, incorporating diverse styles to secure an unprecedented command of the court.

Fans often make tendentious distinctions between pure shooters and one-on-one players. Pure shooters tend to be white and disciplined, testaments to those wretched clichés of the sports world—they're classy and have heart. The same view sees one-on-one players as erratic and selfish; and, curiously, the worst offenders are black. Pure shooters display good "shot selection"; they try to score only when the odds favor them. One-on-one players are children; they shoot the ball even when all their teammates are unguarded and their shot enjoys no chance of scoring. Such classifications obscure most players' performances, because shooters—in the professional game, at least—defy these boundaries. Their profession is to score, a risk they dare in every contest, and their sole interest is to expand their talent to the fullest degree. But their stylistic differences do impart a different attitude toward the game, and this can be observed best in the quietest moment of any contest, when a player is fouled and steps to the line in front of the basket, at his leisure and without anyone guarding him, to shoot one or two shots worth a point apiece.

This is called a free throw, and it is the game's sole instance of a pure match between athlete and skill, comparable—in form at least—to the contest between batter and pitcher. The shooter, a solitary figure at the line, enjoys ten seconds to shoot, and commands the referee's attention. If any player or object distracts the shooter, the referee can let him shoot again. For these reasons the foul line is often called the charity line, and because shooting a basketball is not as difficult as hitting a pitch, it is supposed to be shameful if you miss from there. Chamberlain was a notoriously bad free-throw shooter, and however much he tried to improve his statistics, his bad rap haunted him. Once I observed Frazier trying to break a slump. He had been missing his free throws during the pre-season games, and at the close of one practice he went off with the other players to shoot from the foul line. This exercise ends every practice, and Frazier has probably thrown several hundred thousand free throws during his career, but he concentrated with a child's intensity as he tried to break his pattern and put the ball through the hoop. "Just like the game," he muttered to himself when the ball hit the rim's back edge, and he pressed his lips together and narrowed his eyes, preparing for his second try. "Go home!" he exhorted the ball as he pushed it off his fingertips, and appeared to be deeply satisfied when it fell through the net.

Every player shoots free throws differently. Some players look confused: Kevin Porter, a small, fast guard, always appears befuddled. Others act nonchalant: Mike Newlin, a feisty character, bounces the ball once and chucks it up coolly. Nate Thurmond, a massive center who has played professionally for eleven years, holds the ball high over his head and flexes his wrists once as though he were about to shoot before he actually releases the ball. The first time you see him do this, you think he is hesitating, and it surprises you that a veteran shows such uncertainty; but the gesture is merely his particular quirk. A few players cross themselves before they shoot, and others perform elaborate rituals. The first time Cedric Maxwell—now a forward on the

Boston Celtics, then a center for the University of North Carolina at Charlotte—played in the Garden, he became an overnight playground celebrity because he habitually bounced an imaginary ball three times and shot it before he took his shot. Although he was a stranger to the city, he became such a popular figure that kids passing him on the street would greet him by imitating the gesture, a sign of respect. The most peculiar idiosyncrasy I ever observed, however, belonged to a tall center for an art school. While he stood at the line bouncing the ball, he swayed, shifting from one foot to the other as though he were balancing himself riding the subway. His teammates chuckled at his act, but his shots were true; and although I thought his manner entirely individual, I later saw a number of black high school kids dancing at the line in the same fashion, an inexplicable custom that had arisen out of nowhere. "That's just the way I shoot," the center told me, when I asked him the origin of his strange habit.

Black fans and players especially enjoy such curious styles. The best free-throw shooter at present is Rick Barry. He makes nineteen of every twenty tosses, but I have never heard a black fan praise his accuracy yet. "He's so white," a basketball-loving student of mine once remarked to me. "And his foul shooting. It's *so* white." Barry shoots his free throws underhand; he argues that this method is the most accurate, but only one other player in the league follows his example. His movement is a marvel of physical and psychological economy: he steps to the line, positions himself squarely to the basket, crouches shallowly, bounces the ball and holds it level with his knees as he looks at the basket and exhales. Gingerly resting the ball between his fingertips, he merely flexes his wrists and it sails through the net. Children shoot this way, but Barry performs the act with such precision and knowledge that the movement appears neither embarrassing nor awkward. It does lack all drama, however, and this is the cause of my student's objection to Barry's style: his manner doesn't play for the moment, extend the time, make us feel as though indeed we are the ball poised between his hands and rising through the air, just as many decent baseball hitters don't still and awe the crowd the way Willie Stargell does when he steps to the plate—bat revolving, face scowling, feet rooted.

Fans want to feel the drama of the moment; they desire to see it expressed in some physical form; and great foul shooters—the ones honest kids love—give it to them. Don Nelson, an ex-Boston Celtic who now coaches Milwaukee, used to balance the ball on one hand and throw it like a shot-put; his percentage was extremely high, but every time I watched him I waited for the ball to wobble and fall off his hand. This suspense was mirrored in his face, his forehead lathered with sweat and his eyes two small dots staring at the goal. McAdoo provides the same excitement. He sets himself a little behind the line, bounces the ball too high, and shoots it while jumping an inch or two in the air. "Why do you jump, Bob?" I ask him in an imaginary dialogue every time I see him shoot. "I've got to," he answers me—the same response I received from my shuffling center. Monroe transforms himself into a Cubist painting when he steps to take his shot, his body a series of right angles—legs coming straight up from the floor, thighs sloping down from his waist, torso bent, arms sticking out from his shoulders. He peers at the basket, this extraordinary arrangement of flesh and bones, and suddenly accomplishes something remarkable: he releases a ball through the air and into a basket, winning a game.

Or there is my favorite, Frazier, a study in sensual concentration, grace and intellect. He bends slightly at the knees—the massive muscles at the backs of his thighs supporting his body's weight; extends his arms away from his chest, the angle of his forearm a perfect parallel to the slight tilt of his head. Occasionally he will check himself, assuming the posture and anticipating the players about to leap for the rebound. One starts to jump, but Frazier hasn't yet shot the ball. He will take his time, extending this solitary act, transforming a simple silly event into a memorable moment. He gathers himself again, teasing the clock, stretching his muscles so that even the spectators at the top of the arena can see their lines clearly. His shot isn't as certain as Barry's and statistically it has probably lost more games than that more accurate shooter's. But it is more beautiful, both to watch and to contemplate. After all, the basket is neither a bull coming at you nor a ball being thrown—it's a dumb piece of metal and rope. We would all be fair performers if we shot Barry's way as many times as he has. There's no style to his success—not because Barry lacks form, but because his form risks nothing. To move gracefully at the cost of defying possibility is a triumph; and in a world of percentages it's the only style worthy of the true fan's admiration and perpetual delight.

5. "African Handball"

I

Two-thirds of all professional basketball players are black, as are an equal and growing number of top college stars and the most important high school prodigies—statistics unequaled in any other American business, including sharecropping and domestic work. Black Americans have provided the sport its most famous team—the Harlem Globetrotters; its two greatest stars—Bill Russell and Wilt Chamberlain; and a circus of superb athletes: ringmasters (Oscar Robertson, Lenny Wilkens, Walt Frazier), high-flying trapeze artists (Elgin Baylor, Connie Hawkins, Fly Williams), strong men (Bob Lanier, Nate Thurmond, Paul Silas), balletic stunt men (Earl Monroe, Julius Erving, George Gervin), and hundreds of gifted journeymen who enjoy one glorious night when the star is ill and they trot out onto the spotlit center of the court. Through their skill and effort, these men have claimed basketball as the athletic expression of black culture in America, and the game is so thoroughly associated in the popular imagination with blacks that the black presence has become yet another reason not to watch it. "African handball," Somerville street kids in Boston call it, and I have heard of more than one bartender shutting off a television game because a customer didn't want to watch "the niggers play."

In '69, when I first became a fan, blacks filled the following positions: seven of the twelve players who made the NBA all-star team, the rookie of the year (Lew Alcindor), three of the top five scorers and assist men, four of the top five rebounders. The championship team, the New York Knickerbockers, was pre-

94

dominantly black, and its incontestable star, Willis Reed, was incontestably black. Shortly before the Knicks won the championship, a white, off-duty cop decided to harass a black man driving a Cadillac. He ordered the man to pull over, drew a gun on him, and commanded him to step out of the car. Slowly, the anonymous innocent unwound his massive body from behind the wheel. It was Reed. Before the unsuspecting cop could apologize for his mistake, the New York center gave him two choices: he could leave immediately, and Reed would file charges against him at the New York Civilian Complaint Review Board; or he could stay and get knocked upside his head. The cop chose the first (the complaint met with unaccustomed success at the watchdog committee), and Reed's triumph sweetened my pleasure while I watched the series' final games: Reed was a hero on and off the court.

At the time, I was working as an SDS organizer, and my organization was trying to build alliances with black groups, especially the Panthers. The vision excited me, and I was moved by my introduction to the experience of black people in America. Their lives gave the lie to all the myths and nonsense of our national past, and their understanding of American society suggested a way to change it. Basketball mirrored these concerns. Blacks played with whites, and they viewed the game not as a demonstration of an insufferable collection of stuffy moral imperatives, but rather as an entertainment, an exuberant one, performed by masters.

There were also less principled reasons for my interest and attention to blacks. I admired the image presented by black basketball players—cool dressers, fast athletes, hip talkers—a portrait that now presents them meanly to the white eye. "I really think they do things differently than us," a friend of mine said recently after seeing Earl Monroe play for the first time. My friend meant his comment as a compliment, and I answered it directly by explaining how Monroe had invented a unique style because of the limits of his body and the demands of the game. But my friend wasn't satisfied. "How does he do it?" he kept repeating, trying to mimic Monroe's turns and twists on the street. "They must be different from us."

It has always been thus with basketball. The blacks' mastery of the game has served to prove their essential distinctness from whites. They are taller, faster, looser, stronger, stupider. What other ethnic group would love such a foolish sport? One of my fondest childhood memories is of the afternoon I sat hunched in the back of Loew's 175th Street Theater, eating popcorn and watching twice a film called *Go Man Go,* a chronicle of the Harlem Globetrotters. In one scene, Saperstein is woken up by some madcap black magician dribbling a basketball around his bed. The spectacle delighted me. Who knew the future of the Globetrotters then? Who knew that fifteen years later the show that gave me such pleasure as a child would be characterized as an Uncle Tom festival by athletes and writers who considered it an athletic minstrel show that remained one of the few ways a player exiled from the pros could earn a living practicing his craft? The machine of racism grinds out cruel behavior and foolish judgments. Invariably, it either humiliates its victims or obscures their achievements. The Globetrotters became famous buffoons. Their counterparts, the Harlem Rens (for Renaissance), who averaged one hundred fifty victories a season over their twenty-seven-year life, were forgotten until the recent, sudden interest in black history which rewarded them with a plaque in the basketball Hall of Fame and a New York summer league named after their coach, Robert Douglass, a West Indian who led his squad to more recorded victories than any other coach. Today there is a larger market for black athletes, and the members of the Rens would be the prize of high school coaches, the guests of rich universities, subjects of bidding wars between professional teams, and franchise-makers rating cover stories in sports magazines. But regardless of their professional mastery or commercial importance, a collusion of business, injustice and prejudicial circumstance would inevitably present them as goons, clowns or supermen in the eyes of their white audience, living testimony—as the Globetrotters were—that black excellence in one field, even a minor one such as basketball, comes solely from the fact that blacks are different from us. My friend admired Monroe's talents while a stereotyped racist would scorn them, but Monroe's skills occasioned the same judgment from both: blacks are less inhibited, deliberate and cerebral than whites. In short, they are less civilized.

This stigma is especially visible in basketball, because blacks rule the game. The high number of blacks in the sport isn't a testament to the progressive views of the whites who run the business; rather it gives occasion to prove the ineffable quality of discrimination in America. Relations between blacks and whites off the court are usually tenuous, and white players are often more openly bigoted because of their minority status in the game. Players spend so little time together that one of the reasons the Players Association sends its team representatives on yearly trips is to create a situation in which the black and white members of the union will have to mingle. White players complain that black ones hog the ball; black ones insist that mediocre white athletes are employed only because of their color. In the '74–'75 season, the Golden State Warriors fielded a team of eleven blacks and one white (Rick Barry). The team won during the season, clinched the championship, and was touted as a model of racial harmony. The following two seasons they couldn't repeat their past triumphs, and rumor said Barry and his teammates despised one another: the black players couldn't work with a white superstar, and he couldn't perform with a cast of black jocks.

The predominance of blacks also harms the commercial health of the sport. For big-city arenas, basketball has always been a second sport, the attraction used to fill seats on the nights hockey wasn't played. The black presence in basketball has only exacerbated this situation. An executive from CBS explained its effects on advertising to me: "A lot of considerations make an advertiser decide where to buy time. Say there's a local station broadcasting games in Detroit. Well, Cobo Hall is a war zone after five. It's all the same for a Cadillac dealer if he buys ten thirty-second spots on basketball or the late-night movie. But it's standard practice to throw in season tickets for your advertisers, and this might entice him to buy the basketball slot. Except you'll never convince him to visit Cobo late at night. He just won't do it. So the pinch of gold that might sweeten the pot becomes the straw that breaks the camel's back instead, and he buys his time elsewhere."

The executive didn't consider this decision a racist one because it wasn't founded on personal animus, and this judgment is typical. At present, for example, eighty-five percent of all black youths in

New York City between the ages of sixteen and eighteen are unemployed; the majority who attend college don't graduate, and those who do finish with degrees earn approximately thirty percent less than whites with the same credentials. These facts—culled from the daily paper—indicate the blindness of discussing the effects of race in a purely individual context, but many commentators insist on this tunnel-vision. James Michener, in his book *Sports in America,* for instance, makes the now-fashionable complaint that too many black youths try to succeed through sports. "The athlete," he writes, "picks up his one big contract, pays excessive expenses, lives beyond his means, and faces life at thirty-four forcibly retired from his sport and without a job that pays substantially. He becomes a bartender at the American Legion, and his life income will be that first $500,000 plus little more." This is true as far as it goes, though many retired ballplayers continue in the business, and I suspect few black ones work in American Legion bars. Michener's description of the smart life, however, is just a dream. "The trained man," he continues, "on the other hand, works forty-five years at an average salary of $30,000—or perhaps much, much more—and his life's earnings are $1,350,000, plus an honored place in his community." Who, when, where? The mean income for *whites*, much less blacks, with college degrees is but half of Michener's average salary, and the only successes of the community an athlete gets to meet are well-paid coaches and rich alumni who the player knows would ignore him completely if he didn't average over forty points a game.

To some extent, all managers—high school teachers, college coaches or general managers—consider athletes beasts of burden. But black ballplayers are, with few exceptions, the sons of slaves indeed, and slavery remains the closest approximation to the treatment of young black athletes by the whites who buy and sell them. I spent one winter afternoon sitting behind recruiters from the University of Maryland while they observed players in a six-hour city-wide high school tournament. The players were almost entirely black, as was the crowd. With few exceptions, the recruiters were all white and fashionably suburban, dressed in turtlenecks, Gucci shoes, modest sports jackets, and leather overcoats. When the players entered the court and started their warm-ups, the recruiters all stood, observing the prospects and underlining the names of the athletes who interested them on the roster card that listed each youth's name, age, height, weight and number. They noted each player's physical specifications. Were his legs too thin? His shoulders weak? Would the player have to use weights? How high could he jump? Any exceptionally tall player—even one who fumbled the ball and couldn't shoot—was immediately prized; these men are paid to appraise bodies. Among themselves, they talked about players' attitudes. Was the player "coachable"? Did he have a "good attitude," or was he flakey, a bitcher or whiner? Ah, flakey players—what a bother they could be! Recruiters often tell stories about kids who don't recognize the value of a good education. Carlos is a black Puerto Rican guard who regularly scores thirty points in the New York summer leagues. He went to Idaho State after high school and left after a season, claiming the coach knew nothing about the game. The coach claimed he was a flake. Now Carlos works as a youth counselor. "He don't like white people too tough," his old high school coach, now friend, explains. The coach is white, but he dislikes the idea of being a college coach. "Go around to some punk like him," he laughs, pointing to Carlos, "and beg him to please do me the favor of playing for my school? You gotta be kidding!"

During intermissions between games, the recruiters practice a sort of progressive feudalism, bribing the boys to work for them. "We like your attitude," a recruiter tells a boy. The recruiter is under six feet, a dapper dresser representing a non-profit organization that grosses hundreds of thousands of dollars a year, owns a gym worth several millions, and employs a coach who is a state-wide celebrity. The boy is 6'8", a well-mannered child whose parents come from North Carolina. They have sheltered him, keeping him off the streets. In high school, a white coach has persuaded him to join the team, though the kid performs ineptly. He is reserved, shy, a gentleman. His parents have instructed him to listen politely to older people and respect their views, and he nods slightly while the recruiter praises him, smiles cautiously when the recruiter says he's eager to coach him, shakes his hand courteously when the recruiter promises to be in touch. The recruiter returns to his seat, his cohort asking him about the interview. He shrugs his shoulders for reply. The kid's their fifteenth or twentieth prospect, a last resort if they don't nab the top players they want. The recruit doesn't suspect this. He prances out on the court and sinks three quick shots. He's going to college, all expenses paid!

Already the recruiters have lost interest in the game. They check off one player after another as the cries of high school coaches echo in the gym. "That's your shot, Mango, take your shot! Goddamnit, he's too good, that kid. He's too disciplined. Shoot!" The recruiters yawn, discuss the best routes back to their schools.

After the game, the coach brings over Mango. He wears doubleknit red pants, an iridescent sports shirt, fake suede coat, and sneakers. His dream is to be the first Puerto Rican professional ballplayer, and he hesitantly shakes hands with the recruiter, this powerful man who can aid his career. "Pleased to meet you," he says, tucking his head as he bows away from the man. A black high school coach approaches the recruiter. Has he seen his forward play? The kid's great; wonderful attitude, good specs. He'll love him. "No chance," the recruiter informs him. "Try Albany State," he suggests, wanting to be helpful, and scans the people leaving the court for the coach of the tall kid he spoke to. He spots and stalks him, introducing himself with a firm handshake. "Ah," says the coach, "am I glad to see you!" They retreat to a far corner, conspiring over the kid's future. No buying or selling is transacted; this meeting is to investigate the goods before the final auction of bodies and attitudes.

The unfortunate career of Darryl Dawkins exemplifies the manipulation by whites of young black ballplayers. A huge twenty-one-year-old, weighing two hundred eighty-five pounds and standing seven feet tall, Dawkins signed a six-year contract for one million dollars with the Philadelphia 76ers when he was graduated from high school. He was one of the first high school seniors to become an NBA player. For years the NBA had refused to sign any players with less than three years' experience in college ball. In its struggle with the NBA for superstars, the ABA resorted to signing some players who hadn't yet finished their junior year in college and, the year before Dawkins entered the pros, had even signed Moses Malone, a talented tall rebounder fresh out of high school. The NBA branded its competitors renegades and changed its rule: its teams also could sign eighteen-year-olds. Some managers and coaches refuse to work with these young men because they believe the lack of college experience leaves them irretrievably undisciplined. But Philadelphia and Atlanta—one rich, the other poor; both desperately needing a winning squad—immediately signed teenagers.*

Dawkins attracted attention quickly. His sheer bulk demands interest, and he's an aggressive and talkative person. During his first year, he played rarely. In his second season he began to exhibit his youthful talents at shooting and defense. Still, strength was his main contribution to the team, and he intimidated opponents, much to the delight of the television commentators. Anxious for playing time and a feared reputation, spurred by his own pride, Dawkins battered players until, in the second game of the championship series against Portland, he provoked a fight with Maurice Lucas.

Lucas is a forward who plays with authority and precision, an example of what sports people like to call a "cold competitor": triumph is the sole expression of his nature. When Dawkins squared off with him, Lucas stood his ground. His challenge startled Dawkins; who else had ever stood up to this giant in the schoolyards where he had played only two years before? The attitude of his teammates also flustered Dawkins. He obviously believed this sort of fierce display was expected of him, but his colleagues didn't cheer him on or join him. They wisely backed off; Julius Erving just hunkered down on the court, staying out of harm's way. Confused, Dawkins danced toward Lucas—bobbing and weaving, as the saying goes—while the older man waited for him. A referee stepped between the two before Dawkins threw a punch. Both players were expelled from the game, and Dawkins

---

*Atlanta bought the services of Bill Willoughby, a lanky, long youngster who played little for them and has since been traded to Buffalo. Willoughby first met his professional colleagues at a summer fund-raising game before the season began; he asked a television announcer to introduce him to the stars who were now his teammates. "They awed him," the announcer said. "It was a high school kid's dream come true."

rampaged through his team's empty locker room, busting walls and toilets. The following day Commissioner O'Brien imposed large fines on both players, and the series resumed, Portland eventually winning the next four games while Dawkins sat on the bench. The fight and his abortive rage afterward had been the highlight of his young career.

I rooted for Lucas during the battle because of my unrelenting antipathy toward the Philadelphia team, but Dawkins claimed my sympathy after it was over. Throughout the year, sportswriters and broadcasters had devoted copy and time to his brawn. Brent Mussberger, the CBS announcer, unrestrainedly joked about his appetite. Steve Mix had invited the kid over for supper, Mussberger chortled, and lost his week's pay. Occasionally someone mourned Dawkins's lost youth or praised his ability to play, but these appreciations were rare. Mussberger exclaimed over Dawkins's size even during the fight.

Once the fight was over, however, the press turned on Dawkins—not only was he bad for the game; he was a coward. Tasteless jokes followed. Pete Vecsey reported in the *New York Post* that Dawkins had busted his typewriter in a rage. Vecsey had befriended Dawkins, but in spite of his liking for the athlete, his comments were thoughtless. "I guess he thought the typewriter was alphabet soup," he quoted another sportswriter's quip about the broken machine. A week later, he jested again: "A black coach," he wrote, "calls Dawkins the 'Forerunner of Man.'"

Such ugly and ungrateful comments aren't unusual. They flavor the simplest remarks of white commentators. Interviewed during a Portland–Los Angeles contest, Curry Kirkpatrick, a writer for *Sports Illustrated*, appraised Jabbar's lackluster play: "I don't know what's the matter with Kareem. Perhaps he's packed his bags already and left for Africa." Another harmless joke, but would he have suggested that Ernie DiGregorio was preparing to fly back to Capistrano? Robert Lipsyte says that basketball became too black for white sportswriters in the late sixties, and certainly even black baseball stars are presented by management and press as essentially American in a way denied to black basketball players. Joe Morgan, Willie Mays, Satchell Page have become characters in the endless pleasing drama of the game's heroes and flakes—lusty, peculiar men who, like their white brethren, performed wonders on the field and occasional strange deeds off it. But the portrayals of black basketball players always stress their alien natures. Kareem Adbul-Jabbar is pictured as weird—his height, name, religion. Marvin Barnes is caricatured as extravagant, childish, vicious, criminal. Walt Frazier is feline—moody, distrustful, tricky; a primitive Narcissus. Calvin Murphy is crazy, a battler, boastful and mean. Connie Hawkins is dumb. Among blacks, Dawkins is merely a manchild, that curious person, deserving of sympathy and stern rebuke, who is big enough to affect the world but who lacks the experience to know how. For whites, especially those who make their living off him, he's a beast. Throughout the weeks when the fight was news, I kept remembering a comment by a 76er executive, a man who conducted daily business with Dawkins. Did he have any qualms about Dawkins not attending college? I asked, expecting a neutral response. The man sneered at me. "He has enough money to *buy* a college," he corrected me. The answer was false and contemptuous both of Dawkins and of my concern, and its spirit reveals Dawkins's experience with the white professional world: considered a savage, he was treated viciously; yet when he acted wildly, he was condemned.

II

There's a long-standing debate over whether or not Negroes are more naturally equipped for athletics than Caucasians, and some people argue that blacks dominate basketball because the game demands so many different physical talents. The point about the game is true, but the rest of the argument is specious. Blacks neither played basketball better than other sports nor loved it more dearly until black athletes became the game's greatest stars. Then blacks trained to become basketball players because they knew mastery of the game would earn them money.

Contrary to its present image, basketball was one of the last sports to integrate. As early as the twenties, Paul Robeson played football for Rutgers—the college game was more important than the professional one then—and Jackie Robinson, one of the nation's few black collegiate *basketball* stars, broke the ban on blacks in baseball in 1947 (turning the game into a truly national pastime). But basketball teams and leagues were entirely segregated throughout the sport's infancy and adolescence. White teams sometimes challenged black ones—the Harlem Rens beat the two most famous white teams several times—but no white in sports seems to have ever taken a heroic stand against the jim crow laws and attitudes that prevailed.

With few exceptions, the nation's colleges helped enforce this policy. Basketball has never organized a farm system such as baseball's or hockey's. After the '52 scandals, Maurice Podoloff, the NBA commissioner, spoke vaguely of plans to start a minor league for the sport, but nothing came of his announcement, and with good reason: colleges already were fulfilling the task. College recruiters scout all the best high school players, and college coaches train them rigorously for three or four years, preparing them for the pros. Basketball teams are possibly the cheapest investment a college can make, and more than a few schools have risen to sudden national prominence by fielding a winning quintet on the court. A decade ago, Long Beach State in California played in the NCAA semi-finals, and the network televising the tourney showed a six-minute special on the school's art program during a half-time break. Stephen Horn, the president of the school, figures that more people were informed of the college's activities through that small special than through all the newspaper releases since the school was founded.

Blacks have starred regularly in these games, but only since the civil rights movement. One of the ironies of that struggle for social justice is that the state universities which most fiercely fought for jim crow policies in the fifties now pride and enrich themselves on their largely black teams. The "triplets," three speedy black players who led the University of Arkansas into the NCAA's '78 semi-finals, couldn't have been ballboys for the junior varsity ten years ago; and Jack Givens, a small, powerful black forward, won the championship game for the University of Kentucky, whose team, under coach Adolf Rupp, didn't include any blacks until the early seventies. Northern and midwestern schools weren't much better. In the late forties Dolly King became the first black player on the Long Island University squad. Presumably, Clair Bee, the

Blackbirds' coach, didn't care about a man's color, only his playing ability; but King ate in the kitchen when the team was on the road, with only the assistant coach for company. The famous "grand slam" CCNY team of 1950, still remembered today by some as a model of democracy, had only two blacks, both exceptional talents: Ed Warner, whom coach Nat Holman called the best pivotman he ever coached; and Floyd Lane, a tall, lean guard known for his enthusiasm and his knowledge of the game. (The forty-eight-year-old Lane still plays in semi-professional leagues today and, in a pleasing proof of the adage that what goes around comes around, is the present coach of the CCNY team.) The great teams of the midwestern schools—Oklahoma, Kansas, Bradley, Colorado, Illinois—had no black players: the photos of those championship squads show only spiffy white players, models from *Life* magazine dressed in gym suits. A story about Wilt Chamberlain reflects the attitudes of those days. In 1955 the coach of the University of Missouri, trying to recruit the star, decided to appeal to the lad's racial pride. "Boy," he asked, "how would you like to be the first Negro to play at the University of Missouri?"

Haskell Cohen claims that the lack of good black college ballplayers is the primary explanation for the all-white rosters of the NBA's early years. But the league also had a more commercial reason. The NBA didn't attract large crowds then, and the teams relied on the pre-game shows of the Globetrotters to make a profit. In return, they agreed not to sign blacks, leaving this one-tenth of the population the private reserve of Abe Saperstein. In 1952 the Boston Celtics broke the agreement by drafting Chuck Cooper, a black player from Duquesne. Ever since, Auerbach has insisted that Cooper was simply the best player available. However, the decision to draft him was also an obvious challenge to Saperstein and coincided with the NBA's new general aggressiveness: part of their own announcement that they planned to become the nation's premiere basketball attraction.

Most of these pioneer players—Walter Dukes, Cooper, Sweetwater Clifton, Ray Felix—were giant forwards or centers who acted as their teams' musclemen. Dukes is still considered one of the roughest men ever to play the game, and Clifton was so strong he had to be coached on how to use his massive strength: he was afraid he might hurt other players. Although fans had become accustomed to big centers such as Mikan and Bob Kurland, none of the black ones ever became stars, and few black players were picked to be guards, the players people considered the brains and quarterbacks of the team.

The first players to break this mold were Bill Russell and Wilt Chamberlain. Russell played center for the University of San Francisco, a Jesuit school; and under his leadership the team won the national championship twice. They also won fifty-five consecutive games, a college record then. Chamberlain, the first heralded black high school athlete, played at the University of Kansas, one of the game's midwestern shrines: his coach, Phog Allen, had been passed the mantle by Naismith himself. Russell and Chamberlain never played against each other in college, but as pros their regular duels claimed national attention, and their rivalry remains the game's most dramatic—a testament to the neologic quality of basketball history. The two men set the terms of the game's great theoretical debate between the respective importance of offense and defense, offered unprecedented athletic performances, caused rule changes, and presented an extraordinary contrast of personalities at the moment that black performers began to enter sports' center stage.

Russell was independent, responsible, meanly intelligent, insistently dignified. He discussed every contradiction he felt: playing his heart out for white audiences he despised, denouncing the NBA quota of three blacks per team, demonstrating for civil rights while buying a plantation in Liberia. He was an intensely competitive athlete—he vomited regularly before important contests—and a powerfully embittered man. In his autobiography, he speaks more frequently about race relations in America than about basketball. One story gives a sense of the man. In the fifties, he drove a thousand miles without resting while taking his kids to visit their grandfather in Louisiana: already a wealthy national star, he refused to patronize a jim crow diner or motel.

Russell fills his book, the first intimate autobiography of a sports star, with such incidents. He insists on his own humanity, as though he believes that announcing his frailties—his fears of death, dreams of plane crashes, smarts from racial insults—will awaken the slumbering compassionate instincts of his readers. Voted the league's most valuable player five times, having led his team to eleven championships in thirteen seasons, he dismisses the games that are his claim to glory: "1963–64 was a horrible personal year. I felt the world coming to an end for me. I was on the verge of a nervous breakdown. . . . I had to get away, but I was trapped in a world from which there was no escape. . . . The planes always lay one day ahead of us. . . . How I did it, I don't know. But gradually, it ebbed. I woke one morning and the play-offs were beginning and suddenly it was all right and I was whole again. . . . What else can I tell you? About the long series of championships? You'd be bored."

For Chamberlain, however, the games are everything. Athletic achievement marks him as special in the world, and he can't stop reminding us of his victories. He tells the same tale endlessly. A coach insulted him, a reporter claimed he was a choker, a new audience expected him to fail; instead, he scored fifty points, grabbed thirty rebounds, made fifteen assists. He recalls his statistics obsessively, the scores of his high school games, his college performances, every major NBA contest, even the box scores of his youthful summer match-ups at Kutscher's Country Club. Other players also cherish their triumphs. Rick Mount, an Indiana college star, took a friend of mine on a tour of his old school gym, pointing out the spots from which he had scored in one important contest. Mount never succeeded in the pros, and this failure obviously causes him to prize his victories—a Proustian reverie I've seen in other unfortunate ex-stars. But Chamberlain doesn't share the unhappiness of these men. For years, he was the dominating player of the league, the measure of every other performer, a constant attraction and headline, the country's highest paid athlete, the greatest offensive player of the sport.

Still, he continually feels the need to prove himself. In his autobiography, he defiantly presents himself as a world-eater. He singlehandedly halts segregation in diners and motels throughout the Midwest, decides the players' strike in 1964, uses all the owners who hire him, beats all the players who challenge him, fucks all the women who want him. He turns Russell's lonely journey across the South into an epic: Chamberlain drives non-stop across America because he doesn't need anyone. "I particularly like to drive cross-country—out there alone, racing the wind, with no one bothering me. I once drove the 1,620 miles from the Muehlebach Hotel in Kansas City to the freeway exchange in downtown Los Angeles in 18 hours and 12 minutes—an average of 90 mph. I've also driven from Harlem to Nob Hill in San Francisco (3,041 miles) in 42 hours flat, and from New York to Los Angeles (2,964 miles) in 36 hours and 10 minutes. . . . I never stop for meals or sleep on my cross-country drives. I pack a hamper of gourmet sandwiches and get a few gallons of orange juice and 7-Up, and I take off. I don't even get out of the car when I stop for gas; just 'fill 'er up' and *whoosh!* I'm gone. Although I don't take any passengers with me, I do take a bouquet of flowers along—just in case I happen to meet a pretty young lady along the way."

No record satisfies the man. The only ambition that spurs him is the desire to prove himself to others. He wants us to believe that his sense of himself as a giant sets him above the businessmen who owned and traded him, but he knows that the one quality they value in him is his physique, and he protests too much: like Jacques Tati's Mr. Hulot, his attempts to do right always prove him wrong. I was a serious college student, he complains, and paints himself as a huckster; the Globetrotters are dedicated ballplayers, he insists, and shows that they're girlhounds; I'm not a choker, he bellows, and becomes a whiner instead. Statistics become the only answer to the calumny of his experience.

Fans used to choose between Russell and Chamberlain—who was the greater player? Russell was a champion of the sport and, in the social world, a fighter for civil rights who told the truth. He existed to deny every white myth about blacks. He was wise, precise, dedicated, sentient. Chamberlain proved the truth of every racist stereotype. He was vain and lazy, a sucker for every mark, a madcap consumer, a stud, a brute whose only intelligence was his strength. Compared to Russell, he was a patsy and a sell-out, a man guided solely by greed and flattery.

During the sixties Russell won the contest. But, curiously, players speak more admiringly about Chamberlain than Russell now, perhaps because he first suffered the increasingly terrible process which turns young black athletes into commodities, and time has flattened the different features of the two stars. After leaving the Celtics, Russell became coach of the Seattle Supersonics (he was the NBA's first black coach) and worked unsuccessfully to better the team's record. He made several suspect trades, bickered with his players, and was forced to retire. He refused his induction into the Hall of Fame, married a white woman, attended a Panther trial but wouldn't declare his support for the group, and performed in a series of highly successful commercials for Bell Telephone. He ends them all with the high mad crackle of his laugh, his personal stamp. In his book, he writes that during a tour of the Socialist countries, Auerbach once ordered him to stop laughing. "I have a laugh which I suppose can be grating. But it's mine. I've been using it for years. When I laugh, I laugh. It was nothing new to Auerbach. But someone said something funny and Auerbach started yelling: 'Russell, you be quiet.' I said it succinctly and to the point: '—— ——, Red. Don't say anything to me. Not ever.' "

Chamberlain also tries to coach, but his old team prohibits him; he pursues a series of lawsuits, challenging them and the league in a fantastic one-on-one legal battle he's certain to lose. The Knicks claim they want him, but his aging body costs too much; he slowly retires from the game, spending much of his time organizing a women's volleyball team. He presents a contemptuous mien to the public, but his glory days are finished. He too appears in a commercial. A beautiful white woman appraises him as he orders a beer. The bartender serves him, calling him shorty. "Shorty?" Chamberlain answers, flirting with the woman, and turns to face a man even taller than himself. Like Russell's laugh, his foolishness is his stock-in-trade, the stamp of his character. Always, he's the clown who's bested. In the end, both are isolated: Russell stranded on the island of his character, Chamberlain alone in the fort of statistics he's constructed to protect himself against critics. And Russell's laugh and Chamberlain's height, the very symbols of the humanity for which they struggle both gravely and foolishly, become symbols of their own unending servitude.

Both Russell and Chamberlain fought against bigotry in the game. By 1965 they each were paid hundred-thousand-dollar-a-year salaries, the highest in the business, but their battles never extended beyond their teams. Neither was suited to become a public leader; Russell's individualism was too threatening to whites, and Chamberlain's was too thoughtless. Besides, regardless of the respect they won on or off the court, Chamberlain and Russell hadn't yet escaped the stigma of being giants. Indeed, in 1960, when Oscar Robertson graduated from the University of Cincinnati and joined the city's pro team, Russell still played in the shadow of Bob Cousy, the quarterback and wonder worker whose presence assured the necessity of having a white guard run the team, no matter how many big blacks banged up against one another under the boards.

Within his first year of pro ball, Robertson challenged Cousy's dominance; he was the first black to command unequivocal respect as a player. In his rookie year, he played more minutes than any of his teammates, shot close to fifty percent from the field, grabbed over 700 rebounds, made almost an equal number of assists, and scored 30.5 points per game—a record bested only by Chamberlain and Elgin Baylor. At 6'5" and 205 pounds (he gained weight as he grew older), Robertson was better equipped to play ball than Cousy; he was both taller and stronger, and his eyes were unusually set, allowing him a wider range of peripheral vision than the Boston player. Capable of performing all of Cousy's admired tricks, Robertson was also a deliberate, fastidious player who scored more frequently and more regularly (remarkably so) than Cousy while achieving feats—especially in rebounding—that none of the other famous white guards had even approached. By his second year, his performances became the game's standard of excellence, and his magical craft erased the last reservations against blacks in basketball, an approval that was signified when Auerbach, Cousy's own coach, stated that Robertson was simply the most complete ballplayer ever to appear on a court.

Intellectual, coolly judgmental, Robertson was also the first black star who didn't mold his character from white attitudes. Unlike either Chamberlain or Russell, he acted with a terrific self-assurance, neither fawning in the presence of whites nor bridling with anger; and his poise and confidence helped him influence the game off the court. After its first major skirmish with

he owners in 1964, the Players Association decided to start an
organizing drive. The militants of the union suggested that a black
be president of the organization, and Jack Twyman and Tom
Heinsohn recommended Robertson for the job. They prevailed
upon Robertson, and after considering the proposition for several
days, he accepted the responsibility. His appointment occasioned
significant developments. Before Robertson assumed command,
the Players Association had been limited largely to stars, players
whose talents assured them of contracts and let them risk angering
their bosses. After Robertson became president, the struggle for
recognition by the Players Association took on the aspects of a civil
rights fight. Many blacks who had previously shunned the
organization now joined it, putting pressure on their white
colleagues to follow them. Their presence, pioneered by
Robertson, dramatized the conflict between the players and the
owners. Was sports a form of business or a kind of slavery? Were
players free laborers or chattel? Were owners feudal lords or
modern entrepreneurs? The entire relationship between owners
and players changed from the false good fellowship that had
previously been maintained into a forthright mutual distrust and
antagonism. "Oscar's influence on the Players Association was
enormous," says Larry Fleischer. "He never trusted anything the
owners said." Bill Bradley has stated that the black leadership of
the Players Association was directly responsible for the diligence
with which the organization fought the owners and its steadfast
refusal to compromise with them. With the dramatic increase in
the number of professional teams, blacks became the top stars of
the game; and basketball assumed its current status as the nation's
number one black sport.

III

Triumph breeds its own problems, however. Like heroes in
nineteenth-century novels, the young blacks who excelled in
basketball found themselves the centers of intricate plots for
wealth and power. They were alternately ripped off and catered to,
and their careers became the stumblings of innocents in the big
city. They were Pips confused and guided by mysterious Jaggers,

Rastignacs bewildered by Vautrins. Spencer Haywood's talents occasioned two multi-million-dollar lawsuits; Julius Erving caused the collapse of two businesses and a half-million-dollar fine; George McGinnis left in his wake a feud between the Knickerbockers and the NBA, a major revision of the standard player's contract, and the eventual demise of the ABA. These battles caused dismay among management, press and fans; and the players who occasioned them, practically every recent major professional talent, began to be characterized unfavorably in the popular mind. They were greedy and childish, the argument went. They never developed their skills to the maximum; they played the game using instinct, not craft. Certainly, they were superb individual talents, but as players they diminished the game.

This point of view is not mere nostalgic griping. It is nourished by racial bias. At one Net game, I met two friendly young white suburban kids who were both basketball nuts. We talked through a dull contest, and I asked them which ballplayers they liked. The kids were knowledgeable fans, but not one black ballplayer —neither Julius Erving nor Earl Monroe nor Kareem Abdul-Jabbar—passed their test. It wasn't that they thought blacks couldn't be good players, they argued; blacks just didn't play good ball. Another white fan I met at a high school shoot-out was less guarded. "I like Paul Silas," he told me, and looking around the largely black audience, he added in a whisper, "You know, there's no nigger in his game."

The theoretical expression of these prejudices is the concept of black and white ball. The game has suffered generally, the argument goes, because the majority of its new stars are black and blacks tend to play one-on-one ball while whites perform as part of a team. "In general," Thomas Jefferson concluded his notes on the black race, "their existence appears to participate more of sensation than reflection." Fans employ the same primitive racial stereotypes to distinguish between the two styles of play. In their view, the performances of black ballplayers are seen as a sort of athletic representation of the id—spontaneous, demanding, destructive. Whites are characterized as deliberate and clever (but not sneaky), their mental powers compensating for their lack of physical prowess. Black ballplayers grab rebounds; white ones position themselves to catch them. Black ballplayers leap four feet in the air and dunk the ball; white ones smartly elude their opponents and score on an uncontested lay-up. Black ballplayers reject shots, slamming them back from the basket; white ballplayers stifle their opponents, not letting them shoot in the first place. Black ballplayers steal the ball; white ones force the men they guard to throw it away. Black ballplayers must be lazy, because their physical equipment is so superb that only stupidity accounts for their losses; white ballplayers must be intelligent, because with their pathetic builds, how else can they survive on the court?

Most importantly, black ballplayers can't devote themselves to defense, the single-minded concentration on your opponent and the readiness to help your teammates stop the other side from scoring. Does your man drive only to the right? Does he lose control of the ball while taking a lay-up from the side? Does the right forward regularly slide by the man guarding him and move unopposed to the basket? Defense is the anticipation of all the possible and probable moves the five men playing against you might make. Requiring poise, intelligence and selflessness, it is considered the sign of maturity in a ballplayer, and the aspect constantly lacking in the game of every major black ballplayer in the pros during the last ten years. The phrase, "Yeah, but he can't play defense," is the damning sum of all their villainies, and none of them escapes the charge. Charlie Scott? Yeah, he can lead the fast break and bomb from outside, but he can't play defense. Bob McAdoo? Yeah, he's a great pure shooter and he's not a bad rebounder, but, God, he can't play defense! David Thompson? Jesus, can he jump! Yeah, but he can't play defense. Indeed, some of these players are lax defensively, and ballplayers do score more frequently now than they did twenty years ago; but the individual players are largely not responsible for either of these faults; and, curiously, white players don't suffer them. Paul Westphal? Christ, he's a leaper! Yeah, and he plays defense. Kim Hughes? Dear God, I've never seen a worse foul shooter. Yeah, but he plays good defense. Alvan Adams? Look at that kid's poise! Yeah, and he plays tough defense. The litany is endless and indiscriminate, a Hail Mary of the game ensuring white superiority.

Occasionally, players slip into their opposing camps. When Pete Maravich first entered the league, he was considered a "black" ballplayer, though his Eastern European name contradicts the claim; and Adrian Dantley, a stalwart black rookie forward, was hailed as a team player, though bad press notices began during his second year. Still, players inevitably change their styles from black one-on-one to white team ball, and their evolution as athletes always coincides with their personal development. They mature, as the sportswriters like to say—natives whose mastery of the mother country's tongue earns them a citizen's status.

In practice, this scheme proves false. Basketball is a team sport—you can't play it well and be blind to your mates—and black players and teams have demonstrated this just as well as the all-white squads produced in colleges twenty years ago. Indeed, blacks have propelled most of the advances in the game over the last two decades. Good and bad players and styles of play simply refuse to be grouped by color. For his time, George Mikan (white) was as large as Wilt Chamberlain and matched that black star's vanity and clumsiness. Bill Russell (black), thought to be the game's greatest defensive player, was a driven competitor, while Jerry Lucas (white) was often considered lazy by his colleagues on the court. Ernie DiGregorio (white) is commonly called "Ernie no-D [defense] Gregorio," and Oscar Robertson (black) leads all professional players in assists. John Havlicek's body (white) is an enduring masterpiece, allowing him to play over thirty minutes a game at the age of thirty-seven, while Earl Monroe (black) is all thin flesh and bones at thirty-four, a sinewy canvas of sores and bruises stretched over shin splints, exposed nerves and fractured bones. Dave DeBusschere (white) was called "the butcher" for his physical play under the boards, and 6'10" John Schumate (black) is considered a patsy because he doesn't belt his opponents around.

Still, the division between black and white styles of play is common parlance in basketball, and foolish talk, well-meaning or vicious, maintains it. After the Knicks won their first championship, Pete Axthelm wrote an original and spirited book, *The City Game*. It explored the spirit of New York (read black) basketball. "Basketball," he wrote, "is . . . often a major part of the fabric of ife. Kids in small towns—particularly the Midwest—often become superb basketball players. But they do so by developing accurate shots and precise skills; in the cities, kids simply develop moves.' Other young athletes may learn basketball, but city kids love it." Axthelm meant his comments affectionately, but absolute perversion perverts absolutely, and within a few years his tentative and charming reflections on the relationship of black people to the game became new excuses for insults. The following is from *Have Jump Shot, Will Travel,* a novel written some six years after Axthelm's book by a white ex-ballplayer about a fellow in the semi-professional league: ". . . [Basketball] is their [black kids'] game, and the only means of defining themselves without stealing anything or killing anybody. . . . Basketball is the black Doomsday weapon—the niggers will jive, juke, head-fake, and dribble their way to the turret, the bedroom, and they already work in the castle's boiler room."

Still, the theory of black and white ball isn't an entirely errant expression of racial prejudice. The present black players are probably the most gifted group of performers in the history of the game, and the overall quality of their games is generally higher than ever. They aren't guilty of the faults laid up to them in the popular view, and even within their limits, they are masters at the sport. But many of them remain in some way undeveloped. They don't achieve the greatness they promise in their youth; instead, they become caricatures of themselves, trapped in their prowess, and often seemingly incapable of extending it.

Spencer Haywood is an example of such a "black" ballplayer. Haywood should be one of the game's great forwards. He possesses all the right physical equipment. He stands 6'8" and weighs 220 pounds; his arms are exceptionally long, and when he leaps and stretches them, he can block Abdul-Jabbar's hook shot, a feat beyond the reach of any other current player. Twenty-nine years old, he claims lots of victories: a star of the '68 Olympics, a college All-American, an MVP of the ABA, an NBA all-star. He's smart, proud; and basketball is his life's work, his talent and craft. He's a better player than early basketball fans could imagine, and yet he's an incomplete one. His performance is hampered by the belief that only by his efforts can the team win a close game—which causes him to shoot too frequently, or to think the team has lost because he hasn't shot enough; this attitude puts him under a terrific pressure, largely self-created.

Haywood's history is enlightening. Ball is his life. He was the last child in a large poor southern family, and his father was killed shortly before Haywood was born. "You see," he explains, "I was never supposed to live, so everyone was surprised when this big baby came out, and then they'd say, 'Damn, you're like a duplicate of your father,' and I thought I was a duplicate. And because of this, I always imagined I was special and imagined myself a sort of savior and that I could do anything, and my mother encouraged that. I wanted to go to law school or be a ballplayer, and my mother would say, 'Well, maybe you will go to law school.' " The family was so poor that the children fought for food at the table. "My older brothers would say, 'What the fuck is this runt doing at the table? Get out of here, motherfucker!' " This competition led to fierce rivalries. "Even now when I play my brother in a one-on-one game, we play to win because I still want to beat those motherfuckers. One went to school in Chicago, and after a couple of years I went north to meet him. The first time he saw me, he didn't recognize me. He expected to see the chubby kid he had left. But I was 6'6" now and weighed 212 pounds. We went out to play and we played for three days, and from then on he was like my manager. He got me into a high school, and from there I went to Trinidad [a junior college] and when the Olympics happened I was confident. I measured myself against the other guys and my confidence just kept growing."

A hero of the '68 Olympics, Haywood attended the University of Detroit, an urban college where he attracted crowds but not glory, and left after his sophomore year for the ABA Denver franchise, which had offered him a multi-million-dollar contract. The star of the Denver team, he quit them after several years, selling his talents to the NBA's Seattle franchise, another expansion team that needed a big scorer and gate attraction. When Russell became the Seattle coach, he befriended Haywood, but the relationship didn't stick. "I'm in awe of Russell," says Haywood, "but the fans in Seattle weren't interested in men playing. They wanted boys. They like guys who act like clowns, running around with things on

heir head, shit like that. They wanted boys, and for his own
·easons so did Russell, so he never complained when the press
presented us as boys."

After several seasons, Haywood was traded to New York, a team
suddenly desperate for a strong rebounder and high scorer. Once
again, he found himself cast (and cast himself) as a savior, the player
whose efforts would transform a loser into a contender. New York
continued to lose, and Haywood grew anxious as the team bought
more stars to help it win. Haywood became the team's top
substitute; and though this role—the traditional sixth man—is
honored in the sport's tradition, he rebelled instinctively against it.
His knee nagged him throughout the season; he played infre-
quently, lost his concentration, and was bothered by rumors that
New York had offered him to every team in the league without
getting a bite. Approaching what should have been his best years as
a player, he found his future a dead end.

While the particulars of Haywood's story are unique to him, of
course, his flawed development as a player is typical of many
young black players, and no single aspect of any of their careers
accounts for this problem. One of the most frequent discussions
among basketball people is where black players go wrong, each
coach shifting blame onto the other. Sometimes these talks are
merely expressions of the general prejudice ruling the game, and
the participants can't find answers because they don't want any.
But even when the discussions are objective, they are inconclu-
sive, and no one answer is ever completely satisfactory.

The experiences of players in college provide examples.
Although college coaches often claim that they are helping produce
professional athletes, only a few schools regularly contribute
excellently prepared players to the pros: Kentucky, some of the
Atlantic Coast Conference colleges, and recently the West Coast
schools, with a smattering of independents such as Marquette,
Notre Dame, and that ersatz academy, the University of
Nevada–Los Vegas, whose players, coached by Jerry Tarkanian
("Tark the Shark"), were the market's hottest item last year. Even
players from these schools, however, commonly complain about
the transition from college to the pros, noting the differences
between the college and professional games and pressures

particular to each. Still, on examination, none of these factors is
substantial enough to block a player's development.

One rookie complaint is that the professional game is more
physical than the college one. Referees probably make more calls
on physical contact in college than in the pros (hand-checking is
presumably prohibited in college), but most of these are cosmetic,
covering the damage that has already occurred. This is especially
true of the notorious basket-and-foul call, when the ref awards the
goal and lets the other team shoot a foul for taking a charge by the
offensive player. Some of the most vicious games I've ever
witnessed were college contests, and the general roughhousing
that's part of the court spectacle is mitigated by only one fact: a big
man in college fights fewer equal opponents than a big man in the
pros. Like Dawkins, most strong college players frequently
haven't met players their own size, and the sudden equality of
strength they experience on the pro court shakes them up and
forces them either to quit or to fight harder. This adjustment,
however, is one of degree, not of style, and pro scouts quickly
eliminate the players they believe too flimsy or gentle to play the
professional game.

Similarly, the much discussed demands of defense don't
constitute a qualitative difference between the two games. Unlike
the pros, college and high school teams often play zone defenses;
i.e., players guard a section of the court rather than a single man.
Some people now argue that college players trained in the arcane
study of zones can't perform well once they graduate into the pros,
where the science is banned, but this theory lacks practical
substance. The principles of zone defense don't differ significantly
in fundamentals from those of man-to-man; indeed, successful
coaches insist that a player can't play zone without first mastering
man-to-man. Using either a zone or a man-to-man defense, the
members of a team must still stay on their feet, follow the ball,
know when they should and shouldn't guard a man not assigned to
them, alert their teammates to the other team's changes of tactics,
cut off the lanes. Zones exist to facilitate these practices, not hinder
them; and most college zones depend on the defensive abilities of
one or two players who know the principles and practices of
defense quite well. These are the only ones on the court the pros

vill even consider. Logically, playing defense in the pros should be
:asier for them, not harder, because they can rely more on their
eammates.

The third difference is the most dramatic but of the least
mportance. In college ball, the team is not under an injunction to
,hoot. Pro games are ruled by the clock. This seemingly severe
lifference has no practical effect on most players. College games
tre eight minutes shorter than pro contests, and the difference in
he scoring averages of the two equals almost exactly the difference
n playing time. There are college teams that play an extremely
leliberate style, but they have not produced fewer professional
)allplayers than run-and-gun college teams. Both Al McGuire and
Lou Carnesca, redoubtable examples of coaches who insist on a
)atterned game, produce a large number of professionals.
Carnesca has figured that the average time that elapses between a
)all being in-bounded and shot is exactly seventeen seconds in
)oth the college and the pro game.

The business aspects ruling college games don't explain the
:reation of incomplete ballplayers either. All schools with large
tthletic programs demand that their coaches win, and basketball
:oaches in particular are under the gun. It's estimated that
:hree-fifths of all college coaches will be fired within five years of
:heir first day on the job, and coaches feel and respond to this
;queeze in two ways. Often alumni just want to see triumphs on
:heir alma mater's court. Colleges are notorious home-court
`avorites; several schools boast of 88–2 or 93–5 home-court records
)ver the last several years. The coaches arrange schedules in which
)ther teams come to them—Christians to the lions. Coaches also
:ry to get a star—just one does the trick—who will thrill the
;pectators and whose heroics will give the school a name. Seton
Hall, for instance, has fielded Glenn Mosley, a good rebounder
tnd offensive center, for the last four years. The school played a lot
)f home games, often against weaker teams, and Mosley's record
was inflated until the school could crow that he was one of the
:ountry's top rebounders. Alumni like the coach (and school)
because the team wins; the coach likes the player because he
makes the coach a winner; and the player likes the coach because
he turns him into a star. Meanwhile, the player routs his inferior

opponents, and winning becomes habitual with him. When he tries himself against tougher opposition, he is suddenly shaken: has he suffered a bad day, or is his game really faulty? Instead of honing his competitive edge, the arrangement dulls it, an effect similar to the one suffered by stars who play on expansion teams.

Still, coaches mostly love to coach. They believe they know more about the game than any of the *wunderkinds* they command, and they like to impress their charges with their knowledge. They're bossy, demonstrative people (successful ones, that is), and they enjoy glory. Coaches will always tell you about the players they've "made": the triumphs of the athlete are an additional reason for the coach's immortality. Regardless of the pressures they feel to produce a winner, they should want their players to become masters. When Bob Cousy coached the Kansas City Kings and decided to turn Nate Archibald into a scoring star, he also warned him to pass the ball whenever a player had a good shot, and Archibald ended the year as the league's high scorer and assist man. Players act habitually, and few of the prideful young masters of the game balk at improving their talents if the extra work means winning more games.

And any attempt to quantify a particular kind of coach who works successfully with black players is hopeless. There are ebullient short ones and tall cool ones, tough guys from gritty urban backgrounds, and ministers from the Midwest. Black coaches are, of course, a rarity among major schools, but even changing this shocking fact wouldn't by itself alter the development of most players. Indeed, most black players have taken counsel from some black coaches in their youth—often community center directors—and their presence still hasn't changed the player's career.

The reason that empirical analysis fails to find a single cause for the production of incomplete ballplayers is that their flawed development is a general function of the industry. Men in the business frequently call their players gladiators—"they're the new gladiators." The men using this phrase never include themselves in the image. Rather, they remove themselves, looking down on the kids for wanting to be ballplayers, dismissing the crowds for paying the players to perform, separating themselves from the entire spectacle. Their attitude is similar to that of a young white professional I met the day after the mass looting that accompanied the 1977 New York blackout. He had been in a bar at the time and had passed some looters on the way home. They had offered him a color television set for seventy-five dollars and he had bought it. Still, he had only contempt for his beneficiaries. "Those animals tore up everything," he told me. "It wasn't a good night to be out if you were white." His amorality accurately reflects the way many whites feel about the game of basketball; they enjoy their home team's performance and simultaneously reject any claims the players make upon their respect. They consider the players fools, clowns, children, uppity weirdos, preternatural do-gooders, aliens—everything except performers whose masterful craft and superior knowledge add to our enjoyment of life. Not surprisingly, the theory of black and white ball arose at precisely the moment blacks achieved real dominance over the game and became its most powerful force. A business financially controlled by whites, basketball has helped to confirm the theory's bias, producing athletes who possess extraordinary talents but little capacity to extend them, the quintessential "black" basketball players of recent years. Fans of opposing teams loved to see the New York and Philadelphia squads defeated in the '76–'77 season; the two teams were collections of the most highly paid black stars of the industry, and the scoreboards in Phoenix and Houston used to flash the cost of the New York front court while the team was losing. But the problems encountered by New York and Philadelphia in creating a winning ensemble from their individually gifted stars didn't arise simply from greed, stupidity or laziness on the part of the players. They resulted from an opportunistic business, and the situation won't change as long as superb players continue to emerge from the ghettos, and white fans continue to pay to see them and be happily disappointed in their performances.

Black athletes respond variously to this situation. For older ones, basketball is part of their claim on the world. It is one of the few areas they have been allowed to explore, and they look upon their conquest proudly. People's creativity pops out in strange places when you try to squash it, and for these men the game is part of their history and testament. They don't want their accomplishments washed away by a sea of vituperation, and although white coaches complain that young black athletes can't hear appeals to tradition and pride, it remains to be seen whether they'll listen to similar requests from black veterans.

But for the younger players, the situation is simply confusing and unhappy. They are feted, paid exorbitant salaries—and simultaneously made to feel worthless. Cynicism and apathy are their answer to the conundrum. During one of the hearings on the players' suit against the league, Bob Lanier was asked whether he agreed with Bill Bradley's comment that he believed the league should always preserve a "competitive balance." Lanier answered exhaustedly: "I'd rather trounce people than be in competition with everybody, everybody kicking me. I'd rather be the guy that's on top of the hill, instead of fighting with everybody to maintain. Who said that anyway? Bill Bradley? He's a politician." Fans don't like to hear such attitudes expressed; they resent them fiercely. But young black athletes like Lanier can't see basketball except as a business, and their behavior and attitudes on and off the court mirror that vision. For them, sports are work and mastery, disappointment and betrayal; and the virtues of sports—loyalty, honor, courage—are privileges to be bought and sold. They cannot become millionaires by investing in oil or be famous by discovering a polio vaccine, and they can't change the social realities that create and maintain this situation. But they can spoil our pleasure at watching them perform by making us aware of their bitterness. "If you're from the ghetto, it doesn't matter what you do or how you get it, only if you got it," said Spencer Haywood in 1968. "What loyalties you got? To your family. To your brothers and sisters. But to basketball? To some team? Forget it." Nine years later, Julius Erving announced the same truth. "John Q. Cash did it again," he explained when asked why he had left the Nets for Philadelphia. He turned the fan's pastime into a nightmare; neither heroic nor admirable, his revenge was the only one he could execute.

6. In Court—
Scenes from a Season

The stories of this chapter begin in early fall at a professional team's training camp and end six months later at an amateur tournament held in a dilapidated church gymnasium. The characters are men for whom basketball is both a passion and a livelihood—owners, players, general managers, announcers, coaches, apprentices. Entries from the journal I wrote while researching this book, the scenes are encounters in their professional lives and occur in a variety of cities and towns. Neither the participants nor the locations are identified. Like any social community, the world of basketball is a court, with kings and princes, jesters, adventurers, scheming false advisers, disinherited noblemen, even peasants pounding on the castle door—all of them ruled by a strict set of manners and morals. Individuals fill these roles and enforce the rules, but any of these parts could be played by others without notice. In this world, individuality serves only to make people more typical. Here they speak in their own voices, present themselves both cautiously and unobserved. Their public passions are reflected in the won-lost column; these are tales about the tempers and logic of their private dramas.

$\varnothing \quad \varnothing \quad \varnothing$

During the fall training camp, the team practices at the new gym of a suburban school. Each day the players drive their cars from the local spa to the gym and scrimmage for two hours. They shower, lunch, rest, return for another session. The schedule continues for two weeks as the coach forms his team. Behind a door opening onto the school's vast parking lot, students watch the athletes perform. "Have they made the cuts yet?" a girl asks her beau, sociology and

French texts cradled in her arms. From the forty men who arrived the first morning, the coach and general manager pick twelve who will play the season. Unsigned players envy the stars with no-cut contracts; veterans work to ensure their positions.

"I was working as a clerk in the financial district, and I didn't know what to do," says a young player who tried out unsuccessfully for the team several years ago. "I decided to make a living at ball. I had played around by then, and guys had told me I was pretty good. Anyway, I felt I was a player. A friend of mine told the coach about me, and he called me up. He said they'd give me a shot and pay for me while I was at the camp.

"The first day we scrimmaged. I was guarding their first-round draft choice, and he tried to come around me. He tripped and hurt his ankle. It wasn't my fault, but I felt terrible—his ankle didn't heal that whole season, and they traded him at the end of the year. Putting him out of action was the most impressive mark I made on the team.

"I stayed until the second cut, when the team was down to twenty men. The first night, all these guys who had tried out before asked me to go drinking with them. I realized then I was in terrible shape, because I was so beat I couldn't move, and after drinking all night they still played like world-beaters. But I guess I never seriously thought I would make the team. When the trainer taped my ankles, he told me there were stories of guys like me who had come out of nowhere and succeeded. 'Just go out there and play,' he told me. 'You're here because you're a player, and you just go out and show them you can do it.' But really, I never thought I'd be offered a contract. The fact is I considered myself lucky when I started earning money playing ball in the semi-professional leagues and overseas."

The team now hosts sixteen players. Four must be cut before the season starts. The athletes are divided into two teams, red shirts and blues. Ten of them execute plays on the court while the others sit scattered along courtside benches. Coaches and g.m.'s (general managers) claim they give players every opportunity to prove themselves, but players know whether they're in or out of favor long before they're actually told.

You can see their futures in their faces. One looks perpetually unhappy. Two years ago he was the team's top draft choice. Ever since, he has scored few points, played only a few minutes a game, suffered intense public humiliation. "He'll be all right if he gets his defense together," a veteran says, rooting for him; but the player knows he's been ruled ineligible to practice his vocation professionally again. Another is irrepressible. He entered the league as a third-round draft choice of a newly created club and has worked for five different franchises in the past four years. One term of employment lasted but eleven days. "The coach of another team told me about him," says the g.m. "The kid wrote me a letter, and I invited him to the camp. But I said this was his last chance. If he didn't make the team, I insisted he promise to give up ball." The player is jolly, jokes with everyone. He halloes the g.m. as his employer walks past, and they converse privately for some moments, the player slapping hands with him when they end their talk. That night the team announces they've cut the first player, signed the second.

The coaches wear baggy shorts and sweat shirts. There are three of them, two assistants and the head coach; all are in their fifties, ex-players, well-preserved athletes. They stroll up and down the court in thick-heeled shoes, observing plays and individual movements while the teams scrimmage. A star shoots and the head coach blows his whistle. The players halt. "That was a stupid shot," the coach reproaches the star. "I was open," the star explains. Their conversation is a chat between colleagues. The play resumes, and one of the team's fumbling big men sinks a lay-up. A veteran on the sidelines claps as a joke. "All right," says the coach, a fifth-grade teacher, "who's the wise guy?"

The coach nods to his assistants and walks toward the g.m., who has stationed himself at the baseline, kibitzing with newsmen who will interview players after the practice. When the g.m. sees the coach approach, he goes to meet him halfway, where they can discuss business privately. Each season starts with alarms and diversions: players refuse to report, insist on being traded, fight with their coaches. The g.m. keeps track of all changes and informs the coach of developments. "He's asking that much?" the coach exclaims. The g.m. shrugs. They're two garment manufacturers deciding to buy or sell.

Behind them, the teams practice plays away from the ball, performing patterns of movements that will free players for shots during games. No one guards or dribbles. They take their positions on the floor. "One mississippi, two mississippi," a player mouths. He pirouettes, bends his knee, moves right, turns left; another counts to five, steps to the top of the circle; a third runs up the side of the court, halts, braces his body, runs back; a fourth cuts across his path; a fifth player bounces the ball to him and he shoots. Their performance is a silent *pas de cinque*.

"All right," the assistant coach announces. The players repeat the pattern, this time with the other team guarding. "San Antonio, San Antonio," calls a guard, naming the play as he passes the ball in-bounds. Voices explode in the gym. "Cut, cut, pick left, down here, hey!" A veteran pushes a rookie center away from the basket. The assistant coach blows his whistle. "Lean back on him, goddamnit!" he yells at the rookie. "Use your strength!" The next play, the rookie intercepts a pass and dunks the ball.

One veteran suddenly clutches his calf and hops off the court. The assistant coach waves a player to come and replace him as the veteran hobbles around, talking to himself. "Motherfucker cramp! Get out of here! You've got five to leave!" He hits the wall with his palm and slowly sets his bad foot on the floor; gingerly, he starts to walk on it, exhorting himself in a low mumble. "Come on, Arthur, come on, this mother's going! You chump, you fool, this mother's going!"

The team's superstar sprints downcourt. Last year he performed unevenly, and the sportswriters swore he'd be traded. This season he's lost weight and prances as he runs. "Hey, hey!" he shouts when one of his teammates grabs the rebound. He catches a long pass and makes the lay-up. The coach ends the scrimmage; the superstar stays on the court, loosening up, as the players gather in groups of three at separate baskets to practice foul shots. The star bends over, his body a liquid curve, and bounces off his toes sideways across court, the tips of his fingers brushing the wood.

One by one the players leave for the locker room. As they depart, the newsmen call after them, shouting their names to attract their attention, asking for interviews. "All right," agrees

one veteran, "but we'll have to talk while I shower." The coach and
g.m. continue their conversation at mid-court.

Alone, one player practices jump shots. "I grew up in a small
southern town. After I finished high school, I took a bus here. An
aunt lived in the city. I worked downtown, and one day a guy said,
'Man, you're tall—why don't you play ball with me?' My game was
nothing then; being tall always made me special in my town: My,
the old ladies would say, you're such a *big* boy—stuff like that—but
I played other sports. I started to play every afternoon when I got
off work, and that summer I joined one team in the semi-professional league. The coach here heard about me and came to see me
play. He told me he liked my game and that I should keep at it. For
two years I came to training camp and got cut. But they told me to
stay with it and keep getting my game together. One day in
mid-season, I came home from my job and the phone rang. It was
the general manager. He offered me a contract. Man, I put that
phone down and exploded.

"The first season, the coach was training me. I could see why I
didn't get that much playing time. The year before last they used
me pretty well, and I set one team record and figured that the next
season I'd be playing twenty-five, thirty minutes a game. But I
didn't. I don't know why. I didn't have any injuries, and I thought I
played good, but my main thing is defense, you know, and it's hard
to play good defense when you're only on the court for five or eight
minutes. This year I hope things will work out better. There are
some guys I really want to lock up, just leave them gasping for
points. But I don't know. They're playing a lot of rookies, trying out
new things. My contract with the team expires this fall, and my
agent talked with the general manager over the summer. We're
asking for a no-cut; if they don't give it to me, I'll go to Europe. The
level of play isn't as high, but the money's good, and it's tax-free."

As he shoots the ball, his fate is already decided. The team has
refused his demand and is trying to trade him; they won't let him
leave for Europe until they've exhausted the last possible use of his
talents and worth. He can't hide the anxiety and disappointment
he feels. Off the court, he seems a star: handsomely proportioned,
shoulders back, head steady; on court, even shooting by himself,
he appears without confidence, his stance a slouch, a perplexed,

unhappy expression on his face, the portrait of a lonely boy in a schoolyard hopelessly trying to become as good as the stars. He misses a shot and the ball bounces toward the g.m. walking away from his conference with the coach. The g.m. picks up the ball and tosses it to the player. The g.m. has earned a living from basketball his entire life, and his motto is to act nicely toward everyone because you never know if you'll need them two years from now. "Hey," he says smiling and calls the player by an affectionate nickname.

Outside, the players start to ride back to the spa. Two college kids look admiringly at a superstar's Rolls-Royce as the owner approaches it. "Can't afford that," one remarks to the other. The superstar stores his gym clothes in a soft leather over-the-shoulder bag. He enters the car with a tired grace.

Other players gather by a beat-up red Volkswagen. The owner earns well over $100,000 a year, but he acts like a teenager nursing a jalopy and looks like a grasshopper as he squats to check his oil and battery. "I don't know how the four of us fit in this car," the veteran with the cramp complains to his colleagues. He berates the owner. "And you got all this shit in it. Man, when are you going to clean the shit out of this car? Your heap is the filthiest one on the block. Your wife is ashamed of you, your kids are ashamed of you, your car is ashamed of you." The owner puts down the hood and rises. "Oh, shut up," he answers tiredly. "Whose lap are you going to sit on today?"

On the gym steps, some rookies wait for their ride. All young black men, they look unfriendly and uncertain. Only the rookie center is sure of his job. In the small plaza before them, reporters interview the remaining veterans. A reporter approaches the center, introducing himself. The other apprentices look warily at the journalist: why aren't they the subject of his piece? The rookie speaks guardedly on the morning of his new career, a cadre articulating the party line. "There are some differences between college and pro ball. In pro ball you have the clock, and there's the schedule, and there's more physical contact. We work on things like that. I just do what my coach tells me to." The player who will drive the rookies back to the spa arrives. He's a young man who has played in the ABA for a large contract, but his position on this team isn't secure. Still, he drives an all-white Eldorado, with cushiony leather seats and his monogram all over the car. He gestures with his head toward his chariot; the rookies rise. The center apologizes to the reporter for leaving so soon. "It's confusing, huh?" the reporter suggests sympathetically about training camp. The rookie center opens the car door and answers immediately: "No. I just do my best, follow what they tell me. I started in college on the bottom and climbed my way up to the top of the ladder. Now I've just got to begin that journey all over again."

◐　◐　◐

The new stadium is located in a suburb of a large city, and a generous expanse of lawn and parking lot surrounds it. In the lobby, neatly dressed young people work the concession stands where you can buy everything from hot buttered popcorn to icy whiskey sours. Inside, the arena is a perfect coliseum, banks of seats circling the court without one beam blocking the view. Hanging from the roof over mid-court, a large scoreboard directs the reactions of the crowd. Before the game starts, the scoreboard lists coming events, welcomes Boy Scout troops, displays ads, illustrates the national anthem—fireworks ("the bombs bursting in air"), a flag snapping in the wind ("Oh, say does that star-spangled banner yet wave"), a boy beating a drum, and an eagle soaring ("O'er the land of the free and the home of the brave!"). During the contest, it exhorts the crowd to yell defense, flashes the word *Charge!*, presents *pointilliste* portraits of the players who have just scored, tests the audience with "hoop quizzes": "What players used these nicknames? Trooper, Golden Arm, Chink, Pogo, Hambone?" A quarter of an hour passes before the lights shine the answer. The crowd is comprised of teenagers and families; few members of the audience have grown up with the game. "I told you they called Ray Scott 'Chink,' " a father boasts to his son. "It's because of his eyes."

The game is an exhibition match, one of the last contests before the teams set their final rosters and the season begins. A local fan calls his hometown squad fools. "You're the fool, man," a young well-built black-haired fellow sitting behind him answers. "You paid to see them play." The young man drinks several beers while rooting for them, calling the players by their first names. "Give it up, Snake! Get down, Ralph, get down! All right!" At half time, he joins the kids at courtside and waits aimlessly for the players to return to the court. The kids don't want autographs; the players entertain them regularly, and the children only desire to shout out encouragement or blame, slap hands, give their heroes a pat on the back. "Hey, hey, Ralph!" the black-haired fellow cries when the player troops out. "Hey, Ralph!" The player doesn't see him, confuses his voice with the cries of the kids, and passes him by. Sullenly, the black-haired fellow returns to his seat. In the third quarter, he berates the coach. "He's a fool. He doesn't know how to teach a press, call a time-out, make a sub. He's a nobody." The fan sitting in front of him turns and disagrees. "Don't tell me, man," the black-haired fellow answers. "Until yesterday I *played* on that team. I know."

❂   ❂   ❂

"It's like a hobby," an owner says, describing his basketball team. He's a fashionably dressed middle-aged man who has earned his wealth from real estate. Recently, his company has acquired a publishing house, a television distribution firm, several magazines. The products are displayed in the outer lobby of his office. They are without character, bland, concepts rather than creations, someone's idea of what an audience wants. The only taste that designs them is the desire for money. "Some men fool around, others like the fights, others play the ponies. I enjoy my team."

His inner office is a vast room overlooking the city, a flat plain broken by neutral high rises. His desk is fixed on the bias at the far corner of the room; he sits behind it, signing letters while interrogating a reporter. What magazines has he written for? Why does he want to speak to him about the team? The reporter answers the questions from across the room, sitting on a couch so plush that he can't arrange himself comfortably; every time he readies himself to take notes, feathers and velvet surround him. "Well," the owner says, signing the last letter and finishing the examination. He pushes his swivel chair away from the desk, rises, and sits in a hard-backed chair near the couch. "What can I do for you?"

He owns an expansion team created by the league in the late

sixties when basketball became fashionable. His franchise has suffered a predictable history. It staggered from the gate, wobbling under the weight of inexperience and ineptitude. After several seasons, it collected a group of first-round draft choices and ended two years with winning records. Now fans complained because the team failed to make the play-offs. The franchise named a new goat each year, usually the past season's star. With the regularity of a snake shedding its skin, they traded these victims one by one and entered each fall with vigorous promises. By mid-season, the team wore the same drab colors as the previous year. The season finally came when the squad excelled in the play-offs. "He outshined every star in this town," one gossip reported of the team's owner. "With all the powerful people located here, he still was the man to meet."

He speaks modestly of his involvement with the team and its success. He had heard that the league was offering new franchises and had known that they would like the town he represented. His relations with the team are minimal. He lives and works in another city; rarely sees home games, except for the play-offs. He lets the general manager run the business. "I only tell him how much we can afford, but we've never not signed a player because of money," he says proudly. Occasionally the owner eats with the players.

The reporter reviews the team's history. The owner claims perfect confidence in his general manager. The reporter mentions a player the team traded in one of its yearly sacrifices. The player has excelled since leaving the franchise and is now considered a treasure throughout the league. The owner laughs. "That was a mistake." The reporter refers to another trade. During the interview, the owner has called all the players by their first names. Now he bristles. "I have no regrets about that," he says, ending the discussion, and uses the player's last name. "Sometimes I want a player really badly. I wouldn't mind having . . ."—he pauses, searching for the name. A few months before, Adrian Dantley, a thickly built, determined small forward led the United States Olympic basketball team to victory, his name lighting the sleeping summer world of the game. "Adrian Dantley?" suggests the reporter, his hands pushing down the mounds of couch on either side of him. "That's him," agrees the owner.

He refuses to talk about the team's finances. "Is that important for your article?" he asks the reporter. The reporter shifts position on the couch again, sitting on the edge; if he leans back, he becomes two feet and a head without a torso. The owner wears a distracted expression as the reporter explains the importance of his question. "I don't think the finances of the team are important for your article," the owner answers when the reporter finishes, "whether it makes or loses money. It's not business to me." Then what does the team mean to him? Is it like a charity? "Yes," the owner agrees, "or like a civic association." He gestures pleasantly with his hand, at ease with the comparison.

Later the reporter mentions this exchange to a general manager from another team. "He said that?" the general manager asks incredulously. "He bought that team for half what it's worth now. That team would bring in more that six million now— that's the price for an expansion club, and this outfit's a solid product. And that doesn't include the write-offs he's taken on it."

Mercifully, the reporter rises to leave. The owner is a faceless king. The phone rings, and the owner excuses himself. "All right," he answers his secretary, "I'll talk to him." He negotiates a business deal, assuring the worried man on the other end of the line. He relaxes into his executive manner, crosses his legs, tilts the chair backward. "Look," he explains, "go see the buildings. You know the rent. If you're interested, I'll send you the papers. It's simple." The conversation is the first instance of genuine animation and ease he's expressed during the entire hour.

❦ ❦ ❦

An hour before the practice starts, players amble into the coach's office, two rooms housed in the university's gym, a quaint structure that next year will be replaced by an arena seating ten thousand fans. The arena climaxes the university's scheme to improve its athletic program, a five-year plan that also included increasing the number of athletic scholarships and hiring new coaches. The basketball coach came several years ago, after the previous coach had found it impossible to work with the team's star. "As soon as I got here, I realized it was me or the star. He had already broken the other coach—the man had just left. The star bitched about other players, said they brought down his game, walked off the court, looked away when you told him what to do. I threw him out of practice, threw him off the team. Finally he came around." Last season, the star led the squad to an almost undefeated year and into the national championships; now he's gone—drafted by the pros—and the team's schedule includes many tough opponents. "Ah," says the coach with self-effacing irony, "if I were smart, I would have done this whole thing differently. Win seventeen games the first year, then twenty-one, twenty-three, then the quarter-finals—take five years to bring us where we are today."

A calm professionalism pervades the atmosphere of the coach's office. Pictures of the team's individual players line the walls; one athlete, under twenty years old, makes a telephone call under his own photo. His brother is getting married tomorrow, and he must leave practice early to attend the wedding. A freshman player teases him that he's receiving preferential treatment. "I'm missing the rehearsal and bachelor party," the player complains. "Shit," answers the freshman disgustedly.

The freshman, a tall, bulky kid, sits behind a coach's desk, his hands stuffed into the pockets of his full-length leather trench coat. He has played only a short time with the team, but the coach is already disappointed in his performance. "He'll never be a really good player. Offensively he's all right, but defense takes hard work. For some players the pain of playing defense is worth it to become a good player. But for this kid it's not, and it never will be. He played in a poor league on a so-so team and never matched himself against kids of his own height or build, so he expects things to be easy. We wanted more from him. We just didn't know enough about his history when we took him."

A senior enters and the freshman mumbles hello. "Coach in?" the senior asks the blond secretary, looking around. She shakes her head no; he's at the hospital visiting a player suffering a sudden case of mononucleosis. "Don't plan anything for the weekend," she says. He tells her he's got tickets for Earth, Wind and Fire. "You can't go," she answers with an apologetic smile. "The coach has called an extra practice." The freshman groans. The senior sighs acceptingly. "I thought we were through, but I'll be there." He picks up his tote bag as the team's student manager walks in. "Don't mess with the points today," the senior reminds him, leaving for the locker room. The manager sits on the edge of an assistant coach's desk, near a stack of books including Tom Hayden's *Rebellion in Newark, The Psychology of Coaching,* a volume of essays on the abolitionists, and *The Theory and Science of Basketball.* "What's the matter with him?" he asks the secretary as the freshman wanders out to change into his practice clothes.

Across the hall, a local black kid shoots baskets in the gym while two attendants arrange the practice equipment: a weight-lifting machine, several upright nets set catty-corner to the basket, clocks, timers, basketballs. One of the team's starting guards strolls in with a friend, and they play one-on-one. The attendants ask the kid at the other end of the court to please leave, as the team must practice. "It don't make me no never-mind," he answers and shoots again. The attendants don't want to take the ball from him and provoke a fight. They wait under the basket; when the boy makes a shot, one of them grabs the ball as it falls through the net. "All right," the boy surrenders, and the attendant tosses the ball away from the court.

The gym slowly fills with activity as players enter. One adjusts the weight machine to his specifications and performs deep knee bends and lifts the bar. Others line up behind him. A few run sprints; two shoot jump shots, moving in a semicircle around the basket. An assistant coach runs players through an exercise. He passes the ball to them; they shoot, grab the rebound, toss the ball against the standing net, shoot another jumper from the other side of the basket. For three minutes each player catches, shoots, leaps, throws, catches, shoots, without stop. They add individual touches: hooking, tapping, dunking the ball into the basket. One guard works intently, twisting right and left before flicking the ball. "Go, go!" the coach encourages him. The arena becomes a concert of individual activity, a modern Brueghel.

The head coach enters, dressed like a businessman on a golf date and carrying a clipboard. He has a reputation for wild actions during games, but conducts the practice with absolute command and logic. He divides the players into red and white squads, drops the clipboard to the floor, crouches to watch the action. He barely speaks during the entire two-hour practice, passing his judgments in silence.

The two teams scrimmage on plays, practice shooting, run fast breaks. Most of the practice consists of three fifteen-minute scrimmages during which the student manager keeps score, counting baskets, turnovers, offensive rebounds, steals, blocked shots. The team that loses must perform "the suicide": in twenty-eight seconds they run a third of the court and back, half-court and back, two-thirds and back, the full distance. Any player who takes longer than twenty-eight seconds to finish the course must repeat it. When the whites win the first scrimmage, they exuberantly encourage the losers who must run; when they lose the second by a point, they complain that the student manager has scored the game incorrectly. "I got that steal!" one player insists. The coach checks with the manager, a private conversation over the stat book, and tells the whites to run it. A red player applauds. The whites grudgingly line themselves along the baseline, one player still arguing the case. The coach pretends not to hear him. "Stop bitching," yells the red player. "Just run it. We ran it." The last scrimmage is a fifteen-minute duel, the players exhorting their teammates, arguing over every decision, criticizing themselves and one another for every bad play. No one wants to run the suicide again, so they exhaust themselves trying to win. The buzzer sounds at a tie, and the players stand still, their shirts entirely soaked with sweat, their chests rising and falling with deep breaths. The coach picks his clipboard up off the floor. "All right," he says, expressing more disgust than he feels, and dismisses them.

"When I get my kids on the floor," he says later, after the grueling practice, "they're there to practice. We can talk about the weather in my office. I expect them to be ready to perform, and there are only a couple of ways to make them work if they don't want to—take away playing time, belittle them, make them run the suicide. Those are the ways you get to know who's a player. You take professional football players. Why do they make it when others don't? It's not build or talent. It's because they like it better; they take a greater pride in hitting the other guy. Kids like to play basketball—you don't have to coach them to do it. But mental attitude is everything in winning basketball, and here we train them to be professionals."

◑   ◑   ◑

"My parents always wanted me to be a professional. Physician, dentist, lawyer—at least a CPA, so my father could do his tax returns for nothing. I didn't want to disappoint them. I even studied law for a year and got good grades. But it began to prey on my mind; you're best at what you like to do, and I always had this voice. Maybe I could have been a cantor; I used to hold short services when I was a kid, and the cantors and rabbis of this town like me well enough now—they keep calling me for tickets! People encouraged me. You should use your gift, they said. And besides, I was always a sports fan and wanted good seats to all the big events.

"I was known for being a crazy kid. At school I was the general factotum, cheerleader, kibitzer, the guy who went in for high jinks and fun stuff. I had gift of gab, or b.s.—whatever you want to call it. Let's say I was announcing a college game and saw a cute blonde. I'd get an usher to find out her name. Then I'd announce that there was a message for Miss Abbie-gail, and she'd come over, and one thing would lead to another. When I started announcing for the great man, he let it be known that he wouldn't stand for that kind of stuff. 'If he's as ferocious as he thinks he is, I'll tame him,' he said. He tamed me."

The speaker is an announcer noted for his voice, a mellifluous gravel that puns on players' names and spoofs the calls of the referees. "Twoooo minutes," he chirps, a maniac birdcall; "Frayzzzzier," he intones, rhyming the word with brazier; "Freeee!" he exclaims whenever the Philly long-distance jump-shot artist scores a basket. Small, thin-haired, round-headed, he works days in a downtown ticket office with the great man, his boss for the last forty years. The great man is a legend of the business who has discovered some of the game's most famous players, guided teams to championships, owned one of the league's first franchises. A gathering place for old-timers, their office is filled with mementos of the past when owners knew the game and players were workers, each contributing his knowledge and skill to the high times and tight contests from which they all made an honest living. In this court, the great man is king, the announcer his aide and jester.

"You know that man's a genius," says the announcer. "He made me. One day he came to me and said, 'There are lots of good announcers; you have to do something special to make yourself known.' Well, Lafayette had a player named Tom Gola, and whenever he'd score, I'd say, field goal Gola. Then I thought about it. Gola, goal, goal, Gola. Rather than say the normal prosaic thing, I quipped Gola goal. The audience liked it, and soon the papers picked it up."

His personal mementos include old paperback copies of a book he wrote, redoubtable photos and testimonials, cuff links with his name engraved on them, championship rings. Among the people who have honored him is Huey Long, the Louisiana Kingfish. The announcer opens a jewelry box that contains a tiny golden football and tells the story. "My school was in the Sugar Bowl that year, and I went with them. I followed the team because I worked on the school paper. There was a mix-up and, at the last moment, no one to announce the game, so they called on my services. We led during the first half, and I had my usual fun, but we lost in the second. At the end, Huey Long gave out these little silver footballs to all the members of our squad. Then he said, 'There was a damn Yankee on the microphone all afternoon. He was mighty happy the first half, and plumb sad the second, but he tickled us the whole time.' He called me up and presented me with this golden football. That was a good start for me.

"After I finished college, the great man made a master change, scheduling his team to play in a downtown hotel, and I worked for him. I followed the team everywhere. Oshkosh, Detroit, Chicago. I'd drive one of our cars or go to sleep. Even to this day, I can fall asleep anywhere, and it's hard to wake me up. I'd lie down on the floor, and the guys would just take off their shoes and put their feet on me, and I'd be out. They used to fool me because of my sleeping—practical jokes. One time we were in a jump-seat car, and it was icy. We went off the road, and the car stopped, hanging over a ditch. I was asleep in the back, and when the players saw I hadn't woken up, they all got out quietly and left me there. Then they made a noise and I woke up, staring over this ditch. Another time, the great man was driving us all home after a game at the hotel, and I fell asleep, and he just parked his car and left me inside. I woke up at six o'clock in the morning. I walked home. How could you? I asked him the next day. I forgot, he told me.

"I can't lie to him. He'll always catch me, and he's taught me everything I know. One time a promoter asked me to go around the world with his team. He wanted me to announce and be his chief cook and bottle washer. It was quite an opportunity, but I was doing the announcing for the baseball teams in town—both leagues. I couldn't decide what to do. Me, the promoter, and the great man all met for dinner to discuss the situation. We ate in a fancy place that served two-dollar steaks, and I was impressed, because I was used to eating in a cafeteria where for twenty cents you'd get frizzled beef on toast, coffee, and a sticky roll. I asked the great man what he thought. 'You're grown up now,' he said. 'Make up your own mind. But whenever you leave a job, leave the door open. If you leave, leave with a handshake.' He was right. I took the job with the promoter and I trained an announcer for the baseball teams. Twenty-five years later, when the ballpark had an old-timers' day, they asked me to make the introductions.

"During the war, I landed up in Iceland. I had given this general a smart salute, and he had given me three choices—Alaska, Greenland or Iceland. I stayed there twenty-eight months, putting out a paper, running the officers club, staging shows, fixing up boxing matches among the men. It kept the guys happy. We called ourselves the F.B.I., the forgotten bastards of Iceland; and we still have a reunion once a year. I didn't let anybody get by me; and because I was always nice to them, they always did favors for me. One night a plane landed, and I heard that Bob Hope was on it. I searched around and found this body sleeping in the back. I woke him up, and it was old Ski-nose. He did two shows for us in four hours. Another time, Isaac Stern played there with a quartet. He begged me to let him play on our baseball team but not tell his partners because he might hurt his hands. I've got a letter from him, too.

"Now I do everything—tennis, football, boxing. You have to

gauge your audience. Your tennis audience is a world apart from your basketball crowd. In basketball, you tell the crowd not to throw anything on the court; in tennis you say, 'The management definitely frowns upon any displays of unsportsmanlike conduct from the spectators.' The first time they asked me to do a tennis game, I told them I knew nothing about the sport. 'That's all right,' they said. 'We'll teach you. The first thing you'll have to learn is to keep your mouth shut.'

"I guess I like doing basketball best, because there's so much to say. I don't dream my things up in advance; they just come to me. Freeee! I use that because he's got a high arching shot, and when my voice hits that falsetto, the audience just goes with me. Johnny Red Kerr. He was playing one night and crashed to the floor. As Kerr got up, I said, very softly, Kerr . . . plunk. I came up with Wilt the Stilt, but Chamberlain told me he didn't like it. So one night he slammed one in, and I hit the name Dipper, and I used it. He ran downcourt and gave me the okay sign. Chuck Share—pair for share. Gene Shue—two for shue. Shue once told me that he wanted to play again just to hear me say that once more, and players sometimes come up and request me to make things up about them. Collins . . . Mix: assist. Get it? One time Gus Gerard played. Gerard banks, I said, because that's the name of one of the banks in this town. Everyone in the audience laughed, but Gerard doesn't come from here, and he asked his trainer what was so funny. And I used to love Gar Heard. Heard, I'd say, of Buffalo. So what happens? They trade him to Phoenix."

◑   ◑   ◑

The gym is chilly. The walls are lined with tiles, and some panes of the grated windows are shattered, letting in blasts of cold air. Outside, the gym's light glows over the shriveled grass of the school's athletic field, and the boys' shouts sound ceremoniously joyous. Inside, they run with their arms tucked around them, keeping themselves warm, and yell at the student manager to make the janitor send up more heat.

A short, stocky, vigorous, dark-haired fellow coaches the team. He's a physical education teacher at the school, and basketball is his life. During the summers, he coaches a Puerto Rican team;

winters, he teaches and scouts professional teams for an NBA franchise whose coach is a friend. He harbors great ambitions. He admires the yearbook for the University of Maryland, one hundred pages of advertisements with a picture of Lefty Dreisel, the team's coach, in the centerfold. "That's the way to do it," he argues. Although he isn't the team's regular coach, he has helped form the school's squad. For the last several seasons, the team has enjoyed the services of a superstar, a player wanted by every major college in the country. But the team has never won the city championship. This year is the star's last, and the squad has been bolstered by a tall guard from an upstate school and a 6'6" Puerto Rican who has transferred to the school from a midwestern high school 1,500 miles away. On the second day of practice the guard broke his foot, and now the Board of Education is threatening to rule the Puerto Rican ineligible to play. His family lives in the city, but resides in a distant part of town, so the kid rents his own apartment. The suspicion is that the phys. ed. teacher and the team's coach are funding him to play for the school; otherwise, why should he pick this institution out of all the thousands in the land? "They're full of shit," answers the phys. ed. teacher. "He can live anywhere he wants. He's an emancipated minor." This afternoon the teacher is leading the team's practice because the coach must argue the case with representatives from the Board. "Aw, he's all right," says one neighborhood youth counselor about the phys. ed. teacher. "He's just an eager beaver."

He makes the kids run fast breaks while a friend of his, an ex-college player, looks on. He has come to see the superstar. "This kid's got everything," the phys. ed. teacher says about the superstar. "He was having trouble with his shot, moved in and out with it. I gave him some pointers. He's a sweet kid, coachable. He thanked me." The superstar shakes his head when he hears the tale. "I thank everybody; I thank the milkman. Let them all think what they want to." He shoots jumpers near the foul line and scores effortlessly when close to the basket, scooping and feinting with the ball. The ex-college player studies him admiringly. "He's like Julius with all those inside moves."

A majority of the boys are black; the white kids are sons of German, Irish and Greek immigrants. The smallest player is barely five feet, a tiny black child whom the coach discovered to be a good ball-handling guard during one of his phys. ed. classes. The Puerto Rican hovers over all the rest. The starters act like older brothers toward the sophomores: the magnificent five, one benchwarmer calls them facetiously. "These are your starters," the coach introduced them the first day of practice. They stood next to him on the floor while the other members of the team sat on the bench. "These are the guys everything rests on. I want you to love them and hug them. When they feel good, you feel good; when they feel bad, you feel bad." A sub mockingly wiped tears away from his eyes. The coach caught him. "You think that's funny?" he demanded. The sub readied himself for one of the coach's harmless raging furies; no member of the team respected them because they occurred so frequently. "You're a wise guy," the coach dismissed him. "Run a lap." Sighing, the kid left the bench and trotted around the floor, mugging behind the coach's back. "He told me to stay away from women," the team's superstar says, "—women and weed. Why does he compare women to weed? He came from a woman."

The coach enters the gym, and the phys. ed. teacher halts the practice, waving over the ex-college player as the kids crowd onto the folded-up bleachers that serve as a bench. He puts his arm around the ex-college player and smiles at the kids. "This guy was a great college ballplayer." The ex-college ballplayer is embarrassed by the compliment and looks upward, away from the kids. "You see how tall he is? He gave away five inches to Rudy Tomjanovich, but one night held Rudy T. to six points in the Winter Festival." The kids nod appreciatively. "That's what hustle will get you."

The kids clap, and the coach assumes command, perfunctorily thanking the phys. ed. teacher. He retires with the ex-college player to the edge of the court, skeptically regarding the coach. "Look at his fucking shoes," he says, referring to the coach's out-of-date brown and white wingtips. Envying the opportunity of training the star, he mutters critical comments about the coach's performance. "He talks too much. Look at that—the fucking kids are freezing. You gotta run kids, fast-break 'em. This is psychodrama, not basketball. What the fuck does that guy think he's doing?"

The coach does talk a lot. He's gray-haired, a thin man, consumed by nervous energy. His notes are scrawled on a piece of paper. "All right," he sighs, "where was I?" He looks beseechingly at the kids, who are blank-faced in their endurance. "You know, kids, this isn't an easy job, and sometimes it gets the better of me. I'm human too. I know you're worried about your forms and suits, but don't—I'll take care of that. Just think about the game; that's all I ask you. You know we've had some ups and downs, but that's life." His monologue continues aimlessly, then suddenly stops. "All right, let's do the twenty-two." He names ten players, claps his hands, and the kids jump enthusiastically off the bench. They're merely happy to play, but he smiles, believing he's encouraged them.

Their relief is short-lived. While they stand in position on the court, the coach delivers a relentless diatribe about the defensive zone they're to practice, a talk filled with incomprehensible particulars and seeming contradictions. He lectures each kid except the superstar, and they all respond listlessly. Whoever is the subject of the coach's instructions listens mutely while the others wander around, twirl balls on their fingers, jive with one another under their breaths. The coach overhears one comment. He turns violently. "What are you joking about? You think this is a joke? You think the season's a joke? You think the championship's a joke? This is no joke, you moron!" Even the Puerto Rican receives a dressing down. He starts muttering in Spanish while the coach criticizes him. The coach stops himself. "What are you saying?" the coach asks with sudden concern. The Puerto Rican waves his hand dismissively and starts to stalk off the court. "Wait a minute," the coach calls, running up to him. He places a restraining hand on the kid's broad shoulder. "What's the matter? You look like a madman. Take it easy. What's the matter?" The kid brushes the coach's hand away. "Do this, do that, here, there, I don't know what you want!" The coach grasps his wrist. "Hey, calm down," he says, trying to shut off the kid's speech. "Twenty-two, forty-seven, eleven, thirty-three," the kid continues. The coach laughs uneasily. "Hey, get a drink of water. You want a drink of water? Get a drink of water."

The phys. ed. teacher looks disgusted and wanders outside into the school lobby followed by his friend. "The guy's a mental case," he says. "He's crazy. You see those shoes? Kids don't understand all that talk; this is a running game; they want to run." He must wait until after practice to hear whether the Puerto Rican will play. The ex-college player listens silently. When his friend finishes, he mentions the superstar, comparing him to Julius Erving. "And that schmuck is coaching him," the phys. ed. teacher adds. "Now there's a mystery," the ex-college player suggests after a moment's silence, wanting to change the discussion. "Julius Erving. The greatest player in the world, and he couldn't attract fans. Why do you think that was?" The phys. ed. teacher pauses, but he's in no mood to schmooze. "I don't know," he answers, pulling up the sleeves of his sweater, the hard edge of impatience in his voice ending the discussion. "What are we? On the David Susskind show?"

◔ ◔ ◔

A press photographer arrives courtside at a professional game. He walks behind the reporters and takes his favorite seat, a folding chair at the end of the press table. As the players warm up on the court, he arranges his equipment, loading his camera and taking out a sheet of paper on which he will write descriptions of his photos. A young woman sits down in the folding chair next to his, and he tells her she has no business there. He calls over the man in charge of the press table. "Stanley," he explains, "this young woman works for my paper. She's a very nice girl and I like her, but she's not supposed to be here. Now I won't complain if you say it's all right, but it should be your decision." Stanley calls over his boss, and the photographer repeats his complaint. "Well, let her sit there," the boss decides, embarrassed by the incident.

The game begins, and the photographer sits down. He explains his case to a reporter. "It took us forever to get courtside seats. Originally, they wanted to put us all up in the balcony, but the writers threatened to boycott the games if they did." He sighs. "Now I look like a prick."

He rests his chin on his palm. "This is real barnyard basketball," he comments, and starts sighting through the camera. Desultorily, he shoots a few moments of action, but the incident with the girl has soured him for the night. "I used to travel with the team. Now I

only do home games. They use AP for the rest—it costs them less."
A player stumbles out-of-bounds, and the photographer snaps the
shutter and records the particulars of the play. The arena's own
photographer walks by, asking at which angles the light is best. "It
stinks everywhere," the photographer replies. "Why don't you
take those red filters off the lights up there?" he asks, pointing to
the ceiling. "The horse show was so bad I shot five hundredth at
five point six." He scans the crowd at courtside. "Hey, I think that's
John Wooden. I'll tell my writer. It'll make a great story." But the
reporter is already at the photographer's seat. He's a kid, twenty
years younger than the photographer and as bubbly as his
colleague is leaden. "I got a terrific picture for you," he says.
"Come on, come on! Dustin Hoffman is sleeping behind the team
bench in the third row!"

❂   ❂   ❂

The secretaries greet the reporters in the club's foyer, informing
them when the press conference will start and where they can find
the principals. The club is on the ground floor of the arena. It's
furnished with leather chairs; its walls and tables and the bar are
richly hued woods, a costly, chintzy decor. Reporters gather at the
bar, waiting for drinks, and wander into the dining room, where
television men prepare their cameras, search for electrical out-
lets, arrange the lights. The press relations man hurries about, a
bothersome journalist always accompanying him. The team has
just bought two players from another franchise. One is a superstar,
the other a once-promising dud. The club is struggling and needs
the star to become respectable, and his acquisition has been an
on-again/off-again affair. Just two days ago, the owners of both
clubs announced that the deal was finished. "To tell you the truth,"
says one front-office man, "I'd just as soon we didn't have him.
Even without him, the press has been driving me crazy for seats.
It's going to be a real nightmare now."

Along a counter, Filipino waiters prepare the mix of fondues and
gravied meats that make up lunch. Near them are gathered a
bunch of league executives and front-office men. They joke about
their certainty that the deal was kaput. A man from the league takes
offense. "Hey, wait a minute," he defends himself, "everybody
thought the deal was off. I just know what I'm told." A front-office

man says he wishes the deal hadn't been completed. "I can't remember the last time I got home before twelve. Monday and Tuesday we think he's coming. Wednesday we play a game. Thursday I finally get the day off, and the phone rings at seven and they tell me he's coming in by twelve." The league executive sympathizes. Both are in their mid-fifties and have suffered heart attacks during the past year. "I slept in a hotel three nights this week." The front-office man looks around furtively. "Christ, we almost had them all. Chamberlain, Jabbar, Wicks. How many guys are in the league?" he asks in a low voice. "Two hundred and thirty? We got a closet with uniforms for every one of them."

"All right, boys," the press relations man announces, moving through the room, "we're going to begin." He steps to the podium looking harried; he too has suffered a heart attack this year. He says that the owner, the general manager, two new players and the coach will all speak. After their statements, they will be available for "one-on-one questioning," first with the "pen and paper" men, then with the "electronic media."

The owner takes his place at the podium. "As I was saying Wednesday . . . " he jokes, referring to his comment two days ago that the deal was off. Everyone laughs. The local press has presented him as a hero throughout the last tortuous days. He speaks of the trade as a matter of civic pride. "I went the extra mile for the city. It deserved it. One-on-one negotiations are subjective things. The other owner and I behaved like a couple of guys in a saloon fight." The press applaud and ask no questions.

The general manager takes the stage. He should be smiling, but he has bad teeth and keeps his mouth closed, giving him a taut, determined look, a general saying his men will fight on this line forever. He refers to the players as "kids," says their talents will bring the team "up a notch or two." He introduces the less well known player first; the athlete stands, nods to the press, charming and diffident. He says he was surprised to find out he was traded. "When I met the other player at the airport this morning, I told him to please let me know the next time he was about to be traded." The press all laugh understandingly, but ask him no questions; he introduces the star.

The star is black, tall, lean, dressed in a black turtleneck and black pants. He speaks in a soft southern accent, saying he's glad to be here and that he couldn't concentrate on playing ball when his status on either team was uncertain. The press laugh because the player performed heroically in his last game with his old team. "How do you explain your last game, then?" a reporter asks, setting up the joke. "I wasn't concentrating," the star answers soberly, giving the audience the punch line. Everyone but the player laughs again; he means the comment seriously.

"Not concentrating!" exclaims the player's agent, sitting with some reporters at a table toward the back of the room. "Forty-two points and twenty rebounds! Not concentrating!" He laughs and shakes his head disbelievingly, enjoying his employer's perform-ance, and the journalists all chuckle with him. He's dressed in an expensive gray pin-striped suit and with his blond hair and freshly manicured appearance looks almost a star himself—Robert Redford should play him in the movie.

He repeats the story of the trade to every journalist who asks. A new owner was buying the team. He wanted the star's big contract off the books before he made the purchase. The agent and the star only talked to the old owner. They demanded that some deferred payments be made in cash. Wasn't this a renegotiation? one reporter asks. The word is dreaded. "There were no negotiations," the agent corrects. "The owner only spoke to us once. But he did accuse us of that. He was wrong." He's a lawyer, and he explains the point with sudden energy, as though his enthusiasm by itself will clarify the byzantine difference. "I want you to work for me at the end of your contract. You tell me what you want. Then I agree to it or not. That's the point where we were at. It wasn't a renegotiation; it wasn't during the term of the contract." The reporter begins to question the distinction, but a young woman journalist slides into a seat opposite the agent and says the coach is preparing to speak. The agent smiles at her welcoming look. "His problems are just beginning," she says. The agent warms to the mild flirtation. "With all the shooters on this team, I think he's going to need more basketballs to keep his players happy."

The middle-aged coach is stylishly dressed in Brooks Brothers drab—gray flannels, black shoes and socks, blue shirt, French silk tie, blue gabardine jacket. He speaks in complete sentences. He's glad to have the two players and cautions the reporters not to expect the team to be an instant winner. Again the reporters ask him no questions, and when he sits down, they break to surround the star, one calling the star's first name repeatedly. In this instance, reporting is asking the first question. "Has this whole experience soured you on basketball?" the reporter finally inquires. The star has just signed a contract paying him $500,000 a year for the coming half decade. He looks at the reporter vaguely, uncomprehendingly. "No," he replies.

Across from the throng a young reporter tries to get a story from the coach. "What were you doing when you heard the news?" The coach relaxes, his arms extended along the back of the couch. "I had left the office and was in a restaurant with my wife." The reporter brightens. "And she told you?" The coach smiles. "No. I got a telephone call. It almost ruined my dinner. You want to know what I was eating?" He doesn't wait for the reporter to say no. "Scungilli," he answers himself, pronouncing the word lovingly. "I was eating a cold scungilli salad. You know what it is? It's the meat of a conch. They take out the meat and slice it all up"—he chops the air with the side of his hand—"mix in garlic, onion, parsley, and it's wonderful. I still smell of garlic." The reporter thanks him. "Got what you needed?" asks the coach.

Another reporter sits down next to him. To make room for the new players, two long-standing members of the squad were cut; the reporter asks the coach how one took the news. A displeased look crosses the coach's face. "People ask me how he reacted. How do you expect? I told him myself. I called him up this morning. I think we have the responsibility to do it, but I hate it. Especially that kid, because I used to fool around with him a lot. I think he'll be picked up by someone else. He was playing well for us, and on another team he might start—a lot of these kids do better when they start."

The reporter asks him about the less well known player acquired in the trade. The coach shrugs. "I never really saw him play, except what he did against us, which wasn't much. I don't know how good he is. A lot of these guys find it easier to play center than forward; they played it in college and have to run around more when they're defending against another forward. We'll start playing the two of them and see where we go. What are we now? Twenty-four games into the season? Two games under five hundred? Maybe we should have been playing better ball, but I don't know. We've had a shithouse full of injuries, and then there was all this talk about the trade. It's hard to know if that affects guys. Maybe it did, at least on some"—he searches for the word—"*subconscious* level. You can't tell. You can't worry about it. You play the players, see how they blend, keep going, and don't let it worry you."

His talk is off the record; none of it can be quoted, a rule of the trade. The reporters leave to file their stories. Two meet on the arena's steps. "Back to the typewriter," says one balefully. "What's to write?" answers the other.

◐　◐　◐

The general manager is thin-faced, pinched. He wears aviator's glasses and rarely looks directly at anyone; his glance is normally distracted, his eyes always moving—geiger counters for power and gossip. His office is a large cubicle. A map on the wall has pins stuck into the sites of NBA cities. The other walls display team banners, pictures of his wife and family, and a chart of the rosters of all NBA teams. The letters are movable, allowing him to record all trades immediately. Once every two weeks, he speaks to all the other general managers in the league. "Is it still snowing up there?" he begins his telephone chat with his colleague in Buffalo. His smile is a prefabricated toothy grin.

Two hours before the game, he eats in the cafeteria with the press and other front-office workers. The cold cuts and warm meats dull the palate. He is greeted pleasantly by a broadcaster for the opposing team, and sits at his table. The broadcaster is round-faced, a jovial man, a talker; he eagerly asks the general manager to be his half-time guest and thanks him effusively when the general manager agrees. It's the general manager's policy never to refuse an invitation to speak, and he especially likes question and answer sessions, but the broadcaster takes his agreement as an act of beneficence, not principle.

The general manager asks the broadcaster how his team is performing. As soon as the man starts to answer him, the general manager tunes out; his eyes dart around the room, coming back to rest on the man only for seconds, then taking off again. His occasional spare comments keep the broadcaster yapping. "You'd like our forward. He's good—a Dave DeBusschere forward, a white guy. Strong." The general manager nods as though he's never heard the player's name before, and swallows his last piece of meat. He wipes his lips, promises to meet the man for the half-time show, and is off.

For the next hour and a half—until the game starts—he wanders through and around the arena with an air of fixed purposiveness on missions of absolute insignificance. He possesses a man-on-the-move attitude, as though he's a politician working a convention crowd—glad-handing acquaintances, engaging in short conversations, pulling individuals to the side for brief confidential exchanges, always striding off somewhere to find one person or another whom he does not actually have to meet. He whispers in one man's ear, listens to the answer, leaves to find another, each trip occasioning another twenty-minute parade through the vast arena during which he meets still other admirers and confidants.

On one journey, he reminds himself he must visit the locker room of the visiting team. He greets the coach and a veteran player recently traded to the franchise. "I didn't recognize you," he says to the player. "I'm not used to seeing you wear blue." The coach laments the difficulty of winning on the road. "It's tough," consoles the general manager, his eyes shifting past the players who wait for the trainer to tape their ankles. "Something has to give," says the coach. The general manager's eyes pull back from one player and light on the coach. "Really, really," he agrees.

The team's comptroller meets him in the passageway outside the locker room. They talk while walking to his office. A player wants the team to underwrite a loan for his new house. "How much is he paying? That's a good price." As he steps inside the office, he greets the woman who plays the arena's organ and checks to see that she has organized a half-time show. "No foul-ups like last time," she assures him. He starts to make a telephone call, stops, and leaves the office, making another circuit through the arena. Kids notice him and shout hello—he waves his hand; concession vendors nod respectfully—he greets them by name. He walks down the stairs, around the court, up the other side of the arena, through the passageways to the locker rooms, and into the arena's dinner club, where he drops by the owner's table, shaking hands with everyone. The owner gestures to him with a finger, and the general manager crouches by his side for a five-minute consultation during which his eyes are riveted on his boss. On his way out, the general manager says hello to the team's former owner. The previous owner rises to speak to him, pressing him for gossip as the general manager's eyes scan the filled room.

He returns hurriedly to his office and calls the team's doctor. A player has injured his hand, and the general manager wants to know the prognosis. He relaxes as he speaks to this other professional over the phone. "All right, good doctor, if that's what you say. You coming to the game tonight? We'll fit you in courtside." Two kids waylay him as he leaves. They want schedules. He gives them packets of five hundred schedules apiece. He plans to go to the locker room, but meets a television announcer on the way, a young black man who's having difficulties at his job. "Hey, hey," says the announcer, "three-piece." He rubs the lapels of the general manager's coat between his fingers. "You're coming up in the world." The general manager laughs and suddenly assumes a sober mien, asking the announcer in a low voice about his employment problems. "They didn't give the tryouts enough time," the announcer complains. "I spoke to them about that." The general manager commiserates, and the two of them discuss the merits of different teams as the announcer accompanies the general manager to the locker room. "I've got to go," the general manager excuses himself as soon as he reaches his destination.

Inside, he meets with the coach and the injured player. The athlete wants to play, but the doctor says no. They examine his hand, moving it back and forth. He tells the player he should resume practice tomorrow, snaps his fingers and suddenly leaves; he goes to his office, where he searches for a paperback book. The game will begin in fifteen minutes, and the teams will be walking out for the warm-up in a few moments. He finds the book and positions himself in the passageway outside the visiting team's locker room. His eyes light everywhere as the players start to troop out, a sober squadron of giants. The general manager spots his man. It is the forward whom the broadcaster praised. As the player passes, the general manager steps up to him, calling him by his first name. They both are members of a Christian charitable organization sponsored by athletes, and it would be quite a catch to add the forward's name to the general manager's team on the roster chart hanging in his office. He quickly introduces himself; this man is even busier than he is. "I have this book for you on the environment. I thought you'd be interested in it. I'll leave it in your locker—all right?" The player doesn't utter a word, barely stops walking. He only nods and is gone. The general manager seems satisfied and calls to an usher. He mentions the player's name. "You know which locker is his?" he asks. "Absolutely," says the kid. "You're sure? You're sure you know his?" The kid protests. The general manager sighs and hands the book to the kid. "Make sure it's the right one," he says, and closes his eyes for a second. He opens them and glances around the dark corridor as his face assumes a happy neutral expression. Everything's been taken care of; he can attend to the game.

❂   ❂   ❂

Two recruiters watch a high school practice. They're both young black men, one representing a local school, the other a state university two thousand miles away. The recruiter from the university mentions a big win his competitor's team managed the past weekend. A freshman guard steered the squad to triumph, hitting all his foul shots in the overtime period. The kid's small; he seems to heave the ball, his feet spread apart and off the ground. "He's something," the recruiter says, accepting the compliment. "The coach told him he had to change his style. 'But, coach,' the kid said, 'it goes in.' 'I don't care,' the coach answered. 'It looks like shit.'" They both laugh.

The kids practice in the bare gymnasium, the coach moving back and forth on the baseline, passing the recruiters. The school's star interests them, but the coach keeps telling them about other members of the team. "Hey," he says, "you want a good guard? I got a good guard. This kid Tony's great. Solid." On the next play, he walks past them again. "That kid's a good forward. Terrific talent. He can dunk starting from the sideline—one step and a jump. Good marks, too." The recruiters nod noncommittally. They don't want to get on the wrong side of this man.

The coach suddenly explodes, grabbing a forward by the shoulder. "Idiot!" he yells, his voice screeching. "Idiot! Idiot! Idiot!" He explains a play to the kid again and pushes him back onto the court. He has worked as a teacher twenty-one years; his star is wanted by many colleges; he may never coach another talent comparable to the star's again. "What do I know about basketball?" he comments to the recruiters, passing by again. They smile at the rhetorical question. "I've only been coaching for twenty-one years. These kids know nothing. No brains. They can shoot, but they're idiots about the game."

He blows his whistle, fraught, intense, sets up another play. A thin black kid botches it. The star observes from the sidelines. The coach explodes again. "You want to play more, but you're not tough. Now I want you to get tough. You're a nice kid. You're a gentleman. I don't mean that you shouldn't be. But on the floor it's something else. And if you want to get on the floor, you'd better show me some more!" The kid regards the coach hatefully; sixteen years old, he has become a humiliated child. He walks off the court. The star shakes his head slightly and smiles knowingly. The coach calls another play. "Morons," he complains to the recruiters. "I've got to work with morons."

�℈   ☈   ☈

"I got this job thirteen years ago when we were back in the old arena," says the security guard. I was one of the first Jews they hired; Irish and Germans were the only ones who worked here then. The guy who owned the place was a terrific anti-Semite. You remember in 1939 when the American Nazis held a rally here and a lot of protesters showed up? There's still a newsreel of the Nazis beating up one of them and throwing him out. Who do you think rented the place to them? The owner. He said he didn't know what they stood for, but who could believe him? What was the guy, some kind of schmuck that he didn't know what Nazis were? After that he was a marked man; everyone knew he was an anti-Semite.

"I was working out at the baseball park then. I got thirteen dollars a day for standing in the dugout. They were good to me. The manager was a terrific guy. I froze my ass off with them out there and got rained on—hail, sleet, snow, the works. The manager and I were friends, good friends. Once I drove him home, and another time he visited me where I was down vacationing in Florida when the team was in spring training. Sometimes I used to bring my boy with me to the dugout—four years old, he'd sit on the bench and get his picture taken with the stars.

"You see, I always acted like a gentleman, very polite. What do you want to break somebody's chops for? Then they break yours. I ran interference for the manager. Some guy would come up asking for the manager, and I'd see him coming down the hall. I figured the guy didn't know the manager, but who wanted to insult him? I'd tell the manager there was an emergency phone call for him inside. Then I'd turn to the guy. 'I'm sorry,' I'd say, 'but he's on the phone. Can I take a message?' If the guy was for real, he'd leave one; most of them weren't and walked away, and as the manager picked up the phone, I'd say, 'You don't have to worry about that,' and give him a wink. 'Oh, I don't,' he'd say. I took care of him like that all the time.

"I went to a school in the fifties that was involved with the scandals. Played ball there. During the summer, I worked at a resort as a caddy, and I knew all the guys who were dumping. I was a schmuck—who knew they were on the take? One used to work the boathouse and I would see him with that guy Sollazo they took the money from. The kid would call me up and ask if I could take over for a while. So after I got to the last hole, I'd go down to the boathouse and see this guy drive up in a big Cadillac, and the kid would get in and off they'd go. I never thought anything about it; the kid was a rich boy anyway, a millionaire's son. His family owned a piece of restaurant chain, Sugar 'n' Spice, or Cup 'n' Saucer—something like that.

"Then I went into the service and took some more courses, and after that I got a job as a salesman. Eighty dollars a week—how could I turn it down? Those were big bucks in those days. I've worked there nineteen years, and my boss still doesn't know that I also work here. A couple of nights ago, one of the photographers here took my picture. It was unintentional. A referee blew a call in a college game. Those referees! The coach was giving it to him good, and the fans were going wild, so twenty of us ran over to that side of the court in case something broke out. The next day the photographer tells me my picture's in the paper, because I was standing right next to the referee. 'Oh, Jeez,' I said, 'why'd you do something like that?' That's all my boss needs to know—then I go to ask him for a raise and he tells me, 'Why do you need more money? Work another night at the arena.' 'What do you mean?' the photographer said. 'It's a pretty good picture.'

"All the security guards belong to a union. The arena calls up and they say we need so many men tonight; then I call up the union hall and ask them if there's any work. It's sort of like substitute teaching. Now I'm a regular, of course.

"I do little things to make myself known. Elton John was here a while ago, and I was working the dressing room. I saw his manager walk in and said good evening to him by name. I didn't give him any trouble; I knew he was the manager. The next night I'm up here, and some other guy's working the dressing room. The manager walks up, and the guy won't let him in; he doesn't even know he's the manager. So after the performance, the manager says to the head of security, 'I want the guard who was here last night. Who was that?' They look at their sheet; there's my name. 'Oh, that's him,' they say. 'That's right,' he says. 'I want him.' You see? At the end of the week, he tipped me a hundred dollars.

"Who's to complain? We security guards get thirty dollars a night. At the old arena it was less, and the ushers get still less, but that's because of tips. They make lots of extra money. Even the ticket-takers at the door. Some guy walks up to him and sticks a five in his hand. 'Hello, my friend,' he says. Okay, figure what's the best seat in the house—twelve-fifty. So that's five dollars. Then he walks inside and goes up to another usher and says, 'I'd like a good seat for tonight's game. What'll it cost me?' Say it costs another five; he's spent ten and saved two-fifty. All the ushers do it and split it with one another. We security guards don't get a dime from it. I don't think that's right, because any of us could blow the whistle on the whole thing.

"Some nights you get monsters in here. Kiss is coming Friday.

They're a good group, I hear, but their following is bad—drugs. The girls do it; I thank God I don't have a daughter. They drink Southern Comfort and smoke marijuana, and the combination of the two is supposed to make them sort of float. People get mugged and beaten all over the place: bathrooms, stairways; the poor kids who sell concessions always get ripped off. Nights like that we get forty or fifty assaults in a couple of hours, ship the kids right off down to the hospital.

"Some things you stop. A kid walks in with a bottle under his belt and I see it. 'Excuse me, sir,' I say, 'could you please open your coat?' There's no point in being rude. All right, he's a smart-aleck: 'Hey, what is this?' he says. 'You got a warrant?' I stay cool. 'Now, sir,' I explain, 'we don't have a search warrant, but we do have the right to refuse admission, and I know there's a bottle under your coat. If you leave it with us, we'll give you a receipt, and you can pick it up at the end of the concert; or you can leave it outside or drink it outside, but you can't bring it in.' It's easy once you explain it to them; there's no cause for trouble.

"Of course, they mainly go off and give it to their girlfriends or something. You can't search everyone, and they can get pretty rowdy. A month ago, the guy who works up here with me broke his arm; some kids came tumbling down the stairs and pushed him. Tonight's his first night back. 'John,' I told him, 'you get any trouble, just signal for me.'

"You didn't have that in the old arena; you didn't have the element you have here now. There were a lot of gamblers then, and the whole place was smaller and easier to control. Now these kids will sit anywhere. But I never challenge them; I don't let things go that far. When an usher calls me over to move them, I just get them out. You see, if a guy sits down in one of the back rows of a section before a game begins, you know that the section's sold out. Common sense tells you that if you go to the ticket window and put down six dollars, they're going to give you the front seat if they got it. So if I see a well-dressed couple sitting five rows back from the front and a bunch of kids in the section's premier seats, I know they don't have tickets.

"I'm always polite. 'Look,' I say, 'these seats belong to someone else.' 'No, man,' they say—you know how they talk—but I just ignore any trouble. 'Now you can get up like gentlemen,' I say, 'and walk away, or I'll call twenty guys up here, and they'll escort you from the building.' They look at each other, and I know they're going to leave. 'Don't be stupid,' I tell them. 'Wait until half time. There'll be empty seats then, and no one will bother you.' They leave. I'm not out to bust their chops. Why should I? Look at that bunch. I tell them not to come down here, and they go down the other staircase. Let them go; an usher will come along and move them as soon as they sit down. I can't patrol the whole place.

"For my money, the games in the old arena were better, too. A couple of weeks ago, I worked the locker room for a visiting team. I can't tell you which one, but you can figure it out. They had just lost, and you should have heard this one guy after the game. 'You want to win, just give me the fucking ball. You don't know what the fuck you're doing.' He's the only white guy on the team and a real superstar. I've got a friend who works in another arena, and he says he's heard the same guy complain like that too. Why? Because they won't pass him the ball. That's why this player's going to throw it in this year. Why bother? I heard the same thing between other players. I don't understand it. Sometimes you get to thinking that the blacks must have a conspiracy to run the whites out of the game, you know? I mean, I think that's not really possible, but where are the white ballplayers? They must be somewhere. These guys, they have talent, but they don't know what to do with it. What did Al McGuire say? 'I wouldn't coach any guy that got paid more than I did.' That's smart. 'You know what I got on my team?' a baseball manager once said to me. 'Twenty-eight crybabies.' I mean, get some smart white *Jewish* ballplayers, players with *sechel;* then the good crowds will start coming.

"When they first hired me, they didn't know I was Jewish. I'd worked here one night, and the head of security called me over and asked if I'd like to be put on as a steady. I told him sure. The money was better than at the ballpark, and the hours are shorter. You figure three hours for a baseball game, two hours for warming up, an hour before you leave. Here, I'm in and out within three hours. The only other Jewish guy working here then was an old boxer they used as a bouncer. The first paycheck I got, I see that they'd spelled my name wrong, and I told them so. *'Oy givault!'* they must have said, because they must have thought I was a German or something, and that old owner was really a terrible anti-Semite. Now, of course, a lot of Jewish guys work here.

"It was good extra money then, and I took the job to make a little something for a rainy day. Now, all my kids are through school, but I don't know when I'll quit. The truth is, I love the game. Don't tell them I said it, but I'd pay *them* to work here."

❂   ❂   ❂

Two groups of kids gather at the street entrance to the locker room as the crowd leaves the arena. Three white teenagers discuss the game avidly, angry because their home team has lost. The other is a group of black children, dressed in clothes too thin for the winter cold—corduroy car coats, sparsely stuffed jackets. They raise their collars against the wind and fool with one another. A boy pretends to be a star. "I go round like this," he announces, pivoting as though he were the player. "And I block you like this!" answers his friend. "Kiss her, man, kiss her," a kid urges, pushing a boy toward a girl. The girl shrieks and giggles; the boy tells his friend to shut up and looks away with shame and disgust. One of them spots a celebrity walking with the crowd, an ex-player who towers above the people around him. They call out his name; the teenagers discussing the game turn their heads for a moment and go back to their talk. The kids trail the star, members of the group pushing one child toward him, demanding that he get the celebrity's autograph. The child becomes embarrassed. "He ain't nothing," he says, walking away from their taunts. He names the player he's waiting for. "He's a superstar." They're urchins begging for a touch of fame.

The superstar's car drives up, and they mob the chauffeur, asking him when the player will leave the locker room. The chauffeur walks past them into the bar that's next to the exit. None of them dares follow him, so they gather at the glass, looking into the filled saloon, and see the superstar. "He got by us!" one shouts. "That sucker got past us!" They press their faces to the glass and stare at the star, who sits at the bar talking to a pretty young woman. They pound the glass, calling his name, but he ignores them. "Go on in," one tells a smaller kid. He pushes him toward the door. "Come on, man," he implores. "You be too small for them to chase you out!" The child resists. "Go in yourself." The two tussle playfully, and the three teenagers walk up. "Look at that shit," one of them says. "He's with that chick, warm and nice, and we're out in the cold." His partners agree. "And he didn't do shit tonight."

The kids spot a player leaving the street entrance and run after him. He stops to hail a cab, and they surround him, handing him ticket stubs, old receipts, student identification cards for him to sign. He autographs them mechanically. The kids walk away with the pieces of paper in their hands and ask each other who the star is. "I don't know," one answers, giggling.

A national television announcer leaves from the street entrance, and they cry out his name. "Hey!" he welcomes them, his hands making a halting gesture. They beseech him for autographs. "Not tonight," he repeats many times as he walks away. "You're shit," one of the teenagers yells after him. "You're shit."

The players from the opposing team leave, one by one, the kids running after each. The teenagers stay in place, bemoaning the fate of their club. The cold bites their ears, and their judgments become nastier as they hop up and down to ward off the chill. The black kids depart in groups, and the teenagers are alone when a star from their team strolls out, his eyes staring past them. "Is that him?" one asks the other, although they know his face well; by the time they assure themselves of his identity, the star is at the corner, accosted by the last black child of the group. The teenagers start to leave, and a sub from the opposing team walks out and hails a cab. "Your team's shit," one of the teenagers shouts. "Beat you," the player jokes, stepping into the street and reaching for the cab door. "Hey," the kid calls to the cabbie as the player puts his bag inside the car, "don't take him. He beat us tonight." The player enters the cab, locks the door. "Just wait," the kid cries in a last spasm of frustration. "Wait 'til next time. We'll make you eat the ball."

❂   ❂   ❂

The coach's team is a contender for the city high school championship, and he wants to win it. His work is his avocation. Players he trained ten years ago still ask his advice; he holds parties

egularly for the kids on his team, arranges for them to attend
college, lends them cars, lets them sleep at his house. During the
summer, he works at a camp where he gets them jobs waiting
tables and coaches them daily. The team is black except for two
players, and the coach has had problems with them. "They don't
listen. I'll tell you what the trouble all year with this team has been:
they won't let me use them. When I use eleven men, they win."
During games and practices, he yells and hugs them, pushes them,
curses them, laughs at their jokes. They all call him by his last name
with no mister attached. "Hey," a player tells him during a game,
"I haven't played yet." He has clocked fifteen minutes and has not
performed well. "That's right," the coach answers. "You haven't
played a bit." His team laughs. "You're a super talent, a super,
super talent," he says to one boy, "but you've got no discipline."
He asks a third if he wants to play now. The kid mumbles an
answer; the rest of the team urges him to say yes; the kid looks
embarrassed. "Come on," says the coach, sparing the player
additional shame, "get in the game."

For two hours, the coach works in the principal's office. The
school houses twenty-five hundred boys daily, and kids wander
around. "Are you a cop?" a Puerto Rican student jokes. "No, I ain't
a cop," the coach answers. "Why do you want to know?" The kid
laughs. "I want to cop some dope." The coach runs him out of the
office.

A boy and his mother enter. The kid wants to transfer schools.
He had received good grades in his other school the first term, but
didn't attend class the second. "What are you going to do for us?"
asks the coach. The boy's mother speaks for her child. "That school
wasn't good for him. They played around with foolish things
there." The boy says he couldn't go to class because a gang had
threatened to kill him. "Why?" asks the coach. "I think it would be
different here," says the kid. The coach repeats his question. He
runs his hands through his hair. "Look," he explains to the mother,
"he has to make me want to take him, you understand. So far, he's
not giving us anything. If he goes back to his other school and gets
good marks, then we'll accept his transfer the next term." The
mother protests; she won't send him back to his old school. The
coach explains that the administration of his school simply won't let

the boy enroll. "Can't I see the principal?" she pleads, and the coach hopelessly arranges an appointment.

He makes a telephone call. Earlier that morning, the cops arrested a student for selling cocaine, and the coach must inform the child's father what precinct is holding his son. He speaks curtly to the man, not wanting to involve himself with the case. When he hangs up, a woman teacher comes over to gossip. "I asked my hygiene class what they would do if they saw someone stealing their friend's coat," he tells her, "and none of them said they'd report it." She nods her head. A few days before, a thirteen-year-old boy threw a brick off a highway overpass and killed a woman driving her car. The teacher says her class discussed the incident. The coach interrupts her. "I know what to do with that kid," he says. "Kill him." The woman agrees, but her class didn't. "They said he's a kid and stuff like that. Then I asked them what they would do if the victim had been their mother or sister, and they started changing their minds."

A haggard young man walks in. "Hey, we need some security down in the lunchroom. There are a bunch of guys there, and I don't know what's going to happen." Some black security guards leave, and the coach wanders out into the hall. "Still looking for dope?" he asks the Puerto Rican who teased him about being a cop. "Yeah," he answers seriously. The coach tries to make conversation, asks the kid if he's ever been to Puerto Rico. "What's there?" answers the kid. "You know where you're from?" he challenges the coach. Poland, Russia, he answers. "Why don't you go back there? There ain't shit in Puerto Rico." The coach asks him if his school day is finished, says he should leave the buildings. "Yeah," says the kid, checking his watch, "I'll see if my friend is around so I can score. If not, I'll go home sober."

The coach climbs the stairs to the phys. ed. office two at a time. His team scrimmages with a team from another school today; the other coach is inside the phys. ed. office, his feet on the desk while he leafs through a newspaper. The coach teases his colleague that he won't make the play-offs this year. "Yeah, but next year I'll be unbeatable," answers his colleague. "I have this kid who's 6'2" and unstoppable." The coach knows the player. "You can't play him," he warns, half-joking. "He's ineligible. He should have graduated this year. He's a five-year student. You play him and I'll start an investigation." His colleague dismisses the threat. "I'll play him," he mutters.

They walk to the gym, discussing what they want to practice in the scrimmage. The teams are already in the gym, shooting at the baskets as kids watch from the bleachers that have been pushed together accordion-fashion along the wall. The coach gets out the timer and walks alongside the bleachers, collecting a quarter from each of the kids who wants to watch the game. The school has little money for its athletic program. "I don't got a quarter," one says. The coach passes him by, and the next kid uses the same excuse. "Come on," orders the coach, "pay up." The kid yields the change.

Toward the end of the scrimmage, a fight breaks out between one of the coach's players and a member of the other team. The coach walks onto the court and grabs his player by the arm, dragging him toward the bench. "Sit down!" he commands him. "Sit down!" The player relents and the game begins again. After a moment, the fighter is on his feet once more, calling his opponent names. The coach waves his hand to stop play and stands in front of his player. "Sit down!" he yells. "You never know when's enough!" He pushes the kid, and the student puts his hand on the coach's chest. The coach pushes him again, his face tight and hard as the spectators look on silently. "You're acting like an idiot! Sit down!" The fighter notices one of his teammates laughing. "I don't think it's a joke," he threatens his teammate. "You keep laughing, I'll take your teeth out." The teammate calls him a chump. "I don't see you coming my way. Come my way," he taunts. The coach yells at both of them to sit down. He wants a moment of quiet. "Punk niggers," the fighter mutters, pulling his pants over his shorts. "Faggot assholes. Punk niggers." He's enraged and humiliated, and the coach realizes that his luck's gone bad. There will certainly be a brawl if he doesn't send the boys home. "That's it!" he announces in exasperation. He goes to collect the clock. "You sure you don't want to finish the quarter?" the other coach asks. "No way," he says. The fighter is one of his special projects. "I've been working on him for two years. He was into dope and everything. Always on the street. No mother, no family. A hard case. He's going to college. He'll be all right." The fighter is still cursing his teammates. "Punk niggers, faggot niggers." The coach picks up the clock and a rack filled with basketballs. "My man acted like an idiot," he tells the other coach. "Your kid too. They just don't know when's enough."

❂ ❂ ❂

The television announcer sits behind his desk in the anti-poverty program where he works. The job is a sinecure. "I help put out these brochures and newsletters; and, you know, I'm good for the organization, because I can get in to see people through my association with the team. I talk basketball with them—you know, everybody wants to talk ball—get them tickets, or I can get on the phone right now and call ABC, CBS, or NBC and ask them for a minute-spot because I've done favors for them. Just broadcasting road games on the network, I mention that I work here, and that's three thousand dollars a minute right there. So it's a good deal for both of us." He's in his late thirties, a large man. The features of his face form an African mask. During the winter, basketball rules his life; he reports to the arena every night the team plays, accompanies them on every trip, experiences each contest as though he were playing in it.

"Playing ball was my first love. I went to school, played ball, ate lunch, played ball, did my homework, played ball. In high school, my coach advised me to go to this local college that had never had a black on its team. It was a sort of test; you know, people would say, let's see if this nigger can make it. I had my bags packed for another school, but one morning I decided to accept the challenge. You had to take eight two-credit courses then: accounting, science, literature, history, economics—that was a bitch—business management and two others. I did pretty well, getting almost a B average, and the next year I got some other guys to come to the school; and I made sure they succeeded too.

"When I got out, I was drafted by the pros. To be a basketball player—I thought that was great! And it wasn't the money. They offered me seven thousand dollars. I told them I wanted ten and a no-cut; well, we can't give you that, they said; and shit, I agreed immediately. All my friends were ballplayers—Wilt, Oscar, Satch Sanders. Playing ball was what I lived to do.

"In my first game I scored ten points. Then eighteen, twenty, sixteen rebounds and fourteen points, nineteen, eight, and two. Those are just as good stats as lots of rookies, but the team cut me. The next year another team picked me up, and I played a few games with them, but they cut me too. I joined the Eastern League, and one night I tore up my knee coming down hard. That ended my playing career.

"I was very bitter. Later I realized that basketball's a business. I had never thought about it that way before. It was the man's money. I didn't know why he thought I wasn't as good as someone else or didn't like me, and it didn't matter. There was nothing I could do about it. It was his money, and he thinks dollars and cents; he never forgets it, even when the team's winning.

"I started doing television by a fluke. I was working as a teacher, but went to the games a lot. All my friends were playing. So one day I wrote to the management and told them I would like to do something. Nothing. Then, a while later, I got offered a job as a statistician. Well, you know, everybody put it down. Fifteen dollars a game. I was making good bread as a teacher. What did I need the job for? But I figured I'd get to see the games and I'd have a courtside seat, and maybe something else would come from it.

"I took care of offensive rebounds and turnovers. As a matter of fact, I started the figure that indicates an offensive rebound that's converted into a basket, a little circle with a cross at the top. And, you know, I'd go to the press room and talk to some of the guys, and little by little the men doing the commentary would ask me for some information on the game. My girlfriend even got mad at me: What are you giving away information for? she asked. But I thought I'd be polite, and besides, you never know what will happen. The team's radio announcer kept telling me I should become a broadcaster, and one day he called and said they were auditioning for color commentary. So I went down, and he met me at the door. 'We're going to do an imaginary game,' he told me. I said I had never done something like this before. 'Don't worry,' he said. 'We'll do the Knicks against the Bucks, all right?' I agreed.

"He started. 'Bucks control the tap. Lucius Allen brings it down-court, moving right to left. Passes to Jabbar. Jabbar with the ball, moves right, turns, takes a jumper that's——no good, but he draws the foul.' Then he cued me. 'Well, a classic match-up,' I said. 'Jabbar against Reed. Willis plays Kareem high, trying to keep him from getting the sky-hook; and he tried to keep him to the left. A smart play, but he drew the foul.' Then the announcer took it. 'Jabbar makes both, and it's the Knicks' ball, Frazier moving it downcourt. He pulls up, fakes, shoots—it's good, and the foul.' I came in. 'Another classic match-up, Oscar against Clyde. Clyde had the extra step and got him in the air—a super play.' Then it was 25–21 at the quarter and 50–48 at the half. 'A good first half for the Knicks,' I said. 'They've been shooting well and playing good defense. Kareem's having a super, super game, but the real key here is Dave DeBusschere's work defending against Bobby Dandridge, and that's what we have to look for in the second half.' Then we did the final. 'A super game,' I said. 'Kareem, of course, had an outstanding night with thirty-two points and nineteen rebounds, but at the end he just ran out of gas, and the key match-up was DeBusschere against Dandridge, Dave holding Bobby to eight points when he's averaging twenty a game throughout the league. A great job there and a big win for the Knicks.' A week later they told me I had the job.

"They asked me if I wanted to do television or radio. I said radio. They called me back and said TV. I worked with a guy who had been around a long time. He taught me a lot. He told me to arrive early at every game, and make sure I traveled with the team, so I wouldn't be stranded in a blizzard while they're playing in Chicago. Also, not to bother the players and to get to know them gradually. You know, when a team's traveling, the players sit in the back and the coaches up front; and I heard of one announcer who always sat in the back with the players. So I asked a player about him, and he said, 'Man, that guy was a pain in the ass; he wouldn't leave us alone.' So I took a cue. These guys are tired; they've just played a whole game; so I leave them alone.

"Now I've got my pattern set. On a game night, I walk over to the arena. I see the trainer first to make sure there are no injuries. Then I go upstairs to the press room, talk to the producer and the director, tell them what players to follow and what to look for. They listen to me now. I get a bite to eat, go downstairs, speak to the visiting players and coach, let them fill me in on what's happening with the team. I introduce myself to new players, speak to the players on my team, get ready for my half-time interview. Sometimes I can't, because I don't know who I'll be talking to. Those times, I just hope the guy's got a lot to say so I can think up questions while he's taking a long time to answer them.

"You can't use some things players tell you. Last night, two players said they liked their new coach better than their old one because he commanded their respect. Well, you don't say that. Last year, one player told me he wouldn't sign a new contract with his old team, and I didn't use that. I know when lots of players are unhappy and where they want to go, but I don't say that either.

"My job isn't news. My job is to enhance the image of the team I work for, sell them like you sell a product. Last night, two players were mad that they weren't being played. I knew it, but I didn't say it. I said, 'Well, the doctor wants to be careful with this thing and see how it develops.' I try to help the players in other ways, pointing out when they play good defense, alerting the audience to the things I know they take pride in; and the players like me for that. And I always go into the locker room after a game, whether they win or lose.

"I talk to them about different things. One's very involved in politics. I eat with a couple of others. We have places in Phoenix and San Fran and Milwaukee. You get the best shrimp anywhere in Milwaukee—big fat shrimp, like this—and one guy eats the whole meat dinner and the whole fish dinner. I can hardly finish the meat dinner just by itself. Another player's into tennis. Another one's into jazz; with him I have a special thing going: he hums a tune and I try to name it.

"They call me Mister Blues. It's an inside thing. I play cards with them sometimes on the charter flights. We play blackjack, and I lose—now I'm getting better, but I used to lose. We bet small amounts, you know, but a lot of times they'd be going off for a taxi and I'd be out of change, so I'd say, 'Hey, wait up, lend me some money.' One day this player said, 'Man, you're always crying the blues so much, I'm calling you Mr. Blues.' Now that's my name with them. A couple of nights ago, I got into the bus and started to sit in the middle because that's my policy, as you know. Well, all

the black players were on one side, and the whites on the other
like always, and I was just preparing to read some magazine when
this one brother yelled: 'Hey, Blues, why you sitting there alone,
man? You always sitting alone! Come back here and sit with us.'
And so I did."

$$\bullet \quad \bullet \quad \bullet$$

It's the arena's last game of the season. Huge nets, ropes and
cages hang from the domed ceiling, a shapeless, vast mobile
announcing the circus's arrival in town. A banner saying fare-
well to the team's coach and one of its stars is draped over the
uppermost balcony in the stadium. Both men are retiring, and this
will be their final game. The audience is scattered, the players
lackadaisical. In other towns the fans have honored the coach and
the player, but here in their hometown the arena isn't even filled
for their last performance. They haven't given the fans a winning
season, and the fans, in turn, are refusing them the glory of a
memorable bow.

Around courtside, no one attends to the contest. Reporters chat
with one another. One notices a player's peculiar strut. "He
doesn't move his hips," he comments to a young woman who works
as a secretary for the team and charts the offensive rebounds. She
studies the player's movements for a second. "Writers," she
complains. "If you're not talking to somebody, you're looking at a
guy's hips."

At the half, the statisticians can't get their records right. "Who
gives a shit?" one asks. "It's the last game anyway." Another fools
with a pocket computer, trying to figure shooting percentages.
"I've got it now," he says. "Four-oh-two, seven-seventy-eight."
The scribe takes down the numbers dutifully. "Wonderful," he
laughs. A drunken young fan walks out onto the court. "We're
number one!" He stumbles along the players' bench, sticking out
his hand to each athlete. They look away, the uncomfortable
motion people make to disengage themselves from a beggar's plea.
He stops in front of one of the team's superstars and sticks out his
hand aggressively. "We're number one," he orders. The star looks
at him warily, tiredly. He shakes the kid's hand, his face without
emotion. A front-office man grabs the kid's elbow from behind and

hustles him off the court. "All right. Let's go, let's go."

In the third quarter, the home team shaves the lead, and the fans get excited, but the effort evaporates as quickly as it appeared. Soon they trail by fifteen, and the game's over with a quarter and a half to go. During the first half of the game, the coach called plays, shouted instructions, encouraged his troops. Now he sits silently. The player is retiring because of age, but the coach has been pressured to leave because of his team's losing record. With ten minutes to go, he replaces two of his stars. Have they failed him or he them? They sit at the end of the bench, far away from him, talking to each other as courtside fans berate them.

The only drama is the final moments of the player's career. A few voices call out his name every time he shoots. He has played ball for twenty years now; still, he cannot escape his character. He comes around the key, takes the ball from a guard, sets himself behind a pick, and shoots quickly. The ball falls through the hoop. The crowd chants. A hint of a smile crosses his face, but he has always taken the game seriously, being a somber player, never an exuberant one, and he won't betray himself now. His normal dogged expression returns, and he runs up the court, getting back on defense.

With a minute left, the coach replaces him. The crowd stands and applauds; the sportswriters remain seated. The announcer calls the referees over to the scorer's table, and the coach yells to them: "Give him the ball, give him the ball." The referees hand the ball to the player and he palms it, holding it up to the crowd. The coach takes a piece of gum from his mouth and sticks it under his chair while the referees consult with a player on the court. "Is this the ball?" one asks. "That's it," says the player. The referee tosses the ball to the coach. "That better be the last one we give out," he jokes. "We don't have any more." The coach acknowledges the cheers of the crowd and shouts to the referee, "If I get another T, I'm gonna throw the fucking thing at you." The referee laughs as young players on the opposing team join the applause. "I get the next one," the press relations man jokes.

The banner over the balcony is folded up before the final buzzer sounds. A player heaves the ball from mid-court, and the clock lights 00:00. As the teams walk off the court, security guards chase away kids who try to steal some towels from the bench. "See you next year," one disappointed season ticket holder says to his neighbor. They walk down the aisle, the stands high on either side of them, and into the backstage maze that leads to the street. The huge chamber smells of hay and elephant dung; a tiger roars. "Hey, look at the cats," one kid calls to his friend. "Here, kitty, kitty." A security guard shoos him away.

Outside, kids crowd in front of the street entrance to the locker room. A star walks out: bell-bottom jeans, a wool knit cap, leather over-the-shoulder bag, leather coat. He looks sad and contemplative, and the kids surround him on the street corner like birds around a feeder. He hails a cab, but they plead for his autograph, and he mechanically signs their programs and stubs of paper as the cab drives away. By the time he's finished, no cabs are available; and the longer he stands on the street, the more he's pestered by fans. He fixes the bag comfortably over his shoulder and starts walking to his apartment, not far from the arena. Kids follow him, but no one dares approach him; after several blocks he is alone. He strides through the low life on the avenue: hookers, pimps, junkies; kids handing out brochures advertising massage parlors; drunks; a lost mad old woman sitting on the street in front of a pizza stand; a businessman blinking the lights of his car to notify a prostitute that he wants to negotiate with her. The player looks only straight ahead, and his gaze is so deeply blank, so utterly self-absorbed, that even the few passersby who recognize him take it as a warning not to say hello.

❍   ❍   ❍

The church is a thick drab structure on a street off the main avenue of a suburban town. Kids play in front of it. The tournament is held every year simultaneously with the NBA play-offs, the sponsors hoping that stars whose teams haven't qualified for the professional tourney will offer their services for this amateur one. The strategy has worked in the past, but this year the tournament has been lucky to get stars from the semi-professional league, and few cars are parked in front of the church. It is early evening; the warm air and gentle light announce spring.

Inside, two old men take the tickets that cost two dollars each. "Then he worked in the communicable disease lab," one tells the other. "Syphilis, gonorrhea, warts on the head of your dick. They look like plague, but they're harmless. I had them once."

The gym is an old auditorium. The seats have been removed, and baskets suspended from the walls at both ends. A stage overlooks the makeshift court. When players accelerate on lay-ups, they sometimes must leap onto the platform to keep from smashing their knees. The audience sits in bleachers four rows deep lined against the wall. They are local basketball fanatics, kids who play at the church, friends and lovers of the players. They gossip with one another as the players warm up on the court; a girlfriend waves to her fellow coming from the locker room. "What a place," he says. "Only two showers for all of us and just cold water."

Most of the players hold regular jobs. One works in a bank, another in the Stock Exchange; a third is a doctor; two are truckers, one a phys. ed. teacher, one a jazz musician. Some have gotten work because of their physical talents; a tall red-haired fellow who looks like Bill Walton has an easy job at a bank because he plays for their basketball team. A few still hope to become professionals: a tall forward wearing glasses, a small stocky guard with a receding hairline who plays occasionally with the Globetrotters. They play for an organized amateur team which has a regular coach and is funded by a number of local businesses. Each year the two players try out for the pros, but their stories aren't happy: they are always the last players to be cut. The other teams in the tournament are cut-and-paste, ragtag outfits, players put on squads by the organizers of the tournament or asked to join by friends. One has only seven members and is coached by a man in a CAT hat who knows just two of them. For all the players here, the promise of greatness lies in the past.

The referees come from the semi-professional league. They're preoccupied tonight because the NBA referees have gone on strike, and the NBA has been using men from their ranks to officiate the play-off games. Should they be strikebreakers or not? All of them want to work in the NBA and end the moonlighting and odd jobs they must take to support themselves while they labor as semi-professionals.

The situation has as many crosscurrents as a scandal in a small town. One referee at the tournament is the chief official of the semi-professional leagues. His job is to assign referees to games. Now many of the men who have worked for him in the past are being used by the NBA. He too would love to become a regular NBA official, but he won't scab. "I was down in Washington picketing this morning," he says. "I'm just doing this for a gig. I'm surprised at a lot of the guys who are breaking the strike. I tell you, after this is over, I wouldn't do favors for any of them."

Another referee disagrees with him. He's one of the game's roly-poly characters, a loud-talking funny fellow who walks around wearing a large-brimmed cowboy hat. "He's full of shit," he says about the other referee. "He says he's going to screw all those fucking strikebreakers. So what's-his-name is breaking the strike, but he's still using him. You're screwing everybody, I told him; screw you. There's nobody who's not going to work for the league if they get the call. The league called me about a job, to be a standby. I was away, but I would have taken it. You've got to accept it. It's a once-in-a-lifetime shot. If you were a player and the players were striking, you wouldn't play? You've got to! Three hundred to be a standby, six hundred and fifty to officiate: you've got to be crazy to give up a shot like that."

A black woman sits behind the bench of one of the ragtag squads in the first game. She's the girlfriend of a player and informs her neighbor of her boyfriend's histories and glories. He has thin legs, and his scrawny build has probably kept him out of the pros. The reasons most of these athletes haven't become rich always seem obvious after the fact: one's too short, another bitches too much, another isn't mobile. They play intently, however, running the ball downcourt, sliding into the stands, jumping up onto the stage. The boyfriend's team hurts for members, and toward the end of the third quarter, a friend of the coach walks up and says he'll play if they can find him a pair of shorts. By the start of the fourth quarter, the boyfriend and his teammates are exhausted, and the few players on the bench are afraid to reenter the contest in the game's deciding moments. "Not me," says one. "I'm too cold to shoot."

The girlfriend becomes upset. "Give me a cigarette," she demands. "I'm so tense. He said if he didn't win this game, he'd hang up his sneakers, and I know that would break his heart." At that moment, the boyfriend is cut over the eye. She yells at the coach to replace him. "Goddamnit, I should coach this team. You just don't care." But the truth is, her boyfriend doesn't want to leave the floor, and plays to the end, his team losing by ten points. He approaches her, cupping his eye with his hand. "That fucking white boy just couldn't stop shooting," he complains. "He lost us the game."

The second contest isn't so close. One team is coached by a well-dressed man who works as a sports announcer and carries a small pad on which he diagrams plays. The other has no coach, but they close the first quarter leading by fifteen points. The well-dressed coach tries one play after another, and his team cuts the lead to ten at the end of the half. "We're missing chippies," says one of his players. "We'll get it back." He's wrong. In the second half they're ruined, and the play becomes sloppy. One player shoots the ball from half-court, thinking the game's over when more than a minute is left. An old black man chuckles in the bleachers. He was one of the first black players hired by the NBA and now lives nearby. "My, my, those boys have trouble." They lose by twenty-five.

The players leave for the locker rooms, and their friends and lovers wait for them in the lobby. They take a long time to change because of the single shower, and come out one by one, their hair still wet, their bodies smelling of talc. A svelte black walks up to his white girlfriend who's dressed with a pretty sexiness for the spring night. "Come on, we've got to get to that party." A loser meets his girlfriend, and she takes his hand, consoling him. "What are you doing?" he says, embarrassed. "Si me voy," shouts one happy tawny player to two girls and a guy who greet him with cheers because he's played so well. Another is ambushed by two fellows who ask him if his team wants to play in another tourney—"There's money in it."

The roly-poly referee walks out. "Hey, you got my piece?" he asks the janitor of the church. The old man fetches a revolver from a closet, and the referee stuffs it between his belt buckle and his belly. He waits for a player who's a friend and kids the athlete as he approaches. "You guys wouldn't have even been close if it hadn't been for me. You need a godfather to get you points. If I hadn't called fouls against you, you wouldn't have been in the books." The player tells him to shut up. He has never entertained great hopes of becoming a professional, but these jokes annoy him. He mentions an opponent whose excellent play surprised him. "He used to be the second-best rebounder in the country during his sophomore year," says the referee. "But he lays down. He's erratic. He got his college coach fired." The organizer of the tournament comes up. The player apologizes to him for his team's poor showing. The organizer waves his hand. He's sorry he can't give them any money. "Ah," says the referee, "they don't play for money. These guys, they're junkies. They need their fix. Jo Jo White and Doctor J would climb that stage if they weren't in the play-offs. We're all junkies."

They leave the church. Their voices are the only noise on the street. In other cities, players are walking through crowds leaving nationally televised play-off games, entering their Cadillacs, their young women dressed in suedes and silks, their destinations expensive restaurants, beautiful homes. If things had fallen out differently, the players who shower in holes could be in their places: dressing in rug-lined locker rooms, playing in packed, streamlined arenas, being coached by living legends, cheered by executives, having their moments of excellence recorded in newspapers and on film, providing themselves and thousands of unknown admirers the pure pleasure of triumph. The dream of mastery entices—this promise that all life is changeable, can always work out another way, that the mechanisms tossing you onto a heap will play themselves back and place you on top of the winner's stand. Who doesn't believe that? The mere hint of possibility warms like the spring air. Vagabonds of the court, the referee and player squeeze into a battered Volkswagen and drive off for a pizza.

7. The Styles of Play and the Making of Players

In basketball, you refer to a player's "game." A relative of the street slang signifying a con job—he's running a game on you, jack!—the expression sometimes connotes a player's favorite shots and moves. A kid dribbles the ball behind his back, passes it between his legs, tosses a running hook neatly into the basket: he's into his game, confidence accompanying his every step. The phrase can also mean a player's peculiar talents. John Drew grabs an offensive rebound, George Johnson blocks a shot, Freddy Brown scores with a series of seemingly impossible shots: they're into their games, doing what they know best. In its broadest sense, the idiom conveys the character of a player's performance, carrying the burden of fate. When Bill Walton, a superb player, throws a perfectly timed bounce pass, shoots and hits a fifteen-foot jumper banked off the glass, seizes a rebound and immediately heaves the ball downcourt to the waiting hands of a teammate, he's into his game; and when John Gianelli, a fundamentally inept player, pulls down a rebound, fumbles it, catches the ball again, only to trip out-of-bounds, he's into his. Basketball is an argument of physical logic, matching strength against agility, height against speed, accuracy against endurance; even the "mental game" people talk about—a player's concentration and self-control—is comprised of physical components. In basketball, action is character. The goal of the sport isn't a quality, but a kind of activity—a perpetual, purposive movement of players whose single efforts combine to create a seamless unity. With it, they win; without it, or possessing it less fully than their opponents, they lose. Like Tolstoy's happy families, all great teams are alike—the Celtics under Russell and Cowens; the Knickerbockers with Reed, DeBusschere, and

173

Frazier; the Indiana national champions in '76; the Trailblazers; and, I should guess, the Los Angeles Lakers, presently the Yankees of the NBA, a squad so rich in talent it's fair to say it will fail its promise if it doesn't become the team of the century. A magisterial center directs the attack and defense. A sturdy forward collects errant rebounds. An alert guard spurs his teammates into activity. And around this triune sun revolve the lesser satellites. The brilliant shooters who pass through a game like comets, score eight points in minutes, and return to the bench. The reliable substitutes who struggle to shed the same light their stars radiate with ease. The sixth man, a forward and guard, who rises like a dark moon halfway through the first quarter, just when the opponents think they see daylight. Players bring this perfection into being, producing themselves, extending their talents, restricting their weaknesses. In each practice, game and season, new obstructions hinder their progress—a hostile crowd, a superb opponent, injuries, nerves, a bad referee, a difficult teammate. Players yield to these intruders or overcome them, and from this struggle emerge their "games" and the "games" of their teams, the individual and collective natures of their athletic personalities, the powers and limits of their mastery.

Every contest is a drama of this conflict. Even before the play begins, while entering the arena, we know the basic plot. The players will strive to fashion themselves into a flawless unit, and several stories will be enacted during the quest—a rookie's progress, a duel between two well-matched antagonists, one player's battle with age, another's combat with his own selfishness, a third's attempt to curb his frenzied enthusiasm. Sitting above the court, we are so intimate with the particulars of the story that we feel a strange identification with its protagonists, the players. We associate ourselves with their efforts, cheering and booing their performances, often even imagining ourselves part of the team; at the same time, we can't help them practically: they alone decide the story's end. Experiencing the acts of their performance in a double role, we talk about them, using both "we" and "they" interchangeably.

In the first act, the goal of perfection taunts the team. The players seem unbeatable, executing the plays crisply, grabbing every rebound, making every shot. Ah, we think, they've arrived; but their flaws emerge just as the judgment begins to delight us. Too often, they shoot at a distance from the basket, and while they've been hitting these shots, we know the law of averages can't be broken and that their luck won't last forever. Their opponents play sloppily, but our side can't seem to take advantage of their mistakes. On the last three plays, we've lacked concentration. Our forward commits a stupid foul. Our guard walks with the ball. Our center doesn't see an opponent who cuts to the basket and scores an easy lay-up. In minutes, our team's weaknesses dominate. Can't they do anything right? A rookie grabs a rebound and accidentally throws it out-of-bounds. An entirely mediocre player from the other team penetrates our defense. Watching our men try to perform a play, we suffer agonies. They are incompetent, uncertain, lazy.

In the second act, they regroup. A rookie scores a basket, steals the ball, hits an open man with a neat pass. Superstitiously, we say his efforts don't mean a thing, hoping that the statement will preclude the reality. Our team presses their opponents, dogging their steps all over the court. We don't look pretty, but we're working. We remember a comment by Walt Frazier: "There are lots of nights . . . when . . . you start the game and you just drag. But you gut it out, play your 'D' [defense]; and pretty soon you start to get with it. Maybe I make a steal or Willis Reed blocks a shot, we get a cheap basket or two, and suddenly we're rolling. You forget how tired you are, and pretty soon basketball is beautiful again. The shot you missed by three feet five minutes ago all of a sudden is the easiest thing in the world to make." We keep a running score: 58–52, 60–52, 60–54, 61–54, 62–54, 64–54, circle, exclamation mark! It's the first time we've enjoyed a ten-point margin, and besides, we've held them to five points during six minutes of play. Double exclamation mark!! We cheer as our men troop off the court.

The third act, after half time, begins with a lull, the teams trading baskets. How long can this tedium go on? We notice the way the referee holds the whistle inside his mouth, almost as though he were chewing on an enormous metallic wad of gum. A player sitting on the bench tries to distract the opponents on the court, encouraging them to shoot, telling them they've only got five on the twenty-four-second clock. Why does that fan in the front row keep yelling at the players? He must think he's their coach. Will we win against San Antonio next week? We get a basket; they score two foul shots. With 10:49 left in the contest, the other side makes a move, replacing a guard with a forward. He starts grabbing every rebound, and our lead begins to shrink. Suddenly our opponents are racehorses, straining at the start, and every shot they take falls perfectly into the net. Our players are cold, leaden-footed; in the last four minutes, they haven't scored a point. Our lead evaporates to four, a meaningless margin, and the coach calls a time-out. Around us, people boo, shake their heads, more anxious than despairing, creating a claustrophobic cacophony. There's 5:23 remaining in the game, a lifetime in basketball, but the climax is on us.

The players gather at the bench. Our center sits with a towel draped over his head, an Arab staring vacantly across the floor. Our forward sips juice from a tiny wax-paper cup. Our third guard exchanges angry words with the referee. "Come here, damnit!" the coach yells at him. Two rarely used subs at the far end of the bench raise their eyes for a moment. Perhaps he means them? They think they could right the situation if the coach would let them play; it's a mystery to them why he doesn't use them. They watch him begin to address the five players he'll send back onto the court; the subs return to their stoical silence. The players rise, bend from the waist, bounce on the balls of their feet, shake their fingers, ridding themselves of bad nerves. It's a loose game. They assume their positions on the court as the same crowd that booed them moments before now greets them with cheers. "Get that sucker!" a rookie urges. The referee hands the ball to the player at the baseline. He has five seconds to pass it in-bounds. "One!" the referee mouths, swiping the air with a flat hand, counting the seconds. "Two!" The player holding the ball looks both ways while the opponent standing before him waves his arms like a semaphore. "Three!" The players jostle one another, trying to free themselves to receive the pass. "Move!" shouts a fan. A woman sitting near us neatly presses two fingers to her lips and whistles like a kid on the street. "Call a time-out!"

yells her partner. "Four!" An audible sigh fills the arena as the player lofts the ball high to a forward, who catches it in the backcourt. The twenty-four-second clock begins its new count-down. We ride a lengthening wave of anticipation as the players start to execute a play. Will it break triumphantly or dissolve into defeat on the shores of their prowess?

A team searches for perfection by using different "blends" of players. The term is borrowed from the kitchen. Each player's game is a separate element: one rebounds well but runs slowly, another shoots with unsurpassed accuracy but tries to score too frequently. The coach, general manager and players combine these particular traits into one squad, hoping each talent will accent the best qualities of the other, like ingredients employed to enhance one another's special tastes. Sometimes the dish lacks but one spice to become a masterpiece. In 1968, the Knickerbockers possessed all the elements seemingly necessary for a champion-ship, but success eluded them. In the middle of the year, they traded Walt Bellamy, their center, and Howard Komives, a feisty guard, for Dave DeBusschere, a forward. The trade was a fluke. For several years, DeBusschere had been the mainstay of the Detroit franchise, but the team hadn't gotten to the play-offs with him, and his large public following inhibited the club's new management from making any changes on the squad. The Knicks had faced a similar situation with Bellamy and Komives. Neither had enjoyed strong fan support. But Bellamy's presence had forced Willis Reed to play forward, and Komives had kept Walt Frazier on the bench. This situation was detrimental to both Reed and Frazier. Reed had always considered himself primarily a center; it irked him that people judged him unqualified to play the most important position in the game. Frazier's rookie year had been a roller coaster ride of great and dismal performances, the usual mark of an extraordinary new talent in the pros. In his second year, his progress had stalled. As a substitute, he never had to face the responsibilities of leading his team through an entire game, and he had begun to doubt his own abilities. The trade for DeBusschere solved both problems. Reed excelled as a center, no longer having to guard speedier forwards; warmed by Red Holzman's encouragement, Frazier blossomed as a starter.

DeBusschere, an accomplished athlete, benefited because, although his tasks on the Knicks were more limited than those he had performed for Detroit, the restriction concentrated his brilliance. His presence also created a niche for Bill Bradley in the other forward spot. The trade produced the right blend, letting each player harmoniously exert his most valuable and unique qualities, and the next year the Knicks won the national championship.

The Celtics and Paul Silas present an alternate case. Silas is a strong rebounder, but lacks complete skills as a forward. He's not a good shooter, suffers limited stamina, can't match the speed of many younger opponents. Still, he fulfilled his role on the Celtics perfectly. His rebounding complemented the work of Dave Cowens, the team's center, and when other teams disregarded him altogether as a shooter, he dropped in set shots from twenty feet or drove to the basket, a tactic the Celtics used frequently during their championship series against Phoenix. When Silas left the team (after a contract dispute, a rare instance of Auerbachian stupidity), both he and the Celtics were affected adversely: the team couldn't perform with its previous mastery; and, working with a team that didn't take advantage of his skills, Silas appeared flaccid and expendable.

A good coach lets the talents of his players dictate his team's style of play. He dooms himself to failure if he doesn't. If his players are slow and shoot well from outside, he can't make them play a fast break in which they're running downcourt, going for lay-ups. If they're young and high-spirited, he irreparably damages their performance by insisting they play a slow, highly controlled game. Indeed, one of the ways to predict the outcome of contests is to watch how closely a team keeps to its nature. When a cautious, deliberate team starts running, whatever marginal lead they enjoy will diminish; their play will become sloppy, their stamina will weaken, their concentration will vanish. Similarly, a lead held by a running team will dissolve once they slow down, even if they halt themselves on purpose to preserve their advantage. Coaches win or lose by gambling on the natures of their players. Democracy in basketball is not the liberal variety. If one player hits fifty percent of his shots and another succeeds but once every ten times, the more accurate marksman must shoot more frequently.

With its blend of players, each team develops its own personality. Cellar dwellers blossom brilliantly for a week every season, then return to the shadows. Presently, the New Jersey Nets are the unhappiest of this lot. Their owner, Roy Boe, is a miser, and their game is constructed of spare parts. Without a real offense, they offer the fans single stars—Bubbles Hawkins, Mike Bantom, Bernard King, Kevin Porter, John Williamson. These talents expend themselves until they're exhausted; then they droop like wilted petals and the management pinches them off. A true defensive team performs a ballet of force and finesse; without this ability, the Nets create an ineffective melee. Without meaningful triumphs, they laud themselves for chance flashes of brilliance. During the '77 season, they played the 76ers in Philadelphia. It was the first time Julius Erving had performed against his old teammates. He later said he wanted them to win, but the Nets fashioned their own surprising victory, keeping the score close with individual offensive efforts and their street-fighting defense. Somehow they managed a miracle. With the game tied, Kim Hughes, their center, went to the foul line. Hughes is a likable player, a decent rebounder, one of the game's several centers who, one suspects, keeps his job solely because he is a rarity among ballplayers: a tall white man. He is a terrible foul shooter. During practices that season, he had averaged a good proportion; during games, he had succeeded on but one of every five tries. It was cruel irony to make the outcome of the contest depend on his most atrocious failing; if I remember correctly, the Nets even tried to fool the referee and send another player in Hughes's place. When the ruse didn't work, Kevin Loughery, the coach, covered his face with his hands as Hughes shot the ball. The ball fell through the net, Hughes sank his second try, and the Nets unbelievably won the game. I loved watching the contest, but I knew the Nets couldn't repeat the performance. The triumph was a fluke and a laugh, not an inspiration.

The New Orleans Jazz are several steps up from the Nets. The team revolves around the talents of one man, Pete Maravich, a guard who set every major scoring record in college and is a favorite in the South, where he attended school. Maravich is an extraordinary performer. When he first entered the league, he had the reputation of being a chucker and hot-shot, but with his scoring ability, he shouldn't be handing out assists all the time—he would hurt the performances of his teammates worse than his own. Still, he remains an isolated talent. If he plays to suit his teammates, he ruins his own talents; his shooting becomes hesitant and his passes ill-timed; he exhausts himself on defensive maneuvers when he should be husbanding his energy for spurts of baskets. If he plays without relying on his teammates, he simply runs out of steam. He doesn't have the capacity to raise the other players up to his level, and he can't sink to theirs. The team performs erratically. Gathered behind his excellence, they will win a number of games and just as quickly fall apart. They're a dangerous team to play, because they might explode on any night; but at the end of the year, they'll always post a losing record.

The Cleveland Cavaliers live on the .500 border, a high plane of mediocrity where you win and lose games evenly, a no-man's-land breeding anxious hopes that everyone will come together and win ten games in a row, and desperate fears that the whole team will fall apart and fail in every contest for the next third of the season. There is no margin for error, no relief from the urgency to win each game, no high, happy triumphs or solemn, dignified defeats. Its coach, Bill Fitch, teaches a persistent game, the players slowly working the ball around the sides of the basket, taking chance shots rarely, practicing a methodical defense. The team rarely beats itself, or plays beyond its normal capacity; it lacks those extensions and contractions of spirit that mark other squads. The players are anonymous characters, not flawed, but limited in their talents. This condition seems to affect those athletes with whom they play, athletes who do possess the quirkier temperaments of champions. The tepid quality of the team infects them, and they lose the will to risk triumph or failure. Indeed, the one time the team claimed the divisional championship, on the third rung down from the national title, they were led by Nate Thurmond, an aging determined center who had joined the squad in mid-season. Thurmond had always played under the shadow of greater centers, and he viewed the season as a last testament to his often overlooked abilities. During his stay with the Cavaliers, his statistical performance was negligible. But his presence provided an exemplary leadership on the court that none of his teammates could supply. With it they exerted themselves powerfully, both raising and dashing the hopes of their fans. For that season, his addition to the team created the right blend. The following year, he surrendered, either to age or to the prevailing spirit of the team, and the Cavaliers returned to their previous blandness.

The Washington Bullets are a team who will never win a championship. Of all the league's franchises over the last five years, they have most consistently possessed the best combination of players on paper and should have been a dynasty. Instead, they have continually muffed their moments of greatness. In '75, only the Boston Celtics matched them in talent, both teams finishing the season with a 60–22 record. Washington had split its seasonal matches with Boston, but Washington defeated Boston handily in the play-offs. Their challengers for the national title were the Golden State Warriors, a team that couldn't equal Boston's depth or prowess. Still, Washington simply folded and lost to the weaker team four games in a row.

Elvin Hayes molds their style of play. Hayes is a forward, a lean thoroughbred, one of the league's all-time leading scorers and rebounders. During his college career, he played for the University of Houston and would have been the nation's top player except that Abdul-Jabbar (then Lew Alcindor) was performing for UCLA. In a contest that attracted the largest basketball audience in history, Houston met UCLA at the Astrodome. The game didn't decide a championship, but UCLA had won forty-seven consecutive games and the match was broadcast nationally as a battle of giants. John Wooden, the UCLA coach, calls Hayes's performance during the game's first half one of the great individual feats in basketball. Less spectacular in the second half, Hayes still managed to lead his team to a two-point victory. But the game was his last national triumph. Later in the year, Houston met UCLA in the NCAA tournament and was defeated badly. Ever since, Hayes has been painted as a player who can't win the truly big games, and he has come to resemble the portrait. In decisive moments, Hayes simply gets beaten; and when he stalls, his team comes to a halt.

People often define Hayes's incapacity as a psychological block;

the rap is that he chokes because he lacks the will to win. He is used as an example of a player who lacks a "mental game," inner powers of concentration and discipline. Floyd Lane, a coach I respect greatly, once complained to me about one of his favorite players. "He doesn't have it here," he said, tapping his forehead with his finger. "He lets players beat him, and it's not because he's tired. It's because he just doesn't think."

We like to use such explanations for a player's lapses because they allow us to express our Puritan belief that heroes are people whose will can overcome any obstacle. Still, science suggests otherwise. An athlete can only extend his skills within the limits of his physical being. When players are tired, they perform sloppily, and it does no good to shout that they're not showing hustle. Their slowness isn't a mental problem, but a physiological one: they've sweated a lot, and their systems lack sodium, a chemical vital for the transfer of nerve impulses to and from the brain. With all deference to Floyd Lane's superior knowledge, I still suspect that his favorite player survived more on will than on stamina. Willis Reed was one of the most determined players ever to grace the game; but when the doctors told him he would have to undergo a third operation on his knee, he gave up playing. Even remediable injuries date the careers of athletes. Forty-seven-year-old Walter Dukes still refers to a knee injury he suffered twenty years ago as though it had happened yesterday. For Dukes, the ailment changed his entire game, depriving him of the strength to remain in the air—the "lift," as he calls it, that we see when Erving dunks or Baryishnikov leaps. As happens to many athletes who suffer the same misfortune, Dukes was afraid forever after that any sudden movement to the side would renew the injury, and the fear shackled his game. And the converse is also true. John Havlicek is the wonderman of basketball, still playing thirty minutes a game at age thirty-seven. In '76, the Celtics played the Suns for the national championship, and the penultimate game stretched to three overtimes. The Celtics were losing the second additional five-minute period with only seconds left to play. Havlicek dribbled the ball to the side of the basket, jumped, leaning slightly forward in the air, springing the ball free for a shot that hit cleanly off the backboard and dropped through the net. Havlicek is held up as an example of a "smart" ballplayer, and of course the judgment is right. But only a genetic accident allows him to demonstrate his prowess: his peculiar metabolism gives him reserves of energy unavailable to most other human beings; without it he should have retired several years ago.

Hayes doesn't seem to suffer from any particular physical incapacity. It may be that his team simply didn't combine a winning "blend" when he was in his prime, and that the accusation made against him became a stumbling block which now, with his advance in age, he can't get over. In any event, he can't seem to command his talents when they're most needed, and year after year his team remains unsettled, uncertain, a chameleon that changes with the quality of its competition—dull and uninspired against poorer teams, erratic against average ones, resourceful and reliable against champions, unless the game is a critical win. Without this guidance, they are lost. They bridle at the accusation that they're chokers, but they constantly manage to win only the battle, never the war, always finding a way to snatch failure from the jaws of victory. This is the sign of a losing team, just as the mark of a great one is the ability to discover the road to triumph when most lost in the forest of defeat.*

*Ah, well. . . . At the time I wrote these observations, the Bullets were floundering in the five hundred swamp; when the book went off to the copyeditor, they had managed to crawl onto the firmer ground of the play-offs; when I was reviewing her careful labor, they had climbed onto the perilous ice fields of the Eastern Divisional Championship; and only several days before the manuscript was sent off to the printers, they had overcome all adversity and were camped in position for their final ascent to the NBA Championship, a summit they conquered the following day. Their triumph left me pleased and aghast—I did say I was a lousy prognosticator. Indeed, the Bullet team that won last year relied less on Hayes's talents than the squads I was discussing, and not Hayes but Westley Unseld—the team's center—won the MVP award. Still, Hayes held center stage for me throughout the drama. In a crucial game against Philadelphia, he went flat as the 76ers tied the score and forced an overtime. Ah ha, I thought: yet another example of Marx's dictum that history always repeats itself. Instead, Hayes revived and won the game. These unpredictable swings from greatness to exhaustion marked his play throughout the series, his character seeming to bedevil him as though it were a force separate from himself, like fate in a Greek tragedy. Brent Mussberger, the CBS announcer whose own performance improved dramatically this last year, compared him tellingly with Chamberlain: "Even when he's right, he's wrong," he commented at one point when Hayes was the victim of some unrecognized injustice. But why continue? Justifications of

One of the curious elements in Hayes's play is that opponents with considerably less athletic skill than his match up well against him. Match-ups are the primary tools coaches use during contests to throw their opponents off their game. Most zones used in high school and college ball reduce themselves to several men guarding one man, or attempts to keep a powerful player away from his areas of strength on the court. In pro games zones are prohibited, and each player must theoretically take direct responsibility for his opponent's points. This law encourages the one-on-one contests that often make games memorable—can Maravich best Monroe, Gus Johnson stop Baylor? In practical terms, however, no defense is solely man-to-man, because any good effort must be a collective one; and players constantly sag off on opponents who are weak shooters, cluster around great ones, switch the men they are guarding. Great marksmen—Elgin Baylor, Rick Barry, Erving, Monroe—are unstoppable and manage to discover solutions to any problem, but any team is delicately balanced. Often just making their scorers work harder for their shots or merely holding them several points under their average is enough to create an upset and win the game. In '74, Abdul-Jabbar's last-minute basket won the penultimate match of the national championship series for the Bucks. Their foes, the Celtics, wondered how they would contain the scorer in the decisive and final game. Tommy Heinsohn, the Celtic coach, decided to let two of his players guard Jabbar, leaving Cornell Warner, a Buck forward, free to score. The tactic was a calculated risk. A lackluster shooter, Warner never averaged more than six points a game. He had scored an important basket the night before, but it was only a theoretical possibility that he'd enjoy an extraordinary evening scoring forty points. The gamble succeeded: Jabbar was held scoreless for a quarter, Warner couldn't fill the gap, and Boston won the game.

There simply is nothing theoretically complicated about

wrong predictions are doomed to sound equivocal. I leave the last word to Lou Carnesca, the coach of St. John's. Don't you need good lateral movement to become a professional player? I asked him once. "Lateral movement," he scoffed. "Look," he said, drawing straight lines up and down a piece of paper, "Leroy Ellis played in the NBA for eleven years. During all that time, he only moved up and down, never to the side." He crumpled the illustration into a ball. "In this game, you just can't make rules about talent."

basketball. Auerbach has a favorite demonstration about dribbling. The ball is round, he says, and the floor is flat. If you throw the ball down, it will bounce up to meet your hand. See? He lets the ball fall, and it acts exactly as he has predicted. The same is true for all elements of the sport. You keep a man from scoring by occupying his favorite position on the floor; you pass the ball, making sure the receiver can catch it; you position yourself to grab rebounds; you shoot from the position where your aim is best. The trick is to do it. The game is a simple exercise. During all its years as a national champion, Boston ran but seven fundamental plays. Each formation contained different options, such as a man cutting left instead of right, but the team never won because of their ingenious tactics. They triumphed because they executed the fundamentals of the game better than their competitors.

New fans and people who watch games only occasionally never seem content with this fact. They desire complicated strategies, labyrinthian reasons for a team's loss or triumph. Some coaches supply these demands. Larry Costello, the coach of the Bucks in the Abdul-Jabbar days, instructed his squad in one hundred set plays. Sometimes when a new team wins the championship, people say the victors have invented a fresh style of play. When the Knicks triumphed in '70, everyone spoke of team defense as though Holzman's squad had just coined the idea; Holzman merely instructed them in the game as he had been taught. College coaches are particularly adept at minting new kinds of games. North Carolina's "four corners" offense is the current rage, an offensive maneuver during which four players, positioned you know where, pass the ball, while a fifth tries to get an easy lay-up. But unlike their cousins in football or baseball, such as the shotgun formation or the suicide squeeze, these inventions have no life of their own. The athletes alone breathe the air of triumph or defeat into them, and the genius of great basketball coaches resides in applying fundamental truths, not fashioning them.

Tom Heinsohn's later career demonstrates this axiom. He had played on the famous Celtic teams as a high-scoring forward, nicknamed "Ack-Ack" for his propensity to fire the ball at the basket from any position. Heinsohn was following Auerbach's orders. He endured all criticisms of his performances uncomplainingly, a character trait he also displayed when he braved the threats of the owners and helped organize the Players Association. As a player, Heinsohn never claimed the fame awarded to Cousy and Russell, and their specters haunted him as a coach. Auerbach handed the mantle to Heinsohn only after Cousy had rejected it; the superstar guard was even credited with the strategy that defeated the Bucks. Heinsohn knew differently, and after the '74 series, he insisted on public recognition of his talents. He became known for his unattractive behavior during games. With his team leading by fifteen points, he acted as if his efforts should meet only with perfection and stalked the sidelines, a disgusted scowl distorting his lips. Answering rumors that Auerbach still directed the club, he wrote a letter to the Boston *Globe* enumerating how many plays and options he had invented. Friends reported that he refused to discuss games with them, claiming the contests were too complicated for amateurs to understand. Still, his acumen proved fruitless in the end. The personnel of the team changed in the mid-seventies, and under his guidance the team started to lose. Finally he had to be fired. Strategies meant nothing; he couldn't get his players to perform.

Coaches and managers often say they "made" a player, meaning they developed the athlete's skills. One old-time coach told me he had invented several hundred exercises, each to cure and strengthen a different physical ailment that hinders players. Bad hands is one intractable physical flaw that bedevils some players. They just can't hang on to the ball. I suffer from this—the ball always humiliates me by flying past my palms—and so do a number of otherwise semi-respectable professional players. Other players are gifted with "good hands"; once they've caught a ball, nothing can pry it away from them. This seems to be a natural blessing, but this coach had fashioned a remedy for it. He tied wooden blocks onto a player's palms and made him catch the ball. Similarly, there are exercises for quick eyes, lateral movement, even a player's concentration. Indeed, many people believe that the most important task a coach can perform is getting his players into top physical condition; Auerbach says that in the league's early days he figured that his team would win a number of games on the strength of stamina alone.

"Making a player" implies more than this, though. The phrase suggests the entire ritual of introducing an athlete to the social and psychological rigors of the basketball world, toughening him into maturity. Many of the players from the fifties and early sixties speak of their relations with their owners in this way. Bob Pettit talks at length of his contract-bargaining sessions with Ben Kerner, his employer, as though the meetings were a hard-knock school of adulthood. In some instances, the masters of the game still convey this sense of the sport; they speak of young players ridding themselves of rookie faults and of course the constantly renewed revelation that basketball is a business. But their essential relationship to the game is that the work is play—not an undisciplined or undemanding exercise, but a creative labor of imagination and skill, a task the performance of which is its main reward.

I first realized this several years ago when I taught English at a college in Mount Vernon, a deteriorating New York City suburb. A refurbished warehouse, the school served as the "open admissions" college of the State University of New York at Purchase, a luxurious and expansive campus located some miles away in a well-to-do community. The Purchase campus had a fine gymnasium, but no team. The Mount Vernon students wanted to form a team (the town is a lush grove of talent), but had no place to play. Eventually, the administrators at Purchase acceded to their demand. Two representatives from the mother college played on the squad; the rest of its members came from the colony school down the road. Its coach was a stranger to the players, a young man who planned to write his postdoctoral dissertation on the experience. The largely white middle-class faculty and students of Purchase mainly ignored the team's progress. They measured excellence by their standards solely, and none showed even the slightest interest in the intelligence, diligence or maturity displayed by the students on the court, though for many of the players the game was the arena in which they mastered these qualities, and their experience in the sport was the source from which their general confidence and discipline flowed. The administration ruled the team with a bizarre liberalism. They were afraid that the team would run other people out of the gym, so they restricted it to one practice a week; fearful that the games would become too competitive, they demanded that every player on the squad receive equal time on the court, regardless of his talent.

These pleasantries and dismissals weren't what the Mount Vernon students had in mind; they had anticipated becoming a respectable college club with a band, cheerleaders and admiring alumni. Not to be refused their pleasure, they supplied their own approximations of these frills. The last game of the season, a steel band played while a large crowd from Mount Vernon applauded the street stunts of the players. Still, it was the team that ended the season on a happy note. With a few minutes left in the game, the team's center committed his sixth foul. He tried to fool the referees and stay in the game, but they waved him off the court, and the coach had to call on the services of Myron, a white player from Purchase who had rarely been used during games. (The team regularly dodged the mandates from the administration, since the deans never attended the games anyway.) The students on the sidelines cheered Myron, calling his name, but they all assumed that the substitution would lose them the game. Myron immediately scored. On the next play, he sank another basket and was fouled. "Myron! Myron! Myron!" the Mount Vernon fans shouted, bemused at his performance, and he won the game to the reverberating notes of the steel band.

After the season, they continued to use the gym. Every Friday afternoon, the players drove up with their girlfriends from the school and turned the campus into a playground. Outdoors, the women were taught tennis by two wealthy female professors; indoors, the men ran full-court games. When both were done, they met in the Olympic-size swimming pool whose glass wall looked out on the green hills of a Westchester estate. I joined them occasionally at their encouragement—generous invitations, since my talents and skills were so meager. There was no difference between their athletic and academic personalities. T—a sobriquet for the tongue-tripping Taliafero, the team's center—had little discipline and loved to score points. He always only threatened disaster. He wrote poetry, and once he gave me five minutes to tell him what I thought of his work. His life was a controlled chaos—a wife, a child, and more than one girlfriend. Once he told me he never carried a gun. "You're looking for death when you carry a piece," he explained. Cliff was a reliable, smooth forward who worked hard scoring points and played defense with finesse. The favored of two brothers, he was a science major and handled every task with a competent grace. His younger sibling couldn't match Cliff's accomplishments. He flunked out of school, and his parents exiled him from their house. "I can't do anything," he told me. "The only time I feel good is playing ball, and I'm not even that good at it. I just like it." Several months later, he had weathered the crisis, gotten a job, reapplied to school, and displayed a confidence equaling his previous despair. "I hear you're playing ball," he joked with me. "I'll teach you ball, man. I'll make you stand strong, crash the boards, trigger the fast break; I'll turn you into a Jabbar." My favorite was Antony. A twenty-seven-year-old alcoholic, fat, scant of breath, he was a stutterer who wrote poetry. On the court he floated with a buoyant pudginess, his belly becoming a soft wave he rode up to the basket. He winded too easily to play in the full-court games. I was also useless in those rugged exercises: sixteen-year-olds used to grab rebounds in the air while I had yet to reach the peak of my jump. Antony loved to talk ball, and we would schmooze while shooting baskets. I loved playing with him in two-on-two contests. The two of us made a Mutt and Jeff tandem, but he shot with a superb accuracy and a soft, flawless touch—as long as the ball bounced on the rim, it would fall into the basket. His alchemical ability to turn faults into virtues worked its magic on me. "Take your shot, Lew," he encouraged me, and I became a marksman.

The master of the whole group was James Johnson. A guard, he sported a small bean belly and shaved his head closely, the two orbs giving him a round, satisfied appearance. He had played ball in a New York high school and had expected a scholarship to a major college. None had been offered, and he had attended a small upstate school until he fought with the coach. Now he was stuck in Mount Vernon and didn't know whether his career had a future or should be abandoned.

Playing with the team wasn't an altogether happy experience for James. Good ballplayers go a little crazy when they perform with lesser talents, especially guards—like Maravich—because the perfecting of their abilities depends greatly on their mates. If players miss their passes, foul up good shots, step more slowly than anticipated, the guard's own game becomes fractured. Occasionally, a great guard overcomes the liabilities of his colleagues. When Nate Archibald played with the Nets, he enjoyed some games in which his helpers didn't make a mockery of his moves. A forward would grab a neat pass from Archibald, make a nice basket, and race upcourt almost surprised: did I just do that? More frequently, Archibald simply outplayed his own team. On fast breaks, he had to halt his own forward progress as though he were a plane coming in for a landing, because the only players near him would be his opponents. People often say that Jabbar and players of his stature, both athletically and physically, can lift a team above its own level; and centers can affect a team's play more than guards, because their position gives them greater command of a game's offense and defense. But even Jabbar is ruined by continually bad players. They simply require his talents too much, and he becomes dispirited and exhausted. Guards are even more susceptible to the infection of ineptitude, and James wasn't immune to the disease. The leader of the team, he was also subject to impossible demands; the players counted on him to triumph in difficult situations and complained about his domination of the team when they won.

Still, he never considered not playing with them. His ambition alone didn't make him endure all the petty bickering of his teammates and those generally torturous evenings when his team performed. He still entertained illusions about becoming a pro. I remember one afternoon when he compared his talents to the league's famous guards' and kept saying, "I think I can play there." (In the sports world, people actually say the things you read in the newspaper.) But he had already started taking retrospective glances, those gestures toward understanding which athletes repeatedly perform at the ends of their careers. He wondered about his high school days when he had fought with his coach, and about his maneuvers to secure a good college scholarship. Perhaps he should have worked harder? The progress reports on his contemporaries scared him. One was the best leaper in the Bronx, but had never succeeded in the pros; another could never get his head straight and died of an overdose—would his fate be the same? He remained confident of his powers, but began to speculate on their force: maybe he just wasn't good enough. He was a realistic fellow, adept at recognizing others' faults and virtues, and eventually he acted in his own best interests and gave up hopes for a career in the game, though even then he continued to play, working at his craft.

One afternoon I arrived early at the gym and found James alone. He ran up and down the court ceaselessly, first doing sprints, stopping and starting, then weaving patterns, then dribbling the length of the court. His practice continued, a self-imposed maniacal insistence. For fifteen minutes, he shot consecutive baskets from a semicircle around the net; rested with fifty foul shots; threw the ball against the backboard, jumping to grab the rebounds and tap them back into the net; ran the length of the court, throwing passes to himself off the gym's wall.

I had heard of such crazed displays. Ernie DiGregorio, a respected guard in his rookie days, reportedly spent two hours every afternoon of his youth throwing passes to himself in his parents' concrete garage. DiGregorio's play always seems spoiled to me, demanding, insistent, bratty; even when he's good, a naughty cuteness makes it obnoxious. Watching him, I always remember the vision of his childhood. Those long hours in the isolation of his parents' garage couldn't have been happy ones, and the spirit of his game has never seemed to escape from the concrete walls in which it was manufactured.

James's exercise shared none of this quality. Sweating, out of breath, pushing himself beyond his own limits of endurance, he appeared profoundly at ease in his labor, enjoying it. At the end of his workout, James radiated content. "I love it, man," he said. "You run. You sweat. You cook in your own sweat. It makes you crazy. And then you're ready to play."

James was a player, the term used to denote those athletes for whom the game seems an almost natural activity. I don't mean to romanticize. The struggle to realize this perfection is an arduous one. For professionals, the life often seems thankless, even with their large salaries. The schedule is hard; the idiosyncrasies of coaches, referees, management, agents, fans and press bewildering; the competition physically punishing. There are also psychological hardships. The world of sports is claustrophobic. You must fight to maintain any corner of your own within it—family, particular interests, even the habit of reading the newspaper—and often what you value becomes merely the butt of your colleagues' practical jokes. Fewer athletes than one imagines enjoy any security. They are injured, cut, traded, often for reasons other than poor performances. Larry McNeill, a forward, played excellently when he first joined the Nets. Then the team traded Julius Erving; and Kevin Loughery, the coach, never used McNeill again. In December, the team cut him. The reason was that McNeill shared Erving's agent, though this never came out in the press. McNeill played some games in the semi-professional league, got a short-lived job on the Golden State Warriors, and finally landed a position on the Buffalo team, where he hopes to remain. The lack of regular playing time has already damaged his game; it's possible he'll never succeed as a player, though his ability as an athlete when he began his adventures in the professional world would have indicated a good fortune. The life numbs. Strangely, many of the biographies of the great players revolve around their madnesses. Bill Russell talks at length about his paralyzing fear of death. Bob Pettit begins an account of his career by describing the hopeless feelings that overcame him as he played his last game. Cousy writes that he suffered nightmares so vivid that he would jump out of bed in terror. Finally he ordered his wife to tie him to the bedposts. Before playing his final game as a pro, he spent twenty-four hours locked alone in a room, concentrating on his upcoming opponent, an image of monomania as fierce as any that Melville wrote. The compensations are great and widely known—money, stardom, an entrance into the room the world reserves for people commanding respect. But none of these explains the dedication of players like James to the game or the devotion of most professionals. I once watched a highly paid professional do physical therapy, lifting weights with his leg. The exercise approached torture. Sweat burst from his body each time he fought the mechanical contraptions, the veins in his arms and neck becoming enormous from the effort, and he shouted from the pain. Even so, at the end of the exercise, he appeared exalted. He was no Job, treasuring his agonies, making penance through punishment. He simply took enjoyment from the phys- ical working of his body, a sheer satisfaction in the manifestation of his strength and endurance, his concentration and will. Like James at the end of his frenzy, the player possessed a confident pleasure.

All players (I use the word in the categorical sense) gain this sense of well-being from the game. One friend of mine worked throughout his youth to become a player, exercising every day. He was short, but imagined he could overcome this limitation. In his first year of college, he took a physical education course with the assistant coach of the school's team. The coach considered my friend a hot-shot and challenged him to a schoolyard game. Each took consecutive foul shots until one missed; the winner was the first to make twenty and a basket shot from half-court. If my friend won, the coach promised to give him an A; if he lost, the coach said he would flunk him. The coach went first and managed all twenty baskets, but missed the shot from half-court. My friend then sank all his shots in a row, winning the contest. It was one of the great moments in his young life, and he waited for the coach to award him by offering him a place on the college team. Instead, the coach complimented his prowess and asked him to join the junior varsity. My friend refused, realizing that if this perfect display only commanded such small respect, he would never realize his ambitions. Currently he is studying to become a therapist, his new profession. Still, when he feels the greatest need to revive his confidence and energy, he always goes to the basketball courts.

One of the common discussions in the basketball world con- cerns the inappropriately named "junkies" of the game, players such as Fly Williams who can't make it into the pros and play in semi-professional games, playground contests, wherever and whenever they can. Fly is a thin forward-guard, a wondrous performer, similar in style to George Gervin, the player for San Antonio who is nicknamed the "Ice Man." (His baby is called "Ice

Cube.") Fly is evidently difficult to coach, intractable in his manner. He can't seem to remain on teams that give him a chance: a stubborn and erratically brilliant player, a Christmas cactus of the game. Basketball people often sympathize with his obsession—ah, why can't he leave? He can't be a kid forever. Yet no one would make this complaint if Fly wanted to become a doctor or lawyer against all odds. His drive would be considered commendable, even if foolhardy. Why does the same ambition seem infantile and perverse when applied to pursuits whose social usefulness is less obvious? Fly has devoted himself to his craft. He possesses a unique talent. His performances provide people with an ineffable, nourishing pleasure, a delight and joy. Why should he or they be forced to give this up?

No player presents a more complete contrast to Fly Williams than does Bill Bradley. Bradley was judged the most cerebral of all players and the most disciplined; his game was movement and accuracy, not individual daring. Still, like Fly, he was a player; and he demonstrated this most movingly during his last season of play. One of Bradley's truly remarkable characteristics is his insistence on remaining true to his feelings and judgment, a blunt desire not to falsify his appearance or worth, a demand for a kind of personal integrity so absolute that it occasionally becomes graceless, a self-imposed hair shirt. This quality characterized his last games. Breathing heavily as he ran upcourt, pulling and pushing the man he guarded, his shoulders and chest having lost the alert flesh of his youth, he seemed almost to present himself deliberately as an aging man, demonstrating to the audience the loss of his powers, forcing them to witness his decay. In one of his great poems, "Dejection," Samuel Taylor Coleridge laments the loss of his poetic powers. He writes on a tranquil evening, while waiting for a storm, "the coming-on of rain and squally blast." Nature has inspired him before, and now he wishes the rain and gusts, "Those sounds which oft have raised me, whilst they awed,/ And sent my soul abroad,/ Might now perhaps their wonted impulse give,/ Might startle this dull pain, and make it move and live!" The "dull pain" is his lassitude, "a grief without a pang, void, dark, and drear," and he experiences it while looking at the natural scene outside:

All this long eve, so balmy and serene,
Have I been gazing on the western sky,
*   And its peculiar tint of yellow green:*
And still I gaze—and with how blank an eye!
And those thin clouds above, in flakes and bars,
That give away their motion to the stars;
Those stars, that glide behind them or between,
Now sparkling, now bedimmed, but always seen:
Yon crescent moon, as fixed as if it grew
In its own cloudless, starless lake of blue;
I see them all so excellent fair,
I see, not feel, how beautiful they are!

*   My genial spirits fail,*
*   And what can these avail*
To lift the smothering weight from off my breast?
*   It were a vain endeavour,*
*   Though I should gaze forever*
On that green light that lingers in the west:
I may not hope from outward forms to win
The passion and the life, whose fountains are within.

The lines are a testament to the will-lessness people experience
when their powers fail them, and I like to think that F. Scott
Fitzgerald, who loved the Romantic poets, used Coleridge's image
in his novel, *The Great Gatsby;* the green light the poet can't feel
became the green light on Daisy Buchanan's dock, the image for
Gatsby of the gulf separating him from gaining his desires. Bill
Bradley's performance also was a display of failing powers, but
their disappearance wasn't a mystery or cause for tragedy. "We
receive but what we give," Coleridge writes later, but his
complaint is far from always being true. In his last season, Bradley worked as hard as he had before, but he couldn't
maintain his past standards. His insistence on experiencing this
and demonstrating it was almost ritualistic, homage to his past
prowess, as though he were offering it the humiliation and
exhaustion of his present state. Yet his performance never
suggested that those powers were arbitrary or ephemeral, as

Coleridge implied; rather, he honored them because they had given him pleasure, a pleasure he could cultivate and from which would grow the other satisfactions of his life.

All athletics are essentially innocent activities. We ascribe to them the values we prize in our lives, and they reflect those qualities back to us—the joys of youth, cruel competition, ideal aspirations. Players often say that what happens on the court has no meaning for the world off it, and I am mindful of their caution. In such illusions begin aggravations. Still, all players seem to teach the same lesson; they don't achieve greatness through deprivation or punishment, but by taking pleasure in their powers, exerting them, daring to risk fully all of their prospects, striving to create on the court the game—their "game"—that they imagine within them, a land they see through the mist, a thought they hesitate to announce, yet believe absolutely.

It is their "games" and the "games" of their teams that enthrall the fans. For them, the performances they watch and the activity of the sport encompass a broad range of human nature, express the delights and prejudices of individual character. The lengthy, wandering discussions in which fans indulge are appreciations of the game's bounty, a lingering delight in its moments almost as rich as the pleasure experienced by the players themselves in producing them, a long stroll with friends through a garden on a vibrant July day when the natural world seems a complement to all your best feelings. . . . Ah! here's Detroit with its massive center, Bob Lanier, a plant that's all stem. And this stately tree overgrown with moss is Atlanta. Once its magnificent branches were the pride of St. Louis—Cliff Hagan, Bob Pettit, Charley Share, Ed Macauley, and all of their offshoots—Paul Silas, Zelmo Beaty, Lenny Wilkens, Bill Bridges, Jeff Mullins, Lou Hudson. Here's Buffalo. What seeds buried in such deep snow ever offered such promise? DiGregorio, Gar Heard, Jimmy McMillian, Randy Smith, Bob McAdoo—they made a fluorescent New England garden. At their peak, no team could outmatch them in a single game. Now just Smith and McAdoo seem to renew and grow under the storms of each season. Norm Van Lier, Jerry Sloan, Bob Love, Chet Walker—the soil was too gritty for those crops to be harvested. They worked so hard to break ground that they lacked the strength to bear perfect fruit. Here are the Northwest saplings—Jim McDaniels, Spencer Haywood, Tom Burleson, Marvin Webster. Their coach, Bill Russell, always crowded their growth, and only Freddy Brown, a diminutive guard, seems to have escaped his domination, his wondrous shooting producing ever new creations. These are the cacti of the Southwest. On the Denver plateau, each season sports a fine flower, but the air seems too thin for the bloom to last. In Phoenix, the gardeners want only appearance. They give no care or water to the prize-winning roses they pluck each year, and Connie Hawkins, Charlie Scott, Gail Goodrich, Neal Walk, maybe even Alvan Adams—the youngest of the lot, perhaps the most promising—wither and die. There's the fruit of the city. Los Angeles wins championships by purchasing the exotic giants of New York and Philadelphia. In Philadelphia, suburbanites now spruce up Eddie Gottlieb's longtime hand-tended garden. New York? Will greenery ever last in this city more than three years? Look at Boston, that stately avenue of trees: brilliant maples—Cousy, Sharman and White; deep-rooted elms—Frank Ramsey, John Havlicek; commanding pines—Cowens and Russell; and Auerbach, their impossible gardener. Here are teams unremembered and imagined. The antiques of the past. The Passaic high school boys who won 159 games over six seasons. The Original Celtics owned by Kate Smith. The Buffalo Germans, the Harlem Rens, their faces somberly staring at us from memorial photographs. The anonymous squads of the playgrounds. Was it Chamberlain or Jabbar who threw the ball down so hard on a slam-dunk that it bounced over the eight-foot-high chicken-wire fence, and the crowd went wild? Let it be both. Was it Roger Brown or Earl Manigault who scored the final point, hitting a basket by banking the ball off the top of the backboard? Let it be both. Was it Fly Williams or Connie Hawkins who made so many moves the camera couldn't catch them? Let it be both. Who needs to measure? When David Thompson graduated from college, he was the only player who had a forty-eight-inch vertical leap. He hung so high in the air that his coach was afraid David would one day trip over the head of another player—and indeed he did. Now these leapers leave school by the dozens. In this game, you just can't make rules about talent. Whom would you pick for the perfect team? Jabbar in the pivot? Russell or Walton? There's a fan who still swears by Nate Thurmond, and this one from New York chooses Willis Reed. McAdoo for your scoring forward? Here's Pettit and Heinsohn, Baylor and Erving, Johnson and Stokes, Schayes and DeBusschere. Elvin Hayes? Ah, you'll take him for all but the big games? And who would run your backcourt? Oscar Robertson, in his prime, of course. But was there ever a better college guard than Jimmy Walker?—even if his talents disappeared in the pros. Will John Havlicek come off the bench? Frazier and West, Cousy and K. C. Jones, Maravich and David Thompson, Nate Archibald, Earl Monroe. How peculiarly different they all are. Frazier lets his perfect body sleep twelve hours a night. Randy Smith, the fastest man in the league—scarred arms, scarred knees, patch of white hair on the top of his 'fro—wants to play soccer as soon as the basketball season ends. The perfect team we select is good only for moments. The players change with the game. Who needs to pick gods from this gathering of heroes, unchanging beings, remote, commanding? The natural world supplies enough wonders. There is no end to the making of players. It's a loose game, without constraint or restriction. In this garden, all the insistently varied fruits of nature's will and human desire ripen freely.